The New Nuns

The New Nuns

RACIAL JUSTICE AND RELIGIOUS REFORM IN THE 1960s

AMY L. KOEHLINGER

HARVARD UNIVERSITY PRESS
Cambridge, Massachusetts, and London, England 2007

Printed in the United States of America

ISBN-13: 978-0-674-02473-1
ISBN-10: 0-674-02473-7

Cataloging-in-Publication Data is available from the Library of Congress

For my mother

Contents

Abbreviations

CARA	Center for Applied Research in the Apostolate
CCD	Confraternity of Catholic Doctrine
CFM	Catholic Family Movement
CHOICE	Cooperative Help of Integrated College Education
CIC	Catholic Interracial Council
CMSW	Conference of Major Superiors of Women's Religious Institutes
CORE	Congress on Racial Equality
CRIS	Sacred Congregation for Religious and Secular Institutes
CYO	Catholic Youth Organization
DES	Department of Educational Services of the NCCIJ, also called the Educational Services Department
DMES	Department of Medical Educational Services
HEW	Department of Health, Education, and Welfare
KKK	Ku Klux Klan
LCWR	Leadership Conference of Women Religious
OEO	Office of Economic Opportunity
NAACP	National Association for the Advancement of Colored People
NAME	New Attitudes in Memphis Education
NCAN	National Coalition of American Nuns
NCCIJ	National Catholic Conference for Interracial Justice
NCEA	National Catholic Education Association
NPB	National Placement Bureau
SAIL	Summer Advancement in Learning
SCLC	Southern Christian Leadership Conference
SFC	Sister Formation Conference
SIS	Sisters' Institute of Spirituality

SIS	Sisters in Suburbia
SNCC	Student Nonviolent Coordinating Committee
SUE	Sisters Urban Education
TW	Traveling Workshop in Inter-Group Relations
UAS	Urban Apostolate of the Sisters

Introduction: An Apostolic Revolution

Early in the voter registration drives in Selma, Alabama, in 1963—before Jimmie Lee Jackson was murdered, before Bloody Sunday and the march to Montgomery, before James Reeb died—James Baldwin addressed a mass meeting at Tabernacle Baptist Church on Broad Street, a main avenue through Selma. Among those who gathered to hear the famous author's speech that night were two unseen guests. Next door to Tabernacle Baptist in the mission convent of the Sisters of Saint Joseph two young nuns balanced atop a bedroom radiator with ears pressed to a window facing the alley that separated the convent from the church next door, hoping to catch a glimpse of the famous author and perhaps hear a bit of his speech.[1] Although the sisters spent their days in the company of African Americans at the mission school and hospital, their congregation's customs of enclosure prohibited the sisters from attending the meeting next door. They were not to leave the convent alone and, even then, only on convent business. They were not to have undue casual contact with lay people or to attend political meetings. They were not allowed to enter a non-Catholic church. As one of the sisters recalled: "We did not have a history of going anyplace, so it never occurred to us to go, except to work, to church, to home. We didn't. So we stood up on the radiator in my bedroom and looked through the window and listened."[2]

Two years later, in late March, 1965—after the meetings and protests, after the tragedy of Jimmie Lee Jackson and the brutality of Bloody Sunday—Ralph Abernathy climbed the pulpit of Brown Chapel, a few blocks away from Broad Street's Tabernacle Baptist Church, to give final instructions to those who were about to make the civil rights movement's victorious march to Montgomery. Looking out over the assembly, Abernathy saw women and men, lay people and clergy, black faces and white, and, among them, a number of Catholic sisters. Not only were sisters in the pews of the assembly that day, they also stood defiantly facing sheriff's deputies outside on the "Selma line." They talked with reporters. They drove visitors—lay people, clergy, other sisters—to and from the airport and the mass meetings. They visited "Camp Selma," the makeshift tent-jail that Selma's Sheriff Jim Clark built to detain black youth who were arrested in protest activities, to make sure the young students detained there received adequate food and water while incarcerated. In just a few short years sisters had transformed themselves from virtual inmates of their own religious institutions into public activists agitating for the liberation of others.

In the 1960s, a number of Catholic sisters in the United States abandoned traditional apostolic works within Catholic institutions to experiment with new and often unprecedented kinds of apostolic works among non-Catholics. Women religious who formerly had held typical assignments teaching in Catholic parochial schools or staffing congregational hospitals instead directed those professional skills toward addressing the most pressing social issues of the time. Calling themselves "new nuns," such sisters left the relative insularity of convents and Catholic communities to work among and in some cases live in close proximity to non-Catholics. They joined outreach ministries on public university campuses, counseled drug addicts in addiction recovery programs, assisted labor organizers working to unionize migrant farm workers, tutored adult residents of public housing projects to pass high school equivalency exams, to name just a few examples of these "new works" (as sisters called them). "Why should we be surprised if the Church may call us to bear witness in ways that have never before been essayed?" Sister Gertrude Donnelly, a new nun, asked other sisters in her 1964 book *The Sister Apostle.* "The charity of religious must be a testimony of their own love of God, an act which inspires consciousness of God. God may call us to manifest His love in untrodden ways."[3]

This volume explores this dramatic and often misunderstood shift in the world of American Catholic women religious in the 1960s, a revolution in the religious apostolate of sisters, through close examination of one of the most visible and influential (and shocking to outside observers) of these new apostolic forms, namely the work of Caucasian sisters among African Americans, promoting racial justice. Sisters responded to American white supremacy and racial discrimination in diverse ways in the civil rights era, creating a complex network of programs and activities that I have termed the "racial apostolate." American women religious volunteered to teach at traditionally African American colleges in the South. They held racial-sensitivity training sessions in parish neighborhoods experiencing integration. They sustained urban parish schools after white students left for segregated suburban neighborhoods. They marched at Selma and in Selma sympathy marches. They created summer "free schools" and playground programs for children of color in public housing projects.

This book is not an exhaustive study of the 1960s racial apostolate. The manifold forms and internal diversity of the movement make any such project difficult if not impossible. Rather, this book aims to trace the historical origins of the racial apostolate, to outline some of its dominant features, and to discuss the effect racial-justice activism had on the individual women who engaged in it. This study also attempts, insofar as it is possible, to take readers inside the sisters' worlds, to illuminate the tensions and contradictions that sisters navigated in this particularly fraught historical moment, and to make intelligible the motivations and logic that drove them into such uncharted and, as we shall see, volatile waters. In doing so, I hope to capture some of the confusion and frustration, as well as the exuberance and delight that is so vivid in their writings from this period, that sisters experienced in leaving familiar forms of religious service for new horizons of Christian mission. This book aims to shed new light on the diversity and internal complexity of the lives that sisters created for themselves during a decade of rapid change, replacing outdated popular stereotypes of sisters as either childlike innocents or malicious sadists with more balanced images of their professional competence, complex personal motivations, and the intricacy of their relationships with secular and religious institutions.

I do not in these pages argue that women religious had a substantial influence on the civil rights movement. They did not. Catholic sisters, and Catholics generally, came to the movement quite late, riding the winds of the conclusive demonstrations and legislative developments of 1965 and 1966 when integration was well underway. Though sisters' presence may have been tactically helpful at Selma, providing some measure of protection for others in the final march, their contribution to the civil rights movement remained largely symbolic. Sisters' participation at Selma, in Selma sympathy marches in northern cities, and in later marches for racial justice in northern urban areas lent additional credibility among northern whites to the cause for racial justice. Sisters also attracted media attention, helping to keep the Selma drama in the national spotlight through its resolution in the final march to Montgomery. Sisters' lateness in joining the movement was largely the result of preconciliar norms of enclosure and religious mission that limited sisters' direct participation in most public spheres. It took significant changes to the structure and orientation of the Catholic Church, brought about by the Second Vatican Council (1962–1965), for there to be an institutional context in which American sisters could freely enter into public life and political activism.

While the sisters had an admittedly limited effect on the civil rights movement, the movement had a significant influence upon American Catholic sisters during the 1960s. Not always by design, but always with profound consequences, racial justice and religious reform were intertwined in the experience of many American sisters in the 1960s and 1970s. As this book will argue, public activism and personal transformation were intimately and immediately bound together in the lives of those sisters who participated in the racial apostolate. For many sisters, worlds of religious meaning and institutional purpose were destroyed and then remade through racial activism and contact with African Americans in the racial apostolate. When the period began, the physical, cultural, and intellectual worlds of American sisters were largely confined to exclusively Catholic spheres. But experiences of racial engagement that took individual sisters beyond these familiar Catholic settings challenged and changed them, allowing sisters to fashion new identities as vowed religious and to see themselves, their vocations, and their institutes in dramatically different terms. And, in the final account, it inspired some women religious to return to their congregations and press for thoroughgoing revisions to the norms of religious life in the late 1960s and early 1970s.

"I Love the Church, but I'd Like to Be Able to Respect It"

The racial apostolate of the 1960s was not without precedent among American sisters. Apostolic work that involved crossing geographic, religious, and racial lines to address basic human needs was, at one time, a common facet of life for American women religious in congregations with an active apostolate. Though popular images often portray Catholic sisters as sheltered, naïve recluses who rarely ventured beyond the safe boundaries of Catholic enclaves, such stereotypes mainly reflect the experience of sisters in early and mid-twentieth century, a specific period when canonical regulations limited their activities. In the longer span of American history, contact with a diverse array of people was a natural outgrowth for Catholic sisters in apostolic congregations of their pursuit of works of mercy. As Dana Robert has argued, the earliest plantings of vowed religious life for women in the United States in the early nineteenth century were made by women with missionary aspirations, typically members of uncloistered congregations of European women religious who traveled across the Atlantic at the request of American bishops to establish basic Catholic institutions like schools and hospitals in the wilds of North America. Many of these earliest sisters in the United States did not seek out or intentionally undertake missionary works that involved direct cross-cultural or interracial encounters. Yet the sheer size of the continent and the frontier character of the American Catholic Church (the United States was formally designated a mission territory of the Church until 1908) meant that a majority of American sisters before 1900 lived and labored in frontier settings far removed from the settled villages and established convents of their European homes.[4] In North America those European sisters regularly came into contact with a broad array of people. In a landmark study of the nineteenth-century experience of one such transplanted European congregation, the Sisters of Saint Joseph of Carondelet, Carol Coburn and Martha Smith, note: "In developing and sustaining multiple institutions, the sisters interacted with laity of all ethnic and socioeconomic classes, from clerics, attorneys, doctors, and bankers to soldiers, miners, orphans, and schoolchildren."[5] Throughout the nineteenth century Catholic women religious in noncloistered congregations labored among and interacted with people of diverse background, race, and religious affiliation.

In addition to these transplanted European congregations, several "home-grown" orders of religious founded in the United States in the late nineteenth century claimed a specific charism (or gift of ministry) to live among, serve, and in some cases convert, African Americans and Native Americans. In the mid- and late nineteenth century, African American Catholic women who felt a call to religious consecration responded to the substantial barriers that prevented them from joining predominantly Caucasian orders by forming their own congregations of religious. Working in congregations like the Sisters of the Holy Family and the Oblate Sisters of Providence, African American women religious served enslaved and free people of color, both Catholic and non-Catholic, through a system of schools, orphanages, and hospitals located primarily in southern Catholic enclaves like New Orleans and Baltimore.[6] The efforts of African American sisters were mirrored by members of predominantly Caucasian congregations like Katherine Drexel's Sisters of the Blessed Sacrament, who also lived and worked among people of color, providing education and health care to minority groups.[7] Despite a shared concern for the physical and spiritual welfare of African Americans, sisters of European ancestry and sisters of color rarely cooperated with each other in their apostolic efforts. With few exceptions, individual congregations of women religious were racially specific in their founding and remained steadfastly segregated throughout the era of integration, even to the present moment.

The status of such sisters—noncloistered women who professed private, simple vows of poverty, chastity, and obedience within congregations with an active apostolate—had always been somewhat ambiguous in the larger ecclesial structure of the Catholic church, which until 1900 conferred official approbation only on women religious who accepted solemn vows and papal cloister. As sisters would discover, such ambiguity had certain strategic advantages; official recognition and canonical status, when they came, brought with them new constraints on the autonomy and freedom such congregations had previously enjoyed. Though the 1900 papal bull *Conditae a Christo* conferred official status on religious with active apostolates, it also required sisters to adhere to the restrictions of a partial cloister that severely limited their interactions with the world beyond the convent. The first systematic Code of Canon Law, which took effect in 1918, codified these restrictions as the norm for active congregations, fostering a "cloister mentality" that caused many congregations to turn their apostolic efforts inward toward the Catholic community, where it was believed sisters would be more safely insulated from the polluting influence of the outside world. Required to report their compliance with canon law to authorities in Rome every five years, many superiors of women's congregations from the 1920s through the 1950s rigidly enforced restrictions on sisters' physical movements, access to media and public meetings, and contact with family members, lay people, and even other religious. In a curious juxtaposition, during the first half of the twentieth century when papal encyclicals and American bishops were calling Catholics toward engagement with an ever-broader program of social action, sisters were increasingly required to limit the scope of their ministries to adhere to norms of enclosure. Women religious who felt an apostolic call to minister to non-Catholics and communities of color beyond Catholic enclaves lived with constant tension between the unencumbered movement that such apostolates required and the concrete limitations that canon law placed on them.[8]

Despite the new restrictions women religious faced in the early twentieth century, some congregations managed to continue to pursue apostolic works among non-Catholic people of color in the United States. Such congregations often framed their activities as missionary endeavors, arguing that their work required certain exceptions from the norms of cloister. When members of the Sisters of Saint Joseph (SSJ) of Rochester, New York, moved to Selma, Alabama, in the 1930s to assist Edmundite efforts among black Selmians (the subject of Chapter 5), they traded their usual black habits for white mission habits, marking their work among African Americans as different from the usual teaching and nursing the SSJs performed in Catholic communities in their home state. Sisters in Chicago during the period characterized as the "great migration" of southern African Americans illustrate this dynamic. As Suellen Hoy has documented, congregations like the Sisters of the Good Shepherd, the Franciscan Missionaries of Mary, and the Daughters of Charity found creative ways to engage with newly arrived African Americans in their city, often in marked contrast with lay Catholic perceptions that the migration amounted to a "Negro invasion."[9] "Catholic sisters who linked their lives to those of African Americans" opened missionary schools inside—and occasionally beyond—Chicago's South Side "black belt" while often ignoring pressure from prominent Catholics discomforted that Caucasian sisters would transgress Chicago's "color line."[10] The Daughters of Charity opened Marillac House, a large community center serving a Chicago neighborhood in rapid racial transition. Marillac House not only kept sisters engaged with their African American neighbors, but the Daughters of Charity used senior-citizen programs and a women's auxiliary group to keep white Catholics engaged with the neighborhood even after they had moved away from it. Congregations carefully monitored and regulated these atypical apostolic activities so as not to raise unwanted scrutiny from local bishops or ecclesial authorities in Rome.

A series of changes within the Church and the institution of religious life at midcentury reversed the trend toward insularity among American sisters, prompting some religious to again pursue apostolic activities in communities of color during the later years of the civil rights movement. In the 1950s American women religious initiated a series of reforms that both strengthened and broadened the education offered to women entering religious life. Through the first four decades of the twentieth century, Catholic women joined religious congregations in record numbers in a trend that historians now describe in modern parlance as a "vocation boom." The restrictions of canon law that channeled sisters toward apostolates within Catholic structures meant that sisters were a ubiquitous presence in Catholic parishes at midcentury, outnumbering priests by a ratio of three to one through the 1950s and 1960s. Even in times when vocations were abundant, the demand for sisters' labor had always outpaced the actual number of women religious who were available to staff Catholic schools and hospitals. As the boom waned and the number of women entering religious life began to decline in the 1950s, superiors and members of the hierarchy who were attentive to such patterns of vocation and profession were rightly concerned about the effect that a shortage of religious would have on Catholic institutions dependent on their labor. Partly in response to declining vocations among women, formation directors and major superiors from American communities of women religious implemented reforms that improved the educational and professional training offered to the cadre of young sisters just entering religious life, hoping that such changes would make religious life more attractive to future generations of young women. Through collaborative organizations like the Sister Formation Conference (SFC), congregations of American religious restructured the formation (or formal training) of sisters to stress intellectual development, theological competence, and preparation for apostolic work. The SFC strengthened the already progressive educational opportunities that women religious enjoyed so that, by the mid-1960s, sisters had attained educational levels unparalleled among women—religious or lay—at any previous time in American history.[11]

While American sisters implemented reforms that expanded the educational and professional horizons for the substantial population of women religious, the Church itself was moving toward a renewed engagement with the non-Catholic world. At the conclusion of World War II, the Catholic Church entered a period of serious, sustained reflection on its role in human destiny and its mission in the modern world. Through the 1950s, a group of European theologians—many of whom had been exiled from Europe during the war—plumbed the Catholic tradition for principles that would help the Church respond meaningfully to the challenges that fascism, genocide, and nuclear warfare posed to humanity. At the same time, Pope Pius XII, motivated by a similar concern that the Church not be irrelevant to modern society, quietly pressed congregations of religious to reform any outdated rules that impeded sisters from pursuing effective and relevant apostolates.[12] Building on these foundations, the watershed Second Vatican Council (a meeting in Rome of the world's bishops called by Pope John XXIII) set in motion a process of formal reflection, innovation, and reform that dramatically transformed the culture of the Roman Catholic Church, as well as its central institutions. The contentious meetings of the bishops produced a corpus of surprisingly coherent decrees that called for *aggiornamento* (or modernization) in the Church and exhorted Catholics of all stations to respond creatively and joyfully to the challenges of life in the twentieth century. Stressing the intimate, incarnational presence of a loving Christ over the transcendence of a perfect but distant God, the Council replaced images of the Church as a perfect society with an understanding of the Church as the "People of God," fully immersed in the world as they together strive toward fuller realization of God's desire for the salvation of humanity. The Council mandated reform to such basic elements of the Church as the liturgy and religious congregations, and established goals and timetables to guide the reform process.

Like other Catholics in this exciting and uncertain period, sisters had to negotiate and renegotiate their role within a Catholic theological and ecclesial landscape that was constantly shifting beneath their feet. The national conferences, educational programs, and intercongregational cooperation that occurred through the 1950s in American religious congregations of women prepared them intellectually, professionally, and structurally to respond vigorously and enthusiastically to the thoroughgoing call for transformation that emerged through the Second Vatican Council. American sisters were familiar with current trends in theology, practiced at self-study, and aware of the need to modernize outdated customs in order to remain relevant to modern society. By the early 1960s most congregations had among their members a group of sisters who were prepared to respond to the initiatives of the Second Vatican Council. Indeed, "few groups in the church responded to the decrees of the Second Vatican Council with the alacrity shown by American sisters."[13] Changes that shocked laypeople often were easily accepted and even embraced by sisters.

For sisters, the Council's effects were often felt in areas that related to the religious apostolate. The Council loosened the most severe of the twentieth-century regulations that had restricted sisters' movements and activities, allowing them greater freedom to experiment with new configurations of mission, community, and lifestyle. More importantly, the Council provided women religious with an outward-oriented theology that justified and in fact encouraged direct engagement with social problems. Coming on the heels of the structural and educational changes that American sisters already had implemented in their congregations through the Sister Formation Conference, the conciliar mandate for Catholicism to engage with the world fully revitalized the apostolate among religious in the United States, moving it from the margins to the very center of religious life. Many American sisters interpreted the Council as an affirmation of changes that they had already been pursuing quietly within their institutes for over a decade, particularly those reforms that moved sisters toward more intense or more effective apostolic engagement with the world beyond convent walls and Catholic parish schools. "The Council is the church's public admission of irrelevance in the modern world," commented Sister M. Charles Borromeo, CSC. "But it is at the same time the instrument to find new meaning for the People of God in the midst of God's people."[14] As a result, in the mid- and late 1960s a virtual army of American sisters who had been inspired by the Council to change the world and freed of many of the preconciliar restrictions of enclosure set out to apply their newfound enthusiasm and newly acquired training to fresh apostolic works.[15]

Unfortunately, sisters' embrace of more engaged and relevant apostolic works occurred at the precise historical moment when traditional Catholic institutions offered fewer and fewer opportunities for women religious to have direct contact with people who were poor or suffering. Riding the winds of postwar economic prosperity, Caucasian Catholics achieved unprecedented levels of economic security in the 1950s and early 1960s. Many Catholics moved from traditional urban ethnic enclaves to burgeoning suburban neighborhoods, taking their parishes with them and, by extension, forcing the sisters who staffed the schools associated with parishes to also relocate to the suburbs. This suburbanization of apostolic work for many teaching sisters opened a troubling gap between the emerging apostolic ideals of engagement with social problems and the increasingly affluent and segregated nature of Catholic institutions at the time. "I love the Church, but I'd like to be able to respect it," wrote a sister struggling to reconcile her conscience with the fact of Catholic suburban segregation.[16]

Some sisters, disturbed by prosperity and de facto segregation of suburban parish schools, sought out new apostolic activities that were more consistent with the educational and theological currents moving through religious life in the 1960s, abandoning suburban assignments in Catholic institutions for ones located in impoverished communities of non-Catholics. Many sisters justified this departure from common patterns of the religious apostolate by arguing that such activities, outside of increasingly affluent Catholic communities, allowed them to continue the "works of mercy" that had traditionally characterized religious life. In a racist society that denied economic autonomy, education, franchise, and adequate health care to persons of color, those who bore the stigma of race were often counted disproportionately among the poor. In the years following the Birmingham bus boycott, as the civil rights movement broadened its initial focus on integration toward a broader engagement with issues of racial and economic justice, sisters increasingly found that they shared the movement's overall objectives. Sisters also discovered that the movement for racial justice offered them the kinds of relevant, socially engaged apostolic experiences they had been unable to secure through traditional assignments within Catholic institutions. Thus, the image of a white sister in full religious garb playing dodgeball with African American children on a housing-project playground in 1965 was not as anomalous to sisters as it seemed to the African Americans among whom the sisters of the racial apostolate worked and sometimes lived, nor to white Catholics who were accustomed to the steady presence of nuns in parish schools and Catholic hospitals.

If the civil rights movement provided sisters with a racial focus for the conciliar mandate to "promote human justice," the Johnson administration's War on Poverty made practical and financial contributions to sisters' efforts to reconfigure the apostolic component of religious life. A significant number of the racial apostolate programs sisters created were associated with the Office of Economic Opportunity (OEO) and other related federal agencies of the War on Poverty. Federal antipoverty programs provided a venue for sisters who were interested in apostolic work among poor persons of color but whose congregations would not or could not offer such works under congregational auspices. Because most antipoverty programs provided a modest salary, substituting federal grant money for the financial compensation that Catholic parish schools provided as a matter of course for sisters who worked in Catholic institutions, federal agencies made it possible for sisters to pursue the racial apostolate without becoming a financial drain on their congregations. Participation in these government-sponsored programs, moreover, allowed sisters to utilize the professional training they had received in religious formation and lent public legitimacy to the expansion of sisters' work into new spheres.

Thus, the racial apostolate emerged in a unique historical moment when developments in the Catholic Church, in American race relations, and in the federal government converged to dramatically change the political, theological, and economic contexts in which Catholic women religious pursued the apostolic component of religious life. American sisters' apostolic engagement with race was an organic response to the complex conditions they inhabited in the mid-1960s, a form of creative adaptation to the changes happening within their congregations, the Catholic Church, and in the world beyond convent walls.

The racial apostolate was not a static or singular event. It developed and changed alongside and in relation to the civil rights movement, its fate closely linked with the fortunes and direction of the movement through the mid- and late 1960s. When the racial apostolate emerged in 1965, the civil rights movement was in a transitional moment, poised between initial successes and new challenges. On the one hand, 1965 was a high point of self-confidence for the civil rights movement, when long-sought legislative victories like the passage of the 1964 Civil Rights Act meant that the question was no longer whether integration would happen but rather how, when, to what extent, and to the benefit of whom. At the same time, voices of dissent from the movement's younger members over issues of strategy and tactics that emerged in 1965 presaged the internal ideological conflicts that would ultimately divide the movement in the late 1960s when two of the movements main organizations, the Student Nonviolent Coordinating Committee (SNCC) and the Southern Christian Leadership Conference (SCLC), broke ranks over emergent black power philosophies. Catholic sisters in racial apostolate programs absorbed the optimism of the movement at the time they joined, but they also almost immediately were caught in conflicts within the movement over the role of white activists. From 1965 through 1968, many African American communities were still willing to accept the presence of white sisters among them in exchange for the public credibility that sisters' endorsement lent to the cause of civil rights and for the intellectual and professional resources that sisters contributed to struggling black communities. Over time, as black separatism became more normative in African American communities, sisters learned to recognize and respect boundaries that black communities placed upon their presence and their activities.

The racial apostolate was not the exclusive province of a select few religious congregations. Rather, the 1960s racial apostolate was a widespread but diffuse voluntary effort by a self-selected group of white women religious representing a broad array of religious congregations. Sisters from every region of the country and most religious orders participated. The racial apostolate of Catholic women religious was dispersed across the United States, but there was a higher concentration of these projects in cities of the Midwest. The overwhelming majority of sisters who participated in the racial apostolate were Caucasian. Though there were noteworthy exceptions, for the most part congregations of American women religious remained largely segregated in the civil rights era paradoxically so considering the growing attention the Church paid to issues of racial justice and racial parity in society at large. Sisters who attempted to racially integrate racial apostolate programs ran headlong into logistical barriers linked to the profound segregation of religious congregations in the United States. Writing to inform Sister Margaret Traxler that her congregation would not release her to participate in a particular racial apostolate program, Sister Mary Antona Ebo, FSM, an African American woman religious, tied the racial segregation of apostolic programs to the legacy of white supremacy in American congregations of religious. "Perhaps you can use this as a reply to some of the people who criticize you for not having Negro sisters on the team," Ebo offered, "not only the lack of generosity of those orders who may have a sister to contribute . . . but also the orders who have for so long taken a 'lily-white' attitude toward God-given vocations. Perhaps, some of the rest would have Negro sisters to contribute if the attitude would have been different" (ellipses in original text).[17] Though African American sisters in historically black congregations continued their established works in communities of African American Catholics throughout the civil rights era, the majority of sisters ministering to non-Catholic African Americans in the 1960s were members of congregations composed predominantly of women of European descent. The irony in this situation—so apparent to contemporary readers—that racial segregation proved to be more intractable among vowed religious (even those devoted to integration and racial parity) than it was in American society as a whole was not formally addressed until the National Black Sisters' Conference raised the issue of discrimination within religious congregations at its 1968 founding.[18]

The racial apostolate of the 1960s took many forms. In addition to the representative case studies that are the focus of this book, racial-justice activism among women religious in the 1960s found expression in diverse programs. Some programs were designed to give sisters both practical training combating racial poverty as well as direct experience living in urban slum areas. The Sisters Urban Education (SUE) program of the Department of Educational Services of the National Catholic Conference for Interracial Jusitce (NCCIJ) is one example. SUE offered sisters college credit for participating in three months of training in Chicago's South Side neighborhoods during the summer. Community Urban Environment (CUE) was a similar undertaking in Memphis. Sisters in New Jersey spent summers playing with children on housing-project playgrounds under the auspices of the Summer of Service (SOS) program, based in Elizabeth. The Sisters of Loretto in Chicago instituted the Loretto Educational Advancement Program (LEAP) through which sisters helped African Americans in the South Side Woodlawn area prepare to take the civil service exam. In Chicago the Daughters of Charity organized a program called Summer of HOPE (Help Our People Emerge), which allowed women religious to immerse themselves in local neighborhoods to identify and then address the specific needs of each neighborhood. Sisters of Mercy spent summers throughout the 1960s in "inner city parishes" in Kansas City, Missouri, offering religious education and recreational programs for children. Teaching sisters used their professional training to sponsor educational enrichment programs in black neighborhoods. Franciscan sisters from Minnesota opened a summer "fun school"—the subject of Chapter 5—in Chicago's Cabrini Green housing project in 1965. Mercy sisters in Nashville, Tennessee, successfully fought for racial integration of the exclusive Cathedral grade school and high school. Other sisters attempted to incorporate African and African American history into their classrooms. Sisters in Nashville, for example, added a "Negro heritage" section to their library.

Some programs developed as sisters refused to follow patterns of Catholic white flight to the suburbs, choosing instead to remain in neighborhoods that were rapidly integrating. Sisters teaching in Boston neighborhoods in which African Americans had recently become the majority of residents formed the Association of Urban Sisters (AUS) to coordinate their efforts to keep urban parish schools open. In Chicago, the Urban Apostolate of the Sisters (UAS) addressed the same issues for sisters in the Windy City. Noting the marked decline in the number of urban parishes in Detroit, the Sisters of Mercy selected one parish, Saint John the Evangelist, as the site of their efforts to continue ministry in newly integrated neighborhoods. The Mercies, as they were commonly called, established Project Boulevard shortly afterward, an experimental community in an abandoned nursing convent. Sisters from Project Boulevard dispersed into various apostolic efforts in the neighborhood:

they developed a food co-op, organized a summer day camp, taught music and "uplift" classes, and visited elderly neighbors as they sought to ascertain the specific needs of the neighborhood. At the national level, Project Equality attempted to create economic parity nationally by pressing the Church actively to recruit and hire African Americans for positions in Catholic institutions and to patronize black-owned businesses.

Other programs sponsored by women religious addressed problems of segregation and poverty in the South. Through Cooperative Help of Integrated College Education (CHOICE)—explored in Chapter 6—sisters with doctoral degrees taught in historically black colleges, enabling black faculty to take a summer or a yearlong sabbatical to pursue research and writing. With the motto "A STAR not in the East, but in the South," the diocese of Natchez-Jackson, Mississippi, assigned teaching sisters to summer "centers for basic education" in poor, African American areas throughout the diocese.[19]

Several projects of the racial apostolate worked to foster racial harmony by facilitating encounters between whites and blacks. Summer in Suburbia (SIS) sent African American children from central Chicago to suburban or rural Minnesota to live with Catholic families for the summer. Project Bridge, based in Cleveland, Ohio; Operation Understanding in Newark, New Jersey; and Project Concern in Baltimore, Maryland, were all dedicated to facilitating interracial conversations among either teenage or adult peers. Operation Coffee Cup (OCC) attempted to foster casual conversation between black and white laywomen. Spread Truth, Oppose Prejudice (STOP) was a similar program in Portland, Maine. The NCCIJ sponsored a traveling workshop of "nuns on wheels," sisters who traveled from convent to convent in a station wagon holding racial sensitivity seminars in Catholic institutions.

American Catholic women religious addressed racism and its effects in numerous other racial apostolate programs, many without distinguishing names or titles. Sisters in Pittsburgh ran a remedial summer enrichment program for black high-school students in danger of dropping out. Sisters in Albany, New York, tutored adult literacy in the evenings at the Mount Zion Baptist Church; in Davenport, Iowa, sisters made home visits in African American neighborhoods to locate families needing food; women religious in New Haven, Connecticut, compiled a weekly list of available jobs and job training opportunities and spent evenings counseling displaced black workers. Cincinnati sisters canvassed segregated housing projects to identify residents' needs and then helped organize a neighborhood council to advocate for better maintenance of the homes. Sisters in Toledo set up an activity center in an abandoned storefront, open evenings and Saturdays, for African American children.[20]

One of the most pervasive and telling effects brought on by sisters' participation in the racial apostolate was an increased sense of identification with black women and men. "I feel black. I look at everything through Negro eyes—Negro emotions & Negro pain," wrote one sister after spending a summer in inner-city Chicago.[21] Though at first glance this dynamic might seem surprising, certain similarities between the position of African Americans in American society in the mid-twentieth century and that of women religious in the American Catholic Church at the same time reinforced sisters' identifications with African Americans. Both were depicted as simple and childlike; the inexpensive labor of both was essential to economic expansion and growth in the 1950s and 1960s that largely benefited others. There were clear differences between the circumstances of sisters and blacks at midcentury, to be sure. Sisters voluntarily accepted the stigmatized position they occupied; they were not subject to the brutal violence visited upon African Americans in the name of white supremacy; they occupied a more privileged legal and social position; they had far greater access to education; and they possessed the franchise. Still, sisters recognized something of their own experience in that of the African Americans who became their colleagues and neighbors in the racial apostolate. Sisters identified with the barriers African Americans faced in society, and they identified with the civil rights movement's efforts to overcome those barriers. In the end, the identification of sisters in the racial apostolate with the experiences of African Americans sharpened sisters' criticisms of the male authority structures in the Church and contributed to the dramatic conflicts that flared between American women religious and certain bishops and curial authorities in the 1970s and 1980s.

"A High Price to Pay for Freedom"

This book is divided into two sections. The first section provides a general overview of the racial apostolate as an historical phenomenon, devoting separate chapters to the origins of the movement, the catalytic agent that aided its emergence, and internal dynamics that characterized its operation at the level of the congregation, superior, and individual sister. Chapter 1 considers the changes in the social and religious context of American sisters during the 1950s and 1960s that inspired and compelled sisters to engage directly with issues of racial injustice. Chapter 2 documents the origins and activities of the Department of Educational Services of the National Catholic Conference for Interracial Justice (NCCIJ), the main organization that developed racial justice programs for women religious and placed interested sisters in specific projects. Chapter 3 turns to the internal dynamics of religious communities, paying special attention to the delicate and sometimes painful process of discernment and negotiation through which individual sisters joined racial apostolate programs. The second half of the book is devoted to case studies of three distinct, representative instances of the diverse racial apostolate of Catholic sisters in the 1960s: sisters' involvement in the civil rights campaigns in Selma, Alabama, in Chapter 4; Project Cabrini, a summer "fun school" in a housing project in central Chicago, in Chapter 5; and the National Placement Bureau and the CHOICE program, which often sent sisters into the South, in Chapter 6.

The demonstrations at Selma, Alabama, in 1965 were the most visible and the most confrontational of sisters' involvement in the campaign for racial justice. The violence and the press attention that attended their presence at Selma allowed sisters to sharpen and to disseminate widely among other sisters and their supporters the emergent identity the racial apostolate had facilitated.

Project Cabrini, a summer "fun school" for African American children living in the Cabrini Green housing project in Chicago exemplified the type of apostolic program through which sisters from rural backgrounds entered urban environments. The chapter on the racial apostolate in Chicago explores ways in which the Franciscan sisters from rural Minnesota who staffed the Project Cabrini program experienced race—both their own whiteness and the skin color of the children with whom they worked—in a complex urban environment. The religious habit complicated the race of white Catholic sisters in northern cities, allowing them to inhabit identities that transcended the binary categories of white/black, and ultimately lay/religious and Catholic/non-Catholic.

Northern women religious entered teaching positions in African American educational institutions in the South through the National Placement Bureau of the NCCIJ, an organization dedicated to placing sisters in the racial apostolate. Once in the South, Catholic women religious felt stigmatized, exoticized, and segregated in the Protestant-dominated deep South, and they identified with the alienation of African Americans. The sisters derived comfort both by being included in black communities and from the convergence of black and Catholic cultures in the title "sister" (or "sistah," as the word often appears in their writings). At the same time, sisters qualified this solidarity with African Americans in their reports with anecdotes about the unpredictability of their students, expressing ambivalence and anxiety about blackness and bodies. In writings punctuated by hyperbolic anecdotes about how their students baffled and perplexed them, sisters also testified to profound changes in their own lives.

This project is based upon a close reading of archival documents using interpretive frameworks from the fields of history and cultural anthropology. I also interviewed twenty-four sisters in eight religious congregations. My writing foregrounds sisters' voices, privileging women religious as narrators of their own stories and interpreters of their own experiences when the sources allow this. It is my hope that the prominent voices of women religious in the pages that follow will help orient readers to the perspective of sisters themselves, recovering something of the intense optimism and uncertainty that sisters felt at the time and that they expressed, quite eloquently at points, in their correspondence with one another. Even the best historical writing based on meticulous research is an exercise of recovery and interpretation that trades the immediacy of human experience for the analytic advantage of historical hindsight. Historians hear the thunderous cacophony of the past as faint voices that survive in archive boxes, and then amplify and systematize those whispers into a meaningful story—the most accurate one we can reconstruct—about the past. If cause-and-effect relationships in that reconstituted story seem obvious to us now, if the outcome of historical developments seem inevitable, it is only because our vantage point in the present gives us this advantage over our sources. The voices of women religious that follow stand as reminders that the sisters about whom this book is written lived amid tumult and uncertainty. They were not able to foresee that legal segregation would end or that the Church and the institution of vowed religious life would survive the tumult of the conciliar period.[22]

While this approach is intended to provide readers with close contact with the voices and perspectives of the women religious about whom the book is written, this methodology also at times brings the reader into close proximity with the problematic issues of race and voice in sisters' written and spoken narratives. In several instances, sisters describing specific conversations used a racialized dialect to represent the voices of African Americans. Though this language rightly strikes a dischordant note in the ear of contemporary readers, such passages also open a valuable window into the complexity of orientations toward race among even those sisters who lived closely with African Americans, who were generally sympathetic to the cause of racial justice, and who actively worked to alleviate both the causes and the human effects of racism. These troubling passages remind us that sisters, like other American Catholics in the 1960s, inhabited complex and often contradictory fields of racial discourse in which deep cultural patterns of American white supremacy intersected with Roman Catholic theologies of racial equality as well as longstanding practices of racial segregation in the American Church. Whether sisters employed the convention of racialized dialect to express condescension toward African Americans, to rhetorically distance themselves from African Americans, or, more benignly, to simply represent the differences they experienced in speech patterns, the presence of such language stands as a reminder that sisters in the racial apostolate cannot be uniformly lumped together under a singular mantle of progressive interracialism, nor can they be represented accurately in a one-dimensional portrait of heroic selflessness. Though most sisters in the racial apostolate demonstrated moral courage and an admirable ability to oppose white supremacist norms, it is equally clear that some sisters brought attitudes of white racial superiority to the racial apostolate and retained those attitudes in some form even while working for the cause of racial justice. Paying close attention to the tropes sisters used to represent racialized difference reveals something of the intricacy and diversity of the ways sisters negotiated issues of race, identity, and religious mission in the 1960s.

As with all human acts of narrative, the stories sisters told me in interviews bore many meanings. In hearing, relating, and interpreting these stories I have tried to be conscious first of the events of the narrative itself—the dates and persons, events, context, and consequences that make up the factual content of "what exactly happened"—using archival and printed material whenever possible to confirm the events sisters described and place them within the larger chronological framework of each case study. But I also have tried to be attentive to the larger story that sisters were attempting to communicate to me when they selected particular anecdotes to share in our conversations. When Sister Barbara Lumm, SSJ, spoke with me about the intimidation used against those who attended the first voter registration meetings she interjected a story about the day that Jimmie Lee Jackson, a civil rights demonstrator, died at Good Samaritan Hospital. The sudden welling up of emotion she displayed when she repeated the question Jackson had asked her in his dying moments—"Sister, don't you think this is a high price to pay for freedom?"—reflected the importance she attached to the courage of black activists in Selma and her sorrow at their sacrifices. She was telling me that she knew exactly how high the price was that some of her neighbors in Selma had paid for freedom. In telling me the story of Jimmie Lee Jackson she also was telling me about the relationship between sisters and civil rights martyrs. Specifically, she was telling me that the white supremacist violence she had witnessed had affected her deeply and had transformed her permanently. Her story was as much about herself as it was about the martyrdom of Jimmie Lee, and it is this tale of the inner lives of racial-activist sisters in the 1960s that these pages explore.

CHAPTER ONE

Church and Society: The Emergence of New Nuns

"If anyone asked me today 'What could I get for you?'" reflected Sister Evangeline Meyer, SSND, in 1968 about her ministry in the Lawndale section of Chicago's West Side, a neighborhood that had recently seen three consecutive summers of race riots, "I would say 'A store-front or ground-floor apartment with a glass door.'" What Sister Meyer found most objectionable about her present living quarters in an old convent in Lawndale's Presentation Parish was the blue wooden door and flight of ten stone steps that separated her from the surrounding neighborhood and its people. That big door and the old stone steps simply sent the wrong message. "The place was built to look imposing, and so it does," she observed. "But that was the 'old Church.' Now, accessibility, the 'yes, here I am' approach is in order, especially here."[1]

To Sister Meyer, the steps and doors of the convent symbolized all that was wrong with the preconciliar Catholic Church. The old Church—"settled, solid, sure of itself, insisting on the absoluteness of its own legislation"—had invested prodigious resources in building a "stone and brick" tabernacle that by the mid-1960s stood mainly as a barrier between the Church and the largely non-Catholic, African American residents of Lawndale. Massive structures like the convent she inhabited spoke "too loudly of the smug and static past" of the Church and said far too little about the poverty, racism, and injustice that Lawndale's current residents endured. Determined not to be isolated behind the big, blue convent door or her "long, black skirt and veil," Sister Meyer embraced what she and many others came to call an "open apostolate" of being present in the neighborhood, available at all times of the day and night to respond to whatever needs people brought to her. In contrast to the forbidding Catholic architecture of the parish, she wanted her presence in Lawndale to communicate *"availability to the limit"*: "I will show Christ and/or speak Christ according to the tone and color of the encounter. There must be close, personal contact. Understanding, empathy, compassion, and honesty may be gifts, but they are also simply human—human reactions to human beings."[2]

Sister Meyer's sense that she was creating a "yes, here I am" apostolate in the shadow of a failed and forbidding "old Church" reflects a particular vision of religious life that emerged among American sisters in the early 1960s. Calling themselves "new nuns," these sisters sought to reform what they characterized as the stultifying and impersonal rigidity of the brick-and-mortar Catholicism that had produced a formidable infrastructure of parish schools, hospitals, and colleges by the early twentieth century. In place of a Catholicism defined by its buildings, institutions, and bureaucracy, these sisters envisioned a Church characterized by flexibility and intimacy, one that was responsive to present-day circumstances and that encouraged religious toward passionate apostolic engagement with the "human family" writ large. "New nuns" wanted to replace existing forms of religious apostolate that were patterned on monastic models of contemplation and enclosure, and that often confined sisters' activities to service provision within Catholic enclaves, with a new apostolate that immersed sisters directly and immediately in the most urgent problems of society, particularly racial and economic injustice. Often this meant relocating sisters' work from Catholic institutions in Catholic neighborhoods to programs centered in non-Catholic arenas that had minimal if any connection to the Church.

Some analysts on the recent history of Catholic women religious—particularly those nostalgic for the "good sister" of the 1950s, safely ensconced behind the thick, wooden doors of Catholic parochial schools and hospitals—have erroneously portrayed this reorientation as a radical, illegitimate, even tragic revolution led by a renegade minority of sisters. These critics argue that this minority hijacked the mandate for religious renewal that came out of the Second Vatican Council and used it to overturn timeless and essential components of vowed religious life, thus cheapening both the institution of religious life and the value of religious themselves and, in the process, starving Catholic parishes of the inexpensive labor of sisters.[3] Close examination of the ecclesiastical and cultural context in which this reorientation occurred reveals that this evaluation is incorrect on several fronts. The apostolic transition that occurred within American women's religious orders in the 1960s was one component of a gradual, incremental, and widespread shift in the philosophy, ideals, and aesthetics of religious life among American sisters rather than the work of a small, unrepresentative cadre of sisters. Furthermore, the foundation for the apostolic revolution among American sisters lay at the intersection of simultaneous developments in the Church and in American society that occurred in the 1940s and 1950s. Though the Second Vatican Council influenced the momentum and direction of this broad shift, the ideas and organizational structures at its core both predated the Council and remained largely independent of the Council's agenda. In the end the "yes, here I am" apostolate was not the creation of rebellious sisters so much as it was one particular response (among others) by American sisters to the complex and subtle ways that the ground underneath their feet shifted through the 1950s and 1960s.

This chapter considers the broad historical context in which sisters concerned about racial justice first began to claim identities as "new nuns" in the early 1960s, exploring the unique convergence of changes within the Church and society that prompted apostolic women religious to reimagine the apostolate and their relationship to racial injustice in the United States. Sisters' work in the expanding racial apostolate of the 1960s signaled the extent to which events in the 1950s had conflated an apostolic imperative to "speak Christ" with a "simply human" response of compassion and empathy in the face of human suffering. Like Sister Meyer, "new nuns" often used language that combined theological concepts like incarnational Christology with terms borrowed from the social sciences and the civil rights movement to describe their "new works" promoting racial justice. This discursive bricolage, which apostolic sisters employed to explain their work, reflected the complexity of the world women religious inhabited in the mid-1960s, a world bursting with optimistic new theologies and social theories. Yet this world was profoundly unsettled by shifting demographics of race and class, a place where the heady, sometimes euphoric mixture of new educational opportunities and national conferences that were available to women religious occasionally was overshadowed by looming conflicts within the Church over school and neighborhood desegregation, the religious authority of the magisterium, and the implementation of the Council's mandate for *aggiornamento*. This swirling confluence of changes in the intellectual, religious, social, economic, and political worlds of women religious at midcentury utterly transformed the context in which sisters performed apostolic works, simultaneously altering the meaning of traditional works while opening avenues for new forms of religious engagement with the world.

"Our Lower-Grade Victorian Traditions and Training"

The religious and intellectual context of consecrated life for American sisters changed profoundly in the 1950s through a series of reforms that simultaneously altered the rules governing religious life and the process through which sisters were trained for religious consecration and educated for active ministry. For American religious, this initiative for reform had dual origins: Pope Pius XII instigated reforms for women religious throughout the world that then filtered into American congregations, while in the United States the Sister Formation Conference (SFC) had already formulated its own solutions to logistical problems specific to the American context. Though their point of origin differed, these two reform efforts shared a focus on the religious apostolate, specifically a desire to make sisters more effective in their apostolic works by removing certain obstacles that limited sisters' efficacy, stunted their initiative, or directed their energy away from direct service into inessential details of convent life. For Pius XII, improving the functioning of the apostolate among women religious meant discarding impractical regulations and encouraging congregations toward cooperative action. For the SFC it meant addressing the negative effect the demands of the burgeoning Catholic parochial school system in the United States placed on religious congregations, adversely affecting how they prepared women for religious life and active ministry. For both the Pope and American religious, the effort to reinvigorate the apostolate meant, at a fundamental level, challenging the culture of quasi-cloistered seclusion that characterized Catholic religious orders of consecrated women in the 1950s.

The renewal of the religious apostolate was not an innovation as much as it was a return to a former vision of religious consecration. Throughout the eighteenth and nineteenth centuries, Catholic sisters on the American frontier founded schools, hospitals, and charitable societies in areas otherwise bereft of public institutions.[4] Though tension between religious consecration and external works was a perennial issue for noncloistered apostolic women's communities, prior to 1918

American women religious were able to organize community life in ways that supported vigorous apostolic activities. But in the twentieth century, after the imposition of normative rules of enclosure in the Code of Canon Law promulgated in 1918, the apostolic activities of American women religious were restricted largely to established Catholic spheres—congregational schools and hospitals and diocesan parishes. Reflecting the Code of Canon Law's preference for uniformity among women's religious congregations, for the first half of the twentieth century diverse forms of religious life in the United States had been more or less organized according to a relatively narrow monastic model that privileged the contemplative and devotional cultivation of the "state of perfection" by individual religious over corporate works of charity outside the convent. The Code of Canon Law had framed consecration and apostolate as unequal components of the religious state, defining sisters' identities primarily in terms of convent-centered prayer. The religious apostolate served a secondary role in this model, a poor cousin to the primary work of cultivating an intimate union with God. Thus a "cloistral mentality that stressed separation from the world as the norm" was embedded in the revised constitutions of most orders at the end of World War I, creating an insular "convent culture" that dominated religious life for women from the 1920s through the 1950s.[5] Throughout this crucial time period—often characterized by historians as the apex of American Catholic culture—sisters were carefully trained to view sacred and secular as "separate and distinct realities."[6] Religious regulations and restrictions, customs surrounding mobility and contact with the laity, modes of dress, daily schedules, and limitations on activity all worked collectively to underscore the separateness of religious from the profane world. As Mary Jo Weaver summarized, prior to the Second Vatican Council "sisters lived in consecrated space, closed off from contaminating contact with the world and officially discouraged from dialogue with other women."[7]

This ethos of monastic separation significantly restricted the apostolate of American women religious between the wars, confining sisters to Catholic institutions and then limiting their activities within even the narrow confines of Catholic schools and parishes, lest sisters be contaminated by contact with the world. The development of "closed society" convents created both uncomfortable internal tensions and difficult external circumstances for American women religious between the wars. For many sisters, the physical, intellectual, and social limitations that followed from canon law conflicted with the fulfillment and sense of purpose they experienced through active ministry.[8] This tension between the monastic ideal and the actual experience of religious consecration and apostolic activity could prove especially troubling for women who understood their vocation to religious life as a call to service. Such sisters often felt caught between their desire to minister to others and the requirement that they "keep the rule." As Patricia Byrne has documented, the religious apostolate lived by many sisters in these years was fraught with minor absurdities and, at times, major frustrations. Sisters were indispensable to the parish and its school, yet often were systematically distanced from parish activities—even devotional societies or liturgical celebrations—that did not directly involve children. The salaries or stipends sisters received were so low that often sisters engaged in other income-generating activities, such as giving music lessons or, in the case of one congregation, selling Avon beauty products to pay for basic necessities like food and clothing. Yet sisters often were characterized as dependent on the good will and financial resources of the clergy and treated as wards of the Church or burdens on its finances. Even individual stories—like that of the sister who learned of the assassination of President Warren G. Harding through the milkman because her convent prohibited sisters from reading newspapers or listening to the radio, or the instruction given to the Sisters of Notre Dame in 1930 to limit discussion with laywomen in the parish to child-centered business because talk about family life or domestic troubles "defiles our minds"—underscore how the midcentury premium that convent culture placed on homogeneity and purity for women religious severely restricted the scope and effectiveness of their ministries.[9]

Pius's push for subtle revision to some restrictive regulations in women's orders began a process of reform that softened these sharp distinctions between sacred and secular spheres in the 1950s. Though previous popes had occasionally signaled fleeting interest in the apostolic work of religious, in the latter half of his pontificate (1939–1958) Pope Pius XII turned significant attention to the dual problems of anachronism and intellectual stasis among vowed women, particularly teaching sisters. Responding to the state of religious life in Europe, and convinced that sisters could and indeed must play a unique and important role in addressing pressing social problems in the wake of World War II, Pius XII encouraged specific, limited reforms within women's religious institutes in the early 1950s, aimed at making sisters more effective in their public works. Though Pius affirmed the prevailing view that the canonical profession of contemplative life was the purpose of religious life for women, he also acknowledged that certain elements of religious life needed to be adapted to "moderate participation in the apostolate" to remain relevant.[10] In a measured, cautious tone, Pius asked sisters to consider modernizing or eliminating outdated customs and to improve the educational level of religious in teaching institutions. To facilitate these reforms at the congregational level Pius called religious superiors to Rome for a series of international congresses between 1950 and 1952.[11] Pius used the gatherings to expand and clarify his call for reform among religious, and his addresses at the congresses became guiding statements for early reform efforts in their congregations. Pius encouraged sisters to adapt their institutes to the demands of modern society and to eliminate unnecessarily restrictive regulations. Though Pius urged superiors who attended the Roman conferences to consider limited revisions to outdated rules, he also was careful to maintain traditional norms of religious authority. Addressing teaching sisters at their 1951 conference, Pius urged, "Let superiors and the general Chapters proceed in this matter conscientiously, with foresight, prudence, and courage and, where the case demands, let them not fail to submit the proposed changes to the competent ecclesiastical authorities."[12] The pontiff did not intend these reforms to substantially challenge core principles of vowed religious life, nor did he anticipate the revolutionary effect that his directives—that were formulated largely according to the image and circumstances of women religious in Europe—would have on American congregations.

The influence of the Roman congresses far surpassed the limited agenda set by Pius XII. The conferences, simply by virtue of bringing together superiors from diverse congregations, introduced a novel ethos of unity and collaboration into the reform process, undermining the dominant culture of isolation and competition that existed between religious communities through the first half of the twentieth century. The Roman congresses also set in motion a process of rapid institutional propagation in the United States, creating specialized organizations and conferences of women religious. Following the success of the international congresses of religious in Rome, Pius XII called for similar congresses at the national level. In August 1952 over two thousand American religious—sisters, priests, and brothers—gathered at Notre Dame for the First National Congress of Religious in the United States. "The purpose of this Congress," Francis J. Connell, CSSR, advised in his opening remarks to the assembly, "is to inspire in us a deeper love for our religious vocation, and a more ardent desire to fulfill the obligations we accepted on the day of our profession, to give one another encouragement, to exchange ideas about problems common to all religious societies."[13] Through the 1950s and 1960s American religious created a network of similar assemblies and conferences where religious met to receive guidance and encouragement from the magisterium, and to discuss among themselves common concerns and strategies for reform.[14] Reform-oriented organizations of women religious in the United States included the Conference of Major Superiors of Women's Religious Institutes (CMSW), founded in 1952 to provide a forum for American superiors to discuss common problems, as well as the Sister Formation Conference (SFC), and the Sisters' Institute of Spirituality (SIS). Once established, national organizations of American religious developed their own agenda for the reform of religious life. Often the depth and scope of sisters' critiques of the rules and structures governing religious institutes exceeded the relatively narrow agenda issued by the Holy See. Thus, national conferences of sisters that began as obedient responses to papal mandate often developed into vehicles for the particular aspirations of American women religious. Organizations like the Conference of Major Superiors developed educational programs that brought together sister-superiors from diverse communities for weekend, weeklong, and summer-length institutes and workshops that focused on specific facets of religious life or religious reform. Published proceedings of those meetings, in turn, produced a sizeable literature that circulated in convents and religious libraries throughout the decade, constituting a rich discourse about the theory and theology of religious life that extended the influence of these collaborative efforts far beyond the elite sisters who attended meetings. Through the 1950s and early 1960s these sister organizations and the educational programs they sponsored functioned as vectors for information, quickly and efficiently disseminating research and ideas about renewal through the general population of American sisters. By the time the Second Vatican Council mandated significant reforms within women's orders, American sisters had in place a solid infrastructure of reform-oriented collaborative organizations to help them formulate, implement, and ultimately defend their renewal policies.

The Sisters' Institute of Spirituality (SIS) offers one example of how American sisters translated Pius's modest initiatives into substantial, expansive, influential organizations in the 1950s. The First International Congress on the States of Perfection, which gathered religious from around the world in Rome in 1950, called for the creation of permanent congresses of religious at the national level. The resultant 1952 First National Congress of United States Religious determined that women in congregational leadership needed to receive special theological training and, in turn, created an annual Institute of Spirituality to provide brief but intensive training in the "theology of the spiritual and religious life" to superiors and novice mistresses. In August 1953, 859 sisters representing 159 congregations from all regions of the United States and Canada gathered at Notre Dame for the first Sisters' Institute of Spirituality. Sisters at the inaugural SIS attended lectures by an all-male faculty on topics such as ascetical and mystical theology and participated in a candlelight procession to the Grotto on Notre Dame campus to hear a sermon on "Mary, the model of religious perfection." But they also met in daily workshops to discuss how to apply the ideals proposed in the lectures to the specific circumstances of their own communities.[15] By the 1959 SIS meeting, sisters took the podium as often as male lecturers, and presentations to the 1,135 assembled sisters ranged from theological exploration of the formation of feminine character and spirituality, to a detailed lecture on psychological effects of community structure on individual sisters, to an impassioned appeal for religious to include social work among the apostolic activities of their community. By 1959 the institute also understood itself as part of a growing array of sister organizations; the program chair described the role of the institute as a supplement to the "excellent activity" of the Conference of Major Superiors and the Sister Formation Conference.[16]

In part, American sisters were responsive to Pius's call for modernization and educational reform because his emphasis on removing impediments to effective apostolic work echoed concerns that American sisters already were discussing among themselves. For the American church, the "procrustean requirements" of canon law had served a practical as well as spiritual function, creating a uniform army of "qualified and pliant personnel" to staff the burgeoning Catholic educational system.[17] The rapid proliferation of Catholic schools after World War II placed an enormous financial and logistical burden on religious congregations, which struggled to meet the ever-expanding call for teachers and administrators. The postwar boom in vocations—a 21 percent increase between 1945 and 1950—failed to keep pace with the 200 percent increase in the student population during this period.[18] Stretched almost to the breaking point, congregations increased the size of parochial school classes and placed sisters with little or no training or experience in the classroom in an effort to meet their obligations to diocesan schools. As a result, the education, professional training, and religious formation of women entering religious life often took a backseat to the immediate need for their labor.

Before Pius initiated the Roman conferences, American religious in teaching orders had already recognized that piecemeal educational structures for women entering religious life ultimately compromised the effectiveness of such sisters in teaching apostolates. Beginning with the 1941 publication of Sister Bertrande Meyers's dissertation, *The Education of Sisters: A Plan for Integrating the Religious, Cultural, Social, and Professional Training of Sisters,* and continuing with Sister Madeleva Wolff's revolutionary paper on "The Education of Our Young Religious Teachers" at the 1949 annual meeting of the National Catholic Education Association (NCEA), some sisters had been quietly strategizing about how better to prepare women entering religious life for their professional roles as educators while also continuing to meet the steadily expanding demand for teachers in parish schools. For her part, Wolff saw the familiarity with the outside world of young women entering the novitiate as a resource to be respected and harnessed rather than a potential source of contamination. "They think and move with the instancies of aviation and television. They think in term of superatomic power," she argued. "They are in spirit and in truth the children of God. We must form and educate them in terms of these potencies. We must not frustrate the magnificence of their qualities by our lower-grade Victorian traditions and training."[19] Wolff recommended that communities invest two to three years of education in each sister before placing her in the classroom. Her attitude of openness to the world and respect for the wholeness of women entering religious congregations would come to characterize the movement that grew out of her exhortations, the Sister Formation Conference. Inspired by Wolff's paper, sister-leaders in the NCEA began meeting to develop strategies for addressing pervasive educational deficiencies in young sisters.

In 1952 these early murmurs of reform among American communities intersected with the papal mandates for renewal, accelerating momentum toward wholesale reform in religious congregations. That same year Wolff was invited to address sisters at the First National Congress of United States Religious. Echoing her 1949 address to the NCEA, Wolff proposed to the assembled religious at Notre Dame that all sisters receive one year of training in theology and another in the study of scripture before making first profession. As before, she argued that religious communities should respect, rather than resist, the unique qualities that contemporary youth brought to religious consecration. "The twentieth century girl is a daughter of the age of science. As a religious, she brings to her community the spirit, the aptitudes of her generation that will find their perfect fulfillment in the greatest of sciences," she commented. "As her superiors, her teachers, her older sisters, we must share this great world with her, must even be humble and simple enough to learn new ways to it from her, even from her enthusiasm for it."[20] Her comments signaled a fundamental shift away from the preoccupation with separation and purity that pervaded the convent mentality of the previous decades, and the beginning of a renewed openness to "this great world." Also in 1952, the NCEA sponsored a panel discussion on the implications for American sisters of Pius XII's address to teaching sisters at the 1951 Roman congress. Panelists at the NCEA meeting argued that sisters would be unable to fully comply with the Holy Father's directive that sisters should be as well trained for their apostolic works as their lay counterparts until they addressed the financial and structural barriers that prevented women entering religious life from earning academic degrees before apostolic assignment. Through such discussions, sisters at the 1952 NCEA meeting began to integrate American and papal reform proposals into a single movement of collective self-improvement. Henceforth, sisters and sister organizations that criticized the status quo in religious congregations or who proposed significant changes to the dominant norms of canon law embedded in religious rules could claim papal approbation for their activities.

Education was the common ground between papal priorities and the agenda women religious had set for the reform of their teaching ministries. Discussion at the 1952 NCEA panel, particularly remarks by Sister Emil Penet, IHM, ignited a flurry of organizing as sisters banded together to implement the panel's recommendation that religious collectively create a more coherent and consistent plan for educating and training young sisters. In 1954 this grassroots organization of American women religious named itself the Sister Formation Conference.[21] The SFC advocated a chronological and a philosophical revision of existing patterns of sister education. In the SFC model, previously separate religious and academic components of sisters' education were combined into a unified training program under the rubric of "formation." The concept of formation pioneered by the SFC aimed to respond to the unique desires and capacities of each individual woman entering religious life, replacing the prior emphasis on developing uniformity and obedience in young sisters with a model that sought to nourish and develop the singular and unique potential of each religious as an individual. Sisters formed under these auspices had a clearer sense of personal identity than their sisters educated under the previous system. Their religious instruction stressed the development of Christian conscience and vital engagement with the world rather than simple obedience to "the Rule" or the authority of a superior. Ideally, according to the SFC, communities would replace the "twenty-year plan" with a program of uninterrupted study toward an academic degree, preferably through a college curriculum designed specifically to prepare women religious for the religious apostolate. The SFC disseminated its message through a widely read monthly *Bulletin* that summarized current ideas in teacher education, theology, and religious reform. Its characteristic blue pages were often passed around convents—read by superiors, formation directors, and sisters alike. Sisters involved in formation met in regional and national conferences, and the published proceedings of these meetings also served to further disseminate ideas across religious orders.

The SFC also challenged superiors and congregations to accept and even cherish the unique preconvent experiences and perspectives of novices and postulants. Indeed, young women entering religious life in the 1950s brought with them to the convent ideas, attitudes, and assumptions that were unprecedented in the history of religious consecration. The vitality of Catholic Action among American Catholics during the heydey of Catholic devotional culture from the 1930s to the 1950s meant that young religious entered religious life with a vital sense of the apostolate, of the importance of activity in the world, which they had learned and absorbed through Catholic Action programs in their youth.[22] The Catholic Action methodology of "see, judge, act" for these young sisters seemed an appropriate way for religious, no less than laity, to respond to the problems of the world around them. Such women embraced the apostolic component of religious consecration as a responsibility and privilege shared by Catholics in all stations of the Church, a commitment rendered more rather than less central for women bound to the Church in a special way by their vows. Women entering religious life in the postwar period may have been more aware of their religious responsibilities to the world, but they were also more familiar with the non-Catholic world than their predecessors in the convent. Following World War II, Catholics gradually emerged from the periphery of American society to claim a secure position within the middle class.[23] Historians of American Catholicism frequently claim that in this period the "Americanization" of the Church was finally achieved, as Caucasian American Catholics moved into and then assimilated to the burgeoning postwar suburbs. Thus, the young women who joined religious orders during the postwar years perceived their faith as more easily integrated into the public sphere than did sisters who had previously joined congregations of religious when mainstream American culture had tended to view Catholicism with suspicion. Additionally, many postwar postulants entered religious life well-versed in the ideas and ideals of the American middle class. Indeed, in her study of American women religious sponsored by the Conference of the Major Superiors (CMSW), Sister Marie Augusta Neal documented that a full 20 percent of sisters in religious congregations in 1966 originated from families in which the father's occupation was classified as "professional."[24]

Though not all congregations of religious in the United States were able to fully implement SFC recommendations, many communities made partial alterations to their programs for young sisters, bringing their formation practices into closer alignment with the ideal articulated in the CMSW. Thus, the SFC had specific, concrete consequences for American religious in the 1950s and 1960s. Primary among the effects of the SFC was a marked increase in the number of sisters who were able to attend college full time for a portion or all of their degree requirements. The increase in the number of young sisters attending Catholic colleges created a proportional increase in the number of sisters who pursued advanced degrees (often in order to be able to teach in congregational colleges), many of them at secular universities.[25] "During the 60s the nature and quality of education for sisters took a quantum leap forward," Pat Byrne observed of the SFC's influence on sisters.[26] Madeleva Wolff's passion that sisters receive theological training found concrete expression in the founding of the Graduate School of Sacred Theology at Saint Mary's College where she served as president from 1934 to 1961, "making that college the first in the world to grant advanced degrees in theology to women."[27] Developments in theology and in various fields of the social sciences were broadly disseminated to American sisters through the pages of the *Sister Formation Bulletin* and the published proceedings from SFC regional meetings. Thus American women religious entered the conciliar period with an intellectual and theological sophistication unparalleled in other sectors of the Church. In addition, the SFC had long advocated that Catholic diocese begin to hire lay teachers, rather than rely solely on the relatively inexpensive labor of sisters. Catholic educational institutions gradually shifted toward a more diverse population of teachers, and religious worked alongside lay professionals within Catholic institutions.

Sister organizations like the SFC altered the intellectual world of

American women religious in another way by introducing the concept of expertise into religious life. On one level, the reforms of the 1950s made it permissible for sisters to employ nonreligious forms of knowledge to evaluate the congregational regulations and ministries. Accordingly, sisters began to conduct comprehensive sociological and psychological studies and use the data they collected to inform their decisions about congregational reform. The published proceedings of the 1956–1957 regional meetings of the SFC contained seventy-four different statistical tables analyzing various facets of sisters' teaching apostolate, from "Summary Statistics for Special Education Programs Directed by Sisters, 1950–56" to "Summary of Time Situation for All Groups of Sisters."[28] Additionally, the Sisters' Institute of Spirituality (SIS), SFC, and CMSW applied management and psychological expertise to religious institutes and set a precedent for sisters to use sociology and psychology as tools to evaluate and shape religious life. The 1959 Sisters' Institute of Spirituality focused on a superior's responsibility for the psychological health of sisters under her authority. In the opening address Richard Cardinal Cushing affirmed that "those who exercise authority in religious communities should know something of the fundamental psychology of human relationships and develop certain of the skills of leadership and government which modern psychology has made available."[29] In the early 1960s the CMSW commissioned Sister Marie Augusta Neal to conduct a sociological study of all women's congregations in the United States.[30] These initial studies revealed some common challenges that sisters faced, such as educational disadvantages, health deficiencies, inadequate salaries, and declining numbers of recruits. They also introduced the expertise of a quantitative analysis of religious life into the renewal process and exposed the formerly private sphere of religious to researchers from the social and behavioral sciences.

The reforms of the 1950s fundamentally altered the identity of women religious, making it possible for them to think of themselves as competent professionals, not just nameless servants in the Church. Conferences like the SFC and the CMSW addressed superiors and formation directors as professionals, framing conference activities as an effort to provide superiors and novice mistresses with information and skills specific to their positions of leadership. But the "professionalization" of sisters extended beyond the elite circle of sisters in leadership positions. As the educational reforms of the SFC took hold in women's religious congregations, sisters in lower ranks gained academic degrees, certifications, and professional credentials. Individual sisters who had benefited from the reforms increasingly possessed a sense of their own professional competence, which stood in marked contrast to cultural stereotypes of women religious that circulated in Catholic communities. "Too often, in other writers, one finds a hidden (or overt) picture of 'the good nun,' the meek, humble, docile, otherworldly, and sometimes childish sister whose biggest thrill in life is supposed to be a day at Coney Island or a ride on someone's fire engine," wrote Sister M. Charles Borromeo in the introduction to a collection of essays on new apostolic works. "The sisters who have contributed to this book are, all of them, professionals in some field—tough-minded and competent. The bells of St. Mary's do not ring out in these pages."[31] By the early 1960s American sisters displayed growing confidence both in their status as professionals within Catholic institutions and in their ability to advocate for their own interests in negotiations with male authorities in the Church and secular authorities beyond.

Taken together, the reforms initiated by Pius XII and by American organizations of women religious in the decade before the Second Vatican Council produced two separate but related shifts in the cultural world of sisters in the United States. First, *aggiornamento* signaled a decisive end to the ethos of enclosure that had shaped religious life since the end of World War I. Undergirded by a papal directive to eliminate outdated rules, sisters gradually began to dismantle the system of regulations that had kept all sisters—contemplative and active alike—in a state of virtual, if not literal, cloister. Like removing crucial supports from an architectural foundation, once the ideal of separation from the world was called into question, the whole structure of enclosure became unsustainable. The abolition of the most restrictive regulations led sisters to question the vision of religious life as sanctified separateness from the world, and the model of the religious superior as enforcer of the Rule. In its place, some sisters and sister organizations began, carefully at first but with increasing clarity, to articulate and then to demonstrate a posture of fundamental openness—to the insights and experiences of individual sisters, to new forms of knowledge, to cooperative action across congregations, and to the non-Catholic world. The educational reforms instituted by the Sister Formation Conference reinforced this new orientation among American religious. Because of the SFC, an increasing number of sisters were attending college full- or at least part-time by 1960, some at secular universities. Regional meetings of the SFC brought together sisters from diverse congregations in collaborative efforts. SFC conferences and publications regularly featured academic papers that applied models and insights from sociology and psychology to the institution of religious life, and the SFC's college curriculum for sisters prominently featured the social sciences alongside theology in the course of study laid out for sisters in formation. One sister who left her New England convent for the University of Notre Dame in order to study for a master's degree in mathematics during the summer of 1959 through 1964 described her experience as a "consciousness of moving out."[32]

Strict physical and intellectual enclosure among American religious declined at the same time that the Church's view of the relationship of the apostolate to the institution of religious life for consecrated women shifted substantially. The canonical model of religious life that dominated the first half of the twentieth century considered the contemplative cloister the norm for women religious, emphasizing sanctity as the primary aim of religious consecration. Apostolic works served a secondary role at best in the life of sisters, allowable to the extent that they did not violate the norms of enclosure. Under Pius XII, the apostolic component of religious life moved from the margins to the center of religious life. Pius's call for *aggiornamento* was fueled by his desire for religious to become more effective in apostolic works. His instructions for sisters to eliminate any unnecessary regulations that impeded sisters' work reversed the priorities of the "school of sanctity" model of religious life, empowering congregations of religious to revisit the perennial question of how to appropriately balance religious consecration with service to the neighbor. Organizations of American religious, like the SFC, magnified this reinvigoration of the apostolate. In calling for the education and religious formation of individual sisters to take precedence over the commitments of religious congregations to diocesan schools, the SFC paved the way for the primary locus of the apostolate to be relocated in the vocation and conscience of the individual sister, rather than in the charism or corporate works of her religious congregation. Though some individual bishops resisted the resulting alterations to congregational patterns and regulations for the religious in their diocese, especially given the loss of the sister-teachers it produced, through the 1950s and 1960s it became increasingly possible for American women religious tentatively to experiment with greater contact with the world at large without being immediately perceived as "worldly," and to integrate apostolic work into their identities as vowed religious. In a 1968 essay whose title posed the provocative question, "Can Sisters Be Relevant?" Sister M. Charles Borromeo cautiously responded that "the obvious, hopeful, but very painful answer is 'yes' "—but only if sisters were willing to "personally and communally make profound changes in attitude and practice." To be relevant, sisters would have to continue to address the anachronism of their institutes and customs, and dismantle the barriers that kept them segregated from the laity and that weakened the prophetic witness of their commitment to the Church. "It is interesting to note both sisters and their commentators using images like wax dolls, manikins, hiding in suits of armor, living in a plastic bag," she observed. "The notion that we are otherworldly, out of touch, 'in orbit,' withdrawn, isolated, completely different from ordinary people is very frequently thought and increasingly more often voiced."[33]

Two popular books in this period—Erving Goffman's *Asylums: Essays on the Social Situation of Mental Patients and Other Inmates* and Leon Joseph Cardinal Suenens's *The Nun in the World: Religious and the Apostolate*—were widely read and often quoted by American sisters precisely because they provided skeptics with an explanation for these two massive shifts in the culture of women religious, and justification for the changes to defenders. Goffman's monograph offered sisters a sociological model that supported their claims that cloister had a deleterious effect on the well-being and moral autonomy of sisters. Cardinal Suenens's *cri de coeur* presented a revolutionary theology of religious life that charged women religious with no less than the ability (and thus responsibility) to transform the world by mediating between God and humanity.

In 1961 Goffman, a sociologist, published *Asylums*, an influential account of identity and morality within institutions. In the work Goffman argued that "total institutions"—institutions such as prisons, asylums, boarding schools, nursing homes, and the military, in which people were cut off from wider society—systematically stripped individuals of their identities and reconstructed in their place a selfhood that embodied the institution's need for order among masses of inmates within confined social space.[34] The identities of such inmates, according to Goffman, were characterized by homogeneity, conformity, and restricted moral autonomy. Goffman included religious orders and convents among the total institutions he singled out for analysis and criticism. In the mid- and late 1960s *Asylums* was widely read by American Catholic women religious in a variety of settings. A number of sisters were assigned to read *Asylums* either by their superiors as part of the self-study processes that accompanied congregational reform efforts or by instructors in college classrooms. Some congregations even included the book on reading lists for sisters in formation. Other sisters were introduced to the concept of the total institution in works of prominent sociologist nuns who used Goffman as the stepping-off point for analyses of religious life. In 1966 Sister Aloysius Schaldebrand authored an essay that applied the concept of total institution to the process of reform among religious orders. Her essay included an extensive list of traits that congregations of women religious had in common with total institutions. Schaldebrand's analysis was condensed into a feature article in the *National Catholic Reporter* and published in 1967 in a widely read collection of essays edited by Sister M. Charles Borromeo titled *The New Nuns.*

Sisters in the 1960s lived in a complicated and somewhat ironic relationship with Goffman's characterization of them as inmates confined to a total institution. Sisters were exposed to the concept of total institution through educational reforms by organizations like the Sister Formation Conference (SFC), which had in effect removed them from the total institution of convent culture. Educational reform occurred simultaneously with the development of new apostolates that removed women religious from familiar experiences of themselves as sisters, presenting them with a context in which to develop new religious and moral identities. Though some sisters resisted Goffman's characterization of religious life as hegemonic, even pathological in nature, many sisters recognized in *Asylums* a compelling account of the effect that the rules of enclosure and norms of obedience had had upon American sisters in the early twentieth century. In fact, many sisters accepted Goffman's characterization of themselves as "inmates" of total institutions. Such sisters employed the self-label of "inmate" strategically, claiming inmate status in order to justify drastic revisions to restrictive rules that governed religious life, particularly advocating for an expansion of apostolic works.

Though Leon Joseph Cardinal Suenens, archbishop of Malines-Brussels, might have agreed that "closed society" convents (as he called them) were problematic, his book *The Nun in the World,* which first appeared in English translation in 1963, argued that the damage religious enclosure had caused was far greater than the "stilted, stereotyped, and unnatural behavior" it produced in sisters (the model Goffman offered).[35] Suenens contended that the true tragedy of the climate of restriction among women religious was that it wasted the "apostolic capital" they possessed, depriving the Church of sisters' unique gifts, and humanity in general of sisters' salvific activity. Suenens offered a robust evaluation of the importance of the religious apostolate of consecrated women. He placed sisters at the center of the drama of human salvation, arguing that sisters shared Mary's privileged role of being a "mediatrix between God and the world."[36] The main work of the apostolate of women religious, he argued, was evangelism—"giving God to the world"—not just works of dedication or charity. Thus women were improperly relegated to secondary roles in the life of the Church. Sisters' literal as well as figurative confinement within convents and parish basements in order to care for children and the elderly diverted them from the "direct evangelization" that was their proper role. Similarly, regulations that inhibited sisters' engagement with the world were also contrary to the divine plan for the Church. Suenens wrote, "Anything that dehumanizes or defeminizes the nun lowers her apostolic value."[37] Suenens urged that the apostolate be placed back into the "heart of religious life" and that narrow, rigid models of religious consecration be replaced with a more "supple and open conception of the religious life."[38] "Our nuns, therefore, must be able to situate their work in the social context of our times," he wrote, adding that "all this requires on their part is presence, openness, and readiness."[39]

As a male cleric and a bishop, Suenens possessed both religious authority and a measure of self-expression not available to sisters. Thus his book contained ideas sisters had expressed privately among themselves but had refrained from saying directly or in public forums out of diplomacy and, possibly also, fear of reprisal. In a chapter about the "canonical factor" in the cause of the current situation, Suenens framed canonically mandated enclosure primarily as a feminist issue. "Canon lawyers," he wrote, "have codified the religious life on the basis of the cloistered type of nun, and in the spirit of an age which treated women as a minor to be protected from herself. Canon law still bears the marks of this kind of masculine mentality which has not yet entirely died out." And lest his readers misunderstand his point, Suenens added, "It is well known that what one can only call the anti-feminist tradition has had a long inning."[40] He acknowledged the difficulty that the apparent contradiction between the rules of enclosure and the demands of the religious apostolate added to sister's lives. He used words like "ghetto," "hothouse," and "fortress" to describe the experience of cloister. He called for reforms that went well beyond a simple loosening of regulations, advocating a program of extended "progressive theoretical and practical education for the apostolate" for young sisters, which sounded very much like the programs created by the SFC.[41] It is no wonder, then, that American sisters "devoured" his book, passed it around in communities, assigned it to women in formation, and placed it on countless reading lists. Suenens's message "vibrated in their experience" and gave ecclesial voice to thoughts they had long self-censored.[42] Suenens's book provided the language that many sisters would use to justify new, unconventional apostolic works, and his desire that sisters be able to proclaim "the world is my convent" became their rallying cry.

"Students Are Untroubled by Race and Poverty"

The development of a specifically racial apostolate among Catholic sisters was partly facilitated by these internal changes to the institution of religious life and partly forced by changes in the social and political context in which sisters pursued apostolic works. As the world behind convent walls was being rapidly modernized in the 1950s and early 1960s, the racial geography of American Catholicism underwent similarly thoroughgoing transformations. Postwar prosperity, shifting racial compositions in urban neighborhoods, and growing debates over civil rights dramatically changed the social context of sisters' apostolic worlds in the 1960s. American Catholics enjoyed unparalleled prosperity in the postwar decade. As Catholics entered the middle class they moved from urban ethnic neighborhoods into segregated suburban enclaves, taking their parishes and parochial schools with them. The postwar migration of African Americans from the South to northern cities further altered the racial composition of areas that previously had been predominantly white and Catholic. Meanwhile, the civil rights movement confronted the brutality of Jim Crow segregation in the South, and the 1963 March on Washington brought the depth and pervasiveness of racial prejudice in all regions into the national spotlight. The passage of both the Economic Opportunity Act and the Civil Rights Act in 1964 had a fundamental impact on the legal and fiscal context of African Americans. The various bureaucratic incarnations of President Lyndon B. Johnson's War on Poverty publicly exposed the prevalence of racialized urban poverty while creating complex organizational structures to counter it in the North. The convergence of these diverse factors radically transformed racial geography and political discourse in the United States in the early and mid-1960s, placing the apostolic work of sisters in an equally altered racial and political context. As a result, an increasing number of sisters began to seek out apostolic works that promoted racial justice, often by ministering directly to African Americans.

One axis of sisters' worlds shifted with the postwar migration of American Catholics into suburban areas. White Catholics made significant gains in the economic boom precipitated by World War II, gaining a solid position in the American middle class, the result of the GI Bill of Rights and of the expanding service economy. Through the 1950s and early 1960s Catholics experienced unprecedented upward mobility in education, financial standing, and occupation. John McGreevy notes that by the mid-1960s American Catholics met or exceeded national income averages.[43] Catholic economic mobility had a geographical component as Catholics joined the surge of whites moving from urban areas to the suburbs. As a result, Catholics had to develop new structures for parishes and parish schools.[44] Significant numbers of women religious were reassigned from teaching positions in ethnic parish schools to new suburban ones. Suddenly, religious orders whose apostolic work in the 1930s and 1940s had included ministering to the children of immigrant families who were struggling with interethnic competition, labor conflicts, and economic uncertainty in urban neighborhood parishes found themselves now in enclaves of economic and racial privilege, teaching children who accepted that privilege as a matter of course.

Suburban teaching frustrated sisters, many of whom objected to the racial and economic segregation that characterized suburban life and resented the cultural conformity among the "children of plenty" in their classrooms. "In teaching seniors in a moderately affluent, all-white section of suburbia, it seems very difficult to be objective in discussing either poverty or minority rights," wrote one sister from suburban St. Louis in 1976.[45] Such frustrations contributed to the growing crisis among those sisters who felt that suburban assignments were inconsistent with their religious vocation. "Next spring I would like to step from our middle class neighborhood back into the ghetto where I feel I belong," one sister petitioned in 1969.[46] The racism of white Catholics also disturbed and angered sisters, some of whom joined the racial apostolate as a direct response to the prejudice and complacency they encountered in Catholic parishes. "I do not feel that I would be neglecting the apostolate here if I left," wrote one sister. "The students are untroubled by race and poverty—also largely indifferent to both."[47]

Catholic suburbanization was accelerated by the racial integration of northern urban neighborhoods that formerly had been predominantly Caucasian and Catholic. As John McGreevy has ably documented, this process was fraught with racial hostilities that at times erupted into outright violence.[48] Teaching sisters were caught in the middle of these tensions. If a bishop supported integration of parochial schools, and if in turn a parish school decided to integrate and accepted black students (both Catholic and non-Catholic), sisters encountered angry resistance from white parents and racial animosities in their classrooms. If the school refused to enroll African American students—as many unfortunately did—sisters faced the certain, slow withering of the school as parishioners and students decamped to the suburbs, leaving empty pews, empty desks, and empty collection plates. Caucasian Catholics may have moved to the suburbs for various social, economic, and cultural reasons, but most sisters interpreted the relocations as white flight from integrated parishes and schools. Though not all sisters supported the racial integration of Catholic neighborhoods, many with an interest in race relations and racial justice resisted the gradual withdrawal of Catholics from the central cities of the North and attempted to keep parish schools and hospitals open in those areas. They faced substantial obstacles in doing so. Lay Catholics typically were ambivalent at best about race and racial justice, and diocesan officials resisted investing financial and personnel resources in areas that had ceased being sources of income for the diocese.

The situation among Catholics in the South was not much better. There, too, sisters oriented toward racial justice were frustrated at the incongruity of the behavior they witnessed among local Catholics with the ideals emanating from the Council or from individual prelates. "Msgr. Kourney isn't too forward-looking as you may have gathered. Some segregationist tendencies there, I'm afraid," wrote a sister from Mississippi asking for the Traveling Workshop on Race Relations to come to her region.[49] Sister Margaret Hutton in Jackson, Mississippi, sent off an angry letter to Sister Margaret Traxler in the winter of 1970, attempting to distance herself from forms of religious life that linked sisterhood with the struggle for racial justice. "The fact that we are Catholics should in no way be used to give the idea that we are 'do-gooders' and all that. I wish I could talk to you and explain this to you so that you would understand what I am trying to say," she wrote. "You don't know and understand Mississippi."[50] Other sisters who did know Mississippi noted the same racial situation but interpreted it—and the responsibilities of the Church—quite differently. Writing from Holly Springs, Sister Margaret Mary, IHM, mourned the Church's reluctance to perform a "do-gooder" role in Southern society: "To me the white mentality and what the Catholic Church should truly be are contradictions. Here, however, I see former Northern nuns and priests accepting the divided society and making no effort to change it. What I'm saying doesn't make much sense I'm sure but does disturb me."[51] Reflecting on her summer working in the racial apostolate in Albany,

Georgia, another sister lamented Catholic support for segregation, writing, "There were innumerable intangible benefits both to us and to the black and white communities in which we lived—I say 'communities' for it is just that in Georgia, despite the many gains made in the past few years."[52]

The convergence of these diverse factors radically transformed the racial geography of American Catholicism in the 1960s. Coupled with a renewed national focus on racial justice through the civil rights movement, the racial tensions within the American Church dramatically changed the social context of apostolic work for American sisters, simultaneously altering the meaning of traditional works while opening avenues for new forms of religious engagement with the world.

The Second Vatican Council, convened from 1962 to 1965, issued a profound challenge to familiar Catholic ways of seeing the world and the Church's place in it. The Council's affirmation of ecumenism made possible a new level of religious tolerance for non-Catholic traditions. Ecumenism also placed the issue of Catholic anti-Semitism at the forefront of Catholic social thought, provoking conversation about ethnic and racial prejudice generally. The Council's document on religious life, *Perfectae Caritatis,* called for substantial revision to the rules and priorities of religious orders.

The theological currents embodied in the Second Vatican Council opened the Catholic Church to a novel détente with non-Catholic and even non-Christian religious traditions. The Council advocated new respect for other religions, especially for Judaism. In an address to the American Jewish Committee's annual dinner in April 1963, at the height of the Council's meetings about religious tolerance, Francis Cardinal Spellman, archbishop of New York, issued an unexpectedly strongly worded statement on the problems of religious and racial prejudice. Spellman directly confronted Catholic participation in Christian persecution of Jews, especially through the hateful characterization of Jews as "Christ-killers." "Anti-Semitism can never find a basis in the Catholic religion," Spellman declared. Spellman linked Jewish oppression, specifically the "shameful murder in this very generation of 6,000,000 Jews," with the disfranchisement of African Americans. "The struggle of millions of American Negroes to achieve first class citizenship" testified to the continued existence of racial and religious hatred, he argued, and obligated Catholics to oppose all such forms of prejudice. "By every means at our disposal we must wage war on the old suspicions and prejudice and bigotry which have set brother against brother and spawned a brood of evils," Spellman directed.[53] Because it was both unexpected and uncharacteristic of the dominant public perception of Spellman, his public statement was widely reported in the Catholic media, drawing attention from all corners of American Catholicism. American sisters also noted the archbishop's speech, which was featured in a lengthy article in the *Sister Formation Bulletin.*

Spellman's criticism of Catholic anti-Semitism coincided with an emerging focus in the Sister Formation Conference on Jewish-Catholic relations and, by extension, on prejudice generally. In 1963 three sisters from Saint Louis University, Sister Mary Linus Gleason, Sister Rita Mudd, and Sister Rose Albert Thering, released an analysis of anti-Semitic content in literature used in Catholic schools. The Saint Louis study identified recurrent themes in Catholic social studies and religious education textbooks, including characterizations of Jews as "Christ-killers" and tendencies to equate "the Jews" with "the enemies of Jesus" in Catholic religious literature.[54] That same year the SFC made religious prejudice the focus of its annual workshop, held each summer at Marquette University. The 1963 SFC summer workshop featured Rabbi Marc Tanenbaum, director of the Interreligious Affairs Department of the American Jewish Committee, urging the assembled superiors and formation directors to review the religious education materials used in their congregational schools and eliminate prejudicial content. Tanenbaum summarized the findings of the Saint Louis study and referred to Cardinal Spellman's statement, calling upon sisters to oppose all forms of bigotry and specifically that directed against Jews. Anti-Semitic textbooks, he argued, reflected deeper impulses toward prejudice and "a refusal to identify with the plight of others, a defensiveness which sacrifices charity and sometimes justice to the interests of an unreflective group loyalty." Tanenbaum warned sisters that unless the Church embraced the difficult task of "freeing the vital core of faith from the cultural and temporal encrustations" of centuries of interreligious hatred, the hypocritical contrast between the moral teaching of the Church and the biased behavior of Catholics would spread "skepticism and secularism" in society.[55] Tanenbaum's critique of religious and ethnic prejudice was disseminated among American sisters following the SFC workshop through a series of speaking invitations he received from Catholic colleges. A 1964 issue of the *Bulletin* reported that "following discussion brought about by Rabbi Tanenbaum's lectures at the Marquette Workshop, 15 colleges which include large numbers of Sisters in their enrollment held special convocations featuring Rabbi Tanenbaum as speaker."[56]

The growing attention among certain Catholics to the problematic pervasiveness within the tradition of anti-Semitism led these Catholics, by extension, to a new awareness of equally problematic strains of racism that ran through the history of the Church in the United States and were embedded in some of its current structures. Sisters who had dissected Catholic anti-Semitism noted that bias against Jews had ethnic as well as religious components. Catholics had demonstrated and justified prejudice against Jews on the basis of their presumed racial inferiority, in addition to the expected objections to Jewish religious beliefs. If it was impermissible to discriminate against Jews, it was equally impermissible to discriminate against any group on the basis of race. Criticism of Catholic anti-Semitism led to more comprehensive, and ultimately more racially focused, definitions of social prejudice. Similar to Cardinal Spellman's comparison of the Nazi Holocaust with American racial segregation, the SFC's focus on anti-Semitism eventually led American sisters toward a broader concern with racial prejudice. Thus sisters' growing awareness of Catholic anti-Semitism—coupled with the influence of the social sciences via the SFC and a subtle shift toward devotional ethics of "compassionate solidarity" with the suffering poor—created a context in which sisters could easily integrate human-rights concepts into their understanding of apostolic work. This shift occurred just in time for the transformations that followed the Second Vatican Council and escalations in the civil rights movement that sparked them toward action.

The Second Vatican Council is often characterized by the optimistic assumptions that lay underneath its prescriptions, the documents it produced, and its effect on Catholics worldwide. Reflecting on her congregation's enthusiastic response to the Council, Sandra Schneiders emphasized the active and creative way that she and her fellow sisters tried to respond to the Council's call. "No task was too arduous, no risk too great, no meeting too long as we took up our new identity among the People of God," she wrote. "We poured ourselves into intensive community building, developed new prayer forms, made directed retreats, prepared beautiful liturgies, retrained for new ministries, marched for civil rights and peace, even went to jail to witness for justice."[57] Yet within and underneath all this optimism and activism, the Council also had a deeply disorienting effect on American women religious. The American Church absorbed conciliar reforms unevenly, adapting in fits and starts. *Aggiornamento* was equally complicated in women's institutes. Sisters grappled with language. They struggled with concepts of authority. They described dissatisfaction with religious life and with their communities but had no idea what might replace them, only inklings that something else was out there. Congregations, superiors, and individual religious found themselves ad-libbing their way through revisions to the most basic tenets of religious life, unsure of the rules or boundaries that applied to the reforms, uncertain even of the ecclesial status of their institutes. "Somewhere underneath the noise *we,* the 'average' American nun, stand and, yes, wonder," reflected Chicago sisters at the closing of the Council in 1965. "At times we are merely annoyed. But often we are deeply perplexed, even bewildered at what we are and what role we must play in the post-Council Church."[58]

Theologies advocating the engagement of the Church with the problems of contemporary society circulated widely among women religious, as in the church at large, after the conclusion of the Second Vatican Council in 1965. On December 7, 1965, the Council released *Gaudium et Spes,* the Pastoral Constitution on the Church in the Modern World, which outlined the Council's vision of the public role of the Catholic Church. "This community realizes that it is truly linked with mankind and its history by the deepest of bonds," the document's preface states. The Council declared that the Church, by virtue of its status as the receptacle of divine revelation, had a singular role in human destiny to "anchor the dignity of human nature against all tides of opinion." Affirming "the full spiritual dignity of the person," the Council called upon the Church to "champion the dignity of the human vocation, restoring hope to those who have already despaired of anything higher than their present lot." The Council affirmed as "universal and inviolable" certain human entitlements such as food, clothing, and shelter, as well as more abstract entitlements such as freedom of conscience and the right to privacy. The Council argued that the Church is obligated to advocate that "a more humane and just condition of life be brought about" for those currently suffering physical or psychological deprivations that diminish their essential human dignity.[59]

Certain elements of *Gaudium et Spes* were especially important to women religious who had an interest in the cause of racial justice, and the document's ideas suffused these sisters' writings (as they did those of other lay and clerical Catholics at the time). "Most of the ideas come from Vatican II documentation, which anyone could assemble and disseminate," one sister wrote in defense of her congregation's orientation toward racial issues in 1969.[60] American sisters sympathetic to the cause of the civil rights movement interpreted the statement in *Gaudium et Spes* that the Church "acknowledges and greatly esteems the dynamic movements of today by which these rights are everywhere fostered" as an endorsement of that effort. *Gaudium et Spes* specifically addressed human solidarity, arguing that in the modern world all persons are connected to each other through bonds of mutual respect and assistance. "A special obligation binds us to make ourselves the neighbor of every person without exception," the Council proclaimed, "actively helping him when he comes across our path." Sisters who subsequently joined the racial apostolate applied the Council's mandate for neighborly solidarity without exception to Southern and urban segregation, believing that the Church had called them to create and deepen relationships with African Americans. "We've used the Council documents as themes and would like to have The Church in the Modern World . . . most likely as a theme for all of next year," wrote one sister of her congregation's exploratory chapter meetings in 1966. "Interracial justice, we feel, would be something very pertinent and needed in conjunction with this theme."[61]

Pope Paul VI addressed religious congregations directly in *Perfectae Caritatis* (released October 28, 1965), challenging religious to adapt themselves to the circumstances of the modern world. Developing "general principles of the adaption and renewal of the life and discipline of Religious orders," the document encouraged religious orders to return to the original spirit of their founders as a way of guiding the processes of change. *Perfectae Caritatis* outlined distinct duties and responsibilities for different members of religious orders. Significantly, superiors were asked to reimagine their approach to leadership. The primary role of superior had been to maintain order in the congregation and advance the work of the institute; now, *Perfectae Caritatis* oriented superiors toward the development and well-being of their "charges." Superiors were to ensure that religious in their communities had the proper educational and interpersonal context in these times of change and reorientation in which to pursue the "renewal of spirit." More importantly, superiors were also instructed to educate sisters about the state of the world, promoting "an adequate knowledge of the social conditions of the times they live in."[62] The Second Vatican Council, especially the documents *Gaudium et Spes* and *Perfectae Caritatis,* dramatically accelerated the limited renewal process that American religious had begun in the 1950s. After 1965 most facets of religious life were in flux, open to negotiation between individual sisters and their congregations. Distinctive religious garb, religious observance, enclosure, living arrangements, and the financial maintenance of sisters all were laid open for radical revision after 1965.

Perfectae Caritatis shifted the center of religious life from the order as a whole to the individual religious, and the locus of renewal from religious institutes to persons within the institutes. The renewed emphasis on inner renewal called each religious to a higher standard of human development and spiritual maturity, placing the responsibility for authentic religious life squarely on the shoulders of the religious herself (provided the superior had ensured an appropriate context for such maturity). Within this model the religious vocation as human development and the vows of poverty, chastity, and obedience—the heart of "consecrated" religious life—became occasion for reflection and moment-by-moment choice in each situation rather than a matter purely of adhering to congregational regulations. Thus religious poverty, the document argued, was not achieved by simply obeying one's superior; instead, spiritual and theological "members must be poor both in fact and in spirit, their treasures being in heaven." This reorientation opened the door for sisters to exercise greater autonomy in selecting apostolic work. "Apostolic activity must spring from intimate union" with God, the document continued. A sister who believed that she was being divinely led toward a particular ministry could claim the newly legitimated basis of individual conscience for apostolic preferences beyond the scope of her congregation.[63] This was particularly important for American sisters who were drawn to work among African Americans rather than to teach in white parochial schools.

Perfectae Caritatis also called upon congregations to adapt their collective apostolic work and regulations to modern life. Congregational ministries were to address the particular needs of the historical moment, reflecting "the requirements of time and place, employing appropriate and even new programs and abandoning those works which today are less relevant to the spirit and authentic nature of community."[64] *Perfectae Caritatis* also encouraged congregations to reconsider the rules governing religious life and to adapt inherited regulations to the circumstances of new apostolic challenges. "Communities, then, should adjust their rules and customs to fit the demands of the apostolate to which they are dedicated," directed the decree. Congregations were liberated to reconsider apostolic commitments they had made in the past and select new foci and outlets for their apostolic orientation. The escalation in the civil rights movement, and in particular the catalytic participation of a number of sisters in the historic march from Selma to Montgomery, soon impressed upon individual religious and, in some cases, whole congregations that the most pressing need of the historical moment was the cause of racial equality.

"My Request Is Simply This: Help Us"

There was no uniform response to the civil rights movement among American Catholics, but there was a discernable pattern to the grouping of Catholics who supported and those who opposed the goals of the civil rights movement. In his 1967 study of race relations in Catholic diocese in the United States, William Osborne argued that while the hierarchy generally supported the cause of racial justice and racial integration, the American bishops were uneven in their willingness to implement Catholic social teaching on race in their diocese, and Caucasian Catholic laity, in general, retained definite tendencies toward racism and discrimination. Though Osborne's model oversimplifies the complex range of ideas about, attitudes toward, and practices related to race relations among Catholics in the mid-twentieth century, it does highlight an important tension within the Church in this period.[65] "The position of the Catholic Church on discrimination in employment, housing, and access to public accommodations is clear and convincing," Osborne wrote. "But this is the policy statement of an organization: it is not to be mistaken for the response of the Catholic people, nor even of the bishops or clergy."[66] Osborne observed that while no official sanction existed for segregation, de facto segregation remained firmly entrenched in most Catholic dioceses, in both the North and South, and Catholic support for the civil rights movement was "spotty," despite clear teachings on racial justice from the magisterium. Osborne was unsparing in his evaluation of the "absence of inspirational or charismatic leadership among the Catholic bishops."[67] With the dearth of unambiguously clear leadership by the American bishops on issues of racial justice, the masses of lay Catholics could not be counted on to support desegregation, even of Catholic educational institutions. "It is simply incongruous to expect the members of the typical parish Rosary or Holy Name Society even to discuss non-violent resistance, much less join a picket line," Osborne maintained. As was typical in writings of the time, he ignored a significant segment of the Church in his model of a ideological disconnect between the progressive racial ideas of the hierarchy and the resistance to racial integration among the laity: sisters. Had Osborne attempted to include women religious within this schema, he would have had to locate sisters directly in the middle of this ideological divide or, rather, stretched uncomfortably across it.[68]

American women religious occupied an interstitial position in the structure of the American Church, and this produced contradictory imperatives for them during the disruptions of the 1960s. In the Catholic cosmology that divided the world into distinct categories of sacred and profane, similarly bifurcating the Church into laity and clergy, sisters fit easily into neither category. As nonclergy, technically women religious were laity. However, the Catholic tradition in this period carefully cultivated specific practices that differentiated vowed women from their noncelibate or unvowed lay counterparts, complicating sisters' inclusion in the broad category of laity. As one sociologist of religious life observed, a sister was viewed by the laity as "a 'holy person' with special gifts and access to the spiritual realm."[69] In practice, especially in settings like schools and hospitals where sisters enjoyed professional authority over other laity, the ecclesiastical status of women religious was, at best, unclear. Most Catholics (including women religious) considered sisters to be a category unto themselves in the structure of the Church, distinct from both laity and clergy and positioned somewhere in between them. As outsiders both to the clergy and the laity, sisters found themselves in the unenviable position of having to carefully negotiate between parishioners and the magisterium. In their professional roles as teachers and nurses, sisters represented the public face of the Church's teachings to the lay Catholics they served. Yet their work also required them to understand and respond sympathetically to the perspectives and practical needs of lay Catholics. In the racial tumult of the 1960s, this interstitial location meant that sisters stood at the junction where mounting racial tensions and strong resistance to racial integration in American Catholic parishes collided with new theologies of human solidarity and universal human dignity issuing from the Second Vatican Council and circulating among sisters through organizations like the SFC. Sisters were literally caught in the middle of a problematic gap between the Church's progressive reform ideology and the inert traditionalism held by the majority of its American members in the conciliar era.

Sisters were not alone in this gap between Catholic social teaching and the persistent racial segregation of American Catholics. There were a small but not insignificant number of Catholic interracialists, laypeople and clergy who were committed to the full integration of the Church as a matter of religious principle. The interracial movement among Catholics dates to the early 1930s when Jesuit John LaFarge founded the first Catholic Interracial Council in New York City. Modeled on Catholic Action and nourished by a theology that emphasized the doctrine of the Mystical Body of Christ, Catholic interracialists stressed the essential spiritual unity of Catholics of all races.[70] By the early 1960s, interracialist ideas were beginning to gain currency in the

American Church in the North, particularly among Catholics whose educations had exposed them to progressive theological currents that circulated in elite circles in the period immediately prior to the Second Vatican Council. Catholic Interracial Councils proliferated in cities in the Northeast and Midwest (though, notably, not in the South), and in 1958 the National Catholic Conference for Interracial Justice (NCCIJ) was formed to unite and represent these local councils. Sisters inclined toward apostolic work among African Americans found a natural ally in the NCCIJ and its members, and the organization would play a crucial role in the centralization and dissemination of the racial apostolate. Through the NCCIJ sisters joined forces with Catholic interracialists, and through this partnership sisters were pulled into a catalytic engagement with the late stage of the civil rights movement.

In January 1963 the NCCIJ convened in Chicago a National Conference on Religion and Race on the centennial of the signing of the Emancipation Proclamation. The conference brought together leaders of various religious groups to discuss the perspective of their respective traditions on the racial problems the nation was facing. Conference organizers hoped that through the meeting, which they described as "a religious conference speaking to a moral problem," the national climate would become more conducive to true racial harmony. The conference proposal argued that such a conference could "bring the joint force of religion and religious values to the attention of a country striving awkwardly to correct racial abuses."[71] For their part, the NCCIJ, the Chicago Catholic Interracial Council, and Chicago archdiocesan representatives saw the conference as deeply consistent with the Church's interest in promoting both interracial and interreligious understanding. Responding to Los Angeles Archbishop James Francis McIntyre's proclamation that he was "loathe to make" any comment about the conference or its purpose, Chicago's Albert Cardinal Meyer gently chastised McIntyre for his reticence, explaining that "in the critical area of race relations it was felt that such a conference would respond to the words of our Holy Father, in *Mater et Magistra,* that we should be 'animated by a spirit of understanding and disinterestedness, ready to cooperate loyally in achieving objectives that of their nature are good.' "[72]

As sisters a decade earlier had marveled at the visual diversity of religious garb among the women who attended the First National Congress of Religious in the United States, so also attendees at the 1963 National Conference on Religion and Race were treated to the sight of men and women in the diverse religious garb of Catholicism, Judaism, Greek Orthodoxy, and Protestantism (sisters among them), sitting side by side in the auditorium and mingling in between sessions. Despite the plurality of religious perspectives the delegates represented, conference speakers framed their arguments within what they considered to be a theological common ground of respect for human dignity and a shared guilt for the racial treacheries of the American past. "We are here this week because we feel that the time has come for the three major faiths to speak to the nation with a united voice on what is one of the most crucial problems confronting mankind today," stated Dr. Benjamin Mays in his opening address to the 657 religious delegates who attended the conference.[73] In a strongly worded address, Rabbi Abraham J. Heschel exhorted, "To act in the spirit of religion is to unite what lies apart, to remember that humanity as a whole is God's beloved child."[74] Monsignor John J. Egan of Chicago reminded the assembly that churches, synagogues, schools, and hospitals, as religious institutions, were symbols of God. "The religious institution which remains aloof from its neighborhood, and whose administrators do not involve themselves with the aspirations, causes, and organizations of the neighborhood, are by virtue of their symbolic role denying God in that neighborhood," he argued.[75] Sargent Shriver, the brother-in-law of then President (and Catholic) John F. Kennedy and head of the Peace Corps who would later assume leadership of the fledgling War on Poverty through the Office of Economic Opportunity, spoke of a partnership between religion and the state to create a more just society. "We in government will continue our efforts," he said. "We will move with all the instruments at our command to achieve justice among men. My request is simply this: Help us. If there is to be a social order allowing the fullest possible development of individual personality, if there is to be the widest and deepest fellowship among men of different races, we need what [Jacques] Maritain has called Democracy of the Person. You can bring it about."[76] On the eve of the Birmingham bus boycott, Dr. Martin Luther King Jr. challenged the assembled clerics to assume more visible leadership on issues of race, to be an autonomous "voice" rather than a mere "echo" of the times. "If the Church does not recapture its prophetic zeal," King admonished, "it will become little more than an irrelevant social club with a thin veneer of religiosity. If the Church does not participate actively in the struggle for economic and racial justice, it will forfeit the loyalty of millions and cause men everywhere to say that it has atrophied its will."[77]

With the NCCIJ's National Conference on Religion and Race, the concern for racial justice among American Catholics, which previously had been confined to a loyal but small group of lay interracialists and practiced by a limited number of religious congregations in various missions and projects, emerged into the public spotlight. Sister Margaret Traxler later reflected that the true significance of the Conference on Religion and Race lay not in the attention it drew to religious justifications for racial equality but rather in the way that it brought to light that "there was a relationship between religion and prejudice, a reality that at the time seems clear but at the time was not always acknowledged."[78] On another level, the 1963 National Conference signaled a new outward orientation for the NCCIJ, one that would lead it to build on its existing relationships with civil rights leaders like A. Philip Randolph and the March on Washington Movement (MOWM). Moving toward even closer cooperation with the movement, Catholic interracialists were thus prompted to engage in direct action and nonviolent protest to address segregation beyond Catholic spheres, in American society generally.[79] Later in 1963 the NCCIJ sent a delegation to attend the civil rights movement's climactic March on Washington, and in July of that year the Chicago Catholic Interracial Council (CIC) organized a picket of the segregated Illinois Club for Catholic Women on the Loyola University campus. Six Franciscan sisters participated in the picket at the CIC's urging. Following these initial forays into protest, in 1965 the NCCIJ moved decisively into cooperation with the civil rights movement when Mathew Ahmann, executive director of the NCCIJ, organized delegations of Catholic protesters to go to Selma during the tense days following the "Bloody Sunday" attack by a sheriff's posse on peaceful marchers there. All told, over 900 Catholics—clergy, laity, and women religious—traveled to Selma at the NCCIJ's behest to stand in solidarity with Selma's African American citizens. Among the Catholics who responded to Ahmann's call were fifty-six sisters. The participation of priests and especially sisters in the Selma march generated an inordinate amount of publicity for Catholics, both in the Catholic press and in secular media outlets. Pictures of sisters in full habit on the "Selma line" ran in daily newspapers across the country, and Catholic periodicals featured articles based on the accounts of Catholic marchers. Several sisters returning from the march became minor celebrities back in their northern hometowns, invited even to do radio and television interviews.[80]

The Selma protest proved to be a singularly powerful catalyst to arouse sisters to pursue apostolic works among African Americans. As the image of the "Selma nuns" spread around the country, sisters in diverse locations and in congregations at varying stages of renewal were united in wonder—and sometimes shock—at the new role that sisters had assumed through the protest. Sisters in communities that had not fully absorbed SFC reforms or the emerging ideas about the centrality of the apostolate were confronted with images of the "path not taken." Sisters who had previously felt relatively isolated in their desire to work for racial justice began to feel part of the larger community of racial activists, including both Catholic interracialists and members of the civil rights movement. For sisters who traveled to Selma, the experience proved even more formative. Sister Margaret Traxler, SSND, recounted that many years after the Selma protest her former novice director said she regretted that Traxler left the classroom to pursue the racial apostolate after her experience in Selma (in fact, Traxler would become a central figure in the organizational structure of the racial apostolate). Traxler's response reflects the transformational power that the Selma protest had among American sisters in the 1960s. "In Selma, I saw another classroom," she said. "I met another need and I have never doubted that our founders would have approved the choices that were made."[81] Many sisters were enormously proud of the public witness given by sisters in Selma and were inspired to emulate them. Applications from women religious to racial-apostolate programs increased dramatically after 1965.

Catholic sisters stepped into racial activism through the heady, popular vision of racial and religious unity at Selma and almost immediately found themselves confronting circumstances in which neither religious nor racial cooperation actually existed. Beginning with the 1965 Watts riot in Los Angeles and ending with the riots that followed King's assassination in April 1968, American cities annually erupted in summer violence as African Americans expressed long-held anger over American racism and police brutality. In 1966 there were 43 riots, by 1967 there were 167 separate instances of violent social unrest, and 1968 saw an additional 130 riots. There was a certain irony about the Watts riots. Improbably, the rioting began just as the civil rights movement was beginning to experience clear legislative success. Watts happened a year after the passage of the 1964 Civil Rights Act and less than five days after the 1965 Voting Rights Act was signed into law on August 11, 1965.[82] For Catholic sisters the timing of Watts was even more confusing. The riots coincided with the dramatic conclusion of the Second Vatican Council, a time when sisters were still riding high from their experience in Selma and inspired by the changes happening within the

Church. As such, sisters possessed a kind of unbridled enthusiasm about the possibility for justice that made it extremely difficult for them to comprehend the level of frustration and anger that African Americans felt at the time.

The riots also directly affected the trajectory of the racial apostolate. After Watts, African Americans grew less trusting and open to white "do-gooder" intruders, preferring self-empowerment to outside assistance. When rioting accelerated in successive years, sisters were forced to address the fact that they might be unwelcome in the African American neighborhoods in which they chose to work. For some sisters the riots only increased their conviction that an apostolate addressing racial discrimination and racialized poverty was a legitimate, if not essential, contribution to the mission of the Church. King's assassination and the riots that followed further intensified sisters' sense of urgency about America's racial situation and the imperative for religious to engage apostolically with it. "WHAT A SHOCK Dr. Martin Luther King's death last night was! We have all caused it," a sister in Eau Claire, Wisconsin, reflected in an anguished note. "What can we do—hear us, Lord, we beg you!"[83] A cloistered Dominican contemplative in New Jersey who wanted her community to merge with an interracial community from Alabama attempted to use the King assassination as an occasion to educate women in her community about racism. "We do not have TV," she explained, "but I made a fuss about seeing the King funeral and I won my point." She continued:

> Many of the sisters have been hearing through the years he was a Communist agent (this Birchite stuff) and I wanted them to learn something of the other side of the coin. Then, too, most of them had never seen a non-Catholic religious service before and I wanted them to see how a man who came from a tradition that is non-sacramental and liturgically poor could so personify Christ in his life and his death that he puts us all to shame.[84]

The riots posed more complicated challenges to those sisters already active in African American neighborhoods nearest to the violence. A sister living in central Washington, D.C., during the 1968 riots observed, "As I write this, the curfew begins here in DC . . . 4:00 P.M. The situation is critical, as you know. Less than a mile from here the looting has begun again; it was under control until this morning, late. Several people have lost their lives already."[85] These sisters had to weigh their commitment to solidarity with African Americans against emergent Black Power ideologies that rejected white engagement with black social problems. Another sister writing from the Eau Claire, Wisconsin, convent, struggling to find a comfortable role in the racial apostolate, qualified her own desire to work among African Americans with a recognition that "the colored folks would prefer their own as teachers even when they do not have them readily available. (They show a growing sense of identity and I hope it will soon be realized.)"[86]

If Selma was a catalytic agent that mobilized sisters to seek out apostolic works among African Americans, the federal War on Poverty initiated under the presidential administration of Lyndon Johnson provided sisters with much-needed financial resources to pursue such works. Though planning for a major initiative to address poverty originally began during the presidency of John F. Kennedy, Johnson enthusiastically supported the continuation, and even expansion, of Kennedy's plans when he assumed office in 1963. Johnson invested a considerable amount of his own energy and political capital in pushing through legislation to create a funded mandate for federal action to reduce poverty. The resulting Economic Opportunity Act of 1964 established the Office of Economic Opportunity (OEO) as the central agency to coordinate the antipoverty initiative. Johnson insisted that the OEO be housed in the Executive Office of the President, giving the agency more bureaucratic flexibility to develop a national strategy for the reduction of poverty.[87] Johnson's ambitious War on Poverty created several federally funded programs that provided direct relief, legal representation, education, and job training to the nation's poorest citizens. War on Poverty programs included the Office of Economic Opportunity (OEO), the Legal Services Corporation, Volunteers in Service to America (VISTA), Project Head Start, the Job Corps, and Upward Bound. During its brief ascendancy from 1964 to 1966, the War on Poverty successfully reduced the number of poor people in the United States. It also, improbably, exerted a significant role in the expansion of the racial apostolate among American Catholic women religious.

In February 1964 Johnson appointed Sargent Shriver to be "chief of Staff for the War on Poverty." A devout Catholic with strong ties to the Catholic interracial movement (Shriver was a co-founder of the NCCIJ), Shriver immediately set about implementing a "strategy for fast growth and immediate, visible action."[88] "We knew we had to get the funds out fast" because "the anti-poverty program had to 'prove itself' quickly in the eyes of Congress, the White House, and the country at large," wrote CAP (Community Action Program) administrator John G. Wofford.[89] Shriver announced the first funding opportunities in November 1964, rushing to disperse the first installment of federal money given to the agency. "With the fiscal year ending the following June 30, the Office of Economic Opportunity was faced with the task of obligating $800 million in federal grants in slightly more than six months," Robert Clark, who worked at the OEO at the time, later reflected. "In bureaucratic terms, the task was herculean."[90] In response to this situation Shriver turned to the community he knew well—progressive and interracialist Catholics—informing them about the potential for funding through the agency, encouraging them to submit applications, and even providing some assistance with the drafting of such proposals. William Osborne observed the resulting confluence of federal grants and Catholic communities when he noted that in Detroit "all the diocese in the state are associated with the Federal Economic Opportunity Program. Archdiocesean administrative structures and office[s] are heavily utilized. This is undoubtedly one reason why Michigan seem[s] to be one of the most effective areas in the nation's war on poverty."[91]

Sisters interested in racial justice also took full advantage of this opportunity that the War on Poverty presented. Thus in 1965 and 1966, guided by the Department of Educational Services (a sister-oriented department of the NCCIJ that is the focus of Chapter 2), a significant number of sisters submitted proposals to the OEO for programs that addressed racialized poverty. Because appropriations in those years exceeded proposals, many of the sisters' projects were funded. The Economic Opportunity Act contained seven titles. Most of the racial apostolate programs initiated by sisters fell under Titles I, Youth Programs; II, Urban and Rural Community Action Programs; and IV, Employment and Employment Incentive Services.[92] (Sisters often referred casually to the titles when corresponding about particular apostolic programs.) As a result, the OEO-funded Project Cabrini in Chicago. Sisters participated in an OEO-funded educational program among migrant farm workers in Boca Raton, Florida, with the Job Corps in South Carolina, with Head Start in Detroit, with Upward Bound in Texas, and with VISTA in Louisiana, just to mention a few examples of this phenomenon. In a 1965 address to over 700 sisters in Davenport, Iowa, Mother General Consolatrice, BVM, declared, "What then is the role of the sister in race relations and in the War on Poverty? I see it as one of involvement, of action and of educated leadership."[93] Organizations in the racial apostolate disseminated information about funding opportunities, hoping to encourage other sisters to apply to federal antipoverty programs. Newsletters and publications for sisters involved in the new apostolate included announcements about opportunities for federal funding. "Title I of the Elementary-Secondary Act of 1965 (P.L. 89–10) allows for special programs and services for needs of deprived children," began one such announcement in a newsletter for religious. "Could your school find twenty such children in its enrollment? If so, you are challenged to find space, and a specially trained teacher. Send for 'Education, An Answer to Poverty' (gratis) Community Action Programs, OEO, Washington, D.C. 20506."[94] Sisters and congregations that had successfully secured funding through the OEO in turn advised other sisters how to construct successful applications. Sisters who staffed the OEO-funded 1965 pilot of Project Cabrini in Chicago disseminated their application along with materials about the program, encouraging other groups of religious to emulate them. The following year, the OEO funded six such programs throughout the country.

The War on Poverty and the emerging racial apostolate among sisters fit well together. Because racial apostolate programs often existed outside traditional congregational works in Catholic institutions, sisters who pursued such work among African Americans needed a source of financial support that was independent of the already strained finances of their religious communities. The OEO echoed language and concepts that sisters had encountered through the Second Vatican Council. Its origins in the Kennedy administration (as well as the leadership of the Catholic Shriver) gave it certain credibility among American Catholic religious and, in the end, probably made it easier for sisters to request release from congregational obligations in order to join federal programs. The word "poverty" in its title appealed to sisters whose congregational charism included alleviating poverty, responding to the poor, or "serving Christ as one among the poor." "I asked Mother Charles, my superior at that time, if I could devote this leave to serving in the War on Poverty," wrote one sister of her request to spend a year away from her congregation's parochial school in order to work in a black neighborhood.[95] Another sister listed "serving in the War on Poverty" among her apostolic priorities in her application to a racial-apostolate program. Thus, the War on Poverty functioned as a kind of bridge between old and new elements of religious life for sisters. The federal call to alleviate poverty resonated with sisters' deepest sense of religious mission, and the technocratic deployment of the social sciences, so central to the ethos and tactics of the OEO, also was central to the rhetoric and structures of *aggiornamento* among sisters.

While federal programs provided a bureaucratic and financial framework for sisters in the racial apostolate, employment in the federal government was a decisive step away from sisters' historical identification with work in Catholic institutions. OEO programs carried the interesting corollary of prohibiting sisters from catechizing or proselytizing. There had always been explicitly spiritual and denominational dimensions to sisters' work in parish schools and in the Catholic hospital system, but in federal antipoverty programs the spiritual roots of sisters' participation would have to be no more than an unspoken facet of the sister's spiritual life and vocation. The religious restrictions in antipoverty programs forced sisters to alter traditional conceptions of apostolic work and the relationship of the religious to the people among whom she worked. Thus, in addition to negotiating with her superior about appropriate boundaries of enclosure and financial autonomy, a sister participating in a program of the War on Poverty also had to negotiate with the government about appropriate boundaries for her religious commitments. Religious garb became a focal point of sisters' complicated relationships with federal agencies. Though some agencies, like the OEO, placed no restrictions on sisters' outward religious identification, others, like VISTA, requested that sisters dress in lay attire. Controversies over religious dress occurred at the same time that religious congregations were themselves engaged in a process of revising and in some cases eliminating the holy habit. In a lengthy letter to Sister Mary Peter (Margaret Ellen) Traxler, a seventy-year-old sister from Mankato, Minnesota, described her decision to remain in habit despite the fact that it meant she could not participate in VISTA:

> You'll recall my having asked you to get me into something among the very poorest for the summer months, at least—and I had also mentioned to you that I had applied to VISTA—after much waiting and deliberation on their part they have finally rejected any religious unless they do not wear their religious garb—even tho they had written me that the letter I wrote them in defense of "religious garb" was the best argumentative information yet received and that they were evaluating the possibility of wearing it, they wrote today that the General Counsel had rejected religious from participating in VISTA while wearing a religious garb—so now, my dear Peter, PLEASE get me something down South somewhere.[96]

Though the War on Poverty contributed much-needed legitimacy and financial support to the racial apostolate, it also introduced some unwanted consequences into these works. Participation in OEO-funded programs sharpened the distinction between sisters' work in the traditional apostolate and their emergent work in the wider public sphere among African Americans. The ethos of community-based organizing that was central to the funding priorities of the OEO required sisters to become active members of the communities where their works were performed. Sisters knew that they had to become more public and active in communities and nonreligious organizations in order to be credible recipients of such funding, but this also led to a self-perpetuating dynamic through which sisters became increasingly isolated from Catholic institutions as they simultaneously became ever more identified with and active in nonreligious organizations. Sisters also were aware of the inherent vulnerability in their dependence on federal and other funds. Sisters consciously cultivated relationships with funding agencies and also shared grant writing expertise among themselves, attempting to manage and possibly minimize their exposure to politically motivated fluctuations in federal appropriations to the OEO and other agencies in the War on Poverty. Such measures did not protect them from the sharp reductions in funding that occurred in 1967, leaving many of their proposals to the OEO unfunded.

The events of the 1950s and 1960s together created ideal conditions—a perfect storm, if you will—for a revolution in the religious apostolate. The loosening of restrictions of enclosure and the structural and educational changes initiated by the Sister Formation Conference revitalized the apostolate, moving it from the margins to the very center of religious life. At the same time, changes in racial and economic demographics of American Catholics in the postwar period effectively suburbanized apostolic works that were centered in Catholic parishes, further encouraging sisters to abandon suburban assignments for ones in non-Catholic communities. If the civil rights movement provided sisters with a racial focus for the conciliar mandate to "promote human justice," the War on Poverty provided sisters with countless other resources necessary to reconfigure the apostolic component of religious life.

The swirling confluence of transformations and developments in the Church, in religious congregations, and in American society gave birth to a phenomenon commentators at the time labeled "the new nuns"—sisters for whom the apostolate was at the very center of their identity as religious. Like Sister Meyer whose "yes, here I am" ministry operated in the Lawndale section of Chicago, "new nuns" described these new apostolic forms using terms like availability, accessibility, and responsiveness—words that emphasized the physical presence of sisters in the neighborhood, as part of the community. Writing from a summer position counseling youth in the Job Corps, Sister Lillanna Kopp reflected, "Today poverty for most sisters means simply: AVAILABILITY."[97] "The Sister's role is to *be there for others,*" explained another sister:

> Availability, it seems, is often the measure of love. To be available necessitates *being open* to give whatever the situation calls for, to receive whatever it offers. In this apostolate, the Sister will often serve best as a listener, not only to words, but also to reality, not only to sounds, but to silence.[98]

Sisters framed their reflections on the meaning of this new apostolate to African Americans according to a dialectic of presence and absence. The Church was present in the neighborhood despite the fact that many of its white members were newly absent. God was present in inner-city neighborhoods and rigidly segregated southern cities, despite the absence of justice and peace that might signal divine attendance. And sisters were present to parishioners in a fullness that was not possible in the previous age in which religious regulations mandated their absence from close contact with the laity. Sister Margaret Traxler described the "new works" as a "ministry of presence" that brought sisters into intimate contact with the "joys and the hopes, the griefs and anxieties of the men of this age" (language she borrowed from conciliar documents).[99] Sisters wanted their presence ultimately to lead to such human intimacies, to integration into the community and inclusion in its struggles.

To "new nuns," the concept of presence was an explicitly religious idea, one that resonated with the doctrine of the Mystical Body of Christ and with the incarnational and eucharistic Christologies that preceded it. Presence was not merely the opposite of absence, or even the simple fact of "being there." Rather, presence implied union, manifestation, reconciliation, penetration, and being part of or bound together with others. According to this component of the Catholic tradition, God was immanent in all creation. Incarnate in the world in the person of Christ, God's union with humanity was renewed each time God was made present through the Mass. Shaped by this incarnational religious sensibility, sisters in the racial apostolate saw Christ all around them in their work. One sister evoked Tellihard de Chardin's famous statement of God's immanence—"Nothing is profane; everything is sacred because Christ is transparent throughout creation"—to explain her posture of "encounter and involvement" toward the world.[100] "Christ is always among his people," wrote another sister. "I was glad to come to the inner city where the new church is in birth—a new and truer Christ recognizable by identity with the poor, by compassion and a thirst for justice."[101] For "new nuns," being present in African American communities was a devotional act that acknowledged God's immanence in the collective humanity of the neighborhood. "We may be called wandering nuns," reflected Sister Evangeline Meyer, "but we are wandering among the people Christ is walking with in their patience and hope."[102]

When "new nuns" wrote about their subsequent experiences in urban ghettos or the rural South, they occasionally included detailed, almost lurid descriptions of the poverty they witnessed, the "dope and dirt, drinking, disease, and despair" that were the legacy of white supremacy in segregated areas. Sisters' reflections on the aesthetics and experience of poverty have a devotional character; they were imagined in fine detail and are heavy with nuance and meaning. "Harlem is still in the depression of the thirties," began one such meditation by a sister-sociologist:

> You can smell, taste, see poverty everywhere—dirt, patches on patches, meals of beans and pork-backs, meals of rice and corn bread, meals of barely-fleshed chicken backs that sell almost everywhere at ten cents a pound. Rats live in the crumbling walls. Brittle-shelled roaches literally rain down from the ceiling cracks. Vermin crawl in the soiled bedclothes, the plumbing leaks, gurgles and grumbles constantly, night and day.[103]

Often these passages evoke incarnational Christologies, referring to the suffering poor as "Christ among us." One way of understanding this convention in sisters' writing (and perhaps in their apostolic work) is to see it as an application by sisters of preconciliar contemplative devotional culture to their new apostolic circumstances. As sisters moved out of the convent and into the streets in the 1960s, they brought with them a particular religious imagination that emphasized the spiritual significance of solidarity with the suffering of others.[104] Rather than meditating on the wounds of Christ or the suffering of Christ while sitting in the convent chapel, "new nuns" in new and often disorienting locations meditated on the wounds and suffering that were so evident within Christ's "mystical body" in urban ghettos, in "Christ among the poor." "The Church is the People of God," proclaimed Sister Mary Mercy during a liturgy for sisters involved in an urban apostolate program in Chicago. She continued:

> It is, must be, a flesh and blood Church,
> and flesh smells, and blood spills.
>
> Our Church . . . Not merely Sunday-envelope-altar-and-rosary-home-and-school-good-people.
>
> Our Church . . . the unwed mother, the lonely prostitute, the desparate [*sic*] junkie.[105]

Incarnational theology also provided sisters with a rich discourse to explain their new identity and unconventional apostolate to themselves, each other, and to the magisterium. For "new nuns," not only was Christ present in the Church and in the suffering of the poor, but sisters often described their ministries as an effort to make the incarnate Christ present in and through themselves. Sisters emphasized that "new works" were less about performing specific acts of charity and more about being present, serving other human beings in need, being Christ in the neighborhoods where they lived and worked. In a volume written to inspire women religious to join the new apostolate, Sister M. Charles Borromeo—writing as a sister but under her given name, Maryellen Muckenhirn—challenged sisters to "try out new ways of being Christ for others today."[106] Sisters believed that they participated in the incarnation of Christ, literally "bringing about a Christ who is truly incarnate" in contemporary society and contemporary problems, through their presence in segregated areas.[107] Presence and incarnation were inseparably linked in the apostolic theology of "new nuns." "We must be there to be *Christ* there," explained Sister Lillanna Kopp of the necessity of nuns to penetrate the world.[108] In the next chapter, we will consider the central organization that helped sisters get "there"—to the African American communities where they could enact this new apostolic vision.

CHAPTER TWO

Education and Training: Tools for Racial Justice

On August 26, 1963, John "Jack" Sisson of the National Catholic Conference for Interracial Justice (NCCIJ) met with leaders of the Sister Formation Conference (SFC) to discuss contributions that sisters might make to the cause of racial justice.[1] Though Sisson gave the notes of his presentation the unremarkable title "How nuns can effectively involve themselves in the struggle for interracial justice, a consideration of policy, training, program and so forth," his underlying reason for coming to Winona, Minnesota, to meet with the leadership group of the SFC was more specific than simply to reflect with them on general points of convergence between religious formation and civil rights. Sisson's goal was to initiate a specific partnership between his organization and the SFC.[2]

Handwritten margin notes on the first page of Sisson's prepared comments contain the telling note to himself "Learn the structure of the S.F. Conf. and the Mothers General."[3] Had Sisson already known the structure of the SFC or the Conference of Major Superiors of Women's Religious Institutes (or CMSW, the "Mother's General" in Sisson's note), he doubtless would have reconsidered his trip to Winona. The NCCIJ approached the SFC just as tensions between the SFC and the CMSW were erupting into a full-scale bureaucratic crisis, and Sisson had walked unawares into the thick of the conflict between the two organizations. Within a year of Sisson's presentation, the curial Sacred Congregation for Religious and Secular Institutes (CRIS) would reorganize the SFC into a commission under the direction of the CMSW. This reorganization effectively ended the SFC's status as an independent entity and, by extension, halted the SFC's experimental forays into the social sciences, intercultural relations, and new apostolic works that addressed social and economic inequalities.

Or did it? Philip Gleason noted that, like many reform-oriented Catholic groups of the 1950s, the SFC, "whose autonomy had already been trimmed, effectively disappeared in the postconciliar turmoil."[4] This observation—inarguably true from an institutional standpoint—misses one unexpected and largely forgotten source of continuity (and serendipity) in the story of the Sister Formation movement after 1963, namely the NCCIJ. Though partnership between the NCCIJ and the SFC never materialized in the form Sisson imagined, the NCCIJ developed its own department to channel sisters into the racial-justice movement, naming this internal division the Department of Educational Services (DES). In the immediate postconciliar period the DES continued the SFC's trajectory toward apostolic activities, which channeled the educational advances of women religious toward projects that addressed social problems. In fact, by 1965 the DES had effectively duplicated many of the distinctive projects and perspectives that were purportedly "lost" when the SFC was incorporated into the CMSW the previous year.

The leadership group of the SFC, which Sisson addressed on August 26, was in no state to listen closely to his exhortation and in no position to consider his collaborative proposition. Its members were, unknown to Sisson, divided between the meeting in Winona and a simultaneous meeting of the CMSW in Cincinnati, Ohio. Members of the SFC leadership group in attendance at Winona had spent the morning prior to Sisson's 2:00 P.M. presentation in a stormy session in which they debated how to respond to the complex turn of events within their organization. At the simultaneous Cincinnati meeting, representatives of the curial CRIS were about to "clarify" the status of the SFC, effectively making it a subsidiary under the jurisdiction of the CMSW.[5]

Though the two organizations of sisters had emerged at roughly the same time in response to a mandate by Pope Pius XII that sisters revise certain facets of their institutes, the CMSW and SFC represented very different approaches to the challenge of modernization. The CMSW had been created directly by Pius XII in 1956—despite initial hesitation by American superiors—as a permanent national conference to facilitate dialogue and cooperation between the superiors of women's congregations in the United States. Though its founding statutes defined the purpose of the conference as "the promotion of the spiritual welfare" of American sisters, the assembled superiors of the CMSW broadly interpreted their mission to include a broad array of issues of concern to sisters.[6] In contrast, the SFC was a more-or-less grassroots effort that emerged within a larger professional organization to address a common problem among sisterhoods. After several years of study, planning, and dialogue, sister-educators founded the SFC in 1953 as a special committee of the National Catholic Education Association (NCEA) to improve the inadequate, often piecemeal, training and education young women received when entering religious congregations.[7] The Sister Formation Conference, as its name suggests, focused on the "formation" of sisters—the formal education, spiritual development, and professional training that formed novices into mature religious. Though both organizations of sisters had much in common—both focused on *aggiornamento*, or the bringing up to date of religious institutes, both were comprised of women in leadership positions within their communities, both had organized specifically to facilitate intracongregational cooperation—by 1963 the SFC and CMSW had grown in very different directions. As each organization expanded its own programs, the two bodies increasingly entered territory the other claimed as rightfully its own, and tensions between the two increased from mutual uncertainty to a "polite tug-of-war" to open hostility.[8]

The central issue beneath the conflict between the SFC and CMSW was, in one sense, a straightforward question of authority. The SFC was, in the words of historian Judith Eby, a noncanonical organization that stood "outside the normal jurisdiction of hierarchical authority of that time," whereas the CMSW "stood within the clear framework of hierarchical authority."[9] The SFC's canonical autonomy allowed it to cultivate relationships with sympathetic American bishops, while the CMSW was more closely tied to the Roman Curia through the Sacred Congregation for Religious. Members of the CMSW held that the formation of a sister properly fell under the sole jurisdiction of her superior. Superiors in the CMSW thus believed, by extension, that any organization dedicated to the formation of sisters, like the SFC, should naturally fall under the jurisdiction of the Conference of Major Superiors. However, the SFC resisted being subsumed within the CMSW, believing that its status as an autonomous organization, free from direct association with the doctrinal authority of the Church's hierarchy, was central to the SFC's ability to negotiate on sisters' behalf with non-Catholic and governmental agencies.[10] In what proved to be the last straw, the executive secretary of the SFC, Sister Annette Walters, CSJ, had inadvertently inflamed these tensions over the authority of superiors by arguing in an article in the SFC's *Sister Formation Bulletin* that freedom of conscience, independent of the direction of a superior, was an important component of spiritual maturity for religious.[11]

But differences between the two organizations ran deeper than this seemingly straightforward conflict over the nature of religious authority in the Church. In 1963 the SFC and CMSW embodied fundamentally different ideas about the primary function of the vocation to religious life. At the time, the CMSW operated within the prevailing, preconciliar model of religious life that viewed vowed religious consecration, even by noncloistered women in apostolic congregations, as a spiritual enterprise in which women were to seek perfection through withdrawal from the profane and polluting elements of the world into spheres of religious enclosure in which they devoted themselves to contemplation, prayer, and service to the Church. In this model of religious life as a specialization in sanctity, sisters' identities were to grow primarily from their intimate relationship with God rather than from outward apostolic activities, and much of their apostolic work was to be similarly enacted within Catholic institutions. In contrast, by 1963 the SFC had gradually grown away from viewing religious life primarily as an inward-focused state of consecration based on separation from the world, toward a more fluid vision of religious life as a prophetic, public expression of God's transformative love for the world.[12] Religious life, for women of the SFC, was about being open to the non-Catholic world in new ways. This outward-looking orientation emphasized the active character of the religious apostolate, urging individual sisters to penetrate the world in order to transform it.[13] Articles in the SFC's *Sister Formation Bulletin* during the late 1950s—bearing titles like "Apostolic Action—A School of Perfection," "Religious Women and the Apostolate in the Modern World," "Apostolic Formation through the Curriculum," and "Activity or Activism?"—reflected this apostolic-orientation of the SFC.[14] In addition to seeking to encounter God in the quiet of the convent chapel, these "new nuns" (as they came to call themselves) also believed with renewed enthusiasm that they encountered Christ by attending to the needs of society's most vulnerable and stigmatized members.[15]

This distinctive, outward-looking vision of religious life emerged gradually in the SFC through the first ten years of the organization's existence, as the relatively narrow initial focus on the education of sisters progressively broadened to include questions about how that education should be applied in their professional and apostolic activities.[16] The SFC's vision of religious life contained additional elements that made it uniquely amenable to the kind of work the NCCIJ proposed on that hot August afternoon in Winona. In fact, the SFC's willingness by 1963 to entertain the NCCIJ's proposal that sisters join the civil rights movement was in many ways the logical culmination of a consistent trajectory toward racial-justice activism that the SFC had followed since its inception in 1953. That trajectory had progressively opened sisters in the SFC to new forms of knowledge, then new cultures and peoples, and finally new apostolates, paving the way for the kinds of social activism that the NCCIJ proposed.

Education was, from the beginning, the central focus of the SFC and the source of its institutional vitality.[17] In 1955 the SFC secured a grant from the Ford Foundation to develop a college curriculum specifically for sisters. Named after the town in Washington where sisters met to design the program in 1956, the resulting Everett Curriculum departed substantially from existing educational practices among religious congregations. The core of the curriculum balanced theology (itself a new addition to the training of sisters) and philosophy with a healthy dose of the social sciences and included opportunities for individual sisters to adapt the curriculum to their own educational and professional goals. Embedded in the Everett Curriculum was an expansive understanding of the religious apostolate of sisters. Rather than simply training sisters to be pious contributors to the everyday workings of Catholic schools and hospitals, the curriculum's objective was to train sisters for professional engagement with the world. The social and behavioral sciences were central to this ambitious vision of the religious apostolate because, according to the curriculum's authors, sociology, economics, political science, and psychology offered analytical tools to diagnose and thus remedy specific causes of human suffering.[18] The SFC, in effect, encouraged sisters to abandon the familiarity of physical and intellectual cloister in favor of fundamental openness to both secular forms of knowledge and to new roles in the life of the Church and in human history.

The Everett Curriculum's attempt to combine theology, philosophy, and the social sciences into a coherent academic program was characteristic of the SFC's focus on the "integration" of spiritual and intellectual facets of religious life. Institutes, workshops, and programs of the SFC simultaneously introduced sisters both to new theological currents and new social theories that emerged in the postwar years. The SFC's Instructional Programs in Spirituality and diverse programs at SFC regional meetings introduced sisters to the work of theologians like Yves Congar, Karl Rahner, and Bernhard Haring, applying the *nouvelle theologie* of the time to emerging questions about religious life.[19] The SFC created an annual workshop for sister-professors, held each summer at Marquette University, to study the implementation of the Everett Curriculum by exploring "new knowledges, especially the behavioral sciences, for their relevance to the curriculum for the formation of Sisters."[20] The Marquette workshops introduced sisters to new theories emerging in the social sciences, particularly the work of Erving Goffman and Kurt Lewin. Addresses and papers given at the Spirituality Institute and the workshops at Marquette were reprinted in the *Sister Formation Bulletin,* extending the influence of the meetings far beyond the limited number of sisters who attended. What resulted from these SFC initiatives was a unique cross-fertilization that combined developments in the *nouvelle theologie* with the postwar boom in the social sciences, one that applied directly to the sister-specific question of how women religious could be more effective in their work to transform society.[21]

In doing so, the SFC translated the theological and intellectual developments of the immediate preconciliar period into specific initiatives, turning abstract ideas into concrete programs.[22] In one important example, the SFC responded to emerging theologies that supported ecumenism and interreligious cooperation by creating programs that facilitated cross-cultural encounters between American women religious and non-Catholics, racial minorities, and sisters in foreign countries. The SFC Overseas Project created partnerships between foreign and American communities of religious and at its peak served twenty-eight communities in India, Africa, and Latin America.[23] The SFC also addressed the problematic prevalence of bias against Jews among Catholics, studying religious textbooks for anti-Semitic content and inviting Rabbi Marc Tanenbaum to address sisters at workshops and conferences.[24] The SFC sponsored special programs for sisters at national meetings of the National Catholic Education Association (NCEA), which included lecturers on such topics as "The Sister and Jewish Relations," "Sister Formation and Human Rights," and "The Sister and Civil Rights." Sisters were gathered for the 1963 Marquette workshop when the March on Washington was planned, and during the workshop they watched developments in the civil rights movement closely.[25]

A letter from the SFC to the American bishops in 1963—one of the organization's final acts as an autonomous entity—defended the SFC's characteristic openness to the world, explaining that the Conference "takes its orientation from the openness of the Church to all that is good as it strives to 'build a bridge to the contemporary world.' " The letter stated, "It is an effort to lead Sisters, not to a Crusade, but to a sense of mission based on the present opportunity to extend the loving presence of Christ within the world."[26] By the time the SFC was brought under the control of the CMSW in 1964, the SFC was promoting a robust and expansive role for women religious in contemporary society.

Through programs like the ones described above, the SFC contributed to the emergence among Catholic women religious in the early and mid-1960s of a new apostolate that addressed either the root causes or the social effects of American white supremacy. Though this new racial apostolate (also sometimes called the "social apostolate" or the "urban apostolate" by sisters at the time) resulted from the convergence of diverse developments in the Church, in Catholic demographics, in American race relations, and in the federal government—all of which together dramatically altered the way women religious understood and lived out their religious vocations—the imprint of the SFC on this revolution in the apostolate should not be underestimated. SFC workshops and programs were a "forum where sisters were learning, and at the same time they were acting," recalled Sister Ritamary Bradley, editor of the Conference's *Bulletin.* This convergence of advanced education and apostolic formation influenced women religious, Bradley said, "opening up the minds and experiences of sisters, and drawing them into working on problems like race, not just going into the classroom to teach."[27] The SFC also worked to lengthen the training of sisters, enthusiastically supporting the developing norm of a lengthy "juniorate" period between the novitiate and final profession that gave new religious both time and opportunities to explore social problems like race and to consider ways of making religious life more relevant to them. The SFC laid educational, theological, and professional foundations for the emergence of the racial apostolate, creating a cadre of sisters armed with advanced degrees in the social sciences who were fundamentally open to the world and energized by the prospect of ministering to society's most pressing needs.

Many women who entered the racial apostolate carried with them certain assumptions about their work that had been formed through programs of the SFC. These assumptions would later fundamentally shape the structure and projects initiated under the auspices of the NCCIJ. Such sisters approached the issue of racial discrimination from a perspective that merged theology with the social and behavioral sciences, diagnosing racism both as a rupture within the "mystical body of Christ" and as a form of social pathology that could be remedied through specific action. Education, the starting point and center of the SFC, was also central to sisters' responses to racism. Sisters in the racial apostolate saw education as a powerful tool for changing society, creating educational programs for African Americans to supplement the inadequate schooling available under segregation as well as programs to educate Caucasians about the mythologies and misinformation that lay underneath racism. Just as the SFC operated through channels of extracongregational, intercommunity cooperation among sisters, so the sisters in the racial apostolate often created cooperative programs that joined sisters from different orders. Finally, sisters in the racial apostolate, like the SFC as a body, did not view the individual religious as solely bound to the sphere of her congregation (or the singular authority of her superior), but rather such sisters sought assignments and funding from diverse sources, including those outside of Catholic enclaves. In short, the racial apostolate bore the unmistakable fingerprint of the SFC, which meant that after 1964 the NCCIJ's Department of Educational Services also would bear the SFC's distinctive fingerprint.

It was precisely these characteristic facets of the SFC (also embedded in the racial apostolate) that had alienated and alarmed the Conference of Major Superiors. Though the CMSW would later (in its postconciliar incarnation as the Leadership Conference of Women Religious) champion many of the perspectives and activities that the SFC pioneered in the early 1960s, the more cautious and inward-looking CMSW believed in the early conciliar period that the SFC had overstepped its proper sphere of authority. Formed as religious in an era that understood a sister's primary responsibility as the cultivation of a state of perfection through prayer and religious enclosure, and then charged with the weighty responsibility of guarding the spiritual welfare of sisters in their communities, American superiors, unsurprisingly, were cautious about the possible dangers inherent in unmediated contact between sisters and the world beyond Catholic institutions. From their perspective, the SFC, in its enthusiasm about the renewal of religious life, had breached important boundaries between sisters and the world without considering the long-term spiritual ramifications. The SFC's focus on cross-cultural encounter, the authority it invested in secular forms of knowledge through the social sciences, its enthusiastic endorsement of unconventional religious apostolates, and its pursuit of funding from sources outside the Church all, the CMSW argued, rendered the institution of vowed religious life for women vulnerable to corruption through contact with possibly profane ideas and institutions. It also threatened to elevate the aspirations and conscience of individual sisters over the canonical authority of her religious superior to direct her education and apostolic assignment. From the perspective of superiors, moving the SFC under the auspices of the CMSW would ensure that outward-looking, apostolic facets of formation would be subordinate to the primarily spiritual function of religious consecration, just as wishes of the individual sisters were to be subordinate to the will of the superior.[28]

This is largely what happened in August 1964 when the bylaws of the SFC were rewritten to transfer control of the SFC to the Conference of Major Superiors. SFC offices were moved to Washington, D.C.; the Marquette workshops and many of the other programs listed above ceased; SFC officers were replaced; and the *Bulletin* was assigned a new editor. The expansive agenda of the SFC was trimmed back to a more limited focus on formation and spirituality, and the apostolic components of the SFC, including the fledgling racial apostolate, were quietly downplayed or dismantled.

The effects from the restructuring of the SFC extended downward from the organization and its leaders through its programs to eventually affect the sisters who had supported the changes the SFC represented. For individual sisters, historian Marjorie Beane observes, the restructuring of the SFC meant that the attention to social concerns and the expanded apostolate that had been central to the SFC were "left to the individual sister to develop as the work of the new SFC settled primarily on the spiritual formation needs of the sisters."[29] The reorganization of the SFC thus left an organizational void for sisters who had embraced the new apostolic forms the SFC had first cultivated and then facilitated.

In the fall of 1965 Sister Mary Audrey (Lillanna) Kopp, SNJM—a sociologist and astute observer of religious life—pointed to the void left by the SFC's restructuring when she noted that something crucial was missing from the attempts of American sisters to implement conciliar *aggiornamento*.[30] Kopp observed that despite glimmers of "new ferment" among young sisters and senior administrators, "the great mass of sisters in the middle area between has lacked a catalytic agent" to connect them with the "window opening warmly mandated by Pope John." Put more simply, the majority of existing sisters were at a loss for how to modernize the apostolic component of religious life. It was not so much that sisters were resistant to the renewal process unfolding in the Church and in their own congregations as the Second Vatican

Council drew to a close. Rather, in Kopp's view, women religious lacked practical models for how to implement conciliar changes to the religious apostolate in their communities and, at a more personal level, in their own lives. Most congregations lacked organizational structures to channel religious into new forms of apostolic work. According to Kopp, what sisters needed was a partner who would help them "put their hands generously to the new works of the Church and the temporal society challenging them," an institution that would promote dialogue and experimentation within and among religious congregations. Using language that closely resembled descriptions of the former SFC, Kopp argued that "religious women need and want a neutral catalyst that can assist them [to] reach deeply into the great social issues of the times, a neutral catalyst that can bring to their very doorstep," a forum for dialogue about emerging forms of religious apostolate, as well as opportunities to participate in it. Kopp stressed that this catalyst must be unbiased in its relationship with the diverse congregations of American religious. It should be "an agency close to the interests of every religious community, yet controlled by none."[31] With characteristic enthusiasm, Kopp proclaimed, "This catalyst, now in embryo, I recognize in the Educational Service Department [DES] of the NCCIJ." Kopp envisioned an ambitious range of roles for the DES. Those in the department, she wrote, "can be the pilot project initiators, the creative dreamers of apostolic dreams, the builders of strongly structured patterns for Christian social action in the schools and market places of America."[32]

"Race Relations Needs the Nun"

Seen from one perspective, the NCCIJ's timing in trying to initiate a partnership with the SFC could not have been worse, given the immanent demise of the SFC. Walking blindly into the organizational crisis between Sister Formation and the religious superiors, NCCIJ representative Jack Sisson's address to the SFC leadership group in Winona in 1963 paradoxically promoted precisely the kind of activities that had gotten the SFC into trouble with the body of major superiors. Seen from a different perspective, however, the NCCIJ's timing was nearly perfect. Sisson may have been "preaching to the choir" on that August afternoon in Winona, but the SFC was a choir about to be told, in no uncertain terms, to change its tune.

The organizational crisis between the SFC and the CMSW demonstrates the limits to the reforms and experiments that were possible under the canonical structures of religious life prior to the reception of the Second Vatican Council in the late 1960s. By 1963 the SFC clearly had reached the boundary of permissible innovation to the norms governing religious life, and indeed, at times, had pushed strongly against these barriers. The emergent racial apostolate stood at the outer edge of those SFC innovations and, it was clear, would not be entirely welcome under the auspices of the CMSW. If the racial apostolate was to continue and even to flourish after 1964, it would have to do so outside of canonical structures, finding elsewhere the progressive vision and practical support that formerly had been provided by the Sister Formation Conference.

It was equally true that the SFC, and with it the racial apostolate, had simply outgrown the ecclesial context that had nurtured its impressive early growth. While the racial apostolate benefited from the considerable organizational resources and broad reach of the SFC, it also was limited by accountability to official church structures, the SFC's internal bureaucratic procedures, and the uninvited scrutiny that the SFC's visibility attracted from superiors, the American bishops, and authorities in Rome. As the racial apostolate extended itself beyond Catholic circles, it also suffered from larger non-Catholic (and perhaps anti-Catholic) perceptions that attached to a sisters-only organization like the SFC, namely that its members were less interested in justice per se than they were in the religious proselytization of African Americans. So while the restructuring of the SFC cut loose the racial apostolate from its relatively comfortable mooring within a well-connected, sister-specific organization, the new apostolate was hardly cast adrift. Rather, while the new apostolate was deprived of the benefits of institutional affiliation with the demise of the SFC, it also was freed of certain restrictions that had inhibited its development.

At the precise moment when the SFC (and by extension the emergent racial apostolate) was about to be absorbed into the CMSW, cementing its relationship with and answerability to the hierarchy, the NCCIJ stood largely outside those structures, offering sisters interested in racial-justice activism access to resources that were unavailable and activities that would have been unacceptable within official Church structures. With the creation of the NCCIJ's Department of Educational Services, then, the movement among American sisters toward new racially oriented apostolic forms shifted—largely uninterrupted—from its original proximity to canonical structures to an independent but still Catholic organization that enjoyed both relative freedom within the

Church and proven legitimacy in the larger civil rights movement. Through their affiliation with the NCCIJ, sisters of the racial apostolate were able to secure federal funding as well as remarkably high levels of trust from African American communities. And, in fact, the racial apostolate positively flourished under the sponsorship of the NCCIJ, enjoying a creative vitality that far surpassed its early growth within the SFC. In retrospect, the transfer of the racial apostolate to the NCCIJ's Department of Educational Services stands less as an indictment of the limitations of the SFC than as a reflection of the SFC's success in nurturing a generation of sisters whose educational achievements and apostolic orientation to religious life would ultimately transform the meaning of religious vocation after the Second Vatican Council.

For its part, the NCCIJ also had something to gain from an alliance with women religious. There were specific, strategic reasons that Sisson approached the SFC about creating a partnership with the NCCIJ. Nuns brought instant publicity and automatic credibility to the civil rights movement. The strategic usefulness of sisters was a recent revelation for activists in the racial-justice movement in 1963, even Catholic activists like members of the NCCIJ. Just two months prior to Sisson's address to the SFC, seven Franciscan sisters had shocked Chicago's Catholic community by picketing the Illinois Club for Catholic Women on the Loyola University campus in protest against the club's refusal to admit African American members. Though the demonstration centered on a specific conflict within the Catholic community, the picketing sisters attracted the attention of the national and international media, and photographs of sisters clad in full habit and carrying signs appeared in papers across the country.[33]

The Chicago picket caught the attention of groups like the NCCIJ for two reasons. First, the sheer anomaly of sisters taking a public stand on a controversial issue alerted outsiders that significant changes had been taking place, more or less quietly, within the structures and norms of vowed religious life for women as a result of the SFC. The quietly deferential "good sister" of Catholic lore who split her time between stern lectures in the parochial school classroom and silent rosaries in the chapel had apparently, and without most Catholics noticing, decided to engage with the world beyond parish and convent walls. Second, the remarkable publicity attracted by the Franciscan sisters and the success of their protest—the club, in response, had relented and reversed its policy—alerted civil rights organizers to the credibility and symbolic power that sisters could contribute to the cause of racial justice. After all, an otherwise relatively small battle to desegregate a private club had made national news because sisters were involved. "What an avalanche of letters and phone calls resulted from that action," Sisson reflected to sisters of the SFC in his 1963 meeting with them in Winona. "A million talks or written articles could never have brought up the reaction that seeing the nuns stand up in public against a moral evil did." Sisson acknowledged that the Chicago picket had prompted his efforts to partner with the SFC. "Although we all realize the great role the nun has in shaping our society, still I probably would not be here if it hadn't been for the dramatic example of six sisters in the picket line in Chicago last July 1st," he admitted. "Their witness focused attention on your potential and convinced some of us that many other nuns were probably standing by those pickets and wishing for an opportunity to do something more meaningful themselves."[34]

In addressing the SFC leadership Sisson employed language that was already prevalent in the SFC, framing racial-justice activism as a natural extension of the traditional works sisters had performed in the Church "to establish a Christian order and lead all men to Christ."[35] Sisson argued that works to promote racial justice could help sisters move into more robust engagement with the world. Projects like those proposed by the NCCIJ offered opportunities for women religious to gain firsthand experience outside Catholic enclaves, addressing pressing social problems. Sisson ended his general comments to the SFC leadership group with a direct invitation to the SFC to join forces with the NCCIJ. The NCCIJ would "cherish" the assistance of sisters, Sisson said, "to help in the area of education and health, to develop curriculum and policy, to investigate needs, to feed back information to the sisterhoods." Such sisters could be assigned on a yearly basis, or for shorter terms, to the organization's offices in Chicago. Finally, Sisson proposed a meeting within a month in Chicago to "work out a specific program" of cooperation between the SFC and the NCCIJ. The meeting would include not only representatives from the SFC and the NCCIJ but also "specialists who abound in the Chicago area in the field of social action who would leap at the chance to work more closely with sisters in this whole area of the social apostolate."[36]

The NCCIJ's vision for the role of sisters in the racial-justice movement became clearer in the months following Sisson's meeting with SFC leaders as Mathew Ahmann, the executive director of the NCCIJ, continued Sisson's attempts to woo the SFC into a collaborative partnership. Ahmann and Sisson seem to have remained completely unaware of the changes afoot within the SFC, and members of the SFC with whom they corresponded did not mention the internal struggle that ensued as the SFC prepared for its 1964 transfer to the Conference of Major Superiors. Through the autumn of 1963 Ahmann busied himself building a series of ties between the two organizations, starting with the addition of Sister Claire Marie (Sawyer), OSF, to the NCCIJ's board.[37] Sister Claire Marie was a member of the same congregation responsible for the famous Chicago nun picket, and she would later serve briefly as the first director of the NCCIJ's Department of Educational Services.

A fruitful October meeting of Sister Claire Marie, Sisson, Ahmann, and SFC executive secretary Sister Annette (Walters), CSJ, solidified several channels of cooperation between the NCCIJ and the SFC. Walters agreed to allow Ahmann to lead a panel on racial justice at the SFC's annual meeting in the spring (its last as an autonomous organization) and also promised to arrange private evening meetings for him with key leaders of the SFC at that meeting. Walters also agreed to strategically circulate a letter from Ahmann to sympathetic superiors that discussed possible roles for religious in the civil rights movement. In return, Ahmann offered training materials and travel funding to support the SFC's new initiative: a team of sisters who would travel from motherhouse to motherhouse to "present special course work in intergroup relations for sisters in their juniorate programs." ("Intergroup relations" was a term used often in context of the SFC's focus on cross-cultural encounter. The phrase usually, though not always, referred to race relations.) "Along with the teaching responsibilities," Ahmann reiterated in a letter to Walters on November 5, 1963, "this team would develop some field work possibilities which could give the nuns in training some actual experience with Negroes and race relations." Ahmann was especially enthusiastic about this project and eager to involve the NCCIJ in it. "We have already spent some time trying to develop a list of suggested apostolic apprenticeship experiences which could be organized by a traveling team for follow-up after the team presented its course," he offered to Walters. For her part, Sister Claire Marie had agreed to draft a questionnaire for the SFC to send to motherhouses to inventory what different congregations already were doing in the area of race relations.[38]

Ahmann and Sister Annette Walters corresponded through the winter as they prepared for Ahmann's presentation at the upcoming April meeting of the SFC in Atlantic City. On February 4, 1964, Ahmann sent Sister Annette two letters. The first was brief, informal, and peppered with questions about whether the SFC had made progress on the collaborative projects that had been discussed in the fall, in particular the traveling group in intergroup relations and the survey for superiors. The second letter, also addressed to Sister Annette, was lengthy, formal, and not written for Annette Walters so much as it was crafted for the superiors to whom she had promised Ahmann she would forward it (in order, one presumes, to prepare sisters to be receptive to Ahmann's panel at the NCEA in April). In this second letter Ahmann laid out a rationale for why nuns should join the struggle for racial justice and then listed four "obvious needs" that sisters could fill in the movement.

"Race relations needs the nun," Ahmann declared at the outset of the letter that was to be forwarded to superiors. He invoked the famous Chicago picket as proof that sisters, because of their cultural status and intimate contact with the laity, were uniquely positioned to make a significant contribution to the cause of racial justice. To do this, sisters would have to overcome their relative isolation from the world beyond Catholic institutions. "Almost non-existent is the nun involved in the warp and woof of the lives of people in their neighborhoods," he observed. "They have set themselves apart, and consequently their witness can be irrelevant or can easily be ignored." Ahmann was unsparing in his letter, arguing that there was a widespread perception among Catholic laity that religious life stunted, rather than nourished, the moral development of women who became sisters. "Perhaps it is harsh to observe that there are many people who question whether nuns are permitted to follow their conscience . . . or are encouraged to sharpen their conscience on contemporary issues where Christianity has relevance. But it is true." (His reference to "conscience" surely would have caught the attention of sister-readers familiar with the recent controversy over Sister Annette Walter's article about the relationship between a superior and the consciences of her subjects.) Nuns bear a "heavy responsibility" to make their witness for Christ effective and relevant, Ahmann argued, especially amid the "unprecedented social change" happening in the church and in civil society. "The world of today demands a trained nun with the courage to become engaged in the affairs of men, who will give meaningful service precisely because she is involved."[39]

Ahmann observed that though "countless projects" existed for sisters who wanted to become active in interracial work, there were four specific areas that represented "tremendous opportunities" for sisters to assist with "obvious needs" in the racial justice movement. Unsurprisingly, the needs Ahmann outlined in his letter resemble the projects on which he and Sister Annette were already quietly collaborating. First, Ahmann observed, it would be helpful to collect information about "what particular nuns or orders are already doing in contemporary race relations." (Sister Claire Marie would distribute just such a survey at the NCEA meeting.) Second, one particular order should offer itself as a model for other congregations, sharing information about its training, programs, successes, and failures in this new form of apostolate. Third, someone should coordinate better communication among sisterhoods, and also between advocacy groups like the NCCIJ and sisters, about concerns and developments in the area of racial justice. Fourth, there needed to be formal programs to provide "in-service and pre-service sisters" (language borrowed directly from the SFC) with information about race relations and "apostolic apprenticeships." "We ought to develop teams of nuns who can provide formal training 'circuit riding' to the motherhouses," Ahmann offered. "And then we should devise pilot pre-service projects which will give nuns in training some useful experience."(Again, he described the project on which he and Sister Annette already were hard at work.)[40]

The projects Ahmann described would not, in the end, materialize under the auspices of the SFC. Four months after Ahmann's April presentation to the national meeting of the SFC in Atlantic City, the SFC's bylaws were rewritten to make it a committee of the Conference of Major Superiors. Programs offering apostolic apprenticeship in areas of racial, social, or economic justice would not be a significant focus of the Major Superiors' agenda until the organization's reincarnation as the Leadership Conference of Women Religious in the 1970s.[41] As part of the organizational restructuring that took place in August of 1964, the CMSW replaced Sister Annette Walters as executive secretary of the SFC. Sister Annette left the SFC headquarters in early September, taking a fellowship at the University of Minnesota.[42] Correspondence and documents from the NCCIJ do not reveal how, exactly, the NCCIJ learned of the changes afoot within the SFC. A letter from Sister Annette Walters to John Butler of the NCCIJ, written on Sister Formation letterhead and dated August 25, 1964, described her return to Minnesota in neutral terms, wishing the NCCIJ "continued success in this most important work" and expressing her desire to remain in touch with the NCCIJ.[43] But records from the NCCIJ suggest that by the time Walters' letter arrived at the NCCIJ offices in Chicago, the organization was fully aware of the turbulent transformation happening in the SFC and was making plans to move forward on its own with strategies to involve sisters more deeply in the racial-justice movement. By August 1964 (literally at the same time that the new SFC bylaws were being ratified by the CMSW) the NCCIJ was already organizing its new Department of Educational Services—to be headed by Sister Claire Marie (Sawyer)—to fill the void left by the SFC. The DES immediately set about creating programs to address the needs Ahmann had identified in his February letter to superiors. The DES also recreated under its own auspices the very programs that Sister Annette had been pursuing before she left the SFC.[44]

Though materials from the early months of the DES do not explicitly mention sisters as the *raison d'être* for the new division of the NCCIJ, the department's goals and programs were oriented almost exclusively toward the professional spheres of women religious. The NCCIJ described the purpose of the DES in terms that were bland and opaque—namely, to increase awareness of racial-justice issues among Catholics by improving the visibility and influence of the organization among "persons who were in responsible positions within the Catholic community."[45] If the language was not clear, the implication surely was: by the early and mid-1960s, such persons in "responsible positions" in Catholic schools and hospitals were very likely to be sisters. The DES also copied language and concepts directly from the SFC, and directed most of its outreach efforts at sisters. Though the DES did seek support from the lay-oriented Catholic Family Movement, the bulk of its early efforts to cultivate "meaningful contact" and support from Catholic groups focused on Catholic organizations dominated by sisters, including the restructured SFC, the NCEA, and, surprisingly, the CMSW. The sister orientation of the DES was also evident in the composition of its staff, all of whom were women religious representing major congregations in the United States.[46]

In February of 1965, the DES added Sister Mary Peter (Margaret Ellen) Traxler, SSND, to its staff. Traxler briefly served as assistant director of educational services under Sister Claire Marie, before assuming the director position in the summer of 1965, the summer following the Selma march. A former high school teacher from Mankato, Minnesota, Traxler was a force to be reckoned with. Energetic, ambitious, and a gifted writer, Traxler quickly transformed the DES into the central nervous system of the racial apostolate. She was well-traveled, well-connected, and politically savvy. "Traxler was a sassy Irish woman," recalled her colleague Sister Lillanna Kopp, "she could tell off Irish clergy and they would love it." Kopp said:

> One time there was an article in the NCR [*National Catholic Reporter*] with the headline "Nuns Formed to Buck Bishops." Atrocious! But it was the type of thing Margaret could say to the bishops, and they would laugh. You know, "Buck Bishops." They weren't used to nuns not being totally loyal to the system, but she got away with it, even though she was so outspoken, because she had such a good sense of humor that she never seemed to aggravate anyone but her own community.[47]

More than any other sister, Traxler came to be identified in the minds of sisters with the new racial apostolate. She was present at several significant protests, including the events at Selma. She was the only sister present at the 1966 march in support of James Meredith. As DES director, Traxler seemed to attract media attention, and her propensity to say outrageous things meant that she was often quoted in print. With Traxler at the helm, the DES embarked on an ambitious program of pilot projects designed to channel sisters into the civil rights movement.

From 1964 through 1971 the Department of Educational Services of the NCCIJ functioned as a miniature laboratory where sisters collaborated to create a diverse and ever-expanding array of racial-apostolate programs. DES administrators, especially Traxler, kept a close eye both on the American racial crisis and on the institution of religious life for women (itself undergoing profound changes in the late 1960s). DES staff read widely, attended countless meetings, and corresponded with Catholic bishops, superiors, and school superintendents as well as activists and leaders in the civil rights movement and officials in state and federal government, all in an attempt to keep abreast of the current state of affairs in all these spheres. As they identified specific opportunities for sisters to engage in issues of racial equality, DES administrators set about creating a specific program to address the need or exploit the opportunity. Most of the programs the DES created had no precedent among American women religious but rather grew from the imaginations of DES staff members as they attempted to respond to the contemporary racial and religious landscape. Like engineers creating prototypes, the DES planned its new projects with an eye toward their eventual dissemination into Catholic sisterhoods and diocese and beyond, into non-Catholic spheres. Though many of the programs the DES created were successful enough to continue and even expand from year to year, the real energy of the department always went into innovation—the creation of new programs—rather than the perpetuation of existing projects. The DES was, in fact, eager to "give away" the programs they had created, leaving the administration of programs to local bodies. "As programs evolve," Traxler stated in a 1969 report, "it is hoped that after trial periods and demonstrations, workable ideas and projects can be turned over to school systems and educational associations for adoption and further growth."[48]

The DES purposely established avenues for the dissemination of those models that had proved worthwhile in their pilot incarnations. The department also regularly provided consultation services to groups attempting to emulate DES programs. Success for Traxler and her staff was measured not by the size of the DES but rather by the growth and diffusion of the racial apostolate at the national level. Traxler's regular written reports to the board of directors were long lists of ideas in various stages of development. In any given year between 1965 and 1971, for every program in a pilot or dissemination stage, there were several others still on the drawing board at the DES offices. Traxler always had several irons in the fire, as the saying goes.

Program Goals Have Been Achieved

After the initial inception, research, and general planning of a specific program, Traxler would seek funding (primarily though not exclusively from federal sources) to implement the pilot project. During the pilot's initial year, especially when it showed immediate success, Traxler often invited the press, public officials, and sisters interested in the racial apostolate in other areas to come observe the program. She also wrote colorful press releases touting the effectiveness of the pilot. After the pilot year was complete, DES would evaluate a program and either discontinue it (this happened infrequently) or, more often, expand the range or length of the program. Finally, Traxler offered the pilot as a model for adaptation and duplication for religious in other locations, providing grant-writing and practical assistance to sisters trying to reproduce the DES program in successive years. Using this pattern, the DES enjoyed an impressive fecundity, dispersing various projects it had pioneered in most major cities in the urban North and several locations in the South.

Keeping track of the various incarnations and permutations of DES programs from year to year proves as challenging to the contemporary historian (and her reader) as it must have to the board of the NCCIJ in the 1960s. The limitations of this chapter and academic monograph do not allow for full discussion, much less mention, of all the programs envisioned, created, and either abandoned or disseminated by the DES in the late 1960s. What this chapter attempts to do, instead, is explain the emergence of the racial apostolate in this period by illuminating the central organization through which a significant number of its programs were created and its participants enlisted. A survey of the evolution of the DES also reveals patterns and tensions that were endemic to the postconciliar racial apostolate and that would influence racial-justice programs that were not related to the DES in this period. Though all the major initiatives of the DES will be discussed in this section, two specific programs—Project Cabrini and the Nuns' Placement Bureau—receive only brief mention because they are examined more fully in separate chapters in the section that provides case studies in the racial apostolate.

The tangle of DES programs in the late 1960s is, then, perhaps best understood by dividing the programs into discrete categories according to their function. Some programs attempted to dispel racist attitudes among sisters by teaching them about the moral, social, political, and religious facets of racial injustice in American society, by dispelling dominant white supremacist myths about African Americans, and by challenging sisters to confront their own racial prejudices. (The Traveling Workshops in Inter-Group Relations is one example of the latter type of DES program.) Some projects attempted to counteract white-supremacist elements in the Catholic educational system. (The Textbook Evaluation project was a program of this type.) Other projects facilitated communication among religious about programs for racial justice at the local level. Such programs provided venues for sisters to share with each other what their congregation or community was doing in this area. They also promoted intercongregational cooperation. (The *Nuns Newsletter* served this function.) Other DES programs were designed to prepare sisters for assignments in predominantly African American communities by providing them with information on such topics as the psychological effects of racism on African Americans, the causes of and remedies for racialized poverty, interpersonal and group dynamics, and the structure of social services in a given location (Sisters Urban Education, or SUE, did this). The DES also ran a number of direct-action programs, projects that assigned sisters to specific works that promoted racial justice either by challenging white supremacy among Catholics or by responding to specific needs in African American communities (Project Bridge did the former; Project Cabrini, the latter). The DES also ran "brokering" programs that matched sisters who wanted placement in the racial apostolate with various direct-action programs around the country. (The National Placement Bureau, or NPB, was a DES program of this type.) Finally, the DES over time developed a number of programs that addressed the institution of religious life itself, especially the challenges and conflicts that attended the conciliar-mandated renewal of religious congregations. (The Sisters' Survival Strategy conference is one example of this emphasis in the DES.)

This classification schema becomes slightly more complicated when the interrelationship of these categories is taken into account. The diverse programs created by and run under the auspices of the DES often intersected with each other, so that a sister who came into contact with the racial apostolate through one program eventually would come into contact with one or more other DES projects. The DES functioned as a kind of pipeline, funneling sisters into the racial apostolate.[49] Often, sisters followed a predictable sequence, learning about the racial apostolate from either the *Nuns Newsletter* or the Traveling Workshops, being trained in SUE, and finding placement either in a direct-action program like Project Cabrini or with the assistance of the National Placement Bureau.

Because the DES grew indirectly from the Sister Formation Conference, many of the above categories of DES programs reproduced functions that the SFC had performed prior to its 1964 reorganization. Education, the implicit heart of the SFC, was also the primary focus of the DES, as its name suggests. The DES worked both to educate sisters for work in race relations and to create service programs that capitalized on the teaching skills and experience many sisters possessed. The Traveling Workshops showcased the apostolic applications of the social sciences that the SFC had pioneered. Sisters who had secured advanced degrees through the educational reforms instituted by the SFC served as faculty for the workshops. Like the SFC, many of the DES's programs sought to foster communication and collaboration between religious congregations. The congregationally diverse composition of the DES staff and the Traveling Workshop faculty—immediately visible in the array of habits they wore—modeled intracongregational cooperation. DES publications such as the *Nuns Newsletter* informed sisters about the variety of racial-justice projects in which sisters around the country were engaged, breaking down the isolation that some sisters interested in the racial apostolate felt within their own communities and creating a sense of common purpose among sisters in different congregations. Like the SFC, the DES at times appealed directly to the conscience and initiative of individual sisters in addition to those of their superiors, creating opportunities for sisters to enter the racial apostolate and encouraging sisters to request these assignments rather than relying on their superiors to assign them to such works. Finally, the DES improved on the SFC's largely unsuccessful attempts to secure funding from sources outside the Church. Many of the DES's programs received either federal funding through the Office of Economic Opportunity or supplemental support from private foundations. By perpetuating the SFC's distinctive approach to the active apostolate, the DES effectively extended the influence of the SFC beyond its institutional demise.

A bird's-eye view of DES activities during a single year also is instructive for understanding the internal dynamics of the organization, particularly its ability to sustain diverse programs under a single mandate. By August 1965, for example, just one year after simultaneous restructuring of the SFC and the birth of the DES, the department had fulfilled and, indeed, far exceeded Ahmann's original agenda for the organization. "In general, with one major exception [research]," Traxler wrote triumphantly in her first report to the board, "program goals set up for a two-year period have been achieved in one year."[50] Ahmann's vision of circuit-riding sisters became the DES's Traveling Workshops in Inter-Group Relations, offered by a group of five sisters with doctorates who traveled the country in a rented station wagon conducting five-day workshops that explored the sources of human conflict—especially racial conflict—and strategies for its resolution. And the Traveling Workshops program was just the tip of the iceberg. In its first year alone the DES also provided in-service training in the form of half-day institutes on race relations in sixty-two locations. It developed training materials and a teacher's manual for a teaching unit on race relations and also published four issues of a *Nuns Newsletter*—a mimeographed newsletter that featured page-long narrative descriptions of racial-justice projects written by the sisters involved—that was mailed to 1,100 subscribers, many of them major superiors. The DES mobilized a group of sisters to travel to Selma to participate in the protest marches there following Bloody Sunday in March of 1965.[51] The DES also initiated Project Cabrini, a free day-camp staffed by sisters for children in the Cabrini Green housing project that drew over a thousand children.[52] In addition to projects in the pilot or full-operation stage, in 1965 the DES was also working on plans for "Summer, South and Sisters," a program to train Northern sisters for summer assignment in African American communities in the South; Operation Motherhouse, a program of "self-studies" to uncover and address racial attitudes in convents; a pilot school for curriculum development, an experimental, urban elementary school jointly sponsored with a Lutheran congregation; a teacher training course in human relations to be used in teacher training departments in colleges and universities, along with various prepackaged kits of programs on interracial relations for use in schools and dioceses.[53]

One of the first activities Sister Claire Marie Sawyer undertook as director of the newly formed DES in 1964 was to create a newsletter for the organization. The SFC's *Bulletin* had been an extremely successful tool for broadcasting the group's ideas and programs, and Sawyer rightly understood that the DES would need a similar instrument in order to reach and influence sisters at a national level. In October 1964 Sawyer mailed the first issue of the *Nuns Newsletter* to a preselected list of superiors, Catholic Interracial Councils, members of the NCCIJ board of directors, and superintendents of Catholic schools.[54] The newsletter was free and invited individual religious and their congregations to request continuing subscriptions. In the opening issue Sawyer introduced the DES to readers and explained that the newsletter was an attempt to represent the various existing racial-justice programs she had encountered in her first few months as DES director. "In all of these travels, as well as in the many persons I have met, I am both astounded and thrilled by the tremendously exciting things our Sisters are doing in a direct action kind of program," she commented. "We would like to share some of the experiences of these Sisters with you and in turn ask if you would let us in on some of the things you are doing and some of the things other Sisters are doing about which you know." There were two caveats to her invitation: submissions should be written in a "chatty" style, like a "true letter," and the audience was to be limited to "NUNS ONLY."[55]

The first eight issues of the *Nuns Newsletter,* from October 1964 to April 1966, followed the original format Sawyer had introduced. The majority of the early newsletters' pages were used to print the kind of personal letters Sawyer had requested, in which sisters described and interpreted for other sister-readers their experience crossing racial, geographic, class, and religious boundaries in the racial apostolate. They also are charmingly devoid of layout, design, or illustration. The original *Nuns Newsletter* was a collection of typewritten pages that were mimeographed on colored construction paper and stapled together. Newsletters typically included four or five such letters, followed by a brief section of announcements about DES programs, as well as information about resources and educational materials in the area of race relations, bibliographies, and sometimes book reviews. Circulation followed a trajectory of steadily increasing subscriptions. Sisters often enclosed personal notes with their subscription requests. One characteristic letter from a sister in Fort Wayne, Indiana, explained, "By some good fortune the March 24, 1966 issue of the Newsletter for Nuns Only fell into my hands and I have read it eagerly and enthusiastically! As has been the case with all the activities in which I have participated among our "Inner city" citizens, God has been the instigator—I have only been the instrument. In order that I might be a better one, I would like you to enter my subscription to the Newsletter."[56] By the fourth issue, May 1965, *Nuns Newsletter* had a circulation of 1,100 subscribers. A year later, by March 1966, there were 1,800 regular subscribers. In 1967 the Conference of Major Superiors requested that copies be sent to all American superiors, adding 497 superiors to the subscription list.[57] In addition to direct subscriptions, the publications were often passed informally from sister to sister or from a superior to all in her community. One sister wrote from Arkansas that the newsletter had been read to the entire community "as prayer" in an experimental form of the divine office. "Your letter of June 1968 NUNS NEWSLETTER was read in our chapel this morning to the 150 Sisters at home present," she wrote to the NCCIJ.[58] Another sister recalled posting the newsletter on the bulletin board of the community of which she was the acting superior.[59]

The letters in the first eight issues of *Nuns Newsletter* offer a glimpse into the experiences and perspectives of sisters who engaged in the racial apostolate in its earliest years. Most of the letters are written in first person and contain sisters' reflections on the experience of witnessing poverty and discrimination for the first time, encountering hatred, feeling fear, and trying to make sense of their lives as vowed religious in light of these new experiences. In these letters sisters described the poverty and prejudice in which they were immersed and against which they worked. There is a searching quality to many of the letters published in the *Nuns Newsletter;* sisters raised more questions than they answered and at times expressed frustration at an inability to form coherent thoughts about the feelings that their experiences evoked. In their letters sisters' perspectives are frequently inchoate and ambivalent, full of internal contradictions, and in many letters the issues that strike at the heart of activism and religious consecration—self-identity, institutional purpose, justice and grace—lie just below the surface, indirectly addressed, submerged in stories, appearing as unanswered questions or unassimilable experiences.

The September 1966 issue (the ninth) signaled a change in both the format and the content of the *Nuns Newsletter.* The issue looked significantly different from its predecessors, adding a title and banner across the top and a fold-out format of pages. Interior pages contained both photographs and graphics. The September issue featured a series of images of sisters of the Traveling Workshops in Intergroup Relations captioned by the words "The Color of Truth." But the cosmetic changes also signaled a shift in the purpose of the publication. With the ninth issue the DES newsletter became an official organ of the DES as an organization rather than a forum for individual sisters to share chatty letters about their experiences in unconventional apostolic works. Though the ninth issue still contained narratives by two sisters—one who participated in an OEO-funded program for migrant workers in Florida and another who worked with the Catholic Family Movement—the focus of the revised newsletter was the DES itself. The new *Nuns Newsletter* featured announcements about staff changes at the DES and the NCCIJ, updates on various DES projects, and information about upcoming applications and deadlines for DES projects. It also included, for the first time, poetry, artwork, and reprinted articles from magazines and newspapers about the role of sisters in society. Occasionally, the new version of the newsletter also featured an open letter to sisters from Traxler, reflecting on developments in American society or encouraging sisters that work in race and poverty was important.

One way of interpreting the development of the *Nuns Newsletter* is to observe that by 1966, largely through the efforts of the DES, the racial apostolate had evolved from a diffuse array of discrete projects and individuals into a more-or-less coherent movement among religious who wanted to render the institution of religious life relevant to social problems like race and poverty. The shift from a newsletter featuring individual voices and individual experiences to one that kept members apprised of developments in organizations and shared programs reflected an important change in the perceptions of women religious from seeing the racial apostolate as a form of individual initiative to seeing it as a collective endeavor. A somewhat different reading of this change would observe that the new format changed the focus of the newsletter from the actual ministry of sisters—literally what they were doing and how they felt about it, as described in personal letters—toward the idea of such ministry. In other words, the focus of the new newsletter was not on the work itself but rather on the institutions that supported or the obstacles that challenged the new apostolate. In the former case the central relationship that framed the narrative was that of the sister and the African Americans she served; in the latter it was the individual sister in relationship with the collective movement of other sisters engaged in the racial apostolate. This may seem a minor difference, but it foreshadows a recurrent (and understandable, given the larger context of postconciliar change) tendency of sisters in the racial apostolate to periodically turn their attention toward internal matters of religious renewal. This turn inward was even more clear in the trajectory followed by another DES program, the Traveling Workshops in Inter-Group Relations.

The most successful and influential of the projects inaugurated in the DES's first year of operation was the Traveling Workshops in Inter-Group Relations (later the Traveling Workshops in Race Relations, and after that the Traveling Workshops in Human Relations). In some sense the Traveling Workshops predate the DES. The structure of the Traveling Workshops was devised by Mathew Ahmann and Sister Annette Walters in their early conversations about possible forms of partnership between the NCCIJ and the SFC. When Sister Claire Marie Sawyer arrived at the DES she began the work to bring the workshop idea to fruition. By November 1964 Sister Claire Marie had already secured guarantees from several superiors to release sisters with PhDs to serve as the faculty members for the summer 1965 pilot of the workshop. Reflecting patterns of authority that would quickly change within the racial apostolate, the first faculty members of the Traveling Workshops were primarily volunteered by their superiors for the project, rather than themselves volunteering for such work. Later sisters were contacted directly about joining the workshop faculty and then sought permission from their superiors to participate. "My provincial smiled when I showed her the invitation to join the Traveling Workshop," one sister-sociologist wrote. "Imagine how I felt when she said, 'go ahead sister, we can get along without you.'"[60] Writing to thank one superior for a "generous response" to her appeal for faculty, Sawyer spoke enthusiastically of the "*aggiornamento* in the apostolate" she saw emerging among women religious in response to civil rights struggles. "I am heartened again and again by the dedication and the foresight of the women of God," she said. "I believe that the exciting times we live in are causing us in the Sisterhoods in the United States to examine the meaning of our own vocation in the light of present day needs and demands."[61] The Traveling Workshops remained a central part of the DES's operations throughout the 1960s and into the early 1970s.

More than any other program of the DES, the Traveling Workshops reproduced the structure and focus of the SFC. Workshops generally consisted of a three- or five-day series of lecture-oriented plenary sessions featuring the sister-faculty, supplemented by discussion groups, one-on-one encounter conversations, panels of social-service providers, and, occasionally, site visits to local racial-justice programs. Drawing directly on the educational advances sisters had made through the SFC, the Traveling Workshops faculty was comprised of sisters with PhDs who worked as professors in Catholic colleges. Reflecting the curriculum designed by the SFC, sister-speakers of the Traveling Workshops addressed racial conflict, employing the interpretive tools from disciplines in the social sciences, especially sociology, psychology, history, economics, and social work. The workshops also shared the SFC's focus on the apostolate. The official report of the Traveling Workshops' pilot year lists the first specific goal for the workshops as the "implementation of interracial justice and charity in the apostolate."[62] As we shall see, the workshops functioned as a central conduit for bringing sisters into the racial apostolate.

Over the years the Traveling Workshops program steadily expanded its number of presentations, faculty members, and geographic range. It also gradually broadened its audience beyond sisters to include other Catholic institutions (including diocesan leadership) and eventually non-Catholic groups. In the summer of 1965 one Traveling Workshops team gave six workshops at motherhouses and schools attended by approximately 1,500 sisters and other interested Catholics.[63] The following year, three teams of Traveling Workshops sisters offered forty-five workshops for approximately 14,000 participants.[64] A brochure touting the accomplishments of the 1966 Traveling Workshops paired a photograph of sister-faculty climbing into their station wagon with the question, "Would you believe—fifty thousand miles?"[65] In an odd turn of events, in August 1966 the Traveling Workshops made a presentation to the national convention of the restructured Sister Formation Conference.[66] Other than briefly mentioning that she was "especially pleased" about the SFC workshop, DES records and Traxler's correspondence say little about the SFC presentation, perhaps indicating that the department's origins within the larger SFC-CMSW conflict quickly receded from the institutional memory of the organization. The 1967 workshop program featured four teams of five sisters. By 1969 the Traveling Workshops program had conducted ninety-seven institutes in thirty-nine states; by 1970 it had conducted 110 institutes. Traxler estimated that by 1969 workshop faculty had traveled 400,000 miles, mostly in rented station wagons. "Watch the Fords go by!" she once quipped of the unusual transportation they used.[67]

Through its initial successes the Traveling Workshops gained resources that ensured that the program would continue to flourish through the late 1960s and would continue to serve as a model project to showcase DES operations to Church officials and funding organizations. By its third year of operation, the Traveling Workshops had cultivated a tight-knit network of sister-professors who had served on its faculty, as well as files of glowing and eloquent evaluations of the workshops' efficacy from former attendees. It also had facilitated the development and publication of a growing library of educational materials on race relations and religious life in the United States. As the Traveling Workshops matured, the program gained a measure of freedom to respond to ongoing developments in the Catholic Church and the civil rights movement with creative innovations to the workshops' structure and focus. In 1967 the Traveling Workshops became a year-round program. Though the majority of programs were scheduled for summer months, when sister-faculty were on leave from their respective colleges, the ever-expanding number of experienced workshop faculty meant that Traxler could put together ad hoc teams of available sisters to respond to requests she received for workshops during the academic year. As part of her regular correspondence with faculty members, Traxler mentioned dates and locations for nonsummer programs, requesting volunteers to staff a particular workshop.

Over time, the Traveling Workshops refined its original curriculum, focusing on narrower, more specialized, and specific facets of racial justice. It also experimented with the lecture and discussion format. In 1970 the DES offered workshops on six topics, among them "Black-White America: Uptight," "Renewal in Light of World Needs," "Black Rage–White Apathy: Christian Challenge," and "Spanish American, Mexican American Challenges to Our Christian Commitment."[68] And the following year Traxler introduced a "new thrust" into the workshops that borrowed from neighborhood organizing strategies to create a program that emphasized the practical application of theory and "confrontation through small group dynamics."[69] In 1971, for the first time, most of the workshops were sponsored by the local Catholic dioceses and presented to audiences of laypeople rather than women religious. Calling the new workshops "Action Caravans for the Seventies," workshop faculty designed the new format to "generate ideas that will move people from understanding to action" with specific attention to the unique circumstances of the local community hosting the workshop. As a result of these changes, Traxler reported in her annual report, "Civil leaders in eight cities were given at least 100 specific, localized program ideas to improve race relations in their communities."[70]

Another source of the relative success of the Traveling Workshops was the unique esprit de corps that emerged among its faculty. Workshop faculty spent long hours riding together and sharing guest rooms in what basically amounted to a summer-long, sister-only road trip. By the end of the season, sisters in a particular team had shared with one another anecdotes, stories, and inside jokes, as well as deeper experiences of personal and religious transformation. They also prayed together. Traxler encouraged this unique bond among sister-faculty, writing them regular, affectionate, newsy letters that she addressed to her "Traveling Workshop family." One such letter from the spring of 1967 is characteristic of the humor and intimacy that suffused Traxler's correspondence with workshop faculty. Writing to the 1967 faculty to provide them with a schedule of summer commitments, Traxler opened her letter with a compliment followed by a jibe. "Our Traveling Workshop faculty is growing into what appears to be an impressive senate," she penned. "Who knows, soon one of the economists may insist on unionizing." After introducing new sister-faculty joining the "Workshop family" and providing a list of dates and locations for the coming summer, Traxler indulged in a moment of wry sarcasm. Her comment suggests that, perhaps, the collegiality of workshop faculty at some level sprang from the awareness that in this unconventional assignment, sisters were largely free of the supervision and interference of their religious superiors. "Mother Verda Clare, Sister Margaret Rita's Provincial, reminded us in a letter that when Sister returned to the team in August, she would be tired," Traxler reported. "We assured Mother that we would carry Sister Margaret Rita from place to place in an ambulance and feed her weak broth slowly to return her to health." Then she added, "One more job for the coordinator."[71] In another memo to workshop faculty Traxler emphasized the special relationship the Traveling Workshops sisters played in the overall operation of the DES. "You are sorely needed to be a special board of consultants for the NCCIJ and especially the Education Service Department," she wrote. "I can't emphasize this too heartily for I feel my own poverty in a real sense. This poverty you alone can help allay by giving from your expertise, ideas, and evaluations."[72] With clear affection, Traxler wrote the workshop faculty in 1969, "If God ever gave us a 'temporal reward' for all our hard NCCIJ work, it is the reward of knowing the TW faculty."[73]

Throughout its tenure, the Traveling Workshops program struggled to secure reliable funding. Though much of the administrative cost of the Traveling Workshops was covered by the fee the DES charged for its services—between $200 and $300 per day, depending on the size of the faculty and length of the workshop—workshop faculty typically participated without remuneration. Throughout the late 1960s Traxler pursued outside funding from diverse sources to support the Traveling Workshops and provide stipends for its faculty. Such stipends served as powerful incentive to superiors managing tight budgets to allow sisters to dedicate a summer to serving on the Traveling Workshops faculty. Without it, a superior was literally donating the services and maintenance costs of the sister to the project when that sister could be used elsewhere in congregational works. With a stipend, though, a sister was more-or-less self-sustaining, a contributor to congregational assets rather than a drain on them. Traxler was particularly disappointed by the failure of a 1967 proposal to present five separate two-week workshops for public school teachers under Title IV of the Civil Rights Act, thereby expanding the Traveling Workshops into non-Catholic communities. She later learned indirectly that the proposal was denied for being "too heavily 'catholic' " and as such, in the view of the proposal evaluators, was "not exactly the answer to public school needs."[74] Writing to sisters with news of a funding denial Traxler underscored that she had "longed *really longed* to give each faculty member" a stipend. "Circumstances for 1967 will be as last summer," she continued, "at least all expenses assured with hopeful stipends dependent upon our proposals."[75] The DES did eventually receive funding through Title I of the Elementary and Secondary Education Act (ESEA, 1965) for a joint workshop of public and parochial school principals in Syracuse, New York, in 1968.[76]

In 1967 the DES published the collected lectures of workshop faculty as *Split-Level Lives: American Nuns Speak on Race.* In a private memo to sisters involved in the Traveling Workshops prior to the publication of the book, Traxler, with characteristic mirth, asked for help formulating a title for the collection. "*THE BOOK* which I once referred to as Grimm Fairy Tales because I doubted its publication is going to SVD Press this week," she wrote. "*Nuns Speak on Race* as a title is not a universally-approved title. Perhaps someone can help us. The objection lies in prejudiced people (even nuns) who say they never read books written by Sisters."[77] As a written record of Traveling Workshops presentations, the collection offers a unique glimpse of the information and perspectives featured in the original workshop sessions of the mid-1960s. Taken together, the essays (and thus the presentations at workshops) collectively argued that racial prejudice against African Americans was inconsistent with reason, patriotism, and religious faith.

Several of the essays were crafted specifically to dispel negative stereotypes of African Americans as violent, intellectually inferior, or morally deficient by describing the economic and educational disadvantages black citizens have faced throughout American history. "The rights revolution is, in one aspect, a warfare against all those forces of ignorance, misinformation, and racial myth that deny the oneness of the human family," posited Sister Mary Audrey (Lillanna) Kopp, SNJM, in her essay "The Myth of Race." One italicized subtitle in her essay asks simply, "Are Negroes innately immoral?"[78] Her answer, of course, was that they were not. "One of the most common complaints uttered against Negroes is that they are a lazy and shiftless race," observed Mother Bessie Chambers, RSCJ, in her essay "The Psychological Effects of Segregation." Chambers wrote:

> While the white man rests in his placidity, the Negroes, as people, want to develop their potentialities. Gently, secretly, they try to venture forth, hoping to receive encouragement, or at least to be given a chance. As they apply for one job after another, they are rejected. Each rejection adds to their feeling of uselessness; each time they have to settle for a job which calls for far less than their abilities, they lose faith in their true worth. They finally lose hope.[79]

Often the essays attempted to present the perspective of African Americans (a convention that was later abandoned by the Traveling Workshops in favor of panels featuring African Americans speaking about their experiences after sisters realized the problematic nature of Caucasian religious attempting to speak for African Americans).[80] "How does the system look from the bottom?" asked Sister Mary Heffernan, OP, in her presentation "Equality and 'The System.' " "The system from this perspective is not something to defend, but rather to outwit or to ignore in apathy," she explained.[81] This strategy sometimes left the workshop faculty vulnerable to criticism that they had abandoned a Catholic perspective. Writing to cancel her $5 pledged donation to the NCCIJ, a Benedictine sister from southern Indiana wrote that a sister from her congregation had attended a workshop and "came home feeling very disillusioned—that this is more a black power format than a Christian social justice movement."[82] "Being disillusioned is not a bad thing," Anthony E. Kessel, NCCIJ director of development, wrote in a surprisingly direct response, "being rid of illusions helps greatly in finding solutions to problems."[83]

Other essays attempted to offer less-subjective assessments of race relations in the United States. Historians and sociologists on the Traveling Workshops faculty peppered their presentations with statistics—on topics ranging from the median IQ for different racial groups to the percentage of neighborhood residents typically displaced by "urban renewal programs" to the dropout rate in Watts and the crime rate in Africa—in an effort to quantify large generalizations about the dire circumstances of many African Americans in urban areas. Such statistics were also intended, one presumes, to underscore the professional expertise of a female speaker/author directly challenging the underlying tenets of white supremacist thinking.

Sometimes Traveling Workshops presentations inadvertently validated and reinforced stereotypes about African Americans, even (and perhaps unfortunately) while attempting to undermine them. In her presentation on the fluidity of racial categories, Sister Mary Audrey Kopp, SNJM, offered a portrait of Harlem sufficiently graphic and bleak as to rival those presented by urban segregationists:

> One needs to see Harlem's people, undereducated, underfed, desperately poor, routinely underprivileged, despairing of help, escaping through dope, sex, alcohol, storefront churches with emotional cults. Harlem is so fantastically crowded that two to five families live in a two-room apartment, thirty to fifty persons share a single, end-of-hall toilet and bath. Some beds are never cooled because of shift sleeping. Privacy is unknown to many. Love and intercourse must be before children, rats, and roaches. One needs to see the faces and the eyes of those on the steps of the old greystone-front buildings, the faces and eyes of the idlers, loiterers, old folks, of the lovers, lingerers, children, of the pimps, pushers, and prostitutes.[84]

These grim details did not reflect the innate morality or worth of Harlem's residents, she argued. "On the surface of the Negro ghetto one does see dope and dirt, drinking, disease, and despair," Kopp acknowledged. "But educated persons are responsible for visions or views in depth, are responsible for a search for the whys, are responsible for demanding scientific data with which to reject the naked-eye strategy."[85] Her essay went on to posit both historical and social reasons for the vice and squalor she observed while living in Harlem (squalor that she nonetheless describes with a curious relish). Her writing, surely meant for rhetorical effect, repeated many of the most negative characterizations of African Americans in urban neighborhoods. The historian on the Traveling Workshops faculty, Sister Mary L. Mangan, SL, went one step further than Kopp, arguing that slavery's systematic assault on the family system had produced an "American Negro culture" which, in effect, "disqualified many of its participants for life in modern America."[86] Her point was not that African Americans should be marginalized in American society but rather that white Americans should look to history to explain urban unrest rather than simply blaming it on the presumed moral failings of African Americans. Mangan compared "the current revolt" of urban riots protesting "inferior jobs, inferior schools, and inferior housing" to Nat Turner's revolt against slaveholders.

The overall portrait of African Americans that emerged from essays by Traveling Workshops faculty in 1967 was that of a people profoundly deformed both by their history and by contemporary inequalities. The project of the early Traveling Workshops, then, was not so much to point out to Caucasian listeners the similarities between themselves and their black neighbors as it was to argue that the presumed contemporary deficiencies of African Americans were structural and situational rather than inherent. Workshop speakers challenged white Catholics to support social reforms and educational programs that could transform African Americans into full and productive citizens. Or, in Sister Mangan's words, "if their [the African American] story were fully and truthfully taught there would be a greater chance for racial tolerance rather than intolerance, for patience rather than impatience, for understanding rather than misunderstanding. By such deepened knowledge perhaps the gap between our creed—that all men are created equal, and have inalienable rights—and our actions would be realized and eventually bridged."[87] Ongoing racial injustice in the United States revealed disquieting discrepancies between American ideals and concrete social policies, workshop faculty argued, even as it also reflected a growing gap between Catholic rhetoric of human equality and the white supremacist views of many American Catholics.

In his preface to the collection, Mathew Ahmann explained that the purpose of the Traveling Workshops, and thus of the essays in the book, was primarily religious in nature, to challenge Catholics to act in a manner consistent with Christian principles. "In the area of social doctrine and especially interracial justice, actions of Christians are often the opposite of Gospel mandates," he observed. "Dichotomies between the truths we profess and our actions produce the 'split-level lives' described in this book."[88] Traxler's contribution, "The Ministry of Presence," characterized the racial apostolate of sisters in the inner city as one such effort to put Christian ideals into practice by responding compassionately to racialized poverty in the "ghetto." Sisters who marched in civil rights protests, lectured about human rights, and ministered in impoverished neighborhoods were simply "fulfilling their personhood as religious women," a sacred call to serve society's destitute and grieve their suffering.[89] "In remaining in the inner city to teach and nurse, religious have been given the grace to become new nuns," Traxler offered. "They are what Abbess Laurentia wanted for her nuns—'to stand for something and not to be just nice little things.'"[90]

If Traxler saw sisters as models of how to integrate faith and action, other essays explored in detail the "split-level" hypocrisy of American Catholics on issues of race. Sister Loretta Ann Madden, SL, presented a fierce critique of Catholic apathy in her essay, "Challenge to the Churches." Though public opinion supported civil rights legislation in 1964, such support, Madden argued, proved superficial when African Americans attempted to move into predominantly white neighborhoods. "Resistance to these real estate freedoms is shown most vigorously by the Christian ethnic enclaves within the ghettos of American cities," she observed, referring indirectly to ethnic Catholic parishes.[91] The subsequent rioting in 1965 and 1966 and the "cynicism" of the black power revolution were the direct result of a perception that churches were impotent to influence the behavior of white members in matters of race and justice, Madden wrote. Catholics were doubly indicted by this racist intransigence, she argued, because the sacraments testified to the unity of the human family. "For Catholics, participation in the Mass is a constant reminder that God died for all men," she wrote. "There can be no distinction of race or color in the liturgical community of the Mass."[92] Sister Mary Eric Zeis, SSND, in contrast, argued that the preconciliar Church had directly contributed to the racial crisis by stunting the moral development of Catholics. "The rigid, negative, authoritarian training which unfortunately was characteristic of much religious education in the past" had negatively affected the development of a distinct Catholic conscience, leaving Catholics with an immature moral sensibility that responded to and was deeply motivated by fear rather than by love.[93] "Somewhere along the line people have stopped saying, 'See how they love one another,' of Christians," she observed. But there also were hopeful signs in the Church. "The contemporary insistence on personalism and human diginity is directing us again to the visible witness of love of neighbor in our lives."[94] Conciliar calls for renewal, too, suggested that in the future Catholics would again be able to gain moral maturity within the Church.

The Traveling Workshops served as a central locus for the recruitment of sisters into the racial apostolate. Workshop presentations at convents and motherhouses often served as a sister's first exposure to sustained thinking about racial justice. They also, by extension, introduced sisters to "new nuns," to concrete examples of the renewed and relevant apostolate that the Second Vatican Council had encouraged women religious to cultivate. "I got the impression that for many of the Workshop participants, the TW was providing the first encounter with the 'Nun in the World' [an allusion to the influential book by that name by Leon Joseph Cardinal Suenens] who was willing not only to come out into the world but to stand up in front of mixed groups and strongly and positively state her position," wrote one workshop faculty member of her experience.[95] Other sisters were moved by workshop presentations to want to join the racial apostolate. "During and after the presentation of truth the realization of my personal responsibility to be involved in 'race relations' is mandatory," began one sister who attended a workshop with her community. She continued:

> I cannot be the same again and although I have been involved and committed to the Civil Rights cause prior to this workshop I know that I have reached a new awareness that urges me to work individually and also to make members of my religious and civic community aware of the TRUTH.[96]

Whether moved by the message of racial justice and racial reconciliation or compelled by the new, apostolically driven version of vowed religious life that workshop faculty represented, sisters commonly contacted the DES after attending a Traveling Workshops session with requests for information about specific programs, a wish to participate in the racial apostolate through a DES program, or queries about how to handle specific conflicts within the sister's community. Writing to superiors to promote a new initiative that educated and prepared sisters for urban assignments, Sister Maura Coughlan acknowledged that the new program was, in part, a response to the deluge of requests for such training that often followed workshop presentations. "The constant requests and inquiries following participation in our Traveling Workshop in intergroup relations have motivated Educational Services of the NCCIJ to establish Sisters Urban Education (SUE)."[97] This was, of course, part of the expressed purpose of the workshops, to convince sisters of the importance of racial justice and to motivate them to join the new apostolate. The DES always made information about racial-apostolate programs available at workshops given to religious congregations of women, hoping to match sisters inspired by the presentations with opportunities and openings for service.

One important outgrowth of the Traveling Workshops was a series of annual national conferences sponsored by the DES from 1967 through

1969 that brought together sister-leaders from across the country for a weekend of reflection on a specific facet of religious life. By addressing broader issues surrounding the racial apostolate—namely conciliar change, congregational renewal, the emergent Black Power movement, the revolution in the apostolate, and new forms of community life—the DES national conferences connected the racial apostolate to the massive changes and realignments that were happening within women's religious congregations in the period after the Second Vatican Council. In keeping with her vision of duplicating DES programs under the auspices of other organizations, Traxler initially envisioned that the first conference, on "Adaptation and Renewal," as the pilot for a permanent Traveling Workshops team made up of sisters with experience in community governance or expertise in an academic field related to congregational renewal. They would visit motherhouses and provincial houses to advise congregations about their own renewal process. "The ultimate purpose of these workshops," Traxler wrote to superiors, inviting them to attend, "is to assist Provincials, their counselors and chapter sisters in their efforts to adapt and renew their congregations according to the Decree for Religious as mandated in Vatican II."[98] Along these lines, the conference featured lectures on topics such as the theology of spiritual renewal, the role of liturgy in community renewal, the sociology and structure of religious communities, the history of women religious in the Church, and the psychology of intergroup dynamics, specifically the role of conflict and dissent in collective decision-making processes.

Registration was limited to women in positions of authority—"an elected council member, a directress of formation, or a member of the provincial council"—and, in an effort to bring together sisters representing as many congregations and stages of renewal as possible, no more than two sisters from any congregation were enrolled. (One sign of the success of this effort to include women who were actively engaged in the renewal process is the number of letters sisters wrote to Traxler explaining that they could not attend the workshop because it conflicted with congregational committee or chapter meetings related to the renewal.) Traxler expected that the Conference of Major Superiors eventually would become the primary sponsor for any workshops that might grow from the national conference. "After assisting a team over a trial period, it is the aim of the NCCIJ to withdraw from co-sponsoring, allowing the program to become autonomous," she wrote to superiors about the program.[99] Traxler was more candid with her own staff about her plan to pass the program to the superiors. "Our hope is to pilot this and to develop enough curriculum to 'sell' the Conference of Major

Superiors in September," she wrote in an internal staff report in May 1967. "Presently, our goal is to launch it and then 'give it away.'"[100]

The following year, the DES organized the national conference around the publication of *New Works of New Nuns,* a collection of first-person essays by sisters engaged in new apostolates, edited by Traxler and dedicated to "the thirty sisters on the faculty of the Traveling Workshop." The 1968 conference by the same name explored "adapted apostolates that are entirely new in form and function."[101] Though the edited collection contained essays on a wide range of activities by sisters, from drug addiction counseling to Cursillo retreats to Newman Center campus ministries, the July 1968 conference primarily featured as speakers those authors who worked in urban settings on poverty issues. Writing to sisters from the Traveling Workshops while in the early stages of planning the 1968 conference, Traxler described the rationale for the conference as an effort to respond to the needs of religious congregations currently engaged in the process of conciliar reform: "We receive so many letters from renewal commission people inquiring about a broadened mission that we thought this might serve the sisters."[102] As before, conference registration was limited, accommodating sixty-five sisters who either already were engaged in "new works" or who had been assigned by their communities to study the apostolate. Only one sister from each order was allowed to enroll in the conference. Many sisters who enrolled sent personal notes along with their registration fees, recounting their own experiences in experimental works. A sister who promoted "half-way houses and counseling services to recovering alcoholics" in Montana wrote to urge that the conference address the topic of "new works in prison settings."[103] Another sister who had just earned her master's degree in social work at Fordham University while doing "crisis-oriented" field work in "the seven parishes of Negro Harlem" wrote that she was "intensely interested" in the new apostolates. "Our community, too, is eager for me to share this thinking in our diocese," she added.[104] Another who had worked for the "Clean for Gene" campaign to nominate antiwar Democrat Eugene McCarthy to the 1968 presidential ticket urged Traxler to include "POLITICAL ACTION" (emphasis hers) among the new works. "Seriously, I have found it a great wide open field where precious few sisters have even thought of treading," she wrote. "If our focus points are to be RACE, POVERTY and PEACE a good many more of us must get involved in *the* process which leads to the decisions which fashion the policy of governments. McCarthy's candidacy is a case in point."[105] Though the final program did not feature political activists, it did include several sisters whose projects had received federal funding either through the Office of Economic Opportunity (OEO) or the Department of Health, Education, and Welfare (HEW), including a panel of sisters from DES-sponsored programs, as well as a panel of sisters working in Head Start, Upward Bound, Push Up, and VISTA.[106]

DES sponsored two national conferences in 1969. Growing indirectly from issues raised at the previous year's "New Works of New Nuns" conference, both 1969 conferences reflected the growing complexity of the racial and religious context in which the racial apostolate was situated at the close of the 1960s. The first conference, "The Black Ghetto and the White Nun," was co-sponsored by the NCCIJ and the Black Nuns Caucus of Pittsburgh. Despite a recent assertion in *Trans-Sister* that "New Works of New Nuns are Slum-Oriented," the development of separatist ideologies in African American communities, as well as the emergence of organizations of African American priests and religious in the Catholic Church, raised questions about the appropriateness of racial-justice programs that placed sisters in positions of authority in African American communities.[107] The conference program featured African American speakers, including black sisters, reflecting on the supportive (rather than leading) role that white sisters should play in urban neighborhoods. Two sisters who attended the sessions described the appropriate role of white religious as one of "developing the creative worth of the other, servicing the *real* needs of the community rather than our own psychological needs, and building their community through our leadership rather than perpetuating our own power structure. As the blacks say it 'Come if we want you, do what we want you to, and leave when we want you to leave.' "[108]

The second conference, in May 1969, exploring "Sisters' Survival Strategies," was an effort to address issues that had been raised in the 1968 conference. "Our New Nuns in New Works Workshop brought to light some interesting findings regarding celibacy, prayer, loneliness, tension, and life-styles," Traxler wrote to her staff immediately after the conclusion of the "New Works" conference.[109] In response, the national conference on "Sisters' Survival Strategies" proposed new approaches to the central components of religious life such as formation, horarium, governance, vows, and community structure. The conference program attempted to balance the voices of experts with panels of "informants" who offered experientially based perspectives on the reform of religious life. The conference program thus featured both a plenary address by

Mary Daly titled "The Useful Sisters or Redeeming Religious Women" and a panel called "Young Religious, Ages 20–30," which discussed the "changes necessary in their estimation if accommodation to present times is to be achieved." The conference also included a panel of "minorities and the poor" on which a "hippie leader from Old Town," a drug addict, a "welfare mother of eight children," and a leader of the Blackstone Rangers (an urban gang delicately described as "2,500 young men of the Chicago Ghetto") discussed "how Christian Religious could respond to the anguish of oppressed people." The 1969 conferences hinted at the growing unease that developed among women religious at the close of the 1960s as religious congregations increasingly found themselves in open conflict with local bishops and the Roman Curia over the conciliar reforms to the structures of religious life. The darker mood of the 1969 Sisters' Survival Strategy seminar was evident even in its liturgical component. Whereas earlier DES conferences had ended with a closing liturgy, the 1969 Survival seminar ended with a "Mass for Perseverance."[110]

"The City Is Our Classroom"

If the Traveling Workshops initiated sisters into the idea of the racial apostolate, and inspired them to join it, the DES's Sisters Urban Education (SUE) trained sisters specifically for this work, preparing them for eventual immersion within African American communities. SUE was created and run in its pilot year by Sister Maura Coughlan, CSJ. Coughlan was added to the DES staff in July 1966 as associate director of educational services. Though Coughlan's primary responsibility was to oversee administrative details of the DES, freeing Traxler to devote more time to developing future projects, Coughlan almost immediately began planning her own pilot project, SUE, which used sisters who already were engaged in urban apostolate programs to train other sisters for this kind of work. The idea for the program originally came from Monsignor Vincent Cooke of the Chicago Archdiocesan Charities, who suggested that the DES send sisters to "live with one inner-city group of teaching nuns, or in a cluster of such convents."[111] Through the fall and winter of 1966 Coughlan worked to develop a curriculum for the project and orchestrate logistical details. She expanded Monsignor Cooke's plan beyond Catholic spheres by recruiting institutional partners for SUE from a broad spectrum of community-based social-service agencies, including the YMCA, the Salvation Army, the Urban League, and the Cook County Office of Public Assistance. She also developed an educational program that introduced SUE participants to "the history, sociology, psychology, and theology of poverty and the inner-city" through three weeks of intensive study that combined assigned readings with guest lectures by faculty from the Traveling Workshops.[112] In the end, Coughlan's SUE pilot offered sisters two months of specialized training in urban apostolic work while they lived in an inner-city convent—"so that the participants could see first-hand the problems of life in such a situation"—and worked as apprentices for local community-service programs. Writing to introduce the program to superiors, Coughlan argued that summer assignments like SUE presented superiors with the opportunity to train leaders to successfully respond to the unique needs of the growing number of "inner-city and transitional parishes." "Our schools, our apostolates, our sisters are deeply influenced by the challenges of race and poverty in the central city," she wrote. Sisters who participated in SUE would return to their communities armed with invaluable education and expertise to meet such challenges, she argued.[113] Coughlan's appeal to superiors netted a pilot-year class of ten SUE sisters. Many of them came to SUE with some form of prior experience living in impoverished urban neighborhoods or working in racial-justice programs. Upon learning of her acceptance into SUE, a fifty-three-year-old sister from East St. Louis wrote to Coughlan that she hoped to gain skills during her SUE summer to be more effective in her neighborhood—"an area where the church has really done nothing." "I hope to get a bit of experience, general knowledge of problems, what can be done about them, observation of others' techniques, and so on from this program," she explained. "I like what I saw in the tentative schedule which Mother Provincial forwarded to me."[114] The 1966 pilot was successful, and SUE became a permanent addition to DES programming.

The following year, 1967, SUE was redesigned and expanded under the joint leadership of Sister Mary Francis Briggs, SBS, a sociology professor from New Orleans, and Sister Prudence Moylan, BVM, a professor in the humanities program at Mundelein College in Chicago. The revised program still combined education about urban problems with apprenticeship in community-service agencies but also emphasized direct encounter with the city of Chicago and its residents. "Before our society can be changed it must be understood as it is, in its strengths and weaknesses. This will be our summer work," Moylan wrote to SUE participants about the program before their arrival:

> I propose that we experience life in the city from top to bottom: from the top of the Prudential Building to the caverns of Lower Wacker Drive, from the magnificent mile of Michigan Avenue to the rubble of West Madison

> Street, from City Hall to the West Side Organization, and from the North Shore suburbs to the South Side ghetto. We'll examine the institutions of the police department and parish. We'll visit schools, playgrounds, and juvenile courts. We'll read papers and meet the people of Chicago. And when we come to summing up these six weeks, I hope we shall find ourselves shaken to the foundations and confirmed in hope.[115]

Two sisters who participated in SUE that year summarized more simply, "the city is our classroom."[116] Also, starting in 1968, participants in SUE were eligible for six academic credits from Mundelein College. To be eligible for credit, participants were required to write an original funding proposal requesting assistance for an urban program and undertake an intensive study of a neighborhood near the SUE residence.

SUE followed a familiar trajectory for DES programs. Following a pilot year, a successful project typically expanded to include more sisters, diversified a general focus into multiple-issue specific themes, involved laypeople and non-Catholic organizations in its operations, and proliferated its model through the creation of duplicate programs in other cities. In its third year of operation, 1969, under the direction of Sister Mary Sparks, OSF, SUE became a year-round program, offering fall, spring, and summer sessions. This session enrolled sixty-seven sisters who, because of their numbers, had to be split between two locations. SUE continued its academic affiliation with Mundelein College, standardizing the core curriculum and reading list and increasing academic credit from six to nine credits for completion of the course. It also offered graduate credit through Loyola University. For sisters who could not secure a three-month leave from their regular assignments to attend the full course, Sparks sponsored eight seminars on weekends covering topics related to poverty and race. With DES assistance duplicate SUE programs were opened in Youngstown, Ohio; Paterson, New Jersey; and Philadelphia, Pennsylvania, in 1969.[117] SUE also began to serve nonreligious and even non-Catholics. The Central States College Association, a consortium of colleges in the Midwest, hired Sparks to conduct a version of SUE for college juniors. Margaret Traxler was particularly enthusiastic about this extension of SUE into the general population, believing that proven programs should be disseminated as widely as possible. Reflecting on the meaning of the college association's adoption of SUE, Traxler commented, "NCCIJ will thus be serving an ever broadening milieu of people in society who find themselves enmeshed in a chaotic urban scene yet not understanding the societal patterns and institutions which either succeed or fail in interacting for stabilization and harmony of man in this world."[118]

The most successful DES program, measured in terms of replication outside of the NCCIJ, was a program that created free "fun schools" for children in impoverished urban neighborhoods during the summer months. The program's main goal was to provide a safe, fun, and enriching environment for children who might otherwise be unoccupied during the summer recess. The program and its curriculum closely replicated the Freedom Schools established across the South by a coalition of CORE (Congress on Racial Equality), the SNCC (Student Nonviolent Coordinating Committee), and the NAACP (National Association for the Advancement of Colored People) during Freedom Summer, 1964. The pilot for the DES version was Project Cabrini (the subject of Chapter 5), a joint effort of the DES and the Sisters of Saint Francis of Rochester, Minnesota, named for Cabrini Green, the Chicago public housing project that was home to most of the children the school served. Project Cabrini was federally funded, through a $9,450 grant from the Office of Economic Opportunity and staffed by fifteen Rochester Franciscans. The sisters offered classes in reading, Spanish, math, science, sewing, typing, speech, art, "Negro heritage," and music to neighborhood children during the day and held programs for adults in the evening. Classes met in a parish school that had recently been closed by the religious congregations who founded it when the neighborhood became predominantly African American. The most modest estimate of attendance at Project Cabrini stated that the 1965 pilot drew over a thousand children into its classrooms and programs. By all accounts the program was extremely well-received in the neighborhood. Children crowded its classrooms and, through the children's enthusiasm, parents also became involved in Project Cabrini operations. Over the course of the summer, the sisters, children, and parents together spontaneously created a host of additional activities—an art show, a community newsletter, evening classes, sing-alongs, even tutorials in résumé writing for adults. "Never before has anything so interested the citizens of this area," reflected Ed Narvot, community relations director for Cook County public assistance. "There is no other word to describe Project Cabrini like the word 'electric.' The current is strong and everyone knows it's there."[119] The Franciscan sisters in particular found something deeply satisfying about the experience of the Cabrini Green pilot. They wrote passionately enthusiastic letters back to their superior and fellow sisters in Minnesota. Outsiders also took note of the unique situation developing at Cabrini Green. Traxler estimated that "about one hundred adults came weekly to tour the classes" at Project Cabrini.[120] *TIME* and *Extension* magazines, the *Chicago Daily Sun,* and local television stations all produced features on the project.

Like many racial-apostolate programs, Project Cabrini capitalized on the fact that many sisters who were parochial school teachers were free to take other assignments during the summer. The timing of summer racial-apostolate programs made it easier for the DES to attract participants because superiors could release a sister for an experimental project without losing her services in schools to which the community already was committed. For a sister who felt numbed by the familiar grind of the Catholic classroom or who was discontented with her regular assignment in an all-white suburban parish, programs like Project Cabrini offered the chance to teach in an entirely new environment, interacting with a very different kind of student. Traxler was acutely aware of the potential labor that sister-teachers could contribute to the racial apostolate through summer programs like Project Cabrini. "Given the fact that of the 140,000 teaching sisters in America, approximately 70,000 sisters have varying weeks of free time during each summer, there are potentially hundreds of such free schools that could be organized," she reflected at the close of the pilot.[121]

The clear success of the Project Cabrini pilot inspired the DES to duplicate the program in several locations the following year. The bishop of Charleston, South Carolina, was so taken with the idea of Project Cabrini that he invited Traxler to Charleston to confer with community leaders about the possibility of establishing a Cabrini-type program in that city. He also invited the teachers from the original Project Cabrini to staff it. As a result, in the summer of 1966 Charleston initiated Project SAIL (Summer Advancement in Learning), a summer fun school taught by the now-veteran Sisters of Saint Francis from Rochester. Traxler offered consulting services, training, and assistance writing OEO grant proposals to any congregation or group wanting to replicate Project Cabrini. "Consultation consisted of writing the proposals, staffing, and on-going advisement of these programs which are in all instances located in the heart of poverty pockets," Traxler reported to the NCCIJ board of directors in 1966.[122] In the summer of 1966, in addition to Project SAIL in Charleston, there were eleven "OEO-funded remedial and enrichment schools in ghetto areas," including Philadelphia, St. Louis, and New York.[123] In Chicago alone the DES ran four OEO-funded summer schools that summer. In 1967 the SAIL program in South Carolina blossomed into four complete sections enrolling 3,000 children. According to Traxler's estimates, Pilot Cabrini enrolled over a thousand pupils in 1965, and replicate programs enrolled 8,000 students in 1966 and 16,000 in 1967. As the summer enrichment schools developed their own momentum in locations across the country, the DES stepped back from operations and consulting, investing its resources in the development of other pilot projects.

Though early DES projects focused on the urban centers and suburbs of the North, by 1967 the DES was ready to pursue projects that addressed the racial situation in the South. The NCCIJ already had a department that focused on southern issues, the Southern Field Service, and the DES drew upon field service resources and contacts to develop a pilot program specifically for the South. As with other DES programs, the primary goal of the southern pilot was to channel the skills and training of sisters toward particular needs either in African American communities or in the larger movement for civil rights. The OEO-funded summer enrichment schools modeled after Project Cabrini had created racial-justice placements for sisters who were teachers at the elementary and secondary levels during the school year. This left the considerable number of sisters with advanced degrees, most of whom worked as professors in Catholic colleges, without similar opportunities to channel their professional skills into racial-justice programs. The Traveling Workshops provided some placement opportunities, but the number of volunteers for workshops faculty always far exceeded the number of positions in the program. One legacy of the SFC was a marked increase in the number of women religious earning graduate degrees in the 1950s and 1960s. By 1967, sisters with PhDs were the backbone of a burgeoning system of Catholic colleges and universities. They also were, Traxler realized, an unexploited pool of talented labor for the racial apostolate.

In 1967 the DES piloted CHOICE (Cooperative Help of Integrated College Education), a program that matched northern sister-professors with historically black colleges in the South. (The experience of sisters who joined the CHOICE program through the National Placement Bureau is explored Chapter 6.) Sisters who participated in CHOICE agreed to teach summer courses in small Southern colleges, thus expanding the course offerings of such colleges and allowing "Negro faculty" at the schools to devote the summer to research and writing. Sisters in CHOICE either taught regular courses or participated in Upward Bound programs that prepared high-school seniors to enter college in the fall. CHOICE sisters were paid expenses only, and their salary was given to the teacher they replaced. During the 1967 pilot year, thirty-five sisters were placed in fifteen southern campuses through CHOICE.[124] Most CHOICE sisters lived on the campuses where they served. In some cases, they were the only white faculty at the school. Many sisters who participated in CHOICE reported that their interactions with students in historically black colleges were intense and challenging but also satisfying. "I have the organizer of the Black Militants in my class," wrote Sister Mary Mangan from Miles College in Birmingham. "One night he asked to talk with me which we did warmly and cordially until after midnight." Sisters at Florida A&M University in Tallahassee reported that they were asked by students to join the student council meetings, from which all other faculty were barred.[125]

The pilot was a resounding success, and Traxler immediately began planning to "considerably enlarge" the program.[126] She cultivated relationships with administrators in historically black Southern colleges, crafted formal processes for application and placement of sisters in the program, and recruited volunteers for the summer of 1968. She mailed promotional materials about the program to Southern colleges and Northern religious superiors. "MAKE NEXT SUMMER YOUR *CHOICE* SUMMER," encouraged one announcement about CHOICE that ran in the *Nuns Newsletter.* In 1968, seventy-three sisters served in CHOICE positions. In 1969 the program placed 361 sister-professors. As an outgrowth of the program, a number of sisters decided to extend their stays in colleges where they were placed, committing themselves to teaching for an academic year or longer. In 1969, in fact, seventy-two sisters served as full-time faculty in southern colleges through CHOICE. In a 1969 report, Traxler enthused, "In November, a Choice professor became free due to phasing out of her Peace Corps education center. A letter to Black Administrators about her availability brought seven offers for immediate placement with full professorial status."[127]

CHOICE also gave birth to an unanticipated new program within the DES, the National Placement Bureau. The DES had always brokered racial-apostolate assignments for interested sisters on an informal basis. Often sisters who had attended a Traveling Workshops session or read the *Nuns Newsletter* would write to Traxler afterward requesting information about the racial apostolate or placement in a particular program. Or superiors would write on behalf of a particular sister who had become interested in the new apostolate, asking for advice about how to satisfy the sister's desire for such work. Similarly, organizations creating specific racial-justice programs wrote the DES seeking to attract sisters to their staffs. In January 1966 alone, Traxler and her secretary responded to over 500 letters of inquiry about programs and placements. Until 1968 most of these were handled on a case-by-case basis, with Traxler and other DES administrators matching sisters with programs that fit their interests and training. As interest in the racial apostolate blossomed in the late 1960s, and as programs for these works proliferated across the country, the role of the DES as a clearinghouse for information and the brokering of individual placements became an increasingly burdensome drain on the limited resources the DES possessed—resources that the department preferred to invest in the development of new programs. The administrative structures the DES subsequently created for placing sisters in historically black colleges through CHOICE provided a much-needed solution. In 1969 the DES modified the application form first used for CHOICE in 1968 to make it appropriate for matching sisters with a host of other programs. The form carried the new title "Application for NCCIJ National Placement Bureau" and contained questions about the sister-applicant's education, current assignment, teaching competencies, flexibility regarding living arrangements outside a convent, superior or provincial contact information, and time frame available for placement. Sisters were asked to rank their preferences for placement in the following programs: an OEO-funded school in an impoverished area, a parish Catholic school day camp, CHOICE, Summer in Suburbia, Head Start, and Upward Bound.[128] The DES announced the National Placement Bureau (NPB) as if it were a new program, publicizing it in various sister periodicals, much as it had other initiatives. "The NCCIJ is pleased to announce: A National Placement Bureau for American Nuns," one such advertisement read. "This National Placement Bureau is established to assist nuns who wish to remain within the embrace of their religious communities and yet to make the fullest use of their personal gifts in a broadened education and healthcare service in a humble effort to right the wrongs of mankind."[129] With the creation of the NPB in 1969, the system through which interested sisters were assigned to the racial apostolate became standardized and efficient, making it possible for the DES to process hundreds of such applications each year.

As the Traveling Workshops, SUE, Project Cabrini, and the NPB clearly demonstrate, the DES played a significant role in the development of the racial apostolate at the national level by facilitating and encouraging the proliferation of programs modeled on its own initiatives.

In some cases, the DES paired with established local organizations to create sister-specific programs promoting interracial justice. In 1968, for example, the DES partnered with Project Bridge (also known as Ethnic Leadership in National Parishes) in Cleveland, Ohio, to create a program that extended Project Bridge's work in inner-city Cleveland into area suburbs. Funded by the Ford Foundation, Project Bridge was a lay-led organization that addressed racism in urban Catholic ethnic parishes in Cleveland, particularly in neighborhoods undergoing racial integration, through programs that attempted to dispel negative attitudes among white ethnic Catholics about their African American neighbors. Together, Project Bridge and the DES initiated a pilot project called Summer in Suburbia (SIS) that sent women religious into suburban neighborhoods—"the white ring around the black inner city" of Cleveland—to make "house calls" performing "attitude surveys" as a way of initiating discussions about racial prejudice with suburban residents. SIS attempted to harness the latent influence and authority of women religious among fellow Catholics toward a "broad thrust into all-white suburbs, confronting residents with the urgency of the racial crisis, enlightening them on the issues involved, and challenging them to positive programs for action."[130] Margaret Traxler recruited sisters as volunteers for SIS, inviting those who did not receive placement in the DES's CHOICE program in 1968 to apply for work through SIS. (This was a significant number of sisters. In 1968 there was an unusually high number of applications for the CHOICE program but a substantially reduced number of available positions because colleges working with CHOICE cancelled academic summer sessions in response to decreases in federal funding for Upward Bound programs and also in response to increased student unrest—or "tension," as Traxler called it—on college campuses.) In order to sell work among northern white suburbanites to sisters who had originally applied to teach African American students in historically black colleges in the South, Traxler had to convince sisters that the Northern suburbs were as crucial to the fight for racial justice as locations more closely associated with African American communities. Citing the Kerner Report's attention to the pervasive, destructive nature of white racism, Traxler urged, "the issue of race and poverty must be faced especially in the suburbs where large portions of the Catholic population have migrated to escape these very issues." This increasing crisis of suburban racism, she continued, "must be met head on—NOW—this summer—through the efforts of religious women willing and eager to engage themselves in the struggle for the human rights of all men."[131]

Traxler's bait-and-switch strategy worked. In SIS's pilot year seventy-three sisters participated in the program, making 30,811 house calls in suburban parishes around Cleveland. Sisters who participated in the 1968 SIS pilot reported a significant number of negative interactions. For example, one sister reported being told by a young boy who answered the door, "My mother said to say she's not home. You know what else she said? She said you could go to hell." Still, enough sisters reported positive responses to convince the DES to expand SIS to additional cities the next summer.[132] Writing to thank Traxler for "one of the most worth-while and enriching experiences of my life," a sister who participated in the SIS pilot in Cleveland reflected this optimism about the ultimate effect of the project, despite the generally chilly reception sisters encountered in suburban homes. "Although immediate conversion to Christian principles did not result from SIS contact and efforts," she wrote, "good triumphs in many forms, I am certain."[133] In 1969 the DES partnered with Catholic colleges in Baltimore and Memphis to create duplicate SIS programs of "action-research and one-to-one education confrontation" in those cities. The resulting programs, Baltimore's Project Concern and Memphis's NAME (New Attitudes in Memphis Education), employed seventy-five sisters in the summer of 1969.[134] Both Project Concern and NAME offered sister-participants college credit for their work.

The development of NAME in Memphis is instructive about the fate of racial-apostolate programs that developed through the collaboration of the DES with local organizations. NAME's eventual codirector, Sister Adrian Marie Hofstetter, first contacted Traxler in early 1968, asking simply "if there is a place for me in social justice programs where I can accomplish more than I can here" at a Catholic college in suburban Memphis. Rather than inviting Hofstetter to apply for placement through an existing DES program, Traxler instead encouraged her to create a program modeled on Project Bridge's SIS in her native Memphis. "Perhaps something like Project Bridge is the answer," Hofstetter wrote in reply. "However we do not have a whole task force in Memphis so we are going to need considerable help."[135] In the end, both the DES and Project Bridge provided NAME with practical advice and much-needed financial support through its first summer of operation. Hofstetter's correspondence with Traxler in preparation for NAME's first year reveals the extent to which Hofstetter relied on the DES and Traxler for guidance about both the small details and large challenges of establishing a suburban encounter program. "The big problem at our meeting last night," she wrote Traxler in a characteristic letter, "is who will receive the funds" the program had requested from various agencies.

Later in the same letter she asked, "Are we supposed to limit our task force to Sisters? I suppose so, if we are going to use the name 'Sisters in Suburbia'?"[136] Traxler personally recruited sisters to NAME's staff, writing to a select list of superiors sympathetic to the racial apostolate, asking each to release "a Sister or two" for service through NAME. In typical form, Traxler phrased her case to the superiors in prose that bordered on hyperbole:

> The current issue of America conjectures editorially that there were times in the French and Russian Revolution when, if major policies had been changed, history might have been spared a blood-bath. It seems now in the global racial revolution, each of us has the opportunity to stem the tide by contributing as religious teachers in this Adult one-to-one education program. Above all, it underscores the important role of religious women in today's society.[137]

By May 1969 Hofstetter had assembled a solid coalition of sisters and community activists to NAME's governing board, secured sisters from fifteen states and Canada to staff the program, arranged for sisters to receive six credits from Siena College for their work at NAME, and, most importantly, secured the endorsement of Bishop Joseph Durick of the Nashville Diocese for the project.[138] Stable funding eluded her, however. In the end, NAME's first year was financed by a $3,000 grant from Project Bridge and private donations from "interested friends." Money remained tight through the summer.[139] Writing to sisters accepted to the NAME program with details about the orientation schedule, Hofstetter quipped, only half in jest, "Those with veils will get free transportation on our public air-conditioned buses. If you still have a veil you might want to bring it along in case our transportation money is scarce."[140] Despite scarce funds, sisters working through NAME in the summer of 1969, contacted 4,845 households in suburban Memphis, and were able to engage residents in "prolonged visits" (defined as any conversation lasting between thirty minutes and three hours) in 805 cases.[141]

In 1970 the DES further expanded the program, partnering with local groups to offer suburban education programs in Baltimore, Minneapolis, Philadelphia, Memphis, and Milwaukee.[142] In each location the DES cultivated partnering relationships with local organizations to cosponsor duplicate programs modeled on the SIS pilot from 1968. Project Bridge and the DES generated an interesting additional program, a college course on "Man in Urban Society" taught through Saint John College in Cleveland and taught by five sisters from the Project Bridge staff. Designed in part to "develop an understanding of how urban life shapes the personality of man," the course featured a Traveling Workshops-style rotation of sister-professors lecturing on historical, anthropological, sociological, and psychological facets of urban experience. Lecture titles ranged from "Nineteenth Century Solutions to Urban Problems" (Sister Mary Paul Norman, OSB), to "Anomie and Alienation in the Megalopolis" (Sister Roberta Steinbacher, OSU), to "The Welfare System in Practice" (Sister Loretta Ann Madden, SL).[143] Students in the course were required to engage in a series of "encounters" in which they were to "live the city" through "personal contact with those areas and aspects of the city you may not encounter in your ordinary daily experience." Encounter opportunities suggested in the assignment include price and selection comparisons between one urban and one suburban grocery store, visiting "various areas in the city where transients move about," or interviewing ministers in inner-city churches.[144]

Having achieved pronounced success in creating program after program, the DES also created spin-off programs within the NCCIJ itself. The largest of these internal replications of the DES was the NCCIJ's Department of Medical Educational Services (DMES), created in 1967 after a joint meeting of the NCCIJ and the Archdiocese of Atlanta identified segregation in Southern hospitals as a significant, ongoing challenge within the Catholic Church. In response to a call that a special team of Traveling Workshops sisters be organized "to present institutes to administrations and staffs of Southern hospitals," Mother Regina, RSM, of the Mercy Sisters at Bethesda, Maryland, offered the NCCIJ the use of several Mercy sisters who had experience providing human-relations seminars in the congregation's hospitals. In seeking funding for the new health-care initiative, the NCCIJ took advantage of the close relationship that the DES had cultivated with federal agencies and Catholic organizations, particularly the Department of Health, Education, and Welfare (HEW) and the Catholic Hospital Association. Because, unlike the OEO, HEW did not have a legislative mandate that allowed direct funding of the types of services the NCCIJ wanted to offer the medical community through the newly formed DMES, HEW worked with the NCCIJ to find alternate sources of funding. In 1966 the NCCIJ submitted a proposal to the Surgeon General of the United States requesting funds to allow HEW to hire a special team of Traveling Workshops sisters to present a workshop on race relations and desegregation to hospital administrators in Atlanta, Georgia. "The suggestion for this method of government support came from HEW,"

Traxler later reported to the NCCIJ board. "If the Atlanta institute proved successful, further HEW contract arrangements would be a definite possibility."[145] The NCCIJ submitted a similar funding proposal to the board of directors of the Catholic Hospital Association. Anticipating a favorable decision on their funding proposals, Traxler hired Sister Maureen Mulcahy, OSB, in February 1966 to the DES staff to begin organizational planning for the medical department. In April of that year the NCCIJ's board officially authorized the creation of the DMES as an autonomous division within the organization, separate from the DES, to help "bring an end to the discrimination in the field of medicine, and to stimulate programs to meet the serious public health needs faced by minority groups in the U.S." The board simultaneously appointed Sister Mulcahy to be director of the new program.[146] In 1967 Sister Rose Claire Teeling, FSPA, took over as director of the DMES, a position she held through 1968.

The DMES duplicated for sisters in nursing many of the programs and services that the educational services department had created for teaching sisters. In addition to creating a Traveling Workshops team that specialized in issues related to the desegregation of hospitals and health-care settings, the DMES also organized conferences on racial justice in the health-care system, published a newsletter for religious congregations involved in medical provision, advised religious congregations how to craft proposals for federal funding, channeled sister-nurses interested in racial justice into positions in hospitals and clinics serving primarily African Americans, fielded requests for information and advice from nursing sisters, and advocated for the full integration of Catholic hospitals and health-care facilities. Soon after founding the new division, Sister Mulcahy wrote letters to nurses informing them that "nurses are needed at Good Samaritan Hospital, Selma, Alabama," a hospital owned by the Edmundite fathers and staffed by the Sisters of Saint Joseph of Rochester, New York, and asking sisters to "consider working for one year" at the hospital.[147] The DMES placed special emphasis on the full integration of the Catholic health-care system and the "remaining problems of segregation in the administration of a corporal work of mercy."[148] DMES pressured superiors, hospital administrators, and even bishops to complete the full racial integration of Catholic medical facilities. One such effort by Sister Teeling prompted a curt letter from Charles Greco, Bishop of Alexandria, Louisiana, arguing that continued racial segregation at Saint Francis Hospital in Monroe, Louisiana (brought to the attention of DMES by HEW), was due to the intransigence of the lay staff, not the Franciscan Sisters of Calais who ran the hospital. The sisters "needed no one to tell them what was the 'Christian' thing to do," the bishop chided, "but for their [*sic*] very existence of their hospital, they had to abide by the attitude of their staff."[149]

The development of suburban encounter programs like SIS, Project Concern, and NAME, as well as the medical version of the DES, reflects the flexibility that characterized the DES's approach to the racial apostolate. Traxler kept close tabs on developments in the Church, American society, and the civil rights movement, always looking for new opportunities for sisters to be relevant to the cause of racial justice in the United States. She was quick to identify potential obstacles or pitfalls developing within the racial apostolate. As the 1960s progressed and members of the Black Power movement increasingly criticized the interference and patronizing attitude of whites within the civil rights movement, it became increasingly clear that sisters needed to reconsider their approach to racial justice. Racial-apostolate programs like Cabrini or CHOICE that emphasized the presence of white sisters in black urban neighborhoods and on historically black college campuses would need to find a way to serve these communities while also honoring the black community's demand for autonomy and unfettered self-determination.

To accommodate these changes in the movement, the DES first became more careful not to speak for African Americans in public forums. In place of lectures by sisters who described the black experience in America, the Traveling Workshops added panels of "local ghetto residents who 'tell it like it is'" to workshop programs. Through the national conference, "The White Nun and the Black Ghetto," DES also tried to educate sisters about African American perceptions of the work white sisters were doing in black neighborhoods.[150] SUE also added sections on the ethos and goals of Black Power to the academic portion of its program. The section on reverse racism in the 1969 SUE syllabus bore the arresting subtitle, "Whitey—Go Home and Educate Your White Brother."[151] By 1970 an increasing number of sisters were inclined to heed this request to "go home," or "stay home," pursuing apostolic works in Hispanic and Puerto Rican communities and among the displaced Appalachian poor instead. Writing to the DES to decline a second summer of placement in CHOICE, a sister in Eau Claire, Wisconsin, echoed these sentiments as she explained that she had recently come to "the realization that I had better stay home this summer and see what I can do to help the poor in this area." Though her

CHOICE summer at Paine College in Augusta, Georgia, the previous year had been "a great experience," she was persuaded by the voices—both black and white—in Georgia that had questioned why she had come so far to teach when there were students who needed her at home.[152]

In addition to the large projects listed above, the DES also undertook a number of smaller projects, many of them designed to provide resources on race relations, poverty, and segregation for Catholic educators to use in the classroom. In some cases, DES edited and packaged materials from programs like the Traveling Workshops to make them usable by individual religious. One announcement explained:

> One of the aids that can assist a teacher in her scrutiny of her own attitudes, knowledges and understandings in the area of race relations is a lecture followed by discussion. The Department has developed a sample outline of a discussion that could be used. This is available in a special packet designed to aid in teaching race relations and contains materials pertinent to the teacher's outline . . . Also included in the packet are helpful hints and suggestions for Catholic teachers working with CCD, CYO, CFM, and other lay groups.[153]

The DES offered bibliographies on various facets of race and sold reprints of central articles about race and education. It maintained a library of books, audiotapes, and films about integration and "Negro Heritage" that it made available to sisters who came to the NCCIJ headquarters in Chicago. The DES also offered a "Brotherhood Week Kit" for teaching race relations to middle- and high-school students and a "Do-It-Yourself-Institute" that replicated an in-person visit of the Traveling Workshops through audiotapes, discussion questions, and supplemental reading materials. In 1967 the Pflaum publishing company, which printed the "Brotherhood Week Kit," sold nearly 3,000 copies of the kit.[154] The DES also commissioned a study of social-studies textbooks "to examine their treatment of minority groups and the presentation of their role in American history and society."[155]

One of the earliest publications to grow out of the DES was a curriculum unit designed for the purpose of preparing Caucasian students for racial integration. Titled "Lessons in Race Relations," the fifteen-lesson teaching unit written by Sister Joan Carmen (with the assistance of Sister Claire Marie Sawyer, the first director of the DES) encouraged students to understand the interpersonal and attitudinal facets of racial prejudice as well as its larger historical and structural roots in American society. Several of the units were designed to dispel specific myths about

African Americans. In one example of how "Lessons in Race Relations" was implemented within the Catholic educational system, sisters in San Antonio met privately with the superintendent of Catholic schools for the diocese to request that the unit be introduced in all diocesan schools. After gaining the endorsement of the superintendent and the approval of the board of directors, the unit was implemented in diocesan high schools in 1967 and then revised for later implementation at the elementary level, exposing some 46,000 Catholic students, by one sister's account, to the unit's message that "each man's intrinsic dignity is not measured by his utilitarian value in a society, but rather by his status as a creature of God."[156]

Members of the DES also regularly were invited to give lectures on race and the apostolate, to participate on panels at professional conferences, and to run half- and full-day institutes for congregations of religious. In 1965, a year when the DES was just establishing public visibility, DES director Claire Marie Sawyer gave twelve major public lectures addressing groups such as the Institute for School Desegregation in Houston, Texas, and the Brandeis Forum in Louisville, Kentucky. She also led three spiritual renewal groups for religious congregations, provided two commencement addresses, and addressed thirty-two other "special groups." She addressed seven colleges and universities, five professional organizations of teachers or nurses, three groups of seminarians, the NAACP, the Catholic Youth Organization (CYO), and two "Mothers' Clubs." Traxler, then acting as assistant director, also gave thirteen public lectures on behalf of the DES that year.[157] All staff of the DES were pressed into service as public speakers.

In addition to formal programs and speaking engagements, Traxler and the DES also fielded countless informal requests for information, advice, and materials. Some requests were straightforward and closely related to DES work. "I've been asked to help put together a summer program for eight parishes in inner city or ghetto areas. The archdiocesan commission on religion and race is trying to get as many Sister volunteers as possible in intercommunity cooperation," wrote a sister from San Francisco. "Would you send anything you have on successful programs/projects?"[158] Other letters requested information not clearly within the purview of the DES, such as that of the sister who wrote to ask simply, "Do you know of any societies or the like that offer financial aid to Sisters for their continuing studies in religious education?"[159] Letters like the following one from a sister in Cuyahoga Falls, Ohio, sought information about a specific development in the racial apostolate, believing that the DES was monitoring developments all over the country (in most cases, it did). "After your talk with us at St. John College last Spring, I wrote to ask information about the experimental mobile convent in South Carolina. You suggested contacting a Sister in Troy, New Jersey. After receiving no response from her, I wrote directly to Rev. Creston J. Tawes, the Vicar for Religious in the diocese of Charleston. He did not know anything about it," she wrote. "Was it an unsuccessful venture? A wish? . . . some of us up here are quite interested in this experiment."[160] The frequency and anxious tone of requests for information that arrived on Traxler's desk reflected the anxiety that attended the demographic shifts within Catholic neighborhoods and institutions in the 1950s and 1960s. As the integration of Catholic schools and medical facilities proceeded, requests for information on interracial dynamics poured into DES offices from sisters and school administrators trying either to encourage racial integration in their facility or to prepare students, faculty, and parents for this eventuality. "I have been assigned to a committee which is supposed to provide guidelines for attitudinal change among high school students," wrote Sister Mary Lourdes, SSND, in a typical request. "How do you 'prepare the soil' for physical integration? Once you have the beginning of a shared facilities in the city and county schools, how do you inculcate further attitudes of respect for members of different races, especially Negroes?" Helpful in this regard, Sister Lourdes wrote, would be "any sociological studies that would enable us to understand either the Negro high school student or his white counterpart."[161] The simplest requests that arrived at the NCCIJ office asked for educational materials that the DES had produced and publicized. "My sincere thanks for the bibliography on Negro and African History. If at all possible, could I please have about two dozen more?" asked a sister in Cleveland, Ohio. "Many of our sisters who are principals of inner-city schools are interested in receiving the bibliography also."[162]

Other requests were far more complicated and time consuming for DES staff. The most complicated involved requests for guidance about the process of renewal unfolding in communities of women religious after the Second Vatican Council. The 1966 papal directive for implementing the conciliar decree on religious life required congregations of religious to hold a special general chapter within three years to implement conciliar reforms and also to begin the process of drafting new constitutions. Many American congregations embarked on a complicated process of participatory consultation and self-study, assigning committees to study specific facets of religious life and formulate suggestions for revision of existing norms. The DES had partially opened itself to engaging with this process through its national conference, "Sisters' Survival Strategies." After 1967, requests poured into DES offices from members of committees studying the apostolate, asking for information about opportunities to work in impoverished areas. "This fall we are making a study of deeper development of Community life and involvement in the needs of the Church. As chairman of our group of fifteen Sisters, I am searching about for ideas that I can present to our Community when we have our general meeting at our Motherhouse at Christmas," read one typical request sent to the NCCIJ by a sister in North Dakota in 1967 who had heard about Project Cabrini. "Would you please send me material and information concerning the necessary preparation for this type of work? Would there be an opening for members of our Community to work in this field?"[163] More problematic were those letters asking for advice about the direction a congregation should take or the choices it should make about specific facets of community life. A sister from Lena, Wisconsin, wrote the DES explaining, "Our community has launched out on our self-study and it is my task to write a position paper on the needs of the inner city." Her community seemed ill-suited for such works, she thought, given its status as a diocesan community in a rural area. Still, she raised a series of questions for the DES: "a) Should we send sisters as workers into the inner city? b) What kind of Christian apostolate (teaching, social work, organization, etc.) is most vitally needed in the inner city? c) Do people of inner city need us, want us?"[164] Another sister who had just been elected to represent her community at a congregational meeting in France "to refine our revised Constitution" wrote Traxler, "This is an SOS!" Sisters had been empowered to seek the advice of experts. "Since so many of us have been inspired and encouraged by your words and your works, we feel that you would have much to offer us at this time," she wrote. "Would you be able to make a critical reading of our revised constitution and make any suggestions—changes, additions, omissions, etc—which you deem necessary and/or advisable?"[165]

On top of the voluminous correspondence that crossed her desk and numerous programs, both large and small, to coordinate, Traxler took it upon herself to reach out to civil rights organizations, media outlets, and the academic community, thus generating additional responsibilities for herself and the department. In one year alone, Traxler reviewed fifteen books for various journals, on top of her other responsibilities.[166] Reports to the board were regularly peppered with ad hoc accountings of Traxler's various activities apart from official programs, often delivered in a matter-of-fact tone. "In the past six months I have written eight bibliographies for professional journals, have published seven book reviews and have written ten project evaluations and proposals," Traxler casually mentioned in a section on publications and teacher aids in her report to the board.[167] It is not surprising, then, that from time to time Traxler became overwhelmed by the demands that the vitality of the DES placed on her as director. In a confidential memo to her staff in July, 1968, Traxler expressed frustration at her inability to pursue the development of programs she considered important. "I am seriously hampered by lack of funds which presently deter any progress whatsoever in our Textbook proposal, year-round traveling workshop, and CHOICE development. An assistant is an absolute necessity at this time," she wrote and then continued to describe opportunities in the apostolate that were unmet for lack of adequate staff. "We sent a letter to the Major Superiors of Women giving them an opportunity to request information about each of our education programs. It brought a deluge of requests with each letter reply asking for all program descriptions. There is a great need and the Superiors are eager to receive help."[168]

"I Am Wondering if Your Emphasis Is Entirely Educational?"

From its earliest days, the DES had the difficult, if sometimes exhilarating, challenge of guiding and facilitating an unruly and unpredictable religious apostolate. Much of the racial apostolate's volatile nature was the result of its proximity to simultaneous revolutions occurring in the Church, the civil rights movement, and in American society in the 1960s. The fortunes of the Department of Educational Services—and the racial apostolate along with it—rose and fell in relation to developments in these spheres. The DES experienced vigorous growth from 1965 to 1968, buoyed by the aftermath of the march in Selma and the passage of the Civil Rights Act, a generous influx of financial support from federal antipoverty programs, and the enthusiasm and optimism with which many Catholic sisters embraced the reforms of the Second Vatican Council at the time of its close. As the sixties progressed, the civil rights movement fragmented into factious disagreement about tactics, riots became a regular feature of the urban landscape in the summers of 1967 and 1968, congressional appropriations for the War on

Poverty progressively shrank, and the conciliar renewal of women's religious communities collided headlong with the male hierarchy in the Church, sapping energy and initiative away from apostolic innovations. As a result, the DES had lost much of its momentum toward racial justice by 1972. This momentum toward advocacy and innovation that the DES had cultivated among American sisters did not so much dissipate in the early 1970s as it simply and gradually shifted its focus away from racial injustice in American society and toward gendered oppression within the Church and, by extension, away from African Americans and back toward sisters themselves.

The racial apostolate was always closely tied to the rapid changes occurring in women's religious communities in the period immediately following the Second Vatican Council. From its inception the racial-justice focus of the DES spilled over into issues that were internal to congregations and communities of women religious. The apostolate was central both to conciliar renewal and to the attendant upheaval that occurred within women's communities in the wake of the Second Vatican Council. In particular, programs like the DES that pushed for dramatic revision of the apostolate also advocated, indirectly but inescapably, for loosening of restrictions on the dress and mobility of religious, for the right for religious to determine their own apostolic placement, and for experimental forms of community life. And all of these issues placed sisters in conflict with the male hierarchy.

In May 1967, Sister M. Roland Sornsin, OSF, was just a few months away from finishing her bachelor's degree in social sciences. As her graduation approached, she began contemplating the kind of work she would like to perform for her congregation once she made the transition to full-time apostolic assignment. She had written Sister Maura Couglan at the DES for information about opportunities through its programs. Reading the materials Coughlan had sent her, Sister Sornsin had become "vitally interested" in the training offered through the SUE program. But Sornsin had one question she needed Coughlan to answer before she could proceed to lay plans for after graduation. "I am wondering if your emphasis is entirely educational?" she asked Coughlan in a second letter. "Presently I am teaching Junior High but am anxious to be trained to use my Social Science preparation in work of a social nature other than classroom teaching. Do you prepare sisters for social work with the inner city poor?"[169] Sister Sornsin's confusion was understandable. The exact nature of the work promoted by the DES was not always clear—even to DES staff. Though the NCCIJ's Department of Educational Services was initially created to serve sisters in teaching apostolates—as its name implied—the department's programs far exceeded its original mission (and its name). To be sure, the DES offered programs for teachers, as well as programs that engaged with educational policy—the National Placement Bureau, Project Cabrini, and the Textbook Evaluation Project all reflect a continuing focus on education in the DES. But the DES also sponsored projects that, at least on the surface, had little to do with education, schools, or teachers. While some Educational Services programs fit comfortably within traditional Catholic institutions like parish schools, much of the work of the DES extended into uncharted territory beyond both Catholic spheres and the traditional works sisters had performed in them. Sornsin's confusion reflected a more general uncertainty among American women religious at the time about what limits there were, if any, to the kind of apostolic work that was considered legitimate and acceptable. Was it permissible to challenge white supremacist attitudes among Catholic laity? Was it permissible to openly criticize bishops and Catholic school superintendents for continuing segregation in Catholic schools and hospitals? Was it permissible to live in apartments in ghetto neighborhoods rather than in convents? Was it permissible to march in public demonstrations or, worse, to be arrested? Underneath this ambiguity lay another, more threatening uncertainty among sisters in the racial apostolate as to who possessed the proper authority to decide what kinds of apostolates were legitimate and acceptable: An individual sister? Her superior? The bishops? The Sacred Congregation for Religious and Secular Institutes in Rome?

With the 1964 transfer of the racial apostolate from the SFC to the NCCIJ's DES, the new apostolate had been freed of the supervisory authority of the Conference of Major Superiors. From its strategic position outside canonical structures, the DES was free to experiment with an ever-expanding array of new forms of service for sisters, creating pilot projects whose primary purpose was to respond to specific needs within the racial-justice movement, with secondary thought, at best, given to precedent or current norms within religious congregations. The DES never prejudged whether certain types of apostolic activity were inappropriate for vowed religious. Rather, the organization offered sisters opportunities to engage in a range of programs promoting racial justice, letting sisters themselves (and at times their religious superiors) decide which works were acceptable and which were not. While the freedom of conscience implied in the DES's open invitation to sisters to join the racial apostolate could be liberating and exhilarating, especially for sisters in congregations with unusually strict norms of hierarchical authority, such departures from normal procedure also proved confusing and at times exasperating for those sisters who had to navigate the complicated process of securing permission and leave from congregations in order to join DES programs, especially when congregations and superiors were already embroiled in conflicts with male diocesan or curial authorities. It is to this experience of the individual woman religious, and the intricate process of internal discernment and congregational negotiation through which many sisters entered the racial apostolate, that we now turn our attention.

CHAPTER THREE

Vocation and Negotiation: Congregational Dynamics

In the spring of 1972, Sister Jeanine Jacob, SSND, paced the hallways of Madonna Convent in Tampa, Florida, trying to "listen to the Spirit." Ever since her congregation's retreat two months earlier with Father Maurice Ouellet, an Edmundite priest who had directed a mission to African Americans in Selma, Alabama, during the 1965 protests, Sister Jeanine had felt new ideas "jangling around inside" her. Father Ouellet had challenged the sisters from Madonna Convent to look beyond their walls and to become engaged with the problems of racism and poverty in society. His message was not well received. "He was so committed to the poor and to racial justice," Sister Jeanine later recalled, "that he really threatened us. I resented it terribly." But as weeks and months passed, Father Ouellet's message stayed in her mind, coming back to Sister Jeanine in quiet moments and in prayer. When Sister Margaret Traxler, a fellow School Sister of Notre Dame, visited the convent to give a lecture on race relations, the new ideas in Sister Jeanine stirred in a way that confused and encouraged her at once. Though she had always felt "frightened and repulsed" by social work, Sister Jeanine wondered if God was calling her to do something like it, leaving her teaching apostolate. "'What I should be doing' is the big question I am struggling with," she wrote in a long letter to Traxler two weeks after her visit:

> I know I want to be an SSND; I don't know how or where—our school situation seems a little unrealistic at times. It isn't idyllic, of course, but even in problem times we seem very far distant from the graver problems of our

> country and world. In this past year I have grown more conscious of social problems and more concerned—but always from a safe distance myself. I really don't know exactly how deeply involved I should be, but when I read the gospels, I feel it must be more than I am now. To be as radically involved as Jesus was is really frightening, and I guess that is why I never even seriously considered it before.[1]

In the midst of her confusion, Sister Jeanine found encouragement in thoughts of either going to Chicago to work with Traxler or joining a sister-run program working with African American teenagers in Washington, D.C. Profoundly uncertain about what it would mean to be directly involved with "graver problems"—much less how to go about it—Sister Jeanine looked to Traxler for guidance. "If you have a job, I'm certainly willing. If you have any suggestions, please tell me. If you think I've gotten carried away with all this, tell me that, too," she wrote. Sister Jeanine assumed a posture of expectation, open to her own uncertain thoughts, Traxler's counsel, and the leading of "the Spirit."

The thoughts and fears "jangling around inside" Sister Jeanine, her uncertainty about how to go about changing her apostolic focus, and even her fear and ambivalence about doing so were common among American sisters in the mid- and late 1960s. For many women religious, the initial decision to join the racial apostolate was the result of complicated processes of reflection and even personal hardship. Because a sister's religious conviction about racial justice often intertwined with other dissatisfactions she may have had with traditional forms of religious life or specific frustrations she may have had with her religious congregation, the process of discerning a call to work for racial justice frequently raised deeper, uncomfortable questions about the meaning of religious vocation or commitment to a particular canonical institute. Furthermore, the close association of the expanded apostolate with hotly contested issues of *aggiornamento* and renewal within religious life raised the stakes for individual sisters, as well as for their superiors, congregations, and even their bishops. But the decision to participate in new apostolic forms was just the beginning of the journey for such sisters. The process of obtaining a position in a racial-apostolate program, gaining permission from superiors to participate, negotiating the terms of the new assignment, and then navigating the complicated emotions that often accompanied experiences in racial-apostolate programs all tested the creativity and resilience of individual sisters. Though the process was for some sisters exhilarating and inspiring, for many, it proved confusing, exhausting, and even dispiriting.

"Over and Over Again I Ask Myself, Why Be a Nun?"

News of the racial apostolate spread among women's congregations through diverse networks of communication among sisters, some related to the NCCIJ's Department of Educational Services, some separate from it. Word about the new spheres of apostolic work often traveled by word of mouth among like-minded sisters in a community. News also spread from congregation to congregation whenever sisters gathered for national conferences and assemblies. Summer educational programs through which young sisters pursued bachelor's degrees also proved to be effective forums for the dissemination of news about the expanding apostolate. Though access to secular media was still restricted for many sisters in the early 1960s, some sisters learned about the racial apostolate through articles in Catholic newspapers and periodicals, which were widely available to sisters. The participation of sisters in the 1965 demonstrations at Selma, Alabama, attracted such widespread press coverage in both the Catholic and mainstream media that even women in insular communities learned of it. The events at Selma, in particular, generated interest in race and justice from sisters who found in the public witness of the Selma sisters a compelling model of religious activism.

The National Catholic Conference for Interracial Justice (NCCIJ) assumed a central role in the racial apostolate, coordinating the placement of sisters in various programs amid the confusing accumulation of Catholic and secular apostolic programs in the early and mid-1960s through its Department of Educational Services (DES). Within the DES, Sister Margaret Ellen Traxler, SSND, was a central locus of information about sisters and race. Through her job disseminating information about racial-justice activities, Traxler became a symbolic figurehead for the racial apostolate, a face that sisters could attach to the new style of apostolic engagement. Traxler's prominence was such that sisters interested in working among African Americans often turned to her with questions and problems. Even if sisters didn't know what to call this new apostolate or how to organize it, much less how to ask permission to be involved, they knew they could write to Traxler or to the NCCIJ for more information. The correspondence Traxler received provides a detailed portrait of the excitement and the problems that attended the experience of individual sisters who joined the racial apostolate in the late 1960s. Letters to Traxler reveal just how complicated and uncertain the situation of American women religious was in the immediate postconciliar period. "I know that God works in—to us—strange ways," wrote one sister to Traxler, "but this new working of his confuses and encourages me at once."[2]

Traxler's mail read like an advice column, with letter after letter arriving from sisters asking advice about how to cope with resistance to renewal in their congregations, or how to convince a superior to allow apostolic experimentation, or how to become involved in racial apostolate, or what to do after dispensation from religious vows. One sister stated simply, "In the event I leave the Ursuline Order, I shall need a job."[3] The letters have the feel of women unburdening themselves in the presence of one with whom it is safe to say thoughts normally held close to the heart. "Do you feel like Abby?" one sister wrote after asking for Traxler's advice about problems with her superior.[4] Some letters even contain statements to the effect that the writer expected no response but that the catharsis of expressing to Traxler thoughts that could not be shared within their religious congregations was the only outcome a sister desired. "I know you're very busy. If you can't answer, that's okay. It was good just to write you and let you know," wrote a sister who was questioning her own vocation after several friends left the convent.[5] Anticipating a sympathetic ear in Traxler, another sister wrote, "I really want to be a Religious—a *good* one—a mature one—and really serving the *poor* of the Church. I know you understand this."[6] To the extent that sisters trusted Traxler, they opened up to her about very personal issues surrounding religious life, questions about the purpose of institutes, and even doubts about a vocation. "I just don't know where to begin this correspondence," wrote one sister, addressing Traxler by her religious name. "I open myself to you, Sister Margaret Ellen, for advice."[7]

Echoing the "problem that has no name" that Betty Friedan identified among American women the 1950s in her groundbreaking book *The Feminine Mystique,* sisters in the 1960s also struggled to find words or concepts to explain their emerging desire for an expanded, more meaningful apostolate. Many sisters wrote to Traxler in the hope that she might hold some clues as to where to find the changes they desired but could not fully describe. Lacking an official name for apostolic work in racial justice, most sisters wrote around the concept or gestured toward it, describing the work itself in very general terms, or referring to a "new" type of assignment. "This paper is frustrating me tonight," wrote one sister. "I just cannot express what I would really like to say. I sincerely desire to serve the people of God (and who aren't?) and at the same time profit in a way which may benefit this Province. Thank you for ploughing through this."[8] Another sister began her letter requesting assignment in the South with the simple sentence, "I have no idea what to call this summer work."[9] Women seemed comfortable with the amorphousness of their requests and self-explanations to Traxler, and many wrote lengthy, open-ended letters to her. "I have continued to feel a 'vocation' to some sort of religious commitment and dedication to the people of God," wrote a sister who recently had left the convent. Though this sister could describe her openness, she could not formulate a more specific request than simply that Traxler correspond with her: "Since this is all so vague and I really don't know exactly from what angle to write—I will close with the hope that you will write to me. I am open to new ideas and am ready for a new form of commitment."[10] "I feel that at this time of my life (52) that I want to be more actively involved in an apostolate where there is a greater need," wrote another. "I hope you will have the answers to the where, how, and what."[11]

The tentativeness of sisters' language reflected the instability of sisters' worlds generally during and immediately after the Second Vatican Council. In the mid- and late 1960s, women religious faced many more questions than they could readily discern answers for—the structures and orientation of the Church and of religious life were in a state of profound transformation, longstanding regulations and basic bureaucratic processes within congregations were being reformed and replaced, and new forms of religious life had not yet taken concrete form. The provisional language sisters employed mirrored the uncertainty that characterized the process of renewal and change following the Council. American sisters grasped at language. They struggled with concepts of authority. They described dissatisfaction with religious life and with their communities but had no idea what might replace them, only inklings that something else was out there. Congregations, superiors, and individual religious found themselves ad-libbing their way through revisions to the most basic tenets of religious life, unsure of the rules or boundaries that applied to the reforms, uncertain even of the ecclesial status of their institutes. It was a creative but at the same time deeply disorienting moment for sisters.

The racial apostolate complicated sisters' relationships with their own vocations and with the institution of religious life. Work in the new apostolate caused some sisters to abandon traditional vocations in favor of noninstitutional forms of religious service. Participation in the racial apostolate at other times reinforced a sister's commitment to religious life or to a community that was otherwise reluctant to modernize. Sometimes participation in new apostolates prompted sisters who remained in canonical religious institutes to reconsider the basis of their vocation. Two years after her immersion in the racial apostolate Sister Lisieux Wirtz—whose folk and freedom-song neighborhood hootenannies were a prominent component of Project Cabrini in 1965—applied for a temporary leave of absence from her community in order to pursue inner-city work apart from her order. Writing to Traxler to explain her departure, Sister Lisieux stressed her continued commitment to religious life, explaining that she had "no intention at all of leaving for good":

> I don't think I ever will because I know my place in their stage of life is here. However, I have a little "growing up" to do—in some ways I must mature away from the shelter of the Church. I want to get out and get knocked down and about and have to rise to my own inadequacies and limits and face all there is to face knowing I am nowhere near perfect or even mature.[12]

Participation in the racial apostolate at times deepened a sister's sense of her own vocation, either reinforcing elements that drew her into religious life or allowing for individual development within the context of a vocation. After attending a presentation on how to integrate Catholic hospital facilities, Sister Jane Langer wrote to the sister-presenter, "The incidences you mentioned became meaningful and really personal to me, too, as I thought of you and your apostolate as an influential force in my own life as an FSPA [the Franciscan Sisters of Perpetual Adoration]."[13]

The racial apostolate required sisters to take risks, to leave areas of comfort, and to do things that were uncommon in traditional religious life and assignments in traditional apostolates. The racial apostolate required travel and cultural negotiation. It also often required a flexible approach to regulations restricting the autonomy and movement of individual sisters, which had governed religious life for women throughout the first half of the twentieth century. One sister wrote excitedly about attending a conference on "New Works for New Nuns," asking several logistical questions about accommodations and travel, explaining, "I'm thrilled to be able to take part in this workshop but I'm also 'scared stiff' because it will be my first trip alone."[14] The religious habit, too, was a point of uncertainty for women entering the racial apostolate. One sister added a postscript to her letter, "Could you also advise me on what to wear. Here we wear a suit with a veil or no veil. Or is the Holy Habit preferable? White or Black?"[15] Sisters were uncertain what type of dress was best for the new situations they would encounter in their work. Many assignments in the racial apostolate required sisters to leave convents in Catholic neighborhoods and live either in the rural South or in predominantly African American neighborhoods in the urban North. The work itself took sisters outside the familiar dynamics of parochial-school classrooms, often placing them in unfamiliar, informal situations with non-Catholics. For many sisters the racial apostolate was their first significant interaction with African Americans. "How can you capture on paper the wide-eyed greeting of little children who are curious to see whether the ladies in white are really women beneath their habits?" commented one sister of her surprise at encountering children who were unaccustomed to the presence of nuns.[16]

The racial apostolate also lent itself to experimental forms of community. Living outside large convents and often at a remove from a Catholic parish, sisters in the racial apostolate learned to improvise domestic arrangements. "Three of us are preparing to live in an apartment next to the school here to experiment with new forms of community and prayer life during this present school year. Our area is mostly Black, and we hope to find some way to reach people more effectively."[17] Sisters also found new ways to pray. The Sisters of Mercy at the Boulevard Project in central Detroit designed a "person-oriented" devotional schedule so that "activities of the day including prayer and community gatherings took shape around the apostolic obligations and personal needs of all. Lauds, Compline and the celebration of the Eucharist were chosen as an essential part of living though these times were highly adaptive."[18] Other sisters, such as those at Cabrini Green, were able to participate in the Eucharist occasionally, rather than daily, as their schedules allowed.

These departures from the familiar were welcome for sisters who had entered the racial apostolate as a way of pushing against the restrictions of convent-oriented life. Confined by enclosure in Catholic spheres and then separated from Catholic laity within those spheres, sisters often felt isolated within parish settings where their social contacts were limited to the other sisters in the convent and the children in the school. The racial apostolate was one way for sisters to push against those limitations. "We (the sisters) seldom relate to the people here. We are involved in school only," wrote one sister seeking escape from her placement in a white Catholic parish. "I was thinking of holding a day of recollection for all the women of the parish. I want so badly to get involved in this parish."[19] The racial apostolate offered such sisters varied social contacts, a loosening of the restrictions that governed life in many convents, and a much higher degree of autonomy than they experienced in Catholic parish settings. One sister tied several elements together in her letter requesting a year of leave: "I am considering asking my Provincial for an arrangement whereby I can accomplish three things. 1) get out of the type of upper middle-class girls' school in which I have taught for almost 25 years, 2) live in Chicago, 3) move into an area of work and service more directly concerned with the poor and the Negro."[20]

For many women religious the racial apostolate significantly altered foundational concepts of religious life, in particular the idea of religious vocation. Preconciliar Catholic doctrine held that a true vocation to religious life was an irrevocable call from God. "You can deny it and run away from it, but eventually your vocation catches up with you," as one sister put it.[21] Sisters who left religious life carried with them painful stigmas of failure and betrayal. Often such departures were shrouded in secrecy, lest other sisters be similarly undermined. In some communities sisters left the convent under the cover of darkness, their place setting removed from the community breakfast table, their name not spoken in the community, as if they had never existed. Women who had thus "abandoned" their vocation by leaving the convent were expected, if they remained Catholic at all, to return to proper Catholic domesticity, becoming wives and mothers or else respectable spinsters.

The racial apostolate lessened the stigma against women who left the convent by offering to them a way to continue to pursue apostolic activity outside of canonical institutes. Because sisters in the racial apostolate lived and worked among non-Catholics, they experienced the daily devotional facet of their religious vocation apart from congregational regulations and convent enclosure. Many communities limited the requirements for praying the hours among sisters in experimental apostolates. Because sisters of the racial apostolate were engaged in vibrant new forms of humanitarian service, moreover, they experienced the service dimensions of their vocations apart from traditional Catholic institutions. They taught in community centers and private homes, on black college campuses and public playgrounds, rather than in parochial-school classrooms. They nursed and gave health information in neighborhood clinics or in home visits rather than in Catholic hospitals. They assessed and responded directly to the needs of their neighbors rather than waiting for direction from a superior or a parish priest. Working outside the Church, sisters in the racial apostolate experienced a radical challenge to the institutional structures of traditional religious life. Their commitment to poor and marginalized persons occasionally came into conflict with and even eclipsed certain aspects of canonical religious life. In essence, the question was whether the restrictive obligations in their orders contradicted a more fundamental call to love of neighbor. The issue was profound, and it prompted multiple layers of response. Some sisters wondered whether membership within a canonical religious order was essential to living and fulfilling a religious vocation. Others asked themselves if direct work for racial justice actually resonated more with their individual vocation than did the institutions and lifestyle of vowed religious life.

The racial apostolate provided a model that effectively uncoupled a vocation to serve the poor from a vocation to live as part of a traditional religious community. Many women in the racial apostolate ultimately reconsidered participation in congregational religious life, even while their belief in the validity of their own vocation never wavered. "I am leaving one form of religious life while strongly believing in the essence of living a Christ-centered life of dedicated service," wrote Sister Mary McDermott on the eve of her transition from sister to laywoman. "Having learned the value of sharing one's self and talents with others, I hope to continue to give what little I can to those who might make use of what I offer them."[22] For McDermott, the call to service was the essence of religious vocation. The racial apostolate therefore offered her and other sisters who shared her perspective form of continuity with their religious vocation, a way of remaining faithful to a call to service and justice in a new way. Writing to the National Placement Bureau (NPB) to decline a position in Chicago on the grounds that she had decided to leave religious life, one sister stressed the continuity of her commitment to "the Negro people" despite the change in her religious status. "I still am serious about taking a job within the inner-city area in September," she wrote. "My interests are relatively the same as when I was known as a religious."[23] For such sisters the racial apostolate became an alternative form of religious life to traditional religious congregations. Because they identified religious life with service, they saw departure from their communities to pursue an individual commitment to the racial apostolate as leaving one form of religious life for another.

There were other sisters working in the racial apostolate for whom religious vocation, in addition to service, meant a vowed life in community. They nevertheless found existing canonical structures too confining or their religious communities too slow to change. The 1969 founding of Sisters for Christian Community (SFCC)—a noncanonical association of women, most of whom had recently left vowed religious communities—provided an alternate institutional structure for such sisters. One explained, "I have worked hard for renewal in our community, but since it has not been forthcoming with our past chapter of Affairs in June, I have decided to leave the Presentation Sisters and become a member of the non-canonical Sisters for Christian Community."[24] The women in this group retained total commitment to God through vows and a certain, less-structured form of community, but they chose to forego canonical recognition.

Because many sisters in the racial apostolate eventually worked side by side with former sisters or noncanonical sisters, lines of communication between current and former nuns remained open in ways that previously would have been unthinkable. The development of alternate forms of religious life, as exemplified in the racial apostolate, transformed the tenor of the decision to stay for sisters who remained within canonical religious congregations. Proximity to and communication with former sisters also provided women still in congregations with concrete proof that there was life and service, and even possibly vocation, after dispensation from canonical vows. In fact, these dynamics changed so rapidly in the 1960s that by 1967 when, in a dispute with octogenarian Archbishop Karl Joseph Alter of Cincinnati, a large group of Glenmary Home Mission Sisters left the community to form a lay-service organization, the Federation of Communities in Service, the remaining sisters in the congregation wrote a celebratory press release, stressing the developmental and evolutionary nature of the decision and the fact that other communities faced similar decisions. "The Glenmary Sisters have announced that a number of their members plan to move into a new form of life and work," the press statement states. "They are asking for dispensation from their vows and plan to work as a lay, Church-affiliated organization. The new group will be a lay organization living in community, committed to service for human development with a focus on religious and social needs."[25]

The changes accompanying the emergence of the racial apostolate led sisters to a search to clarify for themselves what religious vocation meant and to integrate their understanding of service, religious consecration, and their integral ecclesial identity.[26] Women religious who stayed within canonical institutes knew that they did so by choice rather than because they feared the stigma of being an ex-nun or because they lacked a meaningful alternative. One young sister wrote an agonized letter to Traxler about her "disappointment and hurt that two of the wonderful young people there who also are my best friends have decided to leave the congregation when this semester ends." The departure of her friends had challenged the sister not only to question her congregation's contribution to the situation; it also caused her to reevaluate her own future in religious life:

> It is hard to live with the fact that our chapter's inability to accept people's diversity and respect and appreciate their ideas had something to do with their leaving now. Their decision has made me face my vocation real hard for perhaps the first time. Over and over again I ask myself, why be a nun. I know (or think) it's what I want, but I want to be able to tell myself why and not just stay out of indecision or insecurity.[27]

Knowing that there was an alternative also made some sisters less tolerant of the things they found unsatisfactory or frustrating about circumstances in their order. "I was a pawn by a priest this summer," wrote one sister. "Had I been thinking of leaving, that would have been the proverbial straw."[28] Describing her fears that her superior would not allow her to continue in the racial apostolate, another sister acknowledged to Traxler that leaving religious life was one of several ways she could respond to such restrictions. "I have a job which I feel is a worthy apostolate," she explained, "if only Eunice, et al, will let me stay with it. I am not sure what I will do if they say no. I'd rather get out completely than join another order, but I'd really prefer staying in."[29] The racial apostolate broadened both the meaning and limitations sisters associated with their own religious vocations.

The rapid expansion of the racial apostolate in the mid-1960s affected congregations deeply, altering the structure of apostolic assignments and of established financial and generational patterns within communities. Short encounters with the racial apostolate, like summer programs or conferences, often motivated sisters to seek full-year placement in the racial apostolate. "My experiences here at Xavier have given me a taste for more involvement with the 'nitty-gritty' problems of human survival which our colored brothers endure on so many levels," wrote one sister from New Orleans seeking full-time placement from Traxler.[30] Another sister from upstate New York wrote simply, "As a result of this summer, I have hopes to spend full time doing some work in the black community."[31] Sister Janet Levert wrote Traxler in 1968 requesting help finding placement and housing in Chicago: "I am an Ursuline Sister–senior high English teacher eager to teach and work in Chicago's inner city during the coming school year. My religious superiors have consented to this my request—have, in fact, encouraged me to enter and remain in the field after one year to take up residence in

East St. Louis, Ill. The year in Chicago is expected to serve, among other purposes, as a year of internship."[32]

Some sisters found it impossible to return to traditional apostolic assignments once they had experienced work in the racial apostolate. They missed the autonomy they experienced there or the camaraderie they felt with other sisters and with laypeople. Anticipating the potential losses that would attend being reassigned from their positions in central Cleveland, Sisters Annunciata and Philip wrote, "God had blessed inner-city nuns with one special gift no others seem to enjoy, i.e. the gift of real friendship inter-community-wise. This has been a source of comfort here. It will be a source of pain and loss if we are definitely moved from this inner-city parish. It is in His hands . . . PRAY!"[33] Sisters working in severely economically depressed areas addressing basic and pressing human wants felt needed in those communities. "We feel we have a very real Apostolate here," wrote one sister from such an assignment.[34] Some sisters felt upon returning to their communities that traditional forms of service were peripheral to the central issues facing American society: race, poverty, alienation and hatred, hunger, and insufficient education and health care for African Americans. Work in the racial apostolate had an immediate and profound effect on many sisters, dramatically altering their perspectives and even their identities. For sisters thus transformed, integration back into white Catholic suburban schools was nearly impossible. Many left canonical religious congregations in order to continue their work among African Americans.

Other sisters developed an ongoing commitment to the racial apostolate through a more tempered process of reflection on the meaning of religious vocation. "A great deal of thought and questioning gradually brought me to the conviction that I had to find the meaning in my religious life in the light of service to the Church. Along with this there grew the desire to give this service in some way to the disadvantaged," a sister wrote in 1968 from a Catholic academy for girls in a wealthy New York suburb.[35] Another stated simply, "It is my firm conviction that persons, qualified by their desire to see improved social conditions for all men, must take a position of leadership to effect social change." She added solidly, "This is the vocation I shall follow."[36]

Issues of authority figure prominently in letters to Traxler. A number of sisters contacted her independently of their congregations; many of these women were on the cusp of leaving religious life entirely. Sisters often wrote to Traxler and the NCCIJ's National Placement Bureau (NPB) seeking employment as they left the convent. Much of her mail begins with statements like, "My dispensation came through last week."[37] At times Traxler acted as a buffer between sisters interested in race work and superiors who opposed such work, encouraging the sister while also writing the superior to assure her of the religious foundations of the new apostolate. Some sisters wrote to Traxler without knowledge of their superiors. "I have permission to investigate teaching opportunities in colleges in this country during the scholastic year 1968–1969," one sister confided. "I have received permission to investigate possibilities for teaching in college next year, but not permission to *do* the teaching, Sister, and so I would appreciate your keeping this letter confidential."[38] Others wrote Traxler in open defiance of a superior. "I just wish to inform you that I am no longer at Marinette," wrote one sister, explaining, "thanks to Sister John Louis and a few others who strongly disapprove of you and my contact with you. You see, they happened to see the mail."[39] Sisters unwilling or unable to deviate from the concept, all too prevalent before the Second Vatican Council, that divine direction came solely through the guidance of a superior, sought from Traxler a voice that would speak authoritatively, like their superior, but from the perspective of the expanding religious apostolate. "When it comes to something like this, I just don't know what to think. Would you please write and tell us what to think about all this so I can quote someone who knows more than I do?" wrote a sister struggling with how to integrate new interracial religious textbooks into her religious-education classes, adding that it would "be helpful to me too [*sic*] get some of this straight in my mind."[40]

Congregations and congregational superiors commonly tried to accommodate sisters with an interest in the racial apostolate by offering them leave or provisional release from their given assignment, a "year away" or "year off" from apostolic work within the community. "For a long time I have wanted a more direct apostolate than classroom teaching. At the close of this school year my community will release me to do this," a sister in this situation reported to Traxler.[41] "I have received my Mother Provincial's letter, confirming what she told me on the phone: that she would like to release me next year full-time to further the cause of the black man. (These are her words turned around a little.)," Sister Mary Anthony Scally wrote Traxler from Pensacola, Florida, in 1969. "She also states that I may serve this cause in any way I might wish . . . this is left to me."[42]

Because most racial-apostolate programs were not directly associated with a particular congregation, its charism, or its established programs, requests from individual sisters to be placed in the racial apostolate were a real burden for their religious congregations, which typically already had prearranged service commitments for each sister. By sending a sister into the city or the South on a special racial-justice project, an unwanted vacancy suddenly opened in the staff of the congregation's usual apostolic programs. Demand for sisters far surpassed their numbers, and such sudden vacancies were not easily filled. Aware of the burdens that leaves of absence placed upon her congregation, a sister writing from Rochester, Minnesota, explained that congregational responsibilities had been an impediment in the past to her pursuit of a direct apostolate in public-health nursing and in "just being with the poor." "I have had a desire for many years," she wrote, "and I have not been free to respond because of the position I held in our largest hospital and the great need our Congregation has for nurses in our own institutions of health."[43] At times sisters felt that they had to choose between their own apostolic desires, on the one hand, and loyalty to the distinctive missions and institutions of their congregations on the other. One such sister wrote Traxler from Lexington, Nebraska, weighing the congregational costs of placement "in a apostolate where I could serve more effectively":

> I am aware that our Order may not have an administrator to replace me and this along with other complications may mean the closing of this school which would cause much heartache and consternation. It is then that I wonder if I am doing the right thing—am I bound to a community obligation or to my desire to serve elsewhere?[44]

Sisters who succeeded in securing a year of leave from their congregations still faced the hurdle of finding placement in an apostolic project and financial support for them during the time off. One desperate sister wrote Traxler to inquire about her placement, "As you mentioned on the phone, I sounded "persistent"—I know to the point of bothering you. Maybe better, "losing hope!"—due to the fact that I have permission to be away during next year, but don't have a job settled."[45] Funding was always a problem in the racial apostolate. Most congregations relied on the salary that diocese or individual parishes paid teaching sisters in exchange for their service. The racial apostolate drained necessary income away from congregations who needed such funds to cover basic expenses and care for aged members of the community. But sisters drawn to the new apostolate often resented the financial dependence of their community on the middle-class Catholic parishes that were a reliable source of income for the congregation. They also were uneasy about the close associations with affluent and privileged Catholics and their children that traditional assignments increasingly required, believing that such ties compromised one aspect of religious profession, namely solidarity with the poor and suffering members of society. "We are entrenched in middle-class suburbia and very comfortable," one sister reflected of her parish. "These souls belong to Christ, too, and need a dedicated element in their midst . . . but dedicated to what? Comfort? I am wondering about the numberless others who need hope, friendship and dedication but since they are unable to cushion us, are left alone."[46]

In the absence of traditional forms of financial support, having some form of independent funding—a salary not tied to a Catholic parish or institution—was central to a sister's ability to enter the racial apostolate. Many sisters were given leave from their congregational duties only insofar as they could be self-supporting while away from official works of the community. After informing Traxler of her provincial's approval for a year of leave, a sister from Pensacola, Florida, immediately turned to issues of funding. "Sister, could you help me here?" she began. "I will be expected to provide my own maintenance during this time."[47] Explaining the reason for her letter to solicit funds to support a summer teaching in Mississippi, another sister stated, "Rather than ask my religious community to try to shoulder all my expenses plus the loss of my services for the Summer I have been trying to get some group or groups to help sponsor at least my travel expenses."[48] The NCCIJ received frequent requests from sisters for information about sources of funding for educational or apostolic pursuits. Though some congregations and diocese financially supported programs that sisters developed in poor African American neighborhoods, many simply could not spare the money. By 1970 a significant number of programs in the racial apostolate were funded by the federal government through War on Poverty initiatives.

Even with financial support in place, sisters were aware that superiors could and often did oppose the racial apostolate on principle alone. The proper role for sisters was in Catholic parishes, many superiors believed, promoting Catholic faith directly through teaching and catechism. As guardians of the spiritual well-being of each member of her community, some superiors also held that the new apostolic forms compromised enclosure, exposing young sisters to potentially corrupting elements in society. The reforms initiated by the Second Vatican Council came at a dizzying rate in the early 1960s, and some religious congregations—and superiors—responded by digging in their heels and resisting all forms of change, including experiments with new apostolic spheres. A Benedictine in a progressive community in North Dakota wrote sympathetically about the situation of an Ursuline sister in an insular community. The Ursuline was "dying, with a few others, on the vine," the sister reported. "No communication—no contact with post-Vatican II thought except on her own." Worse, because the Ursuline community was reluctant to change, the sister risked being ostracized if she raised the issue of an expanded apostolate. She could face a "martyr's existence if she tries to get anyone concerned about social problems," the Benedictine wrote.[49]

Sisters in communities uneasy about change or with cautious superiors often strategized about how to ask for permission for time away from the community to work among African Americans, attempting to frame requests in ways least likely to raise resistance from congregational leadership. One sister wrote to the NPB requesting concrete information about an assignment in the racial apostolate before she requested permission from her superior. Her letter began by evoking the transformative experience, for her, of working in summer programs in the racial apostolate. "I have had the good fortune of working in programs through your service the past two summers. As a result of my experiences I feel a need to become more fully engaged in such works," she wrote. She then evoked the apostolic limitations of her congregation as a preface to her request for information. "Since my community has little more than parochial school work to offer," this sister continued, "I would like to seek employment through your services again. I think it will be a more meaningful request if I have something more definite in mind when I request the entire year from my prioress general."[50]

Traxler received a number of letters from women religious seeking placement in secret, apart from the knowledge of their major superiors. "Do you understand when I say I have not checked with the Provincial as to whether I could or could not involve myself in this work if I were accepted?" asked one sister seeking placement in the South. "A wise general and/or foolish private investigates the area before attack!"[51] If the trust and approbation of a superior gave young sisters the confidence to make difficult choices, the disapproval of superiors deepened the self-doubts of troubled, uncertain, or searching sisters. Sister Mary Liam had volunteered for Robert J. Fox's Summer-in-the-City "*much* against" her provincial superior's desires. Though Sister Liam recognized her superior's rationale—"we are short on sisters, true"—she justified her application to the program by citing increasing racial tensions in American urban areas. She wrote, "I think unless Sisters involve themselves with this growing tumor in American society, that the death-dealing blow might reach us, as well."[52] Her superior had responded sharply to Sister Liam's decision, suggesting that Liam was being selfish, even while offering grudging permission to pursue "this work of your own choice." The exchange precipitated an agonized letter from Sister Liam to Mathew Ahmann of the NCCIJ, asking for help sorting through her duties to community, superior, God, and society. "Is it really my preference only," she asked, "or would it be God's preference that we find vital areas in which to concern ourselves?"[53]

By 1967 many congregations were beginning to experiment with revised forms of governance, further increasing the confusion around sisters' requests for leaves of absence. In congregations where lines of authority were unclear, sisters could be caught in unstable, transitional bureaucratic forms. A clearly frustrated sister wrote from her congregation in La Crosse, Wisconsin, in 1967 complaining about the new system of shared leadership in which a team of sisters—rather than single woman—acted as superior to the congregation. Stressing the plurality of "superiors" to which she was required to respond with an underlined "s," she wrote, "this is a mess—a fine example of a bureaucratic operation! My superiors have now decided I should go to school for the summer. Perhaps my difficulty was in contacting three of the six that I have to consult. Ho! Hum! As you can see, life is made up of all kinds of 'ball games'—tossing the ball around."[54]

For a sister who enjoyed good relations with her superior, a request for a year off often took the form of a conversation between sister and superior, with both working together to discern God's will for that particular sister. "I read your letter with prayerfulness," wrote one sister in response to Traxler's offer of summer placement in the racial apostolate. "Then I took it to our Revered Mother."[55] Another sister explained her decision to decline a placement offer, citing the agreement of her own discernment on the matter and that of her superior. "Perhaps I should put a black edge around this paper for this letter will not bring a solution to one of your many problems," she wrote Traxler. "I did talk with Mother Mary Magdalen and the Holy Spirit does not seem to be giving her any message different from the one I hear."[56] When Sister Lisieux considered taking a temporary leave of absence from her congregation, she "visited" with her superior, Mother Callista, to discuss her future in religious life. Lisieux's description of that conversation suggests a high degree of trust and affection between the young sister and her superior.

"Mother and I spoke long about it and she agrees it is what I need at this moment of my life—that I will be a better, more effective Religious if I know what the world is all about—(or at least partially)," Lisieux wrote of the meeting.[57]

Superiors occupied a complicated position in this process. They had to balance the needs of their congregations and their apostolic commitments against the needs and desires of a particular sister, all without alienating more "dutiful" members of the congregation. Even superiors who were sympathetic to the desires of sisters in their charge and supportive of the emergent apostolate sometimes were bound by other obligations and forced to deny requests to release sisters from given assignments. "Somehow your letter dated May 11 reached me just a few days ago," wrote Mother M. Petronilla, CSJ, to Traxler in 1969, "and I have been going over and over summer assignments to see if I could make some change somewhere. Unfortunately, I found it is just impossible; the commitments have been made, and I cannot withdraw the sisters from the work to which they have been assigned." Attempting to soften her negative response, Petronilla continued, "When I tell you I am really sorry about this, it is not just a polite way of refusing . . . Is it too soon to consider us for the summer of '68?"[58] Some superiors did much of the administrative negotiation for sisters, securing both leaves of absence from traditional congregational commitments and placements in new apostolic programs for sisters in their communities who wanted to join the racial apostolate. Though less frequent than direct correspondence with sisters themselves, Traxler's files contain numerous exchanges with superiors about placement opportunities. One superior wrote inquiring about placement for four young sisters from her congregation: three were the "steady stable type" who would gladly accept any assignment, but the fourth was quite anxious to leave parochial-school teaching. "She is restless, with a great eagerness to 'get her hands dirty' working with the poor," the superior explained. "We'd like to see *her* get a *full* opportunity to work with the most needy in a well-established, well-directed group in Chicago."[59]

In 1969 Mother Callista—the superior of the Sisters of Saint Francis who ran Cabrini Green in Chicago—wrote to Traxler to inquire about placement for two young sisters in an apostolic program in inner-city Chicago. Mother Callista's letter reflects the difficult position that many superiors faced in dealing with young nuns who were eager to participate in nontraditional apostolic works. "It is not that Sister is not wanted or needed at home. We need her desperately," Mother Callista explained. "I present this only as a matter that seems very, very important to Sister Mary Stewart."[60] Later in the letter Callista again attempted to reconcile, or at least recognize, the incompatibility of the racial apostolate with the ongoing traditional work of the congregation. "We can so ill-afford to spare these Sisters," she wrote, "but if this experience is so important to them at this time I would like to help them procure it."[61] The two sisters in question did find placement in the Job Corps in 1969. In a later letter Mother Callista was even more forthcoming about her hopes that temporary placement in the racial apostolate would ultimately integrate sisters deeper into their vocation and the work of their congregation, either sating the sisters' desire for direct work in racial justice or channeling that desire into congregational outlets. She wrote to Traxler:

> Both of these Sisters have asked permission to engage for this year in work with the disadvantaged in some capacity. Accordingly we have not assigned them to teaching within the community frame; they are not being considered as on Leave of Absence in the Church context of this term. They are simply being considered as our Sisters, in good standing, on assignment apart from our schools hopefully to afford them an opportunity to engage temporarily in work that may satisfy their need. I sincerely hope that following this experience they will be ready to continue on as members of our Sisterhood, and as teachers in our schools.[62]

Unstated in these letters, but understood by both author and recipient, was the implicit threat that sisters who were thwarted in attempts to join the racial apostolate would leave religious life entirely, as many did, asking for dispensation from religious vows in order to pursue the work on their own. Some sisters used the threat of leaving religious life as leverage against reticent superiors. "Today I received the latest—there was no definite yes or no on my release for the year," wrote a sister from Muskegon, Michigan. "This is a problem many of us face who haven't forced ourselves a bit more. . . . I did tell her [the superior] I seriously consider taking leave of absence if the permission is not given since continuing as a parochial school teacher in my present frame of mind is foolish."[63]

The exodus of sisters from traditional apostolic assignments—and from canonical institutes generally—concerned and in some cases angered parish priests and bishops who faced the difficult task of staffing burgeoning parochial school classrooms with fewer and fewer nuns available for placement. Sisters were a significant financial asset to the Catholic Church during the preconciliar years of rapid institutional expansion. The relatively inexpensive labor of women religious had made the proliferation of parish schools in the twentieth century possible. To continue without them, schools had to hire lay teachers, who, unlike sisters, required substantial salaries and benefits. Threatened by the new forms of religious life and fearful about their ability to maintain Catholic institutions without a workforce of sisters, many priests resisted apostolic expansion, pressuring superiors to similarly resist apostolic reforms in their own congregations. In turn, sisters resented the intrusion of male clergy into matters they considered private to the congregation. "The problem with me at this time is that I am fed up with confrontation techniques which polarize rather than unite," wrote a sister from Paola, Kansas, of her community's conflicts with a local bishop. "I really believe we should continue our efforts to help the clergy and hierarchy realize and appreciate the fact that we are capable of taking care of our affairs but at the same time we surely do not want to alienate them."[64] Not all nuns were so conciliatory in their response to the interference of the male hierarchy. "It seems very hard to get the ideas into some of the episcopal minds that women are adults and able to manage their own affairs," wrote one sister angrily.[65] The resistance of priests and bishops to developments within women's orders added an additional layer to the already complicated and conflict-ridden processes of change that were underway.

"A Woman Who Is a Sign of Hope"

Though the goal of the racial apostolate of the 1960s was the creation of a more harmonious and just society, the process through which individual sisters became directly involved in specific apostolic works often was quite volatile. The experience of sisters in these situations was anything but peaceful. The racial apostolate raised to the surface of religious congregations certain latent conflicts and tensions that were normally less visible or less operative in the normal course of the community's apostolic works.

In fact, conflict was to a great degree endemic to the racial apostolate. Work among African Americans often put sisters in conflict with other sisters, with their superiors, or with their congregations. The racial apostolate embodied sisters' criticisms of Catholic segregation and suburbanization, which also was an indirect criticism of white lay Catholics. The racial apostolate challenged traditional ideas about vocation, service, enclosure, and the shape of religious community and consecrated life. It produced controversial reforms that at times deepened conflicts within religious communities and between sisters and the male magesterium. As with Sister Jeanine who began this chapter, sisters also sometimes came to the racial apostolate with profound inner conflicts about the meaning of their own vocations.

Despite the pervasive air of discord that often surrounded it, the racial apostolate also embodied the hope and creativity of sisters in a period of profound religious and social unrest. Sisters entered the apostolate hoping to alleviate prejudice and the human suffering it caused. They created a multitude of programs and organizations to this end and entered into an unprecedented relationship with the federal government. Sisters reached out to people like Traxler and other sisters like her, anticipating that these women would help guide them through the process of entering new forms of religious service. The apostolate gave women religious new ideas about the meaning of vocation, helping them to imagine new forms of religious life, including noncanonical communities. Sometimes the apostolate integrated sisters deeper into their own vocations and their congregations, where they worked to transform their communities into places that supported a vibrant, unconventional apostolate.

The experience of sisters in the racial apostolate was thus one of creativity born of conflict and hope within confusion and frustration. To encounter the experience of sisters from this period is to enter a highly charged world, where the outcome was uncertain—both for individual sisters and the institution of religious life. From her assignment in Newark, New Jersey, Sister Gabriella Bauer reflected on this peculiar pairing of hope and conflict in the new works. "To be a woman consecrated to Christ, a woman who IS A SIGN OF HOPE BY HER VERY LIFE, a listener, a supporter of the poor, a prayerful woman of action who confronts those who set up meaningless programs and middle-income housing—is a rich growth process for the local black community she serves, for the religious community who shares in her Paschal Mystery and for herself."[66] Such growth and change, often painfully wrought, were the final result of the racial apostolate for American women religious.

Franciscan sisters joined a demonstration against racial segregation at the Illinois Club for Catholic Women at Loyola University, July 1963. Publicity surrounding the participation of sisters in the protest drew more sisters into the racial apostolate. Courtesy of Special Collections, Marquette University Archives.

Sister Margaret Ellen (Mary Peter) Traxler, SSND. Courtesy of Special Collections, Marquette University Archives.

Sister faculty of the Traveling Workshop on Inter-Group Relations with one of the rented station wagons they used to travel the country holding seminars on racial justice and integration. Courtesy of Special Collections, Marquette University Archives.

Sister Lillanna (Mary Audrey) Kopp, SNJM, lecturing on the "Myth of Race" as part of a Traveling Workshop program in 1966. Courtesy of Special Collections, Marquette University Archives.

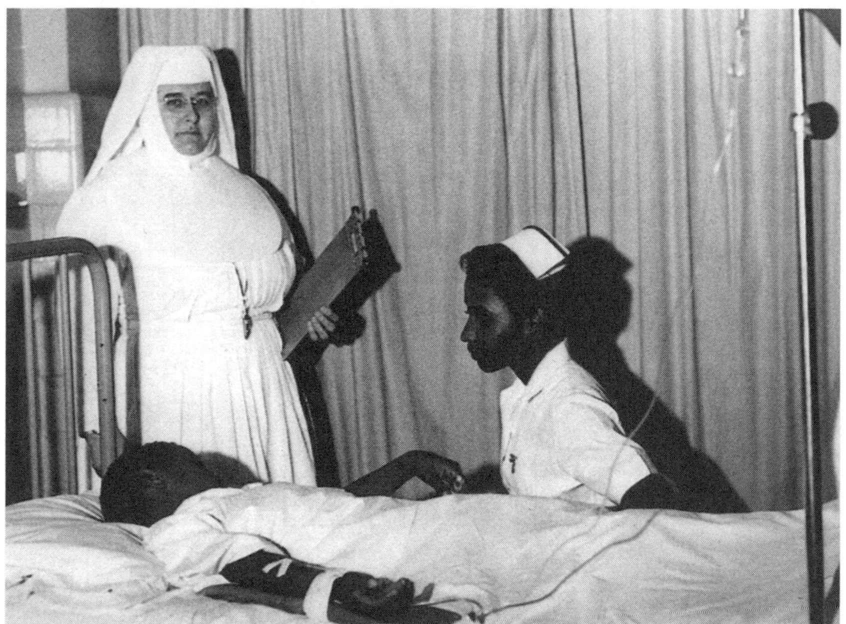

Sister Louis Bertrand Dixon, SSJ, Administrator of Good Samaritan Hospital in Selma, Alabama, in the 1960s. The hospital was one of the few that served African Americans prior to the 1960s. Courtesy of the archives of the Sisters of Saint Joseph, Rochester, New York.

Sister Ligouri Dunlea, SSJ, enjoys a rare snowy day with students from the congregation's Good Samaritan Hospital School of Nursing in Selma, Alabama, in 1962. Sisters wore a white mission habit while working in Selma. Courtesy of the archives of the Sisters of Saint Joseph, Rochester, New York.

Sisters of Saint Joseph picking up visiting Catholic civil rights marchers from the airport. Though they were prohibited from participating directly in the civil rights marches in Selma in 1965, the Sisters of Saint Joseph contributed to the civil rights movement by providing medical care to marchers who were injured by police attacks on Bloody Sunday and by hosting protesters who came from other cities to join the final march to Montgomery. Courtesy of the archives of the Sisters of Saint Joseph, Rochester, New York.

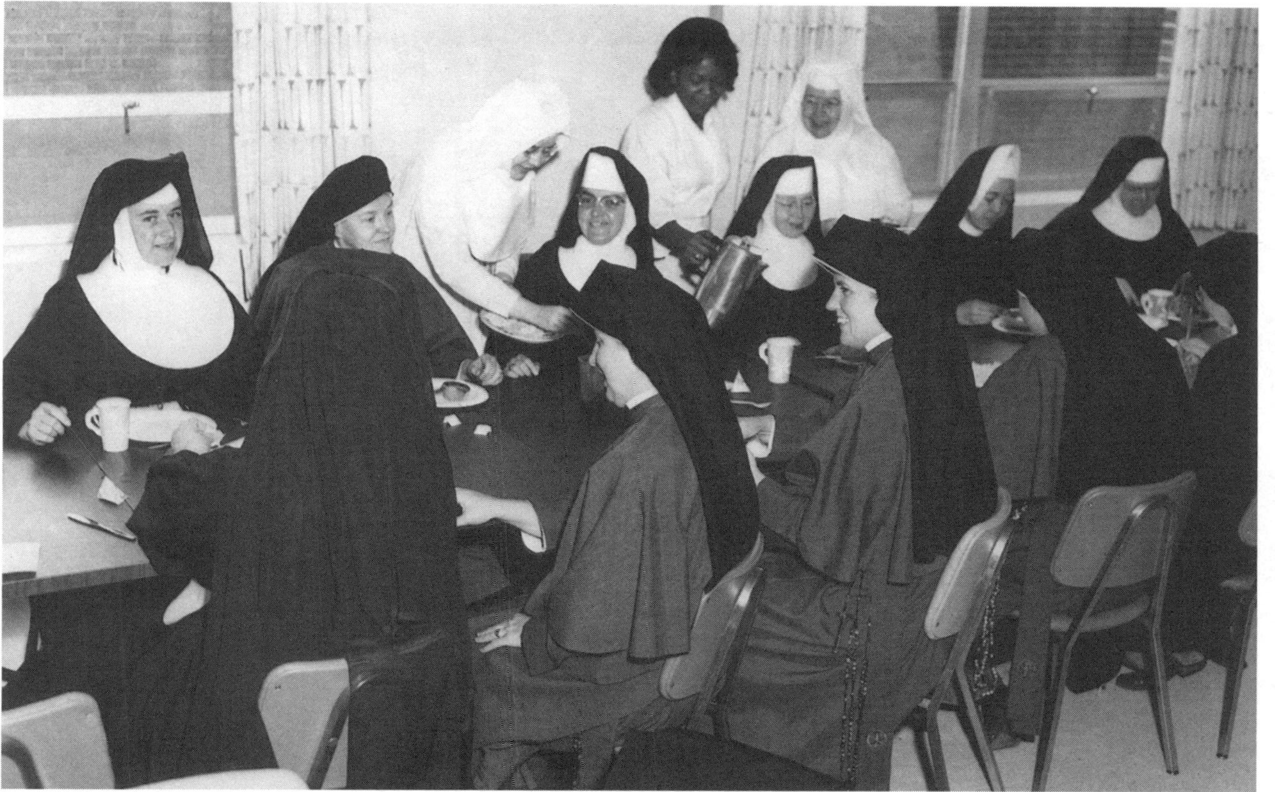

Sisters of Saint Joseph serving a meal to visiting sisters who came to Selma in support of civil rights efforts there in 1965. Note the variety of religious habits among sisters at the table. Courtesy of the archives of the Sisters of Saint Joseph, Rochester, New York.

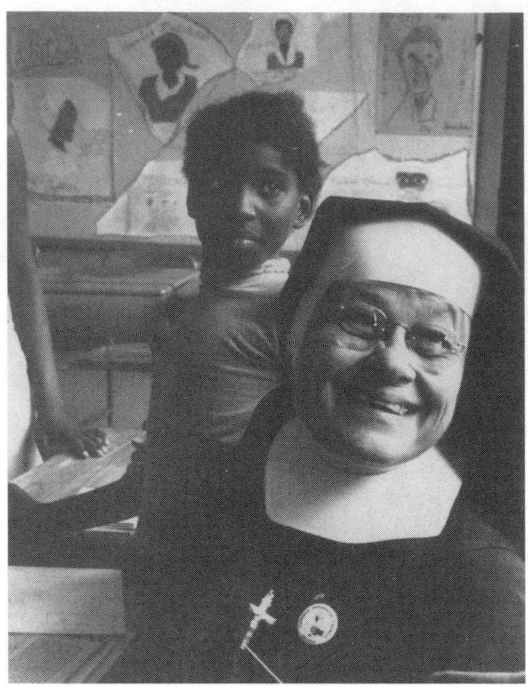

Sister Joachim Von Arx, OSF, with a student at Project Cabrini in Chicago, 1965. Sister Joachim taught courses in "Negro history." Courtesy of Special Collections, Marquette University Archives.

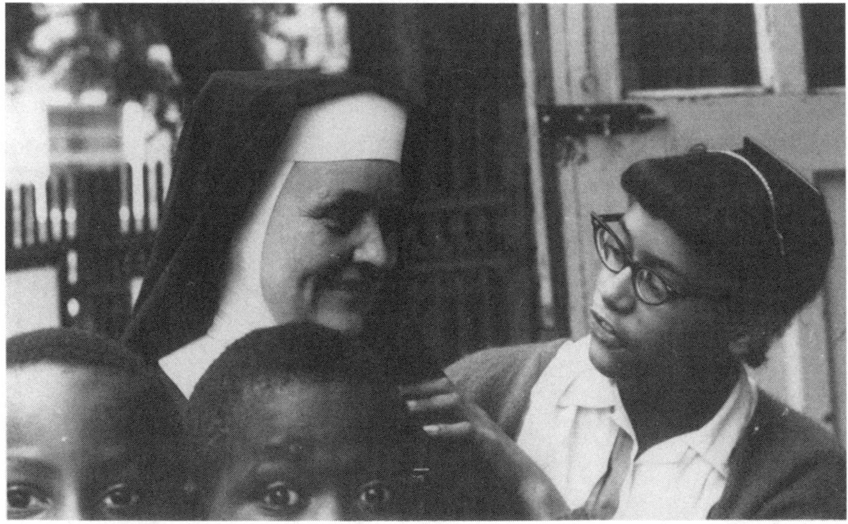

Sister Maigread Conway, OSF, dubbed "chief-in-charge" by the children at Project Cabrini. Sisters enjoyed the informality of their interactions with children at Cabrini Green. Courtesy of Special Collections, Marquette University Archives.

CHAPTER FOUR

Sisters in Selma: Working under Jim Crow

The turning point of the American civil rights movement came in Selma, Alabama, on March 7, 1965, "Bloody Sunday," a clear spring day when peaceful marchers crossing the Edmund Pettus Bridge out of Selma en route to Montgomery, the state capital, were viciously attacked, beaten, and teargassed by Alabama state troopers and a sheriff's posse. Bloody Sunday and the events that followed in Selma brought greater visibility to the civil rights movement, securing its place in the media spotlight and in the political consciousness of the nation. Images of the attack were broadcast widely on American television, causing public opinion among Northern whites to begin to turn toward the movement and prompting President Johnson to push a voting-rights bill through Congress.

In the tense days following Bloody Sunday, religious leaders and civil rights sympathizers (among them a considerable number of Catholic sisters) converged on Selma in solidarity with the movement. Day after day protesters stood in rows against the police barricades that hemmed in Selma's black neighborhood, facing armed police and hostile whites stationed on the white side of the barrier along Sylvan Street. They sang and prayed and talked to reporters, waiting for Governor George Wallace's injunction against the march to Montgomery to be lifted. Brown Chapel, the African Methodist Episcopal church that served as the organizational epicenter of Selma's civil rights push, filled with visiting protesters who arrived in successive waves from the North. Catholic nuns and priests, Jewish rabbis, Episcopal and Greek Orthodox priests, and

Protestant ministers sat interspersed with laypeople, black and white—habits and clerical collars dotting the assembly—as each evening the chapel resounded with freedom songs and speeches.[1] The unprecedented convergence of diverse clergy who came to Selma to support civil rights was the subject of national attention, and no group of protesters attracted as much attention—both positive and negative—as did Catholic sisters. By the time the march to Montgomery was successfully reinitiated almost two weeks after the Bloody Sunday attack, American news reports had carried countless interviews with and photographs of Catholic sisters participating in the Selma protests.

But not all sisters in Selma stood in the "Selma line." Another group of Catholic sisters in the city responded quite differently to the crises of March 1965. Consciously avoiding direct participation in protest activities and attendant media exposure, the Sisters of Saint Joseph (SSJ)—a community of women religious from Rochester, New York, who had lived in Selma since 1940—worked behind the scenes, attempting to stabilize the charged atmosphere in town. Familiar with Selma's segregation and with the violence that supported it, the SSJs responded far more cautiously and covertly, though no less passionately, to the Selma crisis than did visiting sisters from Northern cities. On Bloody Sunday the SSJs nursed wounded marchers at their hospital. Throughout the crisis they visited the Dallas County jail to check on the safety of black youth who had been arrested in the conflict. The SSJs did not march. Rather, they fed, housed, and chauffeured visiting protesters, all the while counseling the visitors to avoid provoking the police and white supremacists. And each night as they returned to the convent chapel for prayer, as was the custom of their congregation, they prayed earnestly for peace to return to their neighborhood and to Selma's streets.

Both responses by sisters to the crisis in Selma—protesting and counseling peace—were incarnations of the racial apostolate, each representing a different strategy Catholic sisters employed in the 1960s to promote racial justice. Drawing on their established roots in Selma and especially their connections to Selma's African American community, the Sisters of Saint Joseph responded to the violence and its aftermath with cautious and subtle community-based service that, for the most part, remained comfortably within the limits, norms, and power structures of Jim Crow segregation. In contrast, Northern sisters who came to Selma in the immediate aftermath of the attack responded to Bloody Sunday by assuming an activist posture, directly confronting white segregationists and consciously flouting Jim Crow social prohibitions.[2]

The willingness of the Northern sisters who traveled to Selma to enter into a highly charged political conflict and to be photographed and interviewed by reporters was a significant departure from the limited public roles that sisters had occupied in the first half of the twentieth century. Selma represented the new articulation of an activist identity that sisters had been developing quietly behind convent walls since the 1950s, through congregational educational practices and in the proceedings of sister-only organizations. Sisters had rehearsed this new identity—the "new nun," as they termed it—in congregational conversations and in the quiet expansion of their charitable work beyond traditional spheres in the early 1960s. But the nuns who marched at Selma brought "new nuns" into the public consciousness and opened the door for sisters to participate in future political protests, as they would in significant numbers throughout the 1960s, 1970s, and 1980s, in protests supporting civil rights and the United Farm Workers Union, and opposing the Vietnam War, nuclear proliferation, and U.S. policies toward Central America.

Though the phenomenon of the sisters who came from the North is the best known facet of the history of women religious in Selma, this chapter treats visiting sisters only as a point of contrast to draw into sharper focus the Sisters of Saint Joseph, and in particular to explore how the latter's familiarity with Jim Crow and their established location within Selma's racialized social structure shaped their actions in 1965.

"I Think of How Naive I Was"

On the morning of March 7, 1965, as people assembled at Brown Chapel in preparation for the first march to Montgomery, Sister Barbara Lumm, SSJ, was finishing her usual Sunday morning shift at nearby Good Samaritan Hospital, a facility run and staffed by her congregation. John Creer, the assistant administrator of the hospital, approached Sister Lumm and asked her to assemble a first-aid kit for some friends who planned to join the afternoon march. She gathered a small package of supplies for the waiting men. "When I think of how naive I was," she later reflected about the contents of the first-aid kit she gave them, "in spite of everything that I knew, how naive I was, that I gave them some aspirin, I gave them something if they got windburned—it was a clear, breezy day and the sun was out—and so I put all these little things in, if they sprained their ankles or got windburned or whatever, and sent them off with this kit."[3]

After her shift Sister Lumm returned to the convent, visited the chapel for prayer, and then sat down to Sunday dinner among the other teaching and nursing sisters. A news bulletin interrupted the regular broadcast on the radio that sisters were playing in the background of the kitchen. There had been violence on the Pettus Bridge and marchers were wounded. The sisters exchanged knowing looks across the table, rose, and immediately left for Good Samaritan, leaving plates and dinner still on the table. "We simply all got up and went to the hospital," Lumm recalled. "We hardly even said anything as I remember, we simply went back to the hospital."[4] The sisters would not return to the convent until late the next morning, exhausted and hungry, their eyes streaming from tear gas.

On the bridge that afternoon a sheriff's posse had attacked the marchers—people of all ages, including children—with tear gas and billy clubs, driving them into a running retreat back into Selma's black district. Marchers were beaten in the melee, trampled by horses and burned with tear gas. In the chaos and panic that followed the posse attack on the bridge, the wounded—over ninety of them, with eleven seriously hurt—were taken to the only hospital in segregated Selma that accepted African American patients without restriction, Good Samaritan Hospital run by the Sisters of Saint Joseph. Sisters from the convent school set up triage in the hospital dining room to separate less seriously wounded marchers—those suffering from tear-gas inhalation or needing stitches or to be calmed—from those with more grave injuries, lacerations, and concussions. The hospital's three-cubicle emergency room overflowed with a steady stream of wounded marchers arriving by ambulance and car, and on foot. Two priests from the sisters' parish, Fathers Maurice Ouellet and Charles McNeice, helped carry people into the hospital as they arrived at the emergency room in private cars.[5] When rumor spread that injured people were trapped inside Brown Chapel, which was surrounded by the police, Sisters Michael Ann and Josepha drove over to make sure all in the chapel were safe. "I never forgot it," recalled Sister Bernice. "I did the best I could. It was horrid. All those people just huddling together. Everybody confused. It was a very hard day. It seemed endless."[6] Tear gas that had saturated the marchers' clothing on the bridge continued to leak from their clothing at Good Samaritan, filling the crowded, chaotic hallways with noxious fumes that burned the lungs and eyes of sisters and marchers alike.

As they tended wounded marchers, sisters slowly pieced together the full story of the attack from the accounts of traumatized patients. Each injury had an attendant story—tales of terror as mounted police rode into the crowd, trampling marchers, of ferocious violence and blatant disregard for women, children, and the elderly. In sisters' accounts of

Bloody Sunday, as they were gathered that day in the hallways and emergency room of Good Samaritan Hospital, descriptions of physical wounds are entwined with stories of the terror that caused them. "The marchers had their heads bashed open," recalled Sister Felicitas, a teaching sister who helped in the emergency. "A lady that I went up to was on a stretcher, she had broken ribs at the time. She had been trying to protect a child. A posse man just came and stomped right into her. That's how they were coming in, terribly frightened."[7] Sister Mary Paul reflected, "The posse rode right into people with their horses, rode them down. One man, John Lewis, had his head split right open. Never thought he was going to make it. I never saw such a bloody mess in my life."[8]

Saint Elizabeth's parish was founded in Selma in 1937 by two priests from the Order of Saint Edmund who wanted to establish a Catholic mission to serve African Americans. Three years later, the Bishop of Mobile asked Rose Miriam, Mother General of the Sisters of Saint Joseph in Rochester, New York, to send sisters to assist the Edmundite fathers in their work in Alabama. In response, Mother Rose Miriam, SSJ, dispatched five sisters to the Selma mission. The number of SSJs in Selma increased steadily over the years so that by the mid-1960s there were eleven whose primary assignment was to the mission.[9]

The first SSJs sent to Selma were "missionary sisters," a designation that set them apart from their peers in parochial schools and hospitals, and that by implication marked Selma as an exotic, perhaps dangerous, place. Whereas SSJs in New York served primarily as teachers in diocesan parish schools, the main work of the Selma SSJs was to convert African Americans. Sisters sent to the Selma mission wore a white mission habit—the same garb worn by the SSJs in their mission in Brazil—rather than the traditional black habit worn by Northern teaching sisters.[10] The object of the Selma mission was not to adapt Catholicism to the circumstances and culture of African Americans in the South but rather to teach Southern blacks to conform to the norms of Catholicism. "I think our style at that time, before Vatican II, was not to honor the black tradition of worship," admitted Sister Barbara Lumm, a nurse at the mission through the 1960s. "In becoming Catholic you became a white Catholic" in worship style.[11] As missionaries, the early sisters at the mission often approached African American culture as an obstacle to Catholic conversion. "On my way to the office this morning I met an old lady who wanted to know what time we held our 'meetin's'," wrote one sister in 1940. "She had a charm around her neck—Sister Anastasia made her remove it and gave her a medal of Our Lady (won playing bingo yesterday)."[12]

The sisters established a convent next door to Saint Elizabeth's parish on Broad Street, the main avenue through the segregated black neighborhood of East Selma. Because the rules of enclosure limited many of the sisters' activities to the convent or its surrounding parish—"to work, to church, to home," as one sister put it—sisters lived almost entirely within the African American world of East Selma, venturing outside it only in limited circumstances. "My world was very small," explained a sister who lived in Selma through the 1960s, "the white doctors being the most extent of white Selma that I knew."[13] Another sister recalled, "We really lived in the black community. We had very, very little to do with any white people because we lived among black people, and white people didn't like it."[14]

Sisters walked Selma's streets, hoping to stir interest among their neighbors. Often, as a matter of course, sisters responded to the physical and material needs of the people they encountered, and these interactions were mainly intended to persuade people to come to the parish for religious instruction. "You hoped that people would see the Catholic Church as attractive, and the Sisters of Saint Joseph as attractive ways of living," explained Sister Barbara Lumm. "It was a small, very small Catholic community. Being Catholic was not a popular thing in the South, and it was not a common thing among blacks."[15] The number of persons who arrived for religious instruction each day was one of the few facets of daily life that sisters of the mission considered important enough always to enter into the spare prose of the convent chronicle.

In the process of making converts, the sisters also performed more traditional "works of mercy," responding to needs within the parish. Sisters founded a parish school at Saint Elizabeth in 1941, shortly after arriving in Selma. At first the school had limited enrollment, mostly Catholic children from the small parish, but as the school expanded, it began to offer its services to non-Catholic children from East Selma. This extended the influence of the sisters beyond the reaches of the parish and into the larger African American community.[16] By the 1960s the parish school had become firmly rooted in Selma's black society and its annual fund-raising picnic was a neighborhood event.[17] The sisters also established a secondhand clothing store, a boys' club, a nursing facility for the elderly, and a school of practical nursing.

In 1944 the SSJs responded to the lack of medical care available to their parishioners by founding Good Samaritan Hospital. "Good Sam," as it was known in the community, was the only hospital in Selma until the 1970s that was fully accessible to African American patients. The early incarnation of Good Sam was a humble structure. "When I first went to Good Samaritan Hospital, it was a combination of shacks put together," Sister Paul Marie remembered. "I used to make arsenic sandwiches for the rats. They used to get into the babies' cribs and steal formula from the babies."[18] The hospital quickly outgrew its initial formation, and in 1947 the sisters built a new brick building to house it. By 1965 the hospital had grown to include sixty-nine beds and a three-bed emergency room. An additional forty beds were reserved for the elderly. At its peak in the mid-1960s Good Sam was staffed by 150 employees, 90 percent of whom were black.[19] Because Good Samaritan admitted African Americans without restriction, it was the place where African Americans were taken in emergency situations, including police shootings and racially motivated attacks.[20] So the sisters who staffed the emergency room of Good Samaritan Hospital saw and treated the victims of the worst of Selma's racial violence in the 1950s and 1960s, including police violence, lynchings, racist beatings, and random acts of terrorism.

Institutions such as the mission school and the hospital would have been taken-for-granted components of parish life in the North, evidence either of the fund-raising talent of a mother superior or the ambitions of the local bishop. But the scarcity of Catholics in Selma, as in much of the deep South, meant that medical and educational institutions run by sisters were unique. And because sisters provided services that otherwise systematically were denied to African Americans in Selma—medical care, education, social services, and vocational training—these institutions also implicitly challenged established social structures.

In fact, sisters in Selma often did things in their work that were considered scandalous within the ethos of Jim Crow. They made social calls to black homes in East Selma. The first sisters often walked the streets of East Selma, stopping to visit whenever invited to do so in their effort to raise the visibility of the mission and produce converts. Typical entries in the early years of the convent chronicle record that "they walked down Lawrence Street and so on, visiting different houses in that poorest part of town."[21] Sisters entered the homes of African Americans, received hospitality from them, and occasionally took meals in the homes of their parishioners.[22] Sisters were particularly attentive to the elderly and the ill, who often required physical care and assistance managing domestic details such as cleaning and cooking. "Yesterday we cleaned the home of a Negro woman paralyzed in both limbs," sisters reported to the motherhouse in New York in one example of this work:

> You can scarcely imagine the condition of the bed in which she lay. In order to make her comfortable we proceeded as follows: We solicited a mattress from a mattress dealer and this, together with blankets which had already been sent, and four sheets which we made, took care of the bed. Then we secured pails, brooms, chlorox, rubber gloves and masks and finally a colored woman to help us. We took the beds apart, cleaned them out in the yard (the water was heated in a large black kettle in the yard), and destroyed the bedclothes. Inside, we brushed down the walls, washed the windows and scrubbed the floor with a broom.[23]

Sisters' unselfconscious presence in black homes was unusual for the time, but their work performing domestic tasks in the homes of African Americans stood in marked contrast to the typical racialized arrangement of domestic labor in the South. Such domestic work was a regular feature of sisters' activities among the Catholic poor in the North. But in Selma, where the domestic service of African American women in white homes reinforced social and class distinctions that accompanied segregation, domestic work by sisters inverted racialized patterns of class and labor, indirectly challenging a presumed arrangement of white dominance.[24] The rigid social boundaries between white and black under Jim Crow transformed ordinary missionary activities—tending to sick bodies, entering homes to give catechism lessons, opening parish schools—into acts of social transgression.

"Are You the White Sisters or the Black Sisters?"

If Selma's segregation altered the meaning of sisters' work, it also affected sisters' racial identification. Until the founding of the Saint Elizabeth mission there was only one Catholic parish in Selma, the Church of the Assumption, a small congregation with a school staffed by the Sisters of Mercy. With the birth of Saint Elizabeth's mission, the two Catholic churches quickly became identified by the racial composition of their congregations rather than by the respective parish names. Saint Elizabeth's was "the black church"; Assumption, "the white church." Townspeople, parishioners, and even the sisters themselves adopted these segregating designations. For example, the convent chronicle reports that the "Christmas crib" display the priests built in the side yard of Saint Elizabeth's attracted much attention, including that of a white boy who "wanted to know if the 'White Church' would have one too."[25] From their first year in Selma, the Sisters of Saint Joseph used the racialized name "white church" to refer to the Assumption parish. In 1940 the sisters wrote about their first opportunity to participate in the rite of confession in the convent chronicle, "We had confession today. Father Dolan from the white church is our confessor."[26] Sisters who had lived in Selma still, today, refer to the Church of the Assumption as "the white church."[27] Sisters employed these labels without irony, seemingly unaware of ways that the labels "white church" and "black church" operated to naturalize segregation in the church, implying that white Catholics and black Catholics inhabited ontologically distinct categories.

Segregated classifications were applied also to the sisters who staffed each parish school: the Sisters of Mercy at the Church of the Assumption were more commonly known as "the white sisters" and the Sisters of Saint Joseph at Saint Elizabeth's as "the black sisters," despite the color of their skin. The salience of race in a segregated social climate and its centrality to classifications and identity in midcentury Selma is evident in how these labels were applied contrary to the obvious, visual fact that the Sisters of Mercy wore a black habit and most of the Sisters of Saint Joseph wore a white mission habit. Thus, despite the fact that in most locations, orders of religious are casually identified by the color of their religious garb—Maryknolls are frequently referred to as "gray nuns," for example—in Selma, the "white sisters" wore black, and the "black sisters" frequently wore white.

The designation "black sisters" complicated sisters' experiences of themselves as religious and further destabilized the already volatile religious and gender identities that women religious inhabited. In the Catholic cosmology that divided the world between sacred and profane and the Church into clergy and laity, sisters fit into neither category. Until the Second Vatican Council officially clarified the ecclesiastical status of women religious, both theologically and in practice sisters occupied an interstitial category in the organizational structure of the Church. Possessing neither lay nor ordained status, women religious occupied a cultural location somewhere between lay and religious realms, a location that unfortunately lacked both the social freedom of the laity and the religious authority of the clergy. Despite doctrines of complementarity that stressed the unique obligations and contributions of male and female religious within the Church, Catholic priests, particularly those in positions of authority, often regarded sisters as wards of the Church rather than as spiritual colleagues. Some priests infantilized sisters, treating them as spiritual charges.

Catholic laity also regarded sisters as markedly different from themselves spiritually. Deference to sisters was deeply embedded in Catholic social practice, as much in the South as it was elsewhere in America.

Such deference was instilled in parochial school classrooms, performed in social rituals and gestures, and perpetuated in social institutions like the parish and devotional societies. But lay deference to women religious reified perceptions that sisters were not quite human. Regulations of enclosure that prohibited sisters from engaging in rudimentary tasks of human maintenance such as eating or sleeping in the presence of laity further reinforced the unearthliness of their image and provided a rationale for their segregation from laity.

The gender of sisters was equally unclear. Though certainly not considered male, sisters were not clearly female either, according to the gender norms of American Catholicism. Because women religious were not sexually available to men for marriage or candidates for childbearing, they stood outside the Catholic ideal that held up Marianism as a model of female identity and equated womanhood with motherhood. Certain conventions of religious life further reinforced such ungendered views of sisters. The substantial religious habit sisters were obligated to wear obscured their physical characteristics, hiding corporeality generally and sexual characteristics specifically. By enshrouding women in layers of black and white cloth, the habit disembodied sisters faces and desexualized their bodies. Furthermore, sisters often were given male names-in-religion. Thus a woman religious was as likely to be called "Sister Bernard" as she was "Sister Bernadette." At times sisters' in-between status functioned as a barrier between themselves and others. Sisters report feeling that, despite the fact that they interacted with diverse groups of people, they never truly belonged anywhere outside the enclave of the convent. The inconclusive race of sisters in Selma added an additional layer to their already liminal religious and gender identities. "We were in every way an exotic bird," commented Sister Barbara Lumm on the social position of sisters in Selma.[28]

Though sisters' in-between qualities tended to isolate them in traditional Catholic settings, in Selma the vagueness of their race and gender enhanced their work by making it possible for sisters occasionally to transcend social categories. Sisters' protean identities functioned as a kind of camouflage that allowed sisters to move unnoticed between discrete racial and religious worlds. If sisters did not fit clearly into one racial category or another—if they were "inconclusively white," to borrow a phrase from Matthew Frye Jacobson—they also were less likely to be perceived as transgressing racial boundaries when they interacted with African Americans.[29] And if Catholic sisters were both inconclusively white and not clearly women, then they definitely were not *white women,* an especially fraught category under the perverse cultural logic of Jim Crow. Thus, sisters' general ambiguity allowed them to fly below the radar of white supremacy, to interact with and live in close proximity to African American men without eliciting violent responses from white supremacists.

Sisters' sense of blackness was enhanced by their historic and theological identification with the poor, most of whom, in Selma, were black. Sisters employed theological language to underscore the bonds they believed knit them together with Selma's blacks—particularly black Catholics of Saint Elizabeth's parish who were, even by the most conservative definition of the Catholic doctrine of the Mystical Body of Christ, co-members with sisters of Christ's Body. Sisters' sense of nonwhiteness was further deepened by their horror at the behavior of Selma's whites. When confronted with acts of violence and terror, sisters drew back even further from white society and the privileges of whiteness.

The designation "black sisters" also affirmed a sense of religious vocation among the SSJs. These sisters interpreted their identification with African Americans as a sign that their mission activities were successful.[30] One sister described her pride at being included in a segregated group of black nurses:

> I was very honored one time—this was right after the civil rights act—and a whole group of us from the hospital went to donate blood at a Red Cross blood bank. It probably was the first time that people had ever come together to donate blood, and so we all donated and then sat down together at a table, and we were ushered to this table and that's where the orange juice was, there were white people around at other tables. And one of the nurses said, "Oh sister, lookit, are they segregating all of us black people again?" And I thought, "Well, I'm included in this and it's pretty nice."[31]

Sisters often chose to describe the interpersonal effects of their complicated racial status through anecdotes about their relationships with African American children (for whom sisters' race might well have been confusing, given the strangeness of the habit and the fact of sisters' residence in segregated neighborhoods). The stories sisters told ranged from tales of a child's uncertainty about a particular sister's race—as when the convent chronicle reported that "little Shirley Mae George" interrupted a hand game she was playing with a sister and, "taking Sister's hand in both her tiny ones, she held it up close to her face and said, 'Sister, why yo hand white?' "[32]—to others in which children resisted the possibility of the sisters' whiteness. In their annual report to Monsignor John S. Randall of the Rochester diocese, the SSJs described a little girl in Saint Elizabeth's school who approached her teacher after class and said, "Sister, if you get much lighter, folks are going to think you are a white lady."[33] A sister's racial ambiguity served in other narratives to underscore the closeness between a sister and a child. Sister Remigia, for example, remembered one conversation with Johnny Manassa, an orphan who lived with the sisters from age four until he died at age twelve. "He had ahold of my finger one day," Sister Remigia recalled, "and he looked at it and said, 'Sister Megia, you fittin to turn white?' I said, 'Johnny, I am white.' I was covered up in the habit and he never realized I was white . . . he used to say 'sister is my mama.'"[34]

The designation "black sisters" did not mean that the SSJs became "black," of course. The salience of whiteness under Jim Crow was too powerful to be so easily erased. However, the SSJs' whiteness was in some circumstances certainly obscured or complicated by their association in the minds of white Selmians with the black side of Selma's racial divide. "We most definitely are NOT neutral," wrote Sister Mary Paul Geck, in a similar vein, from the Selma mission in 1965. "For all practical purposes we are 'Negroes' living in a Negro community."[35]

Because the title "black sisters" identified women religious with African American citizens of Selma, it did serve at times to mark sisters as no longer entitled to the privileges of whiteness in a racist society. In letters to the motherhouse and to fellow sisters in New York, SSJs in Selma told diverse stories of racial discrimination and derision in public spaces. The SSJs grew accustomed to the more benign expressions of racism that some white Selmians directed at them as the "black sisters," including hard stares on the streets and taunts from passing motorists. In one characteristic account of these incidents, Sister Paul Marie Dougherty's memoir relates that a "truck driver, driving down Broad Street, stared at us, even turning around to continue staring at us as he drove along."[36] Sister Remigia and Sister Louis Bertrand reported that as they were shopping one day in Selma in the early 1960s they were approached by a clerk who tartly inquired, "Are you the white sisters or the black sisters?"[37] The SSJ convent was marked in 1950 by a sign hung by the Ku Klux Klan on the convent door that read, "The KKK is watching you."[38] "The work being done here by the Catholic Church is at least gaining local recognition," one sister remarked sarcastically about the incident in a report letter to Monsignor Randall, "for last February our plant was one of a group that were marked with KKK stickers. Several colored people, particularly the more prominent ones, received notices from the same organization to get out of town. No reasons were given—they could be deducted. If you were Colored and succeeded or if you helped the Colored to succeed you have no part in our living."[39] In such statements, sisters acknowledged that their associations with African Americans made them targets of white supremacist hatred.

Sisters were not always passive in these encounters with Selma's white power structure. The Sisters of Saint Joseph learned to manipulate the malleability of their interstitial racial position in Selma and to move purposefully between black and white worlds and between black and white identities, "passing" as black or white as situations required. Racial passing—the intentional manipulation of racial symbols and racial identity in order to claim the social location of a particular racial category—was a strategic practice for sisters. Sisters learned to embrace blackness in situations where they needed to cultivate the trust of African Americans or when such trust attributed legitimacy to their mission. They learned to claim whiteness in situations of duress, or while fund-raising, or when acting in professional medical capacities. This strategic deployment of whiteness was particularly helpful when sisters faced religious and civil authorities such as the bishop or the police.[40]

Sisters' manipulation of racial categories found its clearest expression at the voting booth. By the time the Southern Christian Leadership Conference voter-registration drive accelerated in Selma in the early 1960s, the SSJs had learned to use their racial malleability to attempt to leverage small political concessions for African Americans. Because most sisters were assigned to the Selma mission for a specific number of years, rotating through Selma from the SSJ motherhouse in Rochester and then back, newly arrived sisters at the Selma mission had to register to vote in Dallas County. Sister Mary Paul Geck, the superior at the Selma convent from 1962 to 1967, encouraged Saint Elizabeth's parishioners and Good Samaritan Hospital staff to register to vote, and sisters from the convent often went to the registration office in the company of black neighbors and colleagues from the hospital.[41] Sisters believed that at times their unclear racial status confounded the categorizations that were central to Jim Crow, introducing temporary ambiguity into the registration and voting process and perhaps undermining the wholesale disfranchisement of African Americans. Sisters also assumed that their presence in line, witnessing the actions of officials, occasionally influenced registrars to refrain from more extreme tactics of intimidation. One sister vividly recalled her first attempt to register, including the patterns through which registration officers were "just slowing this down so that they didn't register very many people at a time":

> We went down before nine in the morning—Sister Liguori, and Evelyn Merrit, who worked in our business office and was a woman of color. The three of us went down to register to vote, and we stood in line until three in the afternoon, and the registrars would stop and go for coffee. Then they would stop and take coffee down the hall to somebody else, and they did this all in the very nicest way, as if it were normal, as if this was sane to have a hundred and some people standing in line and you would close your office and leave and say, "Well, it's time for coffee," "It's time Mrs. So and So doesn't have any coffee so we're going to take some down to her." They just, they just did it. And they had the power to do it. And we stayed in line. Nobody left. Everybody stayed there.[42]

Sisters employed their racial ambiguity at the polls, too, and subsequently encountered discrimination. "We were voting over at the firehouse," Sister Saint Joseph recalled, "so, what did they hand out, but pencils that could be erased and we had to write leaning on the fenders of firetrucks. We stayed until all the people who could vote were done. We weren't very popular."[43] Voting officials attempted to prevent all of the SSJs from voting in the 1964 presidential election, claiming that they had failed to pay poll taxes for years in which they had not voted. Sister Mary Paul Geck, who as local superior was responsible for such payments, stayed at the polling site throughout the afternoon, insisting that the sisters be allowed to vote. Dallas County election officials relented ten minutes before polls closed and allowed the sisters to vote after Sister Geck paid the fraudulent fees.[44]

Sisters did not tell such stories in order to suggest that they endured levels of racial discrimination similar to African Americans in Selma. Sisters readily acknowledged that encounters like the ones discussed above gave them a small and admittedly incomplete taste of the experiences of discrimination endured by their African American neighbors and colleagues. Sister Barbara Lumm described the complicated racial position sisters inhabited in Selma in terms of unstable but real racial privilege: "No doubt we were in a position of privilege most of the time, simply by being white, being from the North, being connected to the Church, but it was a shaky position of privilege. I mean, we certainly weren't treated in the way that I know black people were treated. We were never treated in those ways."[45]

Rather, tales of discrimination served a narrative function for the sisters, emphasizing their integration into Selma's African American communities and the effect of Selma on their later perspectives about religious life. Stories of discrimination placed sisters on the other side of Selma's racial division, making them objects of the humiliations and discriminations visited upon African Americans. Stories of voting fraud placed sisters close to the issue that was the central focus of the civil rights movement in Dallas County.

The Sisters of Saint Joseph's identification with their black neighbors in Selma was not absolute. Rather, interspersed among anecdotes about racial solidarity, the convent chronicle contains passages that preserve a definite cultural and religious distance between sisters and African Americans. Mission documents, particularly from the 1940s and 1950s, reflect sisters' awareness that their neighbors were quite different from themselves in some respects. "Life here in Alabama is like living in another country," wrote Sister Mary Christopher to friends in the Rochester convent, "or at least seems that way when you consider the political and religious atmosphere around us."[46]

Tabernacle Baptist Church next door to the Selma convent was the object of much of sisters' initial fascination with African American life and remained a frequent subject of entries in the convent chronicle through the 1940s. Preconciliar regulations that prohibited Catholics from entering non-Catholic churches limited sisters' experience of African American religious forms to what they could overhear from the Baptist church across a narrow ally from the convent. A chronicle passage from the month sisters first arrived in Selma comments: "After our own boisterous services we were amused by the rather boisterous ones next door in the Baptist Church. The pastor sounds amazingly like a bull."[47] The different religious practices of their Baptist neighbors fascinated the SSJs. Sisters listened closely to the Baptists next door, interpreting the sounds of worship that penetrated the convent walls in a comparative framework in relation to their own Catholic liturgical tradition. "It seems to be a big day in the Baptist temple. They had about four Baptisms by immersion," the chronicle records in August 1941. "We could hear the words distinctly pronounced as we say them except for adding 'Amen.' A woman 'got' religion too and let out a blood-curdling scream."[48] To this day sisters from the Selma convent still recall the best locations in the convent for eavesdropping on the religious world next door.

In the chronicle and in correspondence with sisters in the North, the SSJs repeated anecdotes that highlighted cultural differences between sisters' speech patterns and those of their black parishioners. "Lulu Owens came to the convent with two broilers as a gift," one such entry records. "She told us that she 'was rejoiceful to say' that her house was cleaner than it had been when the Sisters made their first visit." The entry then mimics this language, concluding, "The sisters were rejoiceful to hear it."[49] Another passage describes two sisters' conversation with a woman who visited the convent clothing thrift shop "to buy a hat to wear to Mass." Two sisters accompanied the woman to the shop and "fitted her out with shoes and an uninteresting brown lumpy hat which the lady thought 'would suit cuz I'm a settled woman.' "[50] Though the attention sisters paid in their correspondence to linguistic differences was due in part to their desire to describe what was different about Selma to sisters who lived in New York, the prominence of such anecdotes in the convent chronicle, as a document recording both the mundane and the important events in the day-to-day life of the convent, reflected the extent to which sisters were trying, at the time, to explain to themselves how and why African Americans were different than themselves.

These tales were rarely mocking. The tone of the anecdotes was mostly playful and amused, rendering the exotic in a familiar framework, reminiscent of the tales sisters told in other contexts about comical things a particular student might say in catechism class. "It poured and poured all day long," one sister began her story. "While going over to the office I met a little tyke about ten years old without rubbers, umbrella, or any protection against the driving rain. Over his shoulders was slung a potato sack half-full of scattered hunks of coal—picked up on the railroad, no doubt. He walked with me a bit under my umbrella."[51] In some anecdotes, however, sisters found no familiar comparison for their encounters with African Americans, and in these stories sisters described the unexpected in encounters with African Americans in the South through a kind of anthropological curiosity and exoticism. Sisters' occasional sightseeing trips to rural Alabama yielded many such anecdotes, rendered in the language a tourist might use in a foreign country. On one such trip a sister was confused by the complexity of race within families. "We also took a picture of a hut and a colored woman with eight children," she wrote. "Two of the youngsters had blonde hair and blue eyes—otherwise they were like the rest."[52] When the Sisters of Mercy—the "white sisters"—took the Sisters of Saint Joseph on a tour of the countryside between Selma and Mobile, the sisters stopped to explore a "colored cemetery":

> We were surprised to see pitchers, platters, and other pieces of China gracing the tops of the graves. The sister explained that the departed especially treasured these trinkets and it would be a desecration for anyone to use them, hence, they were placed as ornaments on the grave. It makes one feel very far from civilization to hear tales of this nature.[53]

The effect of such narrative practices—which clearly borrow from dominant racialized tropes—was to open distance between sisters and Southern blacks.

Jim Crow segregation essentialized and naturalized categories of whiteness and blackness, insisting that all people and all institutions could, indeed must, be classified as either black or white. Threatened by ambiguity, the cultural logic of segregation resisted nuance, denied exception, and punished transgression. By occasionally transgressing and confounding categories of white and black, the Sisters of Saint Joseph posed a direct challenge to the tidy classifications of segregation.

"A High Price to Pay for Freedom"

Because rules of enclosure typically confined sisters' activities to a narrowly proscribed religious world, sisters frequently experienced Jim Crow segregation not in the public face that people associate with segregation—with prohibitions from public space and public accommodations, or substandard "colored" restrooms, or "whites only" restaurants—but where it intersected directly with their limited spheres of movement within the African American community, in the black neighborhood where their parish, convent, and school were located and on the grounds of the black-oriented hospital and nursing school. Thus sisters most often encountered segregation not as boundaries and prohibitions—or even, most directly, as privileges attached to whiteness—but in its effects on African Americans, in the ways segregation harmed people who were their fellow parishioners or co-workers, their pupils in class, or their patients in Good Samaritan Hospital. In their work providing medical and educational services to Selma's black community, the SSJs witnessed firsthand the many horrors visited upon African Americans under Jim Crow segregation. Sisters saw the violence inflicted daily on the bodies of African Americans, and they understood the relationship between human misery and segregation because they had fed hungry children, stitched wounded workers, and buried murdered men.

Sisters were shocked by the economic deprivation in which Selma's African Americans lived. Their accounts of the Selma mission return again and again to descriptions of this distress. One sister described African American poverty through an anecdote about a student's generosity: "Clarence George, third grade pupil, went home tonight and did some work earning his $.06 which he promptly brought to the convent to put in the poor box. The poor lad was himself wearing a pair of men's shoes."[54] "The parishioners who have remained in Selma are making a living for themselves, but certainly, for the most part, still do not enjoy the financial or social benefits accorded to their brethren who have moved elsewhere," one sister noted. "There are still far too many who have to turn to the Fathers and Sisters for food, clothing and emergency financial help."[55] Sisters witnessed how black families in the South often experienced all at once hunger, illness, inadequate housing, unstable sources of income, and dangers posed either by a lack of heat or from makeshift heating units, and they knew that these multiple layers of poverty-related issues compounded the burden and damage of each upon people's lives.

Most immediately, sisters could see hunger and malnutrition in their fellow parishioners and neighbors and in the children who came to the school and hospital. In the daily records of the convent, stories abound of children who were diagnosed with malnutrition at the hospital. Food was a central component of sister's visits with the sick and typical descriptions of home visits always included food offerings. "We left food for the invalid and her children," a sister recorded of one such stop.[56] Sisters also refused hospitality in the homes of parishioners for fear of depleting scarce food resources. "The mother was getting supper," sisters reported after one visit. "She took a small casserole from the oven. She asked us to stay for supper; of course we said no, making the excuse that we had to get back. We remembered she had four children to feed and food was scarce enough."[57] Sisters also encountered hungry children in their classrooms at the parish school. Hunger was common in the experience of children in the parish school, surfacing even in schoolwork, as the boy whose English composition about Thanksgiving ended: "I hope we will go away for Thanksgiving dinner, because if we do not there will not be enough to go around."[58]

Sisters' representations of the poverty of Selma's blacks often were framed by descriptions of the inadequate houses or shacks in which people lived. Sister Mary Corgan described typical Selma housing in terms of what it lacked. "We ate in poor shacks," she recalled some years later, "inadequate heating, with no screens to keep out bugs and flies, no running water, phone, radio or electricity."[59] Because home visits, particularly to the sick, were part of the sisters' regular mission activities, they also understood the relationship of inadequate housing to chronic illness, the effect on the body of drafty rooms, poor sanitation, no public utilities, and constant battles against insects and rodents. "We now talk about having an 'option for the poor,'" Sister Dorothy Quin commented in a memoir of her Selma days, prepared in 1989:

> I don't believe the majority of us know what poor is. I didn't know until I stumbled into the South—our Alabama mission. We had children living in raw wood shacks up on stilts. Everything seemed to be upon stilts. I never got into one of those old houses until one day Sister Mary Paul asked me to go with her to visit an old, sick lady she was worried about. Sister was bringing her some supper. When we got inside, I saw it was just like the outside, with weather-beaten old rough wood. She lay on a shabby old bed; there was a pot-bellied stove used for heating in which she burned coke. A little dresser was her place to store dishes. I still think of that little room. Near the ceiling were cobwebs which stood out because the coke dust which had settled over them had outlined each one.[60]

Their medical training deepened sisters' sense of the interrelationship between poverty and illness. A typical midwinter entry in the convent chronicle reads: "Visited the sick. Came across a youngster about twelve, sick in bed. The baby of the family was in bed with the patient, under the covers to keep warm."[61] Another January record tersely notes: "Very cold. Visited Emma Gillum—no fire—not cared for, in bed."[62]

At Good Samaritan Hospital the sisters directly encountered the toll that white racism exacted on the bodies of African Americans, particularly on the fragile bodies of African American newborns and the emaciated or burned bodies of older children. Convent records detail alarmingly high infant mortality rates, requiring frequent emergency baptism of endangered newborns. Entries registering baptisms and infant burials are among the most common in the convent chronicle:

> June 29: Sister Frances Marie baptized twin babies at the hospital. Other twin died later without baptism.
>
> June 30: Father Casey baptized three week old baby at hospital.
>
> July 17: Infantile Paralysis boy patient given last sacraments and died.
>
> July 27: In evening Sisters Lucina, Frances Marie and Alma Joseph went to see Sister Anastasia at Baptist Hospital. While there learned of boy dying at Good Samaritan. Returned quickly. Sister Alma Joseph baptized boy.
>
> August 27: Baby died in hospital. Baptized by Sister Anastasia.[63]

The precarious health of newborn black infants in Good Samaritan Hospital required the constant vigilance of sisters, who were religiously obligated to see that none died unbaptized. Johnny Manassa, an orphaned boy who lived at the hospital for eight years, became so accustomed to cycles of birth, baptism, and death in the pediatric ward that sisters relied on his ability to monitor infants and alert them when one was in danger. Sisters eventually allowed Johnny to perform emergency baptisms.

Older children presented a different consequence of poverty to the nurses at Good Samaritan. The open fireplaces that were the main source of heat in many African American homes posed special risks to children, who suffered burns by coming into accidental contact with flames. "As the Red Cross worker carried little Bessie Allen into the children's ward, a familiar but lamentable sight greeted our eyes," one sister wrote in 1951:

> Bessie had been burned at home and came here to join the ranks of those poor, deformed, sad-eyed children, who spend months with us in their fight for life. . . . Her thick long braids had to be cut-off because of the extent of her burns and her frail body is almost completely hidden by bandages. . . . Bessie is often asked how she was burned and her reply is always the same, "The fire jumped on me." In reality she fell into an open fireplace in her home.[64]

Because burn injuries were so numerous and required special care, the sisters reserved a special portion of the children's ward solely for burned children. Sisters understood that poverty marked bodies with fire. One sister wrote, "We have some children who come to us with arms or legs burned off or faces horribly burned and which will result in scars to be carried on them for life."[65] In tending to the bodies of children, sisters encountered the ways that segregation stamped children's bodies with malnutrition, illness, and burns.

In nursing adult bodies, sisters saw up close the violence against African Americans that underscored and reinforced segregation. Stories about racial violence were common elements in the letters of the Selma sisters to the motherhouse in Rochester. Interspersed with reports of stifling heat, mosquitoes, and other elements of life in the South, the sisters' stories of Selma's violence have an air of weary ubiquity in their letters. Seemingly offhand references to racist violence—"A colored man was shot by a policeman out front tonight"—are scattered throughout the convent chronicle.[66] Sister Mary Christopher included the following anecdote in her letter to a sister back in New York in 1965: "A negro child too young to be considered illiterate, just couldn't read the sign at 5 years of age, and so was beaten by the owner of the restaurant whose bathroom facility the child used . . . The sign read NO NEGROES."[67]

Good Samaritan was the place where African Americans were taken in emergency situations, specifically after police shootings or racially motivated beatings. The sisters who staffed the hospital emergency room saw the worst of Selma's racial violence. "I remember a young man who had been beaten up," reflected Sister Barbara Lumm, who served as a nurse in Selma in the 1960s:

> He had been stopped by a group of white men—these are all probably in their nineteens, twenties—this man was probably twenty or twenty-two. He'd been driving at night and had been stopped by a group of seven or eight white youths who had a light on their car so he thought he was being stopped by the police. They beat him up, as a result he lost an eye. He was black and they caught him, and that was what they did to him.[68]

In procedural emergency room interviews sisters heard stories about the randomness and viciousness of white attacks on African Americans for being in the wrong place at the wrong time, or simply just for being. "Just before the Civil Rights Act there was an old man who came in with a broken hip to the hospital," one sister remembered, "and he and his wife told me that this would be the first time in sixty-five years that they had ever slept apart. And the way that his hip got broken was in a gas station, some young white got mad at him for some reason and knocked him over. This was an old man, and it was a young white man who did this to him."[69]

One might think that after forty years such stories would take on a rote quality. But to the sisters who faced the blood, injuries, and the sheer physical brutality of racist violence in the South—whose job it was to stitch wounds and reset bones—these stories continue to resonate with the powerful emotions of sorrow and rage. In interview conversations, sisters pause and at times weep when retelling these stories, perhaps signaling the graveness of the situation, respect for the distress of the victims, and maybe, too, the difficulty of reimmersion in the emotions that attended these experiences. In one characteristic interview conversation about racial violence in Selma, Sister Lumm recalled attending Jimmy Lee Jackson, civil rights demonstrator, while he was hospitalized at Good Samaritan for a gunshot wound suffered while defending his mother from a racially motivated attack following a civil rights march in nearby Marion, Alabama, in February of 1965. Jackson eventually died in the intensive-care ward of Good Samaritan Hospital. "I took care of him for several days before he died," Sister Lumm began with a strong voice, "and he was clear until about the last day or so, and he would say, 'Sister, don't you think this is a high price to pay for freedom?' " Sister Lumm's voice cracked as she spoke the word "freedom," and she paused, looking away and weeping for a moment at the memory. "It just always gets to me," she whispered apologetically and then paused again to weep. "Well, anyway, that was," she began, and then her voice again trailed off into tears. After several moments sitting silently, wiping her eyes and collecting herself, Sister Lumm finally was able to continue her narrative, "that was when the voter registration meetings really heated up."[70] In such unguarded moments it is clear how profoundly the human toll of Selma's racial violence affected sisters. It shaped their experience of the South in the 1960s and their responses to the civil rights movement there, and it left indelible marks on sisters' memories and psyches.

While Good Sam's emergency room exposed sisters to the sheer physical brutality inherent in white supremacy, it also exposed them, in the reactions of police and white doctors, to subtler elements of condescension and intimidation that perpetuated racial inequality. Sister-nurses at Good Samaritan learned about the complicity of local police in allowing, and often conspiring in, violence against African Americans. "One day a man was brought into the emergency room with a gunshot wound to the chest," Sister Paul Marie Dougherty recalled years later. "He had been sleeping in the bus station on a bench while waiting for his bus. A police officer roughly awakened him. The man, confused by sleep, resisted and the police officer shot him in the chest. The life of a Negro was not worth much in Selma pre-1960s."[71]

In their emergency-room conversations sisters also came face to face with Selma's intransigently racist legal system. Describing the emergency-room scene as sisters admitted a young black man who had been brutally beaten in a racially motivated attack, Sister Mary Paul Geck reflected, "There was just no thought that there was any police or anybody to go to make a complaint about this. It just wasn't in anybody's thinking that there was some justice that would happen about this."[72] Sister Lumm recalled the impotence she felt the first time she attended the admission of a beating victim to the emergency room:

> I said to the doctor who was taking care of him, "Shouldn't the police, shouldn't somebody be notified?" He said, "Oh, you don't want to get into this kind of stuff"—this is a white doctor saying this—"There's nothing that can be done." And when you think of any kind of violence like this, you'd expect that the police would be, I mean, there was nobody, white or black, thought that the police were going to do something on behalf of a black victim.[73]

On another level, white doctors exhibited overt racism themselves toward black patients and black colleagues on the hospital staff. One day a black x-ray technician at Good Samaritan talked back to a white doctor. That night the technician came to see Sister Louis Bertrand to explain that he was leaving town before the Ku Klux Klan came to punish him. "He was in such fear," she recalled. "I don't know if this white doctor would have done anything to that kid, he just left. He was afraid something would happen to him or his family—so he just left. They lived in fear."[74] Such incidents revealed the extent to which racial intimidation operated even within a hospital whose purpose was to serve African Americans.

Racial violence laid bare the many layers of institutional complicity among Selma's whites—in the police, the courts, the press, and sometimes even in the white doctors who worked at Good Samaritan—and placed sisters in the uncomfortable position of mediating between African Americans and the white power structure. The hospital, as both a place of sisters' ministry and a place of public accommodation, was the point where the black world of the mission parish and the white-dominated town met. The private world of sisters' religious work intersected with the larger context of Selma's racial polarization in the emergency room of Good Samaritan Hospital; it was there that sisters faced the essential incompatibility of their approach to race—an orientation that was central to their religious work—with the public standards of conduct that were expected of them as white women in the South. The tensions inherent in the sisters' complicated social location, in between black and white worlds, were intensified on the occasions when local plantation owners brought black workers who had been injured in the fields to the hospital for treatment. One sister recalled that her naiveté about the mission hospital was challenged the day that a white plantation owner brought a forty-year-old woman to the hospital:

> She was quite sick, and he [the plantation owner] said to me, "I brought my girl in." So I looked at this woman who was twice my age and was dumbfounded by the fact that he had called her a girl. I said to the doctor who was going to operate on this woman, I said, "That man called her a girl." And the doctor looked at me like I needed a little educating, "There's a little cultural awareness that you haven't taken on." I just remember thinking to myself, "I guess I won't bring that up again." It was very unwelcome.[75]

Caught between the infantalizing rhetoric of the plantation owner and the complicit approval of the doctor for racist conventions, the sister learned that the hospital occupied a different social place than the parish and school. In the annoyed look of the doctor, she also learned the social consequences of questioning racist talk in places considered the public domain.

White doctors at times attempted to train sisters in the ways of whiteness, enforcing rules of interaction in the hospital setting that were common in Selma's public spheres and rebuking sisters who failed to adhere to racial codes. When asked to describe ways that she witnessed interactions among black and white non-Catholics, Sister Barbara Lumm responded with an anecdote about a doctor at the hospital: "I remember there was a legend of one of the doctors who was a very religious person, a white doctor, who said to Sister Remigia, 'Don't you ever "Miss" a nigger to me!' She called one of the nurses Miss So-and-So, and he, in front of whoever was there, said that to her."[76] Because they relied on the professional labor provided by the few white doctors in Selma who were willing to treat African Americans, sisters felt unable to challenge the openly racist behavior exhibited by doctors. To do so, they believed, would have meant jeopardizing the medical care available to Selma's blacks and thus coming "at someone else's expense" as one sister put it.[77]

Though their intimacy with African Americans was accepted by Selma's whites if it occurred within the black neighborhood or black community, sisters who ventured into certain public places in the company of blacks were expected to display their whiteness by not mixing with blacks in ways that would violate norms of segregation. Thus sisters had to learn how to exist within the norms of behavior and the culture of black Selma, in which they were included at times, and they had to learn to manage in a segregated white world that occasionally expected them to adhere to Jim Crow behaviors. At Good Samaritan Hospital, a setting far more public than the mission parish and school, sisters encountered limits to their identification with African Americans and the limits white supremacy placed upon their "blackness." In the hospital, where sisters were in the presence of white doctors and often white police in the emergency room, sisters were expected to enforce segregation, and they were sharply reprimanded when they failed or refused to draw symbolic distance between themselves and African Americans. In the hospital setting, where sisters were expected to tolerate, if not adhere to, racist social conventions, they also learned strategic silence and strategic complicity. On the eve of Bloody Sunday, sisters literally bit their tongues as the doctors who stitched injured marchers chastised the wounded for "stirring up trouble."[78] As sisters learned strategies for managing the conflict between their religious beliefs and the white power structure, they also learned patterns of behavior that would shape their reactions to the civil rights conflicts that would happen in Selma in 1965, and ultimately their responses to the Catholic magisterium in the 1970s.

"You Didn't Know What Was Going to Happen"

Against this backdrop of white supremacist terror and violence, civil rights organizing in Selma accelerated in late 1964 and early 1965. The Student Nonviolent Coordinating Committee (SNCC) had developed a strategy for the state of Alabama that focused on organizing voter registration in rural areas and small towns, where African Americans often were in the majority.[79] SNCC had been present in Selma since 1962, working to organize a grassroots community movement in Selma for desegregation and voting rights. The Sisters of Saint Joseph watched the emergent civil rights movement in their neighborhood and parish, excited and curious about the changes afoot but also fearful of increased violence against African Americans.

Though Brown Chapel on Sylvan Street would become the epicenter of civil rights activity in Selma during the dramatic events of 1965, the initial meetings in 1963 were located in the Tabernacle Baptist on Broad Street, across the convent alley. "They were right next door," Sister Barbara Lumm explained. "The very first one, the pastor of the Baptist Tabernacle next to us, Reverend Anderson, was . . . the only one brave enough at first to let the voter registration people come and use his church."[80] Much as in years past when sisters had paid close attention to the sounds of worship coming from the tabernacle, in the early 1960s the SSJs were able to hear much of the initial voter-registration mass meetings from their "listening places" in the convent. When asked if she remembered anything specific from the meetings, Sister Barbara recalled the speaker inviting the white sheriff, who had come to intimidate the congregants, to join the assembly:

> We could hear whoever was leading it saying to Sheriff Clark, "Sheriff Clark you are welcome here, too. You don't have to stand in the back. You can have a seat." I can just imagine him standing back there with his billy club in hand and his hand on his pistol. He was very macho, very white supremacist. So they were inviting him in, they were very polite.[81]

The narrative juxtaposition of the nonviolence of black activists to the intimidation and violence of the white resistance, evident in this memory, is a common theme in sisters' accounts of the early civil rights meetings in Selma. Sisters' memories of these early mass meetings were shaped by their awareness of the dangers blacks faced resisting white supremacy.

That Sister Barbara imagines Sheriff Clark—rather than remembers seeing him—underscores ways that preconciliar regulations impeded sisters from direct participation in the mass meetings. Limited by what they could hear through the walls or to the secondhand accounts of colleagues and neighbors, sisters had to use their imaginations to fill in missing details about the civil rights movement as it developed in Selma. That Sister Barbara imagines Sheriff Clark with his hands on his weapons reflects the extent to which those imaginings were shaped by sisters' previous encounters with state-sponsored white supremacist terrorism. They feared that the violence that already permeated life in the Jim Crow South would intensify, touching their neighbors, parishioners, and colleagues.

The few images sisters did gain of the early organizing efforts only reinforced their fears about white violence. Though unable to see inside the church, sisters had an unimpeded view of the scene on Broad Street in front of the Baptist Tabernacle and the convent. Through the convent windows they witnessed the gathering of white law enforcement to intimidate those attending the meetings. "Every posseman, every white deputy from three counties around came in plain clothes and cars and lined the streets and stood on the streets, some of them in uniform with billy clubs," Sister Lumm recalled. She described the scene:

> They simply lined both sides of Broad Street. It felt like as far as you could see. It felt like a horrifying sight to see all of this because you didn't know what was going to happen to the people when they walked out into this. As it was, they walked out just as calmly, in absolute silence, and walked out and walked home, past this, these people holding billy clubs. And people out there, taking photographs of the meeting for their employers, or the employers themselves. It was very intimidating, and the people walked as if there was nothing to fear.[82]

The SSJs were not surprised by the terror that was unleashed on Bloody Sunday. They had seen up close the violence that lay at the core of segregation in Selma.

The sisters also were privy to perspectives within Selma's black community and were familiar with the stories that circulated through it. They knew that Selma had a reputation among African Americans for the viciousness of its segregation. Sister Barbara recalled how black nursing students from Mobile, Alabama, seemed surprised by the racial climate in Selma. "In Mobile, they felt like they could breathe," she described.

> They felt like there was a meanness in Selma. They would say "This is a terrible place. This is a terrible place. Segregation here is very different

> from how it is in Mobile." But I remember being shocked and thinking that Mobile is not that far away that they think this is such a terrible place compared to Mobile. So, they had an idea that racism and segregation was maybe more strictly held, or there was a level of commitment to that that they had not experienced elsewhere.[83]

The SSJs also knew that not every black citizen in Selma welcomed civil rights organizing. Some people believed that "it just couldn't happen" in Selma—that the white power structure could not be forced to end segregation and black disfranchisement, and that it would never do so voluntarily. "It was frightening to people," Sister Lumm commented. "Not everybody thought this was a good idea—the people were afraid for their jobs, they were afraid of violence—and rightly. Sheriff Clark had a very iron hand, and there were stories about his brutality against blacks in the jail."[84] Because they had been schooled in the subtleties of segregation—what to say, what not to do—and were reminded of it often enough by white doctors when they stepped out of bounds, sisters also knew that any remarks or actions that disrupted the status quo could bring terrible retribution against blacks in Selma. The SSJs were aware of the fine line that blacks walked in everyday life—and the consequences of misstepping, of acting out, even just once.

In February of 1965, as the movement accelerated in Alabama, the violence everyone feared finally erupted. In Marion, thirty miles southwest of Selma, a large posse of state troopers and sheriff's deputies attacked a night march at the town square, beating marchers—and nearby reporters—with billy clubs. In the fray, twenty-six-year-old Jimmie Lee Jackson ducked into Mack's Cafe, trying to get medical attention for his grandfather, Cager Lee, who was bleeding from blows to his head. Troopers entered the cafe. When one struck Jackson's mother, Viola Lee, Jackson lunged at him. The trooper slammed Jackson against a cigarette machine and struck him several times before another shot Jackson point-blank in the stomach. Jackson was taken first to Perry County Hospital and then transferred to Good Samaritan Hospital in Selma because Good Samaritan had blood transfusion capabilities Jackson needed. Jackson lingered for five days, dying at Good Sam.[85]

In response to Jackson's murder, SNCC and SCLC leaders organized a memorial march from Selma to the state capitol in Montgomery. As described in the beginning of this chapter, on March 7, 1965, marchers led by Hosea Williams and John Lewis set out from Brown Chapel. As they reached the Pettus Bridge (named after a confederate general), state troopers advanced and attacked. Using clubs and tear gas, the troopers pursued fleeing marchers back into Selma's black neighborhood. Footage of the attack was broadcast across the country that evening, raising national awareness of the tense situation in Selma. In response to the attack, Dr. Martin Luther King Jr. issued a call for concerned people to come to Selma to stand in solidarity with African Americans there. Thousands responded. In the days following Bloody Sunday, as representatives from the SCLC and SNCC attempted to negotiate safe passage for the march to Montgomery to continue, people flooded into Selma, filling Brown Chapel and the streets of East Selma. Mathew Ahmann, executive director of the National Catholic Conference for Interracial Justice, put out his own call for members of Catholic Interracial Councils to come to Selma. Among those who responded were a number of Catholic sisters from various orders, including Margaret Traxler.

The Sisters of Saint Joseph did not participate directly in the protests that followed Bloody Sunday. Years earlier Archbishop Thomas Joseph Toolen of Mobile had threatened that any nun who participated in racial protests "would be on the first bus out of Alabama."[86] Obedient to their bishop's restrictions, the SSJs did not march. Instead, they opened their convent and an empty former ward of Good Samaritan Hospital to house visiting Catholics, particularly the sixty-five visiting sisters. "We were so fortunate in that we had this hospital, and we had the school. We had work that had to be done, but when the march happened and people flooded in from all over the country, we had just moved from the old hospital into a new hospital, and we had not done anything with those vacant wards. They were huge spaces and the beds were still there. And so when the people came we had a place to put, probably, eighty people, at least," remembered Lumm. In addition to continuing their work at the school and hospital—which still had wounded marchers from the previous Sunday—the SSJs picked up visitors from the airport, fed them, and coordinated sleeping arrangements. "I remember one sister who came from California, maybe, whose feet were blistered at the end of the day," an SSJ nurse recalled. "And she came back and I put medicine on her feet and bandaged her in the emergency room the next day before she went back out on those same poor feet."[87]

The SSJs were both heartened and frustrated by the visitors. "It was wonderful seeing all of these people. I didn't even know that there were these numbers of orders of sisters," wrote Sister Mary Paul Geck. Though they were grateful for the visitors, especially for the measure of protection that the presence of whites and the press lent to Selma's blacks, the Sisters of Saint Joseph continued to worry about future violence. They feared that the visitors, many of whom were both untrained in the methods of nonviolent civil disobedience and eager to confront Selma's white authorities, would incite further violence. Sisters visiting from the North, on the other hand, had more of a sense of urgency about the situation, wanting the march to go on. These visitors experienced the immediate shock of immersion in the violence of enforced segregation but without the SSJs ingrained sense of the depth and viciousness of violence that was possible. Among pages of hurried correspondence that the Selma mission exchanged with the motherhouse in New York State in the days following Bloody Sunday is a telegraph that reads simply, "Sister Mary Paul is asking the fervent prayers of our Sisters today. Another March is planed by the colored, reinforced by more than 100 clergy from the North of all denominations. Please pray that there will be no violence or bloodshed."[88]

The SSJs experienced the civil rights activities in Selma in a fundamentally different key than the sisters who visited from the North. If sisters from the North experienced March 1965 in Selma as a major key of bright chords of solidarity, confrontation, and ultimately victory, the SSJs of the Selma mission experienced a tune in a minor key, with echoes of fear and anxiety. They held their breath, as did much of black Selma, when the meetings and voter-registration drive started, anticipating the violent reprisals that had, too often in their experience, followed black self-assertions. The SSJs watched, fearfully, as people left the voter-registration meetings. They privately hoped that the marches would be canceled. They listened fearfully to rumors about violence and tried to prepare for its inevitable arrival. And they tried to dissuade visiting marchers from saying inflammatory things. Familiarity with white supremacist violence made the sisters hesitant and fearful: because they were so familiar with, and dreaded, the effects of white supremacist violence, the SSJs were extremely cautious about the protests, praying for an end to the marches at the same time that they prayed for segregation's end. This placed them in a fundamentally different position to the marches than that of the sisters who came from the North to participate. The SSJs knew that, even more than usual, they must be vigilant, prepared to aid black Selmians who were injured by whites. Sister Mary Christopher wrote to fellow sisters back in Albany, "We just wonder what will happen next. We of course are always ready for any alert. If anything happens, it will probably be after dark."[89] In some ways this familiarity with the ways of white supremacy made the SSJs wiser. They knew the nuances of the racial system and they knew how it could be occasionally finessed or manipulated, for example, to get medical releases for black youth incarcerated at Camp Selma to come to Good Samaritan Hospital.[90] Moreover, they understood the deep fear within Selma's African Americans, knew its causes and its foundations and how the fear had been reinforced in countless ways for generations. They knew that fears of white supremacist violence were well-founded. Ultimately, they knew the amount of courage, vision, and hope that Selma's black citizens had gathered in order to confront white supremacy. They knew the price of freedom. They also knew, deeply, the power of solidarity.

The sisters of the mission at Saint Elizabeth's parish in Selma, Alabama, were women religious who entered the racial apostolate by virtue of staying put as the world around them changed. These sisters were more or less unwitting participants in the civil rights movement. They did not consider themselves to be radicals, at least not political radicals (though some sisters understood vowed religious life to be a form of radical religious witness). Many of them, at least in the beginning, did not identify with the civil rights movement or see themselves as part of it. And some were quite bewildered to find themselves at the center of civil rights struggles. Rather, the Sisters of Saint Joseph became engaged in the midcentury struggle for racial justice in the United States inadvertently, by engaging in typical apostolic activities of women religious, by doing what sisters had done for centuries—they visited the homebound, healed the sick, educated children, and cared for members of the parish communities where they lived. And, in a parish where the majority of members were African American, the context of racialized poverty and Jim Crow segregation transformed sisters' activities that were otherwise perfectly normal, and in fact often overlooked as banal, into a form of racial activism.

At Selma in 1965 the African American struggle for racial justice briefly converged with the internal reform of Catholic women's religious congregations, and, similar to the way Selma changed the course of the civil rights movement, it also signaled a turning point in the history of Catholic women religious in the United States. The protesting sisters at Selma attracted the attention of the news media, and Americans were variously shocked and delighted by news images of women religious, dressed in full habit, engaging in previously unimaginable public displays of political defiance. Though such images have become clichés of the late 1960 and 1970s, in 1965 their novelty was arresting. Among fellow women religious, however, the sisters at Selma were neither surprising nor unfamiliar. Though "new nuns" by 1963 already had begun to participate in small-scale projects, the publicity sisters attracted at Selma confirmed for many women religious that profound changes were afoot, and it inspired countless others to undertake similar justice-oriented apostolic works. The words of Sister Mary Peter (Margaret Ellen) Traxler, SSND, penned in 1965—"After Selma, Sister, you can't stay home again!"—reflected a perception among many women religious that Selma permanently had altered the trajectory of religious life for American sisters.[91]

CHAPTER FIVE

Project Cabrini: Becoming Sistahs

The sister walked down the noisy street in central Chicago at twilight, strumming her guitar. Behind her the setting sun reflected off of the Cabrini Green housing project "risers," bathing the unadorned gray concrete towers in an orange glow that warmed their austere dullness. Beneath her feet, the light struck bits of broken glass on the sidewalk and the candy wrappers and newspaper debris that had blown up against the chain mesh fence that separated the flat, black tar playground from the street. The risers cast long shadows that stretched across the neighborhood toward the wealthy townhouses along the lakeshore. In a soft, angelic soprano voice the nun sang:

> Little boxes on the hillside, little boxes made of ticky-tacky,
> little boxes, little boxes, little boxes all the same.
> There's a green one and a pink one, a blue one and a yellow one,
> and they're all made out of ticky tacky and they all look just the same.

As she walked and sang, the sister passed people coming home from work—tired-looking men in dirty coveralls, women balancing bags of groceries as they squeezed through the narrow door of the bus that carried them home from jobs cleaning houses in the suburbs or folding sheets in the basement laundry of a hospital on the North Side.[1] They stood in the asphalt yard of Cabrini Green, waiting for the single elevator that served the entire building to take them to their apartments; or, tired of the long wait, they climbed flight after flight of the open-air, concrete stairs to greet eager children, many of whom who had spent much of the summer's day without the company or guidance of an adult.

The Cabrini Green housing project was a model of the contempt for the poor that was embedded in many of the urban renewal projects of Chicago mayor Richard J. Daley's administration. The eighteen-story building had a single elevator, a service elevator, available to residents. There was no entryway to the building, rather, the elevator opened directly to the outdoors. There was no canopy or shelter over the elevator entrance, so in the rain or snow, people had to stand unprotected outdoors while waiting in the inevitable line to use the elevator. The stairs were not much better. Bare concrete, open to the outdoors, they offered no protection from the elements. Because there were no public bathrooms in the project, and because of the limitations of the elevator and the length of the climb up the stairs, the stairwells often contained the added unpleasantness of human excrement from children who could not make it through the wait or climb to their apartments.

Children often gathered to follow "sistah" on her twilight neighborhood hootenannies, a pied piper in black and white gabardine leading a trail of African American children, singing:[2]

> And the people in the houses all go to the universities
> and they all get put in boxes, little boxes all the same.
> There's a doctor and a lawyer and a business executive
> and they all get put in boxes and they all come out the same.

During the day many of the children attended a summer "fun school" that the Sisters of Saint Francis of Rochester, Minnesota, ran for children in the neighborhood, particularly for those who lived in the risers. At times, the singing sister was accompanied by other sisters from the program who sang or played bongos. The sisters didn't live in the neighborhood. During the school year, most of these women religious taught in Catholic parochial schools in various towns in Minnesota. Though many Catholic schools were long-established fixtures within old Catholic neighborhoods, recently some sisters had been assigned to newer, wealthier parishes in suburban areas. The children that the sisters encountered in their usual classrooms were quite different from the ones they stood beside on the street corners of Cabrini Green. Together, sisters and children sang:

> And they all play on the golf course and drink their martinis dry
> and they all have precious children and their children go to school,
> and their children go to summer camp and then to the universities,
> and they all get put in boxes and they all come out the same.[3]

The sisters were amazed and appalled by the conditions in which the children of Cabrini Green lived, conditions that were markedly different from those with which the sisters were familiar from their typical yearly assignments in Catholic parish schools. Crammed into small apartments in the tall buildings of Cabrini Green, many children suffered the effects of poverty that prevailed in the neighborhood. Of the 18,000 people living in the Cabrini Green housing development, 12,000 were children. Thirty-five percent of mothers in the neighborhood received public assistance. According to the 1960 census, fewer than 24 percent of persons over the age twenty-five in the area of the project had a high-school education.[4] When asked to describe what things surprised her about Cabrini Green, Sister Joachim immediately referred to the poverty in the area. "We fed the children when they came in to school and we fed them before they went home," she recalled.

> A little boy came to school one day and he had a bandage on and it was all sore, and I said, "What happened to you?" and he said that a rat had bit him. And we fixed it up, and a few days later he came all smiles and said, "I fooled the rat." And I said, "What did you do?" He got a cardboard box and he slept in that and when the rat starting nibbling on that he would wake up. I said, "Why didn't you do what I would do? Get rid of the rats!" And he said, "Well, Ma'am, you don't know how rats stays in our house."[5]

This chapter examines the experience of the Franciscan sisters who staffed Project Cabrini in its pilot year, 1965. Exploring the forces and processes that led to the development of the program and the events that shaped sisters' experiences there illuminates the motivations and concepts that led Sister Lisieux Wirtz to stand on an inner-city Chicago street corner and sing folk songs that were sharply critical of life in the suburbs to a group of children from an urban high-rise housing project.

"Do I Understand That You Will Arrange This, Monsignor?"

In 1964 the Sisters of Saint Francis, like many other American congregations of women religious, reviewed the apostolic commitments of the order. Directed by the Second Vatican Council to renew its apostolic orientation and spurred on by organizations like the Sister Formation Conference, the Sisters of Saint Francis assigned a committee to explore whether certain areas of apostolic focus were still consistent with the charism, or the unique work, of the congregation. "It is recognized that there is a need for studying the possibility of extending our apostolate in view of the spirit of the church today and of the socio-economic and other needs of the times," the Committee on the Apostolate reported to the general chapter of the order.[6] The sisters also hoped that a modernized apostolate would preserve the appeal of religious life for young vocations. "Our courage in examining and renewing our apostolate will be an inspiration and a great attraction for young women of our time."[7] Guidance for the renewal process was to come from the rule and constitutions of the order, the spirit and example of its founder, and from the magisterium through the directives of the Vatican Council and the Holy Father. To this end, the committee sent each sister a bibliography and reading materials to prepare her for discussions about apostolic renewal. Sisters must first study the "role of the Christian as it is being defined by Vatican II," the report urged, because the Church's relationship to the world is the foundation of the apostolate. "The apostolic community finds its reason for existence," the report argued, "in the full and effective participation in the Mystical Body of Christ within the limits of the works in which the Community is engaged."[8] In other words, the congregation itself existed in order to contribute specific forms of service toward the unity of the Church on earth.

The report quoted liberally from the congregation's rule, linking passages about the virtue of charity with encouragement that each sister should undergo a process of individual spiritual renewal. "The test of love of God is the practice of charity toward the neighbor," the report quoted from the rule. "That charity may abound in deed it must first abound in the heart."[9]

The majority of the report focused on particular regulations and restrictions that the committee believed interfered with the effectiveness of the congregation's current apostolate. Among them, the committee recommended that the congregation revise rules that limited sisters' abilities to visit homes, attend concerts and lectures, work in missions with fewer than four other sisters, visit doctors and dentists without a sister-companion, take vacations, and have frequent contact with their families. In addition to the congregation's established focus on "the Christian education and training of youth, the care of orphans, and of the sick in hospitals," the committee asked the congregation to consider adding several new works, such as home visits, counseling on secular campuses, conducting classes for laywomen in domestic arts, and performing health education in poor parishes. The last new apostolic work on the list addressed summer months, a time when teaching sisters typically either returned to the motherhouse or took classes. In an attempt to "further work with the poor," the committee recommended, "Sisters, who have received their Bachelor's degree, and who during the summer months would find further study difficult, could be assigned to this apostolic work in diocese in need."[10]

Responding to several requests from sisters in the congregation for such summer apostolic work, Mother Mary Callista Hynes, general superior of the Sisters of Saint Francis, started to investigate opportunities for apostolic programs in Chicago for the summer of 1965. She wrote to Monsignors William McManus and Francis Byrne of the Chicago Archdiocese the previous January inquiring about summer work for her sisters among the "underprivileged" there.[11] She wrote to a Chicago-based organization of Catholic lay volunteers with similar questions and asked sisters assigned to the congregation's two parish schools in Chicago to investigate neighborhoods for such work.[12] McManus suggested that Mother Hynes contact Sister Mary William of the Daughters of Charity, who ran a successful interracial program in Chicago called Marillac House. "A number of our Sisters have expressed the wish to work this summer with underprivileged groups, particularly with children and young adults," wrote Mother Hynes to Sister William in early February. "The type of work we propose is new for us," she explained, "at the present time we are seeking to find our way."[13]

The opportunity for one summer program presented itself when Sister Mary Emmanuel Collins, a Franciscan congregational representative to the SFC, met with Sister Margaret Traxler at the midwestern regional meeting of the SFC. Traxler mentioned to Sister Collins that she was investigating turning an abandoned Catholic school near Chicago's Cabrini Green housing project into a sister-run summer enrichment program for neighborhood children. Traxler wanted to establish a summer apostolate program that could be emulated by other congregations and sister organizations. In a letter to Sister Collins immediately following the conference, Traxler stated her intention that the Cabrini program be a model for sisters involved in the expanding apostolate, especially the SFC. "With proper implementation," wrote Traxler, "this can be an ideal summer set-up and if God blesses it, Sister Formation people can look at it and see in it the matrix for other congregations in other summers."[14]

Upon her return from the conference, Sister Collins wrote to Mother Hynes about the possibility of assigning Franciscan sisters to Traxler's project. "While there I met Sister Mary Peter [Traxler], SSND," she began, reporting about the SFC meeting. "There is a Catholic school in the parish of St. Philip Benizi . . . the pastor of the church would be willing to turn it over to any sisters who would work on the project . . .

They would like the sisters to do remedial work and to teach art and crafts."[15] Anticipating the mother general's reservations about sending sisters into new types of service in a poor, urban parish, Sister Collins described the physical resources of the parish, stressing that sisters would have access to a regular Mass. She extended Traxler's assurance that the Franciscan sisters would be safe there. "She says there is no danger for anyone in the habit," wrote Collins of Traxler, "because the Negroes are religious or if they have no religion then they are superstitious. In either case they would venerate and honor the garb the Sister wears."[16] (This chapter will later touch on the oddly discordant note in this exchange that characterized African Americans as superstitious in relation to the religious habit.) Project Cabrini became one of three racial-apostolate programs to which the Sisters of Saint Francis sent members in the summer of 1965. Other Franciscans went to Marillac House in Chicago and to an inner-city program in Washington, D.C.

Sister Traxler and Mother Hynes spent the spring months establishing the financial and administrative structure of the program that was to become Project Cabrini. Hynes sent letter after letter to Traxler to iron out fine details about the Franciscan sisters' role in the project. Mother Hynes's earliest questions about Project Cabrini were practical in nature, related to how sisters would be able to maintain usual patterns of religious life in the new apostolate. "What are the dates during which the help of the Sisters will be needed? Where will the Sisters be housed?" she asked. "Does the program have the necessary ecclesiastical approval? Or are we to direct the Chancery Office to ask approval of the participation of our Sisters in the program?"[17] Diocesan officials shared Mother Hynes's concern that Project Cabrini not unduly disrupt standard ways of organizing the daily lives of sisters, particularly norms of enclosure, daily prayer, and communion, and clear lines of hierarchical authority. Typical of early projects in the racial apostolate, Project Cabrini precipitated extensive negotiations between the congregation's superior and the Chicago Archdiocese.

One point of conflict between the sisters and diocesan officials was the matter of where visiting sisters would reside during the program. Traxler and Hynes and the sisters who volunteered to staff Project Cabrini agreed that the sisters should live in close proximity to the neighborhood, either in rented apartments within the Cabrini Green high-rise or in a nearby convent. Diocesan officials, particularly Monsignor McManus, balked at the idea of sisters living in such unconventional arrangements. McManus wanted the sisters to live in the two convents of the Sisters of Saint Francis in Chicago, the Saint Juliana and Saint Priscilla convents, a traditional arrangement for visiting women religious.

McManus presented the diocesan position in a lengthy letter to Hynes in May 1965. "Because some of the work contemplated by the Sisters is unusual and may involve some deviations from the Sisters' regular routines," McManus's letter began, "the Bishop has requested that you appoint one superior who would be in charge of all your Sisters assigned to this special work in Chicago during the summer months." In addition to preserving congregational authority structures through a local superior, McManus also preserved the final authority of the Chicago Archdiocese over the sisters by requiring them to meet with a diocesan vicar, Monsignor Raymond Zock, who would advise the sisters "on certain proprieties and precautions that would be in the best interest of the Sisters and their work." Monsignor McManus required that the sisters reside in convents of the Sisters of Saint Francis while in Chicago. "The Bishop and I are both persuaded that this living arrangement is far more desirable than having the Sisters reside in rented apartments in the Mother Cabrini Project," he stated. "We do not see how having the Sisters domiciled at one of the convents where your Sisters regularly live will interfere with their daily activities with the underprivileged who will seek their services at St. Philip Benizi School where Mother Cabrini Project will have its headquarters." Then, softening to a paternal tone, the monsignor offered that such measures were truly in the best interest of the sisters and that the requirements established by him and by the bishop reflected only their concern that "all reasonable standards of propriety and protocol would be observed and that the safety and welfare of the Sisters would be reasonably protected."[18]

Mother Hynes was an experienced superior, practiced in the methods sisters employed to gain concessions from the hierarchy and familiar with the limits of those methods in the face of stubborn bishops. Her reply was a reverently phrased, carefully worded challenge to the monsignor's directive. She began her reply by agreeing to name a superior for the project and to direct the superior to contact Monsignor Zock, as the monsignor had requested. Mother Hynes then took up the matter of housing. She agreed to request permission for sisters to reside in the convents of the Sisters of Saint Francis but questioned the practicality of this arrangement on both logistic and financial grounds. "The only problem may be the time element involved in driving back and forth," she wrote. Mother Hynes gently placed the financial burden of the monsignor's requirement that sisters live some distance from Project Cabrini back with the monsignor himself. "I mentioned the matter of cars in one of our telephone conversations. Your reply was that it would be simple to arrange the use of cars. Do I understand that you will arrange this, Monsignor?" she asked. "Under no circumstances would I feel that we could expect to have the use of a [Saint Juliana or Saint Priscilla] parish car, since I know the demands for their use are many."[19]

Mother Hynes's strategy was characteristic of that employed by women religious in the racial apostolate in negotiations with the male hierarchy: she deflected the sharpness of her challenges by phrasing them in deferential tones and embedded them in statements of obedience and compliance. Mother Hynes presented McManus with her reservations about the practicality of requiring sisters to drive long distances to and from Project Cabrini, couching them within the paternalistic ethos that had characterized his directives. If the monsignor had reservations about the "safety and welfare" of sisters who wanted to reside in Cabrini Green, would he then cover the expenses they would incur by living in traditional convents, some distance away from their work?

Among themselves, sisters were less charitable in interpreting the monsignor's actions. "Certainly the devil must be worried about what is going to happen in the Cabrini Project this summer," Collins wrote to Traxler. "I don't know anyone else who could cause so many misunderstandings and create so many obstacles." Collins noted the arrival of the letter from McManus, "confirming his interference with the plans for our Sisters' residence during the summer. Since Mother Hynes is ecclesiastically minded like all Mothers General it will take a note from the Bishop to counteract Monsignor McManus' machinations." Collins was particularly irritated by the monsignor's uninvited intrusion into a project that sisters had initiated. "Undoubtedly he plans them well," she added, "but it is hard to understand why he feels it is his place to make all those decisions without discussing them with the people concerned."[20]

Project Cabrini encountered a second obstacle—also characteristic of programs in the racial apostolate—when expected Chicago-based funding failed, and the Office of Economic Opportunity (OEO) delayed making a final grant to Project Cabrini. Though the project was jointly sponsored by the NCCIJ and the Catholic Interracial Council of Chicago—"to heal the breach between the members of God's human family,"[21] sisters needed OEO funds to purchase equipment for the project, including typewriters, sewing machines, art supplies, and books, and to rent buses to take children on field trips. Both Traxler and Mother Hynes determined that the program would go forward regardless of whether or not it received federal funding. "We are ready if OEO comes through," Traxler wrote to Mother Hynes the week before the sisters were to arrive. "Somehow all this budget business seems inconsistent with Our Lord's words about 'neither script nor shoes' and the birds of the air not having nests nor foxes their holes."[22] "The sisters will be in Chicago, God willing, by Saturday next," Mother Hynes assured Traxler in reply. "We will plan to give the assistance promised regardless of whether or not a favorable answer comes from Washington."[23] Sister Collins added her own words of encouragement to Traxler as they waited for word about the OEO grant. "I think you would have some very disappointed Franciscans if the money doesn't come through. If it doesn't come through it seems to me that we should go ahead and arrange some way of doing it anyhow," she added.[24]

The sisters moved to Chicago in June uncertain of whether or not their program would be fully funded. OEO approval for expenditures up to $8,800 was granted three days after Project Cabrini was underway. Project Cabrini was one of thirty-five Chicago programs funded by the Economic Opportunity Act in 1965.[25]

Sisters spent the week prior to the program's opening cleaning the school and knocking on doors in Cabrini Green, inviting parents to send children to the "summer fun school." Project Cabrini opened its doors on June 27, 1965, at 8:45 A.M. On a typical day sisters rose for prayers at their respective convents, and then after breakfast they took a rented yellow bus across the north side of town to Cabrini Green. There they taught classes or led play groups from 8:45 A.M. until afternoon. Children over seven-years-old and adults were welcome, and the curriculum included classes in reading, art, Spanish, piano, typing, crafts, "Negro history," math, speech, and dramatics.[26] Sisters estimated that around 900 students visited Project Cabrini each day.[27]

Like other programs of the racial apostolate, Project Cabrini required sisters to be flexible about certain components of their apostolic assignments. After attending a "Boston Tea Party" held by Cabrini residents in her honor, Sister Maigread Conway reflected on her experience adapting to the constantly new array of situations that Project Cabrini presented to her. "When wondering about these things and when I ask for someone who knows for a bit of information, all say, 'Oh Sister you must play it by ear!' I'm sure I will be a great musician if this is the case as I play well by ear now."[28]

From all angles, people who encountered Project Cabrini in 1965 agreed that something uniquely wonderful was occurring there. The project was popular with neighborhood parents and children, who filled its daytime classes and evening programs to capacity. The Chicago Archdiocese proudly claimed the project as a model of Catholic social engagement, as did its sponsoring organizations. And the sisters who staffed Project Cabrini described their experience as transformative, as the fulfillment of their religious vocation.

The summer of 1965, the summer following Selma, was the high point of trust between Catholic sisters and African Americans. Prior to Selma, sisters who entered African American communities to perform apostolic work had to work consciously to cultivate trust and to overcome historically conditioned mistrust of the motives and attitudes of whites. In the immediate aftermath of Selma, it was easier for sisters to establish relationships with African Americans, many of whom associated the religious habit, after March of 1965, with the solidarity evident in Selma. The fact that sisters occupied a supporting role to the African American leaders from SCLC and SNCC in images of Selma also softened African American perceptions of sisters as missionary meddlers interested in changing the community more than in serving its people. Though the tolerance of African Americans for the presence of white sisters in their neighborhoods would lessen with the emergence of Black Power ideologies in the late 1960s, the summer of 1965 was a brief window of easier interactions between sisters of the racial apostolate and blacks in Northern urban areas.

These elements lent a certain feeling of grace to Project Cabrini. Those involved—sisters, residents, administrators, and observers—all seemed to recognize an unusual abundance of good feeling surrounding the project. Those responsible for Project Cabrini immediately recognized the unique euphoria that surrounded the project and publicized it as widely as possible. Project Cabrini frequently welcomed visitors, often brought over by Traxler during her daily visits. The guest book for Project Cabrini listed 169 sisters among twice that number of total visitors.[29] In an early report letter from the project to Mother Hynes, Sister Conway observed, "Countless folks continue to visit us daily. The Sisters and children are doing splendid work, but no different than the work Sisters all usually do during an ordinary school year, but this all seems so fantastic here as far as all of these people are concerned. We continue daily to wonder why. The wonderful spirit of joy we share among ourselves with all seems to be the spoonful of sugar that attracts."[30] Traxler and

Sam Dennis of the Chicago Catholic Interracial Council (CIC) distributed a flier to sisters of the Urban Apostolate of the Sisters (UAS), a group of women religious interested in apostolic work in urban areas, stressing both the unusual spirit at Cabrini and their hopes that the project would serve as a model for others like it. "Because there is obvious enjoyment at *PROJECT CABRINI,*" the flier began, "we invite you St. Philip Benizi School in order that you too may see here the workings of what we hope will bc for you, an imitable plan for future summers in other urban areas."[31] Project Cabrini was covered by the *Chicago Sun-Times* in an article that stated that "the program is a pilot project that may influence future policies of their own congregation and other organizations of Roman Catholic sisters now seeking to adapt their middle-class backgrounds to the changing environment of big cities."[32] Articles about Project Cabrini also appeared in the *Chicago New World, Chicago Daily News,* and *Chicago's American.*

"God Is Black, O My Brothers"

Sisters' stories about Project Cabrini stressed that sisters felt wanted in the neighborhood, appreciated by the residents, and admired by the children. Sister Joachim, who taught "Negro history" in the program, reflected that participating in Project Cabrini "made us, it made me, feel proud that I was sister, that I could help, and I felt Negroes appreciated, they appreciated." She added that "the fact that we were white, this didn't make any difference to them."[33] A press release about the program included a typical anecdote about children's desire to be with sisters: " 'I dreamed about this all night,' the little girl radiated joy as she greeted Sister Maigread at the school door."[34]

Sisters included several anecdotes in each issue of the weekly *Project Cabrini Newsletter* that they sent to sisters back in Minnesota and to various supporters of the program. "So much has happened, both amusing and confusing, it is hard to tell where to start," sisters began the first newsletter.[35] Often the stories functioned to underscore the developing bond between sisters and students in the project. " 'I like you,' Albert age 9 tells each of us in turn," one story began. " 'I not only like you; I love you,' he adds, charming us with his wide white smile and his shining eyes. 'You-all ain't gonna leave us, are you?' He and his friends want to know. 'We wouldn't if we could help it,' we assure them."[36] Anecdotes stressing the close bonds between sisters and children in Cabrini Green gave legitimacy to Project Cabrini, demonstrating its success to readers. Moreover, the stories served as a medium through which sisters shared experiences they found remarkable or noteworthy about the racial apostolate with sisters back home in Minnesota. The evening hootenannies were occasions for such stories. The second newsletter reported that one evening, after the hootenannies had been rained out for two days, the sisters heard a "heavy pounding on the door two stories below. It was some of the children. When we opened the door, they asked, 'Ain't you-all comin' out? The rain's been gone a long time ago.' So we went out," the sisters wrote.[37]

Sisters' anecdotes from the newsletter often described mutual warmth and tenderness between sisters and the children of Cabrini. "A four year old on Sister Viatrix's lap kissed her crucifix and then asked, 'Was his wife there when they killed him?' " the newsletter reported.[38] The story juxtaposed the physical closeness of the child sitting in the sister's lap and the intimacy of the child's gesture in kissing the sister's crucifix with the child's uncanny question. "A little boy came back to Sister Lisieux while she was showing a movie in the gym and asked if he could sit on her chair with her. Once he'd crawled up, he looked at her very seriously and asked: Will you be my sister?"[39] In both stories a child approached a sister openly, without fear or hesitation. Sitting comfortably in a sister's lap, the child then yielded to curiosity, asking an unusually intimate question.

Stories like these echoed sisters' surprise and visible joy at being in a place where they were free to be affectionate with children. At Cabrini, among non-Catholic children, sisters could be more physically expressive than they were in regular Catholic classrooms because non-Catholic children lacked the physical inhibitions that characterized Catholic children. Whereas Catholic children treated sisters reverently, often fearing them, children at Project Cabrini hugged sisters, held their hands, touched them, and climbed unself-consciously onto their laps—all things that Catholic children rarely would have done to sisters in traditional parish schools. Sisters were pleased and even moved by the spontaneity of children's affection for them at Cabrini Green.

At times sisters' anecdotes identified children primarily by their race, attributing to the children specific visual and linguistic racial tropes that were common at the time. In some stories race operated as a form of camouflage that blended children into their urban surroundings. In one tale about the Franciscans' first tour of the neighborhood, sisters compared the color of the children to that of the buildings, while the children's eyes and teeth stood out against the dark background. "While we were walking that day that we heard voices calling, 'Hiya, Sistahs,'" the story began, "and, looking up along the dirt-browned bricks and stones of the building, we suddenly caught sight of eight white eyes and four white grins lined up along a third-floor windowsill directly overhead. The little hands that threw us kisses could not be distinguished from the bricks of the same color, except that the hands moved!"[40] The specificity of race in the depiction of children—who appear as urban Cheshire cats—is characteristic of stories in the Cabrini Green newsletter. The anecdote also is characteristic in the clear warmth and affection, and the informality, with which the children greeted the sisters. Race similarly camouflaged children in a story about some "nasty words" that sisters discovered painted in brown paint on the yellow doors to the school. "Sister Soubrious suggested that the culprit would be easy enough to track down: 'Just find someone with a brown finger.' [sic] (Reminder: there are only 180,000 brown fingers in this neighborhood to begin with!—18,000 population of which 12,000 are under 17 years of age)"[41]

In other stories, the race of African Americans was featured either through uncanny behavior or linguistic patterns. "In Spanish class, the adult students were trying to master a new vocabulary and Sister Baylon was trying to help them by making little sketches; chair, desk, flower, etc," one anecdote related. "Suddenly they laughed and one of the men remarked: 'How's dat? She draws in Spanish too! Who gonna translate?'"[42] One story emphasized the humorousness of interactions between a priest and a resident of the neighborhood: "Father asked a friend of a convert if he, too, wouldn't like to be a Catholic. 'No suh,' the man replied. 'I is already a Negro and that is enough of a problem!'"[43] In another tale a little girl frightened by the array of religious habits worn by a large group of visiting sisters from the Urban Apostolate of the Sisters program declared, "I all thoughts devils and ghosts was here!"[44] This particular anecdote reflected not only sisters' amusement at unexpected phrases in children's language at Cabrini Green, but it also suggests that the children of Project Cabrini may not have been comfortable, entirely, with the level of attention that their interactions with sisters elicited from outsiders—from visiting sisters, Catholic dignitaries, and even representatives of the press.

Sisters' stories about Project Cabrini often concentrated on how African Americans accepted the Franciscans, including them in the life of the neighborhood. "The habit spoke volumes to those people," Sister Joachim commented. "I know with some of them I felt as though they were ready to kidnap me for it, they were so proud of the fact that the sisters came."[45] In her last report letter to Mother Hynes from Project Cabrini, Sister Maigread Conway described the "First Annual Boston Tea Party" given by the North Central Community Committee in honor of the Franciscan sisters. "The 'Boston Tea Party' was given to honor newcomers into the community who were accepted by the folks who reside here. It was an honor to be accepted, I'm told . . . It seemed like a huge crowd and all Negro so one was almost overwhelmed."[46]

In her private files Mother Hynes saved a letter sent to her by "Anthony J. Grant and William R. Copney (And the people of chicaog [sic])," as it was signed. Written by two men who had learned how to type at Project Cabrini, the letter thanked Hynes for sending the Franciscan sisters to Cabrini Green and asked whether the same sisters could be sent the following year. "We all have grown to love them very much," wrote Grant and Copney. The letter is one of the very few remaining archival documents about Project Cabrini in which the voices of Cabrini Green residents were not filtered through sisters' memories or writings. Grant and Copney listed three ways in which the sisters had endeared themselves to people in the neighborhood:

> One Kindness—When they speak to us they speak in a lovele tone of voice this is one of the Things we are not use to. Two Willingness—We have found out that are always willing to help us no matter what it is if they can do it they will. Three they are helping us to find our Individual Potentiality and follow it Through.[47]

The letter testified to the mutually affirming relationships that African Americans and sisters formed through Project Cabrini.

The theology of the Mystical Body of Christ echoed in the streets around Project Cabrini throughout the summer of 1965 in the relationships sisters formed with Cabrini Green residents. The doctrine of the Mystical Body of Christ took a central place in American Catholic understanding through Pope Pius XII's 1943 encyclical *Mystici Corporis Christi,* or the Mystical Body of Christ. Drawing on historical currents within Catholic theology, the encyclical sanctioned the idea that Church was Christ's mystical body on earth. In other words, Christians together comprised a spiritual manifestation of Christ himself, the doctrine held; they literally re-membered Christ's body on earth. Divine love was a unifying force, evident in Christ's sacrificial death, which forever united God and humans together in bonds of love. Divine love found expression in the unity of Christian people, as well. *Mystici Corporis Christi* argued that "the more we become 'members of one another,' 'mutually one of another,' the closer we shall be united with God, with Christ; as on the other hand the more ardent the love that binds us to God and our divine Head, the closer we shall be united to each other in the bonds of charity."[48] In this sense, the doctrine of the Mystical Body of Christ was a theology of human unity. It stressed that bonds of responsibility and good will connected human beings.

Through the 1950s and into the 1960s the doctrine of the Mystical Body became a powerful metaphor in the Catholic world for understanding human relationships. The Mystical Body gained currency in popular Catholic theology through departments of religious education and in theological summer schools attended by both priests and sisters. The doctrine was explained to laypeople in diocesan newspapers and from the pulpit. It appeared in catechism classes and in internal newsletters within religious orders.

The Mystical Body of Christ was a powerful contemporary ecclesiology. It subtly infused Catholic social thought at midcentury, shaping how Catholics defined relationships within the Church and within society, offering a practical, direct metaphor for explaining interpersonal relationships. The concept of the Mystical Body was a flexible ecclesiology; in practice, Catholics expanded its application beyond religious boundaries, using it to define and understand community in a larger sense. Catholics interpreted the Mystical Body in diverse ways, employing it as a metaphor to explain various social relationships, including family structure, church governance, educational settings, national unity, and human solidarity.[49] In the 1960s, when the Second Vatican Council directed the attention of Catholics toward the relationship of the Church to the world, the doctrine of the Mystical Body took on even greater significance for American Catholics.

The doctrine of the Mystical Body of Christ stressed the importance, the preciousness, of each member of Christ's body on earth. "The love of the divine Spouse is so vast," Pius XII argued in *Mystici Corporis Christi*, "that it embraces in His Spouse the whole human race without exception. Men may be separated by nationality and race, but our Savior poured out His Blood to reconcile all men to God through the Cross, and to bid them all unite in one Body." Not surprisingly, Catholic integrationists in particular employed theologies based on the Mystical Body to explain the spiritual significance of interracial harmony within the Church. Catholic integrationists borrowed heavily from encyclical passages like the following, which seemed to sanction interracial cooperation:

> He has taught us not only to have love for those of a different nation and a different race, but to love even our enemies. While Our heart overflows

> with the sweetness of the Apostle's teaching We chant with him the length, the width, the height and the depth of the charity of Christ, which neither diversity of race or culture, neither the wasteless tracts of ocean, nor wars, be their cause just or unjust, can ever weaken or destroy.[50]

Sisters enacted the Mystical Body of Christ in several ways at Cabrini. They affirmed the unity of the divine with the whole of humanity when they acknowledged God's blackness. Singing the song "Kumbaya"together, sisters at Project Cabrini added verses that proclaimed "God is Black, O my brothers, God is Black," "God is white, O my brothers, God is white," and "God is love, O my Brothers, God is love."[51] Sisters took Eucharist in the form of whole-wheat hosts, and in doing so they made God brown. They venerated the presence of a brown Christ on the altar and consumed Christ's brown body in Mass. "Don't you ever wonder if people question God's having made them black or white—whichever He did make them?" sisters asked in one of their newsletters. "Or if Our Savior makes a distinction between white and whole-wheat hosts at Mass?"[52]

Sisters attempted, as well, to teach perspectives based on the Mystical Body to residents of Cabrini Green, and in particular to instill it in children. Several narratives that issued from Project Cabrini involved sisters' attempts to redirect the gaze of people in Cabrini Green away from the interior of their apartments and out the windows. "From the metal-enclosed porch of the nineteenth story of the risers," sisters observed, "one can look out beyond the smokestacks of local factories and over the fire escapes of tumbling tenements that have not yet been replaced by public housing, and see Lake Michigan shimmering in the sun."[53] Sisters reported that they "asked a child who lives on the other side of the building if he ever watches the stars from his window. He had never thought to look, he told us."[54] In looking outward and upward, sisters wanted members of the neighborhood to recognize a common human family in fellow residents of the risers. One sister wrote:

> When we visit their apartments during the day, we invite them to look up the nine rows of windows to one side, and up the ten rows of windows on the other and see hundreds of faces in the windows. It gives us another sense of the mysterious oneness of which our various minority groups: Negroes, Catholics, Puerto Ricans, Mohammedans and Italians are a part. It is just one step from this to the prayer: "that all may be one, Father."[55]

The experience of the sisters at Project Cabrini was profoundly influenced by theology related to the Mystical Body of Christ. The doctrine was present in the exploratory Committee on the Apostolate's focus on charity. It shaped sisters' view of the neighborhood around Cabrini Green and the way they approached residents of the neighborhood in their work. The doctrine allowed sisters to see themselves united with African Americans into a seamless community through their work at Project Cabrini. In their final newsletter from the project in August 1965, sisters took solace from their belief that they were united, irrevocably, to the people of Cabrini Green. "As we go our separate ways," they wrote, "we intend to carry on the work that has begun here. We don't think in terms of being here in spirit only. That's impossible when "We are ONE."[56]

In July, Dr. Martin Luther King Jr. visited Chicago for three days, giving speeches and meeting with local leaders. Prohibited from participating in marches associated with the King visit, sisters from Project Cabrini nevertheless attended speeches and rallies. They watched one of King's speeches from across a parking lot and greeted several other residents of Cabrini Green who were in the crowd. Sisters' reports of the weekend echoed themes of connection and acceptance that characterized their other stories about Project Cabrini. Sisters dubbed King's visit "the weekend that was," and wrote excited, almost breathless accounts of the weekend to sisters back home in Minnesota. King's visit affected the Franciscan sisters. King gave them a sense of the uniqueness of their contribution to the cause of racial justice. He affirmed for sisters that they offered something to the movement that no other group, Catholic or non-Catholic, could offer. Falling well into their weeks at Project Cabrini when the sisters were beginning to feel comfortable in their surroundings and at home with the buildings and people with whom they worked, the King weekend also increased sisters' sense of belonging in the Cabrini Green neighborhood and in the black community, generally.

Representatives of the Chicago Archdiocese had made it clear to the Sisters of Saint Francis when they first arrived in Chicago that they were not to engage in political activity or protest marches during their time in Chicago. Anticipating these limitations from the archdiocese, Mother Hynes had preemptively forbidden sisters assigned to Cabrini to participate in political actions. In June, shortly after the sisters arrived in Chicago, Sister M. Sean reported to Mother Hynes that the diocesesan vicar serving as the director of Project Cabrini, in his initial meeting with Sister Maigread Conway, had cautioned sisters not to become involved in protests. "He expressed the same feeling toward Sisters taking part in marching as you did," Sister Sean reported to Hynes. "His face broke into a broad smile when Sister Maigread anticipated his thoughts and said, 'There will be no marching, Those were Mother Callista's last words to us.'"[57] When King arrived in July, there was no unresolved question hanging in the air as to whether or not sisters would join the protest marches. The matter was settled. For sisters to participate in the visit, they had to find ways other than through political action. "We did not take part in the 'march' which seems to be more and more a 'sign' of Christ's message in our times," sisters reported, "but we did communicate in several other ways."[58]

Over the course of the weekend, Franciscan sisters attended one of King's speeches at a rally held three blocks from Cabrini Green in front of an integrated Methodist church. "Of course we went!" sisters wrote about the rally.[59] Sisters stood some distance from King, across a parking lot, and couldn't hear all of his speech. Their memories of the event were largely interpersonal, focused on interactions they had with African Americans in the crowd. "Two small girls came up and stood in front of us and said, 'Ah cain't see, Sistah,' and stretched out their arms," sisters reported. "We picked them up and pointed out their leader."[60] Sisters described powerful feelings of inclusion and solidarity at the rally. Improbably, they belonged. "'Yes, sir, dat's right,' we wanted to add with the woman standing beside us," they wrote of King's speech. Leaving the rally, sisters were greeted warmly by people who had attended. "On the way out of the lot, a little old Negro grandpa and grandma were leaning on a sawhorse that marked off the area, and Grandma reached out and shook our hands as we walked by."[61]

On Monday, July 26, King led a demonstration march, and though the sisters did not march, they employed the idioms of the Mystical Body to describe the solidarity they felt with those who did attend. "We did not march on Monday afternoon although thousands did," the sisters explained:

> On our way back to the project from supper that night, however, a Negro man passed us and said, "Wasn't it magnificent? So dignified and orderly." We admitted that we hadn't been part of the particular "visible sign." A block further on, a truckful of Negroes was just leaving the vicinity, singing a spiritual, and a young Negro saw us, doffed his hat, bowed, smiled, and threw us a kiss. We smiled, waved, and tossed kisses back.[62]

The image of sisters throwing kisses to men passing by in trucks—something they likely would not have done in their home parishes in Minnesota—suggests that in Cabrini Green sisters felt less bound by restrictions and protocols that characterized their lives within Catholic enclaves.

Writing in the *Project Cabrini Newsletter,* one sister compared her encounter with the man on the truck with the feelings of unity that she had experienced earlier that week at an interracial Mass. She explained that the "impression of oneness in Christ was the same as it had been earlier that week" at a Catholic Interracial Council (CIC) meeting where she had sung and prayed and received communion in a small group of African Americans and sisters. "We received the Lord directly over the altar under the form of whole-wheat hosts, and were united to one another there in a uniquely intimate way," she remembered. "The impression had not yet worn off when we found it renewed at the Negro's greeting."[63]

Monday evening King addressed the CIC, and several sisters attended, including some from Project Cabrini. Sisters summarized King's message to Catholics in their newsletter under the all-capital heading, "WHY WE ARE IMPORTANT, SISTERS."[64] In his address to Catholics, King first evoked Catholic participation in the events at Selma. Paraphrasing King, sisters reported that he believed that "with the presence of nuns in demonstrations and marches such as those at Selma, the Church has spoken Her interest in ALL men in the cause of justice." Singling out women religious, King praised the contributions that sisters had made to advances in the cause of civil rights. Sisters proudly reported that King said he had come to address Catholics in Chicago because sisters "had given the movement an 'unstoppability' and a 'new dimension' which it never had had though ministers and priests were already marching in the ranks. The presence of sisters brought a 'purity' to the fundamentally RELIGIOUS ASPECT of the movement." King's speech affirmed that sisters—more than any category of Catholics, including priests—were important to the civil rights movement. The *Project Cabrini Newsletter* quotes Al Raby declaring that "even non-Catholics got the message of a Sister's 'witness,' which no one else—not even priests—could give."[65]

The King visit made sisters feel that they were on the inside of the civil rights movement and that they had made important contributions to it. King's visit to Chicago fell four short months after the events at Selma in March of 1965—Bloody Sunday, the unexpected influx of Northern supporters, the daily protests and negotiations, and the final victorious march to Montgomery. King wisely chose Chicago to publicly acknowledge the contribution of sisters and priests to the advances made in Selma. Not only had Chicago contributed many religious and lay Catholic supporters to the Selma march; the Chicago-based NCCIJ and the Catholic Interracial Council of Chicago—both sponsors of Project Cabrini—had been instrumental in organizing support from Catholics. Mathew Ahmann, then executive director of the NCCIJ, had sent urgent, pleading telegrams to interracial councils and religious motherhouses throughout the North urging Catholics to dispatch supporters to Selma.

The midwestern cities of Chicago, Saint Louis, and Milwaukee had been disproportionately engaged in the events in Selma compared to cities of the Northeast, and King used the visit to Chicago to recognize and strengthen Catholic support for the civil rights movement in those areas. "This is a marvelous and ecumenical movement—that we are all one in Christ—is due to Pope John and Pope Paul," the sisters reported King had said, "when so many priests and Sisters welcome a man named Martin Luther, it is ecumenical."[66] King used his visit to Chicago to begin mobilizing Catholics to integrate the archdiocese parish school system. In his address King invited the Catholic school system to set an example for public schools by integrating. Chicago, which was 54 percent Catholic, was a good place to start, King argued.

"You Is Sistahs"

As King suggested, sisters did occupy a unique place among African Americans, particularly in Cabrini Green. Sisters did not just stand out physically in the African American neighborhoods; they were also unique to a certain extent in their capacity to transcend racial borders, becoming often the very few whites in an area. Forced to live away from Cabrini Green, sisters moved into and out of the neighborhood daily, crossing borders of race and class as they came and went from the project. What did it mean to sisters to drive into Cabrini each day knowing that they were entering a neighborhood that whites had characterized as dangerous? What did it mean to them when they stood and listened to a speech given by Martin Luther King Jr., knowing that they were among the very few whites trusted to be there?

At Project Cabrini sisters were allowed to enter worlds in which other whites were not welcome. They were invited inside a community that was in many ways closed to others whites. The stories sisters told and still tell about Project Cabrini stress their inclusion and acceptance there.

> Juliet sat in the office window grinding her teeth and muttering: "Ah hates whites. Ah hates dem comin' 'round yere lookin' at us." "But you're nice to us," Sister Maigread said. "We came around looking, too, when we first came." "Well, you-all ain't whites," Juliet said. "You is Sistahs."[67]

The dynamic of sisters being able to enter places where other whites were not welcomed was a reversal of the constraints that sisters experienced relative to Catholic laypeople in usual apostolic assignments. At home in Minnesota, laypeople went to the dentist alone, visited their siblings at will, attended concerts of interest to them. As the Committee on the Apostolate had discussed, the Sisters of Saint Francis were not free to do such things in traditional assignments. In 1965 sisters still went to the dentist in pairs. They asked permission before visiting their families. They weren't allowed to go to concerts. But in Cabrini Green, sisters fit in where other white lay Catholics often did not.

At Project Cabrini sisters' days were bifurcated into one realm where they were limited by protocol and authority and another where they were relatively free of these restrictions. Each day sisters of Project Cabrini awoke in the world of the traditional convent—a place they stayed because protocol and authority had required it—and then they piled into a yellow bus that transported them across the economic and racial boundaries that separated the neighborhoods from each other on Chicago's North Side. Once at Project Cabrini, sisters experienced new freedoms of movement and activity, which contrasted sharply with traditional apostolic arrangements.

Sisters were able to cross borders that other whites could not. More so, at Cabrini Green, away from the prying eyes of the bishop or the fearfulness of Catholic parochial-school children, sisters felt free to create the apostolate that they had been desiring and imagining, the apostolate they felt had been denied them in suburban parish schools. Aided by the Council and the theology of the Mystical Body of Christ, sisters created an apostolate that responded to real human needs and that was characterized by spontaneity of gesture and expression, singing, and even traversing the alleys of Old Town in the company of young adults. At Project Cabrini sisters were accepted rather than restricted or protected. They were relevant rather than antiquated, unique rather than taken for granted, and approached rather than feared.

Sisters particularly described the freedom to be physically demonstrative with children in Cabrini Green. Sisters clearly took great delight in the physical affection they gave and received from the children at Project Cabrini. Photographs from Project Cabrini bear out the physical connections between sisters and students. In the images, smiling sisters and smiling children mingle easily in classrooms, laughing together on playgrounds and in the streets. Sisters told and retold stories about how children addressed them informally with a "Hello Veil" or "Hiya Sistahs." "We daresay, if, after this, we ever find ourselves in positions where a lavish demonstration of affection—especially with children—is frowned upon, we will be out of our element!" wrote sisters from the program.[68]

Sisters took pleasure in conspiring with black children, delighting in their antics and even their antipathy to white police. When asked what sensory memories she carried with her from Project Cabrini, Sister Viatrix answered that she clearly remembered the playfully ominous "Dum, dah, dum, dum" song that children sang when police cars drove by.[69] The *Project Cabrini Newsletter* printed a story about the children shushing an enthusiastic sister in order to avoid attracting the attention of police:

> When sketching classes were coming back to school through Old Town, the students did their best to quiet down Sister Geoffrey who was exclaiming in her best voice how gorgeous an ally-way was that they could just as well have been drawing if she'd only noticed it was there! It seems the police in that part of the city pride themselves on closing in on noisemakers![70]

Related as an amusing anecdote, the story nevertheless suggested that the sister had entered into the children's world in some way. Her companions on a sketching tour intervened to teach her how to move through the alleys as they did, knowing in which parts of the city it was safe to be boisterous and in which parts one needed to be quiet.

Seen in this light, sisters' tendencies to attribute race to the bodies and speech of the people of Cabrini Green in their anecdotes can be understood as a way in which sisters demonstrated to white readers that they were accepted and included inside the black community, a world many white Americans in the 1960s perceived as hostile. At Cabrini, sisters' exoticization of African Americans did not so much serve as a means for sisters to distinguish themselves from African Americans as it did in some of the anecdotes told by sisters in the National Placement Bureau. Race in many of the newsletter anecdotes from Cabrini Green did not signify distance between the sisters and the residents but rather the distance between sisters and the white Catholic world from which they had come. It is in this context that the image of Sister Lisieux Wirtz, walking the streets of Cabrini Green at twilight singing a folk song that indicts the banal privilege in the American suburbs, makes sense.

CHAPTER SIX

The Placement Bureau: Matching Nuns with Needs

In February 1971, Sister Benedicta Claus, OSB, sent greetings "from the deep South" to friends in her religious community in Ferdinand, Indiana. Reflecting on the experience of teaching literature at Benedict College in Columbia, South Carolina, Sister Claus invited fellow sisters to imagine themselves in an environment so foreign—or, better yet, an environment in which they were so foreign—that even their titles, the names to which they responded tens of times on any given day, had become problematic. As she described her circumstances:

> Benedict is a Baptist College, 1400 students, all black. Just imagine what an enigma I was on campus last September: northerner, white skin, fast speech, and a Catholic. To call me "Sister" was nearly incredible for these students, since all members of the *black* community call each other BROTHER and SISTER. By being *white* I was the one person in the classroom that should be Miss, Mrs., Dr., or anything but definitely not "Sister."[1]

Sister Benedicta could not rely in this unusual context on the implicit familiarities of race and religion that had framed her relationships with students in the Catholic college where she usually taught. Rather, at Benedict College, seeing herself reflected in the eyes of students who found her strange, she was challenged to reimagine her identity on different terms. "My one redeeming factor that first week," Benedicta explained, "was that I was a member of the human race; it was there that we had things in common."[2]

Sister Benedicta became an enigmatic presence in a black Baptist college in South Carolina through Cooperative Help of Integrated College Education (CHOICE), a program of the Department of Educational Services in the NCCIJ. Beginning in 1967 the CHOICE program assigned sisters who were professors in Catholic colleges to replace their counterparts in traditionally African American colleges, many of which were located in the South, during the summer session, allowing black professors time to pursue research and writing. The multipage application that the DES used to match sisters with teaching assignments in CHOICE proved so efficient for this task that in 1969 the DES altered the form in order to use it to standardize its informal process for placing sisters in the diverse racial-apostolate programs the DES sponsored or assisted. This new program, named the National Placement Bureau (NPB), matched individual women religious seeking summer work in "new apostolate" programs and organizations that needed the inexpensive and often professionally experienced labor that sisters provided. Though CHOICE remained the central program into which the NPB funneled sisters, the bureau also assigned sister applicants to programs that ranged from small summer day camps run by individual parishes to massive, federally funded projects. Sisters were dispatched to locations as diverse (and, to them, as exotic) as Normal, Alabama; Newark, New Jersey; and Abbeville, Louisiana. Sisters applying to the NPB could choose from among several federal programs, such as Head Start, the Job Corps, and the Office of Equal Opportunity's "poverty schools." In Upward Bound they could tutor "deprived" high-school youth in skills they would need in college, or they could educate white suburban adults about race and racism in the Summer in Suburbia (SIS) program.

In 1966 the Center for Applied Research in the Apostolate (CARA) published a study of "the inner city activities of religious communities of sisters," documenting that 76.4 percent of religious communities responding to the CARA survey had assigned a sister or sisters to teach in inner-city schools. Within many congregations, the study discovered, sisters were engaged in part-time "extra involvements in the inner city," undertaken voluntarily in addition to their primary apostolic commitments.[3] The CARA study offered a carefully rendered portrait of the typical sister engaged in the expanding apostolate of work within racial-justice programs like those in Northern inner cities. She was about thirty-five-years-old, with a BA or possibly an MA degree, and she lived in the East North Central or Middle Atlantic region of the country. She was new to the inner city, having spent less than four years working there, and she likely had not received special preparation from her congregation prior to her first encounter with the urban apostolate. The sister of the new apostolate engaged in such works on a part-time or summer basis, in addition to rather than in place of her "regular work" within a Catholic institution where she typically offered her services as an educator or an administrator or assisted with a "community action activity" such as a visitation program or a housing survey.

However revealing it was of the demographic identity of the sisters who were expanding spheres of apostolic activity in the mid-1960s, the CARA study failed to uncover the motives inspiring them. We know the typical level of education that sisters like Benedicta Claus possessed and even what type of work they performed among African Americans, but we have fewer sources that provide insight into the reasons why sisters like Benedicta wanted to participate in these "new works," what cultural and religious resources they drew upon to formulate new conceptions of the apostolate, or how they understood the expanded apostolate in relation to their conceptions of religious life and to their identities as sisters.

Some tentative answers to those questions merge in the applications and the postplacement evaluations of sisters who engaged in apostolic works among African Americans through the National Placement Bureau, especially in the CHOICE program. By attempting to flesh out with more nuanced detail a portrait of the sisters who crossed these racial, geographic, and religious boundaries to engage in a new, racially oriented apostolate in the late 1960s and early 1970s, this chapter explores the complex ways in which sisters integrated disparate experiences into narratives about the racial apostolate. The hundreds of applications, evaluations, and personal letters preserved in the records of CHOICE and the NPB offer insight into the experiences and perspectives of those sisters already attuned to issues of racial justice and interested in broadened definitions of the religious apostolate. Demographic information in CHOICE and NPB applications suggests that sisters involved in the racial apostolate ranged in age from twenty-six to sixty-nine, distributed in roughly equal numbers across age categories with a slightly larger concentration of applicants between the ages of forty-two and fifty-three. A significant number of sisters were sixty-four or older. With few exceptions sisters had completed at least one advanced graduate degree; approximately a third held doctorates. Nearly two-thirds of applicants had previously engaged in "inner-city or similar type service," such as voter-registration drives in the South, interviewing applicants for legal-assistance programs, tutoring adults for high-school equivalency exams, teaching CCD in migrant worker camps, or teaching in inner-city art programs.

"It Is Hard to Be Anything but Stilted on Paper"

On February 9, 1971, Sister Mary Paul Krasowski, CSFN, completed an application for the NPB; she had first applied in 1970 but had not received a placement offer. At the time of her second attempt, Sister Mary Paul was fifty-six years old. She held an MA from the University of Notre Dame and had just completed a master of education degree at Duquense University. She was an experienced educator, having taught French and music at the elementary, junior, and senior high-school levels. She had also spent four years, from 1964–1968, teaching in her congregation's elementary school in Montgomery, Alabama, where she had worked "exclusively with the Black People." When she applied to the NPB, Sister Mary Paul was serving as the principal of Lawrenceville Catholic Elementary School in Pittsburgh. She did not know how to drive a car. She was "uncertain . . . but hopeful" that her community would grant her permission to serve a full year, rather than only a summer, in a position gained through the NCCIJ's placement bureau. On the last page of her application, the neatly typed words of Sister Mary Paul's "statement of purpose" spill over the edges of the provided lines, filling blank spaces and pushing into the margins, trailing down the page in a complex tangle of thoughts about the character of black people, the nature of indebtedness, the obligations of the Church (and of herself) toward "the black race," about her own abilities, and about the elements that constitute "success" in an apostolate. Her application states:

> My experience in the South has convinced me that I have a debt to the intellectual leaders, be they teachers, administrators at alia of the black race. My Church has not given all its best; I love the black man, my brother in a special way. I have worked with them very successfully, success in this case being mostly my own development as a person through interaction with the parents and children. I would now like to offset our debt and to grow as a person through my involvement with these warm, kind and happy, basically, people and in my small way to contribute to their needs, to their becoming more themselves. It is hard to be anything but stilted on paper, Sister, I just hope I can help where I feel I am qualified. Since I have experience in many areas of Administrative work, including Supervision, Curriculum Planning and implementation, I want to share. Please let, me, if you can.[4]

Sister Mary Paul's statement was characteristic of those offered by sisters in NPB applications, both in the themes she raised and in the intense and thematically intricate nature of her sentences. Sisters' reflections on their reasons for wanting to participate in a racially oriented apostolate were typically multifaceted, simultaneously articulating diverse conceptions of race, of the sisters' own identities as persons and as religious, of the American Church and its congregations, of how to understand and address the inequalities that resulted from racism, of the needs of African Americans and of their own resources to meet those needs, and of the meaning and appropriate expression of the apostolate of women religious. None of these elements stood alone in the statements; rather, the themes twisted around each other, magnifying and complicating each other. The sheer complexity of these statements renders it imperative to approach them in a way that recognizes the order and integrity within the entanglement and explores the interplay of the overlapping elements. To meet the perceptual worlds of these sisters means to hold many thoughts at once, while avoiding the temptation to still the cacophony.

Sister Susan Elizabeth Fitzwilliam typed her application to the NPB on February 6, 1970, from her assignment at Fort Collins, Colorado. At twenty-eight-years-old, with a bachelor's degree in social science, Sister Susan was serving as the coordinator of the diocesan religious-education program; she had thirty-five teachers under her direction. In six years of active apostolate, she had taught math, science, music, English, literature, social science, and religion to students ranging from grade two through grade eight. She felt competent enough as a teacher, indeed, to write to the NPB that "at the elementary level I could teach any subjects." And she could drive a car. She had spent the 1967–1968 school year teaching sixth, seventh, and eighth graders at an "inner city school in Rockford, Illinois," and now she was asking the NPB specifically to find her an assignment with an OEO-funded "poverty school." Just as Sister Krasowski had done, Sister Susan Elizabeth pushed against the limitations of the lined space on the application form, doubling up lines as she reached the bottom of the page. She explained her desire to participate in the racial apostolate by evoking her current assignment among the middle class, the ways it challenged her both apostolically and personally, and by limning the responsibilities of privilege:

> For the past two years I have been working among the American middle class. If I am to be of any value in this area, I feel the need to spend time periodically with the more unfortunate people of our society. It is only with

> this first hand experience with the "other half" of our society that I can speak with any conviction to the more privileged, about their duties and obligations of sharing what they have. Besides, I see apathy in myself as I lived more removed from real social problems.[5]

The prominence of "I" in Sister Susan Elizabeth's statement is significant. By asking sisters to "please write a brief statement of purpose in applying for a position" and leaving several blanks lines for the response, the NPB application encouraged sisters to construct narratives that addressed each respondent's own unique relationship to the racial apostolate. The application invited each sister to insert herself into the expanding apostolate, to create a narrative in which her own biography converged with the circumstances of American racial politics and the postconciliar Church that had made such an apostolate necessary and possible. Through the application form, sisters engaged in the imaginative act of placing themselves into a larger narrative about race and the apostolate. Many sisters responded enthusiastically to this invitation. In a significant proportion of applications, sisters' statements exceeded the boundaries of the given response space. Sisters wrote in the margins and blank spaces (like Sister Mary Paul) and continued on the blank back side of the page, or they attached extra pages and even personal letters.

Sister Ann Julia Kinnirey wrote to the NPB from Trinity College in Washington, D.C., where she had taught courses in ancient languages and philosophy since 1932. At the time of her application in 1971, she was sixty-five-years-old. She had received a master's degree from Columbia University in 1926 and a PhD from Catholic University in 1935. Her teaching experience was as impressive as her academic pedigree. Though she had taught Latin, Greek, ancient and medieval history, logic, and classical elements in English, her specialty was ancient philosophy and aesthetics. Sister Ann Julia had also participated in expanded apostolate work, teaching night classes in reading to African American adults for three years in the District of Columbia. She had recently spent the summer in southern Virginia tutoring at a rural community center by day and in the homes of adult students in the evenings. She did not drive a car. She stated in her application a willingness either to teach "deprived" students or to do literacy tutoring among adults. Sister Kinnirey rejected the possibility of a Summer in Suburbia placement, remarking, "I don't have the patience to undertake educating white racists." Her statement of purpose blended her desire to help, an inventory of her professional resources, her liking for black youth, a belief in her own insight into them, and a reference to the structures governing apostolic work in her community. She wrote:

> I would very much like to help the black people in our country. My only resources are three months of free time and a certain amount of knowledge of a rather impractical kind, with experience imparting it. I like black people just I like [*sic*] white people; and I have gotten along well with those I have met. Also, I think I can understand the aloofness of young blacks. Our financial set-up in the community is such that I would not feel free to take a job that did not pay at least board and room along with long distance travel. I appreciate the great work you are doing.[6]

Most sisters did not give a well-defined, singly oriented reason when asked why they wanted to participate in placement bureau programs. Rather, they offered several, often phrased in the form of tangled thematic components. The expansion of the apostolate of American sisters into racial activism was thus the product of no single element, tradition, or common experience that sisters could easily or singularly reference in their writing. It resulted from the convergence of multiple contextual factors. Reading the letters sisters wrote to the NPB is to encounter a religious world already touched by conciliar *aggiornamento* and on the cusp of a truly radical transformation, a Catholicism still adjusting to the peculiarities of suburban life, and a racial context touched by the beginning of desegregation, a world on the edge of deepening white resistance and internal fragmentation. The sisters' statements reflected the extent to which individual sister-respondents inhabited inconstant positions within multiple and unstable worlds.

That sisters like Sister Kinnirey gave such imbricated responses when asked about their reasons for applying for positions working with African Americans suggests that for them the racial apostolate remained inchoate, with complex roots in their experience of the 1960s. Sisters' multiple idioms also reflected the transitional nature of Catholic moral and religious language itself at the time of their applications. Situated amid simultaneous transitional moments in Catholicism, the civil rights movement, and the institution of vowed religious life, sisters did not possess a singular, authoritative language to explain the relevance of apostolic work among African Americans. They could not evoke a set of shared, well-established, and normative tropes to express their desire for this type of apostolic work. They were making language—and themselves—up as they went.

The vocabularies of traditional Catholicism and preconciliar religious life were also in transition in this period; newly emergent theological and ethical discourses were still largely tentative and contested. Sisters were improvising a bricolage of diverse languages whose complexity reflected the multifarious and open-ended nature of apostolic expansion at that particular moment. In writing to the NPB, sisters combined the idioms and interpretive resources available to them in the multiple worlds they inhabited simply by being at once women, women religious, white, professionals, Catholics, Americans, and human beings. American women religious borrowed frameworks, symbols, phrases, and words from these multiple positions to craft improvised and provisional "statements of purpose" about themselves and about the racial apostolate.

Sister M. Consolata Grace, PBVM, was fifty-five-years-old when she filled in the blanks of the NPB application, living in a dormitory at the University of Notre Dame while completing a master's degree in music. She taught CCD classes at the nearby Sacred Heart parish and directed the choir at Corpus Christi parish. Though she had taught English, reading, and religion at the high-school level and speech classes at a junior college, Sister M. Consolata specifically requested an assignment through the NPB to teach music theory, music appreciation, or choral and vocal performance. She had had no significant previous apostolic contact with African Americans. She explained her application to the CHOICE program using language that contrasted the educational impoverishment of African Americans with the educational opportunities she had enjoyed, adding that she expected to gain something from being near and sharing the lives of impoverished African Americans:

> It has come to my attention that the students graduating from black Colleges are not receiving the education that we have been given; I would like to share my knowledge. I'm sure I will learn much from them; they are Christ's poor.[7]

The application forms opened space for sisters like M. Consolata to articulate desires and expectations about the new apostolate. Woven among other elements in sisters' statements are the repeated phrases "I expect," "I hope," "I anticipate," or "I would like." These indications of intentionality revealed a sister's assumptions about the telos of the apostolate—her perception of the potential for justice or social change or what she considered to be the most salient aspect of interracial activity. Statements of desire described variously what effect against racial injustice a sister wanted her work to have, how she anticipated that work among racial minorities would transform her, what she hoped to gain from experience in the racial apostolate, and how it might benefit either her congregation or the people among whom she worked. Sister Mary Paul, for example, anticipated that she would "grow as a person" through an assignment among African Americans. Sister M. Consolata anticipated a (possibly spiritual) enrichment through her engagement with impoverished students. Sister Ann Julia wished simply to help black Americans. Sister Susan Elizabeth hoped that an NPB summer placement would make her more effective at educating privileged students about just behavior.

NPB applications also invited sisters to imagine an apostolate free of the problems or limitations that frustrated them in their current apostolic positions. In applying for work through the NPB, sisters stepped outside the customary congregational boundaries, freeing themselves of congregational priorities, institutional obligations, and of the authority structures that often determined sisters' assignments. They were thus liberated to imagine and request types of work that seemed more appropriate to their education, training, or personal preferences. M. Consolata wanted a teaching position congruent with her musical training, for example. Sister Susan Elizabeth wanted a respite from immersion in middle-class students. Such statements indicate not only what sisters thought might be possible in new forms of service but also what they found unsatisfying about their current situations, and thus constituted a moral critique of midcentury middle-class American Catholicism. The expectations and desires woven through their statements suggest that sisters anticipated that the racial apostolate would be a means to articulate, and possibly even realize, hopes for themselves and for the institution of religious life at a time when such matters were open for discussion and revision. Sisters entered these racialized locations with expectations of further personal and institutional transformation already in place.

Sisters improvising this new form of apostolic work had at their disposal a rich array of ideological and theological concepts by which to legitimate change. Their intellectual heritage within the contemporary Catholic church was diverse, offering both pre- and postconciliar ways of understanding the ends of religious life. Because the institution of vowed religious life was similarly undergoing a complicated moment of transition, it presented sisters with several possible explanatory frameworks for expanding the apostolate into spheres of racial activism. The varied professional training women religious had acquired in preparation for the apostolic component of religious life, especially in the social sciences, offered them a language that they could use to appeal to audiences outside the Catholic Church. The civil rights movement itself provided another language—one of racial and social justice—that sisters employed to argue for the importance of a racial apostolate. These disparate explanatory and legitimating languages converged in sisters' writing to create an ethos of reciprocity: they would contribute to the cause of racial equality, and in turn they held a set of expectations about what they would gain from this work.

Theological orientations of the Church presented activist sisters with theologies of charity and social action whose roots were deeply embedded in Catholic tradition. "By social action, I do not mean violence or rebellion," one sister explained. "I mean sharing the belief in the eternal dynamism of the Divinity reflected in the Mystery of the Incarnation; serving God through man, and man through God."[8] The doctrine of the Mystical Body of Christ provided activist sisters with a spiritual language to talk about interracial unity. Sisters discussed their desire to participate in the racial apostolate by evoking theological conceptions of the specialness of the poor and of the spiritual benefits to be gained through service to and presence among them. "I have a deep interest and concern for the poor," a sister explained in her application for the CHOICE program. "It is also an opportunity for me to find Christ and my way to give Christ."[9] Other sisters explained the racial apostolate in terms of a generalized Christian obligation to be socially engaged. In the words of Sister Anne Mary O'Donnell,

> I believe that a Christian humanist must show effective concern for the social problems of one's age. Helping students in a black college to think critically, to write cogently and to respond to literature sensitively seems to me to be an indirect but real contribution towards achieving racial justice in the United States.[10]

Another sister stated more generally that she was applying to the NPB "to be involved in a Christian social service commitment."[11] Sisters frequently presented the racial apostolate as a spiritual enterprise that followed logically from theological conceptions of social justice and service to the poor that they saw as central to Catholic social teaching.

Individual religious communities possessed their own unique charisms, and sisters who participated in racial activism portrayed these, too, as congruent with apostolic concern for racial parity. Sisters' discussions of the spirituality of the apostolate ranged from basic statements about the duty of religious to relieve human suffering—"to serve where there is a human need and a possibility of giving 'witness' in an Apostolate"[12]—

to nuanced arguments about the unique role that religious played in reconciling God and humanity. Several sisters described the racial apostolate as a natural consequence of the intersection of conciliar theologies with the process of renewal in which religious were engaged. "To live totally means to give life to others," explained a sister who was teaching language arts at a parochial elementary school in Prior Lake, Minnesota (then an outer suburb of Minneapolis), at the time of her application. "In very real ways," she continued, "I experience the demand to move to another area of giving this life. Religious giving only pragmatic service to the world is of the past—to touch value systems and possibly impact them is what witness is about."[13] This sister's weaving together of pragmatic service with "giving this life" is characteristic of ways in which spiritual beliefs and practical concerns converge in NPB statements about the racial apostolate. In another example, a sister explained that a summer position through the NPB would allow her to fulfill the apostolic imperative of religious life while supplementing her academic education with an experiential one:

> My membership in a religious order says to me I MUST serve my fellowman in a capacity of Christian influence. For five summers I have been getting my MA from "books." I feel now I should use it for others as well as get an education of experience for myself.[14]

Some sisters were drawn to the racial apostolate for reasons directly related to their education or their profession as educators. These sisters viewed African Americans less as "Christ's poor" and more as persons who had been unjustly denied access to adequate education. "I want to be of service to people who have been deprived of the advantages of a solid education. I feel that serving in a 'deprived' school is the best way to do this," wrote one sister.[15] These sisters frequently explained their desire for placement through the NPB in terms of their own competence as teachers. "Any classroom is a piece of geography whose chalkdust I breathe as native air," commented one sister, "and any brand of youngster, whatever the color, is still familiar scenery."[16] Another sister stated simply, "I would like to share any knowledge, competence, etc. with others, especially those suffering from prejudice and deprivation."[17]

Sisters who used professional language to discuss the racial apostolate believed in the transformative power of education and, by extension, in the efficacy of the teaching apostolate to remedy racial injustice. Sisters wrote passionately about education in their applications. "Education today is the area where the revolutionary action can be, where one can shape the world of today and that of tomorrow," proclaimed one sister. "As a religious who is an educator I have an incarnational imperative to contribute to those who need what I can give—college teaching."[18] Indeed, the generations of sisters who applied to the NPB had either lived through the transition from pre-service to in-service education of women religious that the SFC had accomplished or had directly benefitted from this prioritization of education for sisters. These sisters had also experienced firsthand the power that their orders had gained relative to the male hierarchy as the result of increased professionalization. Sisters also, no doubt, understood that it was largely their own professional expertise that would gain them apostolic entrance into African American institutions, where their professional status was valued and needed. When sisters evoked the transformative power of education, they were speaking both as educators and as women who had gained a measure of autonomy and empowerment through education. "From a theoretically-liberal sociological 1940s viewpoint on blacks," wrote one sister, using language borrowed from her own educational experience in the social sciences to explain her NPB application, "I have come to a committed desire to help them through education."[19]

By equating racial injustice with educational deprivation (and then proposing to remedy the deprivation) sisters of the racial apostolate framed racial inequality in terms that echoed rhetoric in the larger civil rights movement in the South—equal opportunity, pride, empowerment. One sister wrote:

> I believe that the Negroes, both in the North and in the South, have been given an inferior education. It is only through the development of reading and writing skills that they will ever achieve the power to succeed in American society. This power will certainly do much for their self-image. Since I have the background and experience in these areas, in justice I must share it with those who have not had these opportunities.[20]

Sisters did not conceive of racial justice in abstract terms; instead they asked how the lives of African Americans would change by creating the context for them to experience self-actualization, economic success, and autonomy. These women religious intended the work of the racial apostolate to itself create justice by compensating blacks for injuries they sustained in slavery and segregation: "I am intensely interested in trying to even the score for the Negro," Sister Celestine Hoedel wrote in 1968. "My modest attempts in this direction may help, however slightly, to atone for centuries of injustice."[21]

Sisters shied away from discussions that focused exclusively on abstract conceptions of racial equality, preferring to join race and justice with spiritual and pragmatic concerns. One sister gave a detailed account of the complicated position she felt religious must maintain relative to African Americans in order to help them achieve. "To understand the black, one must work with them, observe them and learn from those who are working with them," she explained. "We must help them but to help them we must learn how to handle them so that they can achieve. They are bright, they need help. I want to learn how I can help them."[22] More often, sisters' evocations of racial justice entailed specific plans for the racial apostolate to provide African Americans with what they had been denied under segregation and then for sisters to step out of the way.

Sisters generally explained their desire to participate in the racial apostolate by combining theological, professional, and activist languages. "I believe there is racial injustice," wrote one sister in her statement of purpose. Then she linked racial justice to the obligations of religious life, saying "as a Christian I believe that I have a duty to be concerned, and as a religious, my duty to be concerned is doubled."[23] Another sister incorporated theological concepts in her perception of African Americans in this way:

> As a practical application of my conviction that a Christo-centric life must also be socio-centered, I strongly desire to give myself and whatever talents I possess to help in some way the movement towards social justice. This motive has been strengthened during my contact with Negro people of our inner-city, whose culture, warmth, and dignity I love and respect.[24]

Such statements describing the racial apostolate in multiple terms reveal sisters' diverse motivations for engaging in work among African Americans. One sister simultaneously evoked her competence as an educator and her desire for new apostolic experiences in applying for the CHOICE program:

> I feel that I could gain much for myself in this experience, and give a good deal in my teaching. I enjoy teaching and I have this desire right now to be of a greater service than I have been in the past. I am at the place in my thinking (right now) where I feel I must get out and help those less fortunate. In replacing one of the southern teachers, I could really be doing two things: (1) giving that person a wonderful chance to better himself or herself, and (2) give of myself in my teaching and presence on a Southern campus.[25]

When sisters worked these diverse languages into statements of purpose they produced an explanatory rhetoric that characterized the racial apostolate in terms of reciprocity conceived on several levels. Most often, sisters described a reciprocal relationship between what they would give and what they hoped to gain from racial activism. "I believe that there is much to be learned from the exchange with persons in a new environment," wrote one sister.[26] Such characterizations of the racial apostolate suggest that these sisters understood the apostolate not solely as a form of service or witness but also as a venue for religious and, just as commonly, for personal development. Racial activism was a form of apostolic engagement by means of which sisters could expect to gain greater personal benefits than they would in traditional patterns of religious service. "I would learn a great deal" in an NPB assignment, one sister predicted. "These experiences would add to my development as a person."[27] Another version of this reciprocity combined racial justice with the theological concept that Christians were spiritually enriched by interaction with or nearness to the poor. According to this ancient Catholic ethos, sisters would gain specific, efficacious spiritual benefits from apostolic work among African Americans because they were the most stigmatized members of contemporary society. On another level of reciprocity, some sisters who employed professional language described racial activism as an obligation entailed by the educational advantages that sisters had gained in religious life:

> In the past few years I have been given the opportunities to obtain an education and to travel rather extensively. I'd like to be on the giving end for a while. Presently I teach in a school near the inner-city. We have some white-black problems. I would like to learn more from the Black community, as well as give some of me to them.[28]

The racial apostolate also provided reciprocal opportunities for sisters to gain interracial experience that would make them even more effective advocates for racial justice. Sisters moreover evoked apostolic reciprocity to describe their hopes that an NPB assignment would remedy unsatisfactory elements of their current circumstances. "I would like to make a contribution to the cause of interracial justice but do not feel qualified to serve in the areas of inner-city work," one such sister wrote. "I am also interested in a change of scenery and situation on a temporary basis for my own development as a teacher."[29] The exchanges of goods that sisters expected to realize in the racial apostolate reflect the languages and expectations that had influenced their desire for such work in the first place. Each idiom was oriented towards a specific end—spiritual enrichment, professional expression, personal development, or the creation of racial justice. When sisters described racial activism in reciprocal terms, they harmonized these disparate elements and allowed for several ends to be fulfilled at once.

Several NPB applications from sisters contain deep, devastating critiques of American Catholicism. Currents of frustration and anger ran underneath and through the sisters' sentences, as they distanced themselves at various times from laity, from the Church, and from their own congregations. "Last summer I taught in a program at Dunbarton College that was designed to prepare CCD teachers," one such criticism began. "If am correct, it was one of the most unrealistic projects in the world."[30] Sisters criticized the complacency of laity regarding racial justice and the complicity of the hierarchy in perpetuating social inequities. They criticized their congregations for privileging a safe, predictable, traditional apostolate over one that addressed contemporary social problems, for failing to embrace conciliar reforms quickly or completely, and for prioritizing congregational apostolic obligations over individual sisters' apostolic inclinations. A sister who taught reading, science, math, music, art, and spelling at a parish school in Lorain, Ohio, described how her congregation's institutions limited her desire to teach particular subjects and particular levels. "I enjoy the adventure of sharing through literature but lack the opportunity during the year," she explained, "[because] we have no high schools or colleges."[31] Another simply stated, "I am not satisfied personally or professionally in teaching at the high school level."[32]

What most troubled sisters inclined toward the racial apostolate was the increasingly suburban nature of American Catholicism. Though a few sisters portrayed the entire parochial school system as a stifling professional environment, most sisters objected to placement in schools whose student population comprised mainly middle-class, white Catholics. By teaching in the Catholic schools that had sprung up in metropolitan suburbs in response to the migration of African Americans into former Catholic neighborhoods in the city, some sisters felt that they were themselves complicit in the injustice of de facto segregation. "While at the present time I am in suburbia," wrote a sister who taught high-school biology on the outskirts of Baltimore, "I believe that I could be more effective away from the religious scene & suburbia and put my life where my lips are."[33] Some even argued that suburban assignments had a deleterious effect on sisters, as did one sister who listed the ill effects of her placement in a suburban school. "I have been working in a suburban high school for three years," she recounted. "The atmosphere in the school is not conducive to active involvement in the social problems of the day nor to creativity or initiative in the performance of my work."[34]

Some sisters sought NPB placements as a way to escape or at the very least to balance their apostolic assignments among the middle class. "I currently teach in a college which draws its students from an upper to middle class, white, suburban population," one such sister wrote. "I would like to have some contact with students from other stratas of society and fell [*sic*] that the CHOICE program would allow me to have this contact along with doing something positive to assist in the improvement of education for the negro by pinch-hitting while the negro teacher is furthering his education."[35] Other sisters employed the moral language of reciprocity to argue that an NPB placement offered experience and knowledge not available in a suburban-oriented apostolate. Some sisters, accepting the inevitability of a white, middle-class apostolate, described suburban teaching as a missionary endeavor, arguing that even temporary experience in the racial apostolate would fit them to be more effective in teaching racially and economically privileged students about justice. "I would like to obtain, through experience, a better understanding of the needs of minority groups," one sister argued. "In this way I could better communicate a desire for social justice in the students I regularly teach."[36]

Sisters' desire for a racial apostolate reflected their frustration with demographic changes within American Catholicism and with their congregations and, more generally, with the institution of religious life. Some sisters believed that their congregations were failing to provide meaningful apostolic work that would be more congruent with individual sisters' preferences. "I am now serving in a Negro community, in an area of need to them, but in an area foreign to my professional training and my own job satisfaction," a sister wrote the NCCIJ in 1970. "I plan to continue here for another year, but I would like the opportunity to teach in my own fields and yet continue to work with the people I have learned to appreciate and respect."[37] Another wrote to request NPB placement in order to live outside of congregational institutions: "I am just completing three years in administrative work as Directress of Education in my community. I have been living at the Motherhouse during this time and feel quite out of touch with the larger Christian community whom I wish to serve."[38] An older sister described how her own sense of the apostolate had changed over time and no longer matched her long-held assignment: "I feel the need to express my apostolate in a manner different than my present status allows. After 25 years in the classroom, I feel the need to seek a deeper, more committed manner of serving others."[39] "I really want to get 'involved,'" wrote a twenty-year-old sister, "and I feel in my present structure I am too restricted. The high schools administered by my community are too static and provide a stifling atmosphere—I want to be free to grow & develop in a open spirit of Vatican II!"[40] Thus the racial apostolate provided a way for sisters who felt stifled or limited by certain facets of religious life—an unsatisfying apostolic placement, lagging *aggiornamento* in a particular community, a tense relationship with a local superior—to remain in their congregations. Racial activism offered, potentially, a middle path for sisters trying to avoid both conformity to the congregational status quo and disillusionment with the institution of religious life.

"They Respected Me as a Person"

One sister, in a letter to Sister Margaret Traxler, recounted the acceptance and freedom she felt in her racial-apostolate assignment:

> My students accepted me in a most wonderful fashion. I did not wear a religious habit at any time during the summer . . . it was entirely up to me to do what I wanted to do, and was used to doing. I made the choice not to wear it and in talking freely with the students during the summer, I have learned from them that they were delighted to have a Sister teach them. They respected me as a person—someone desirous of helping them. They were so very grateful that I took my time (!) to come and be interested in them. It was the first time for most of them to even be associated with a Sister. This was great experience for them and for me personally. I cannot sing their praises enough!![41]

For many sisters the racial apostolate was a type of mirror in which they were able to see themselves and the institution of religious life apart from the norms of the Catholic world which they normally inhabited and which ordinarily constituted the horizon of their vision. The expectations and desires sisters expressed in their applications shaped their perceptions of the African Americans they encountered in the eventual assignments they went to in the racial apostolate. The expectations also determined the meanings sisters attached to these experiences when they reported them to other religious. Sisters were alien and strange in black communities in the South and in the racialized inner city, and their anomalous presence often provoked questions about identity or motive among those with whom sisters interacted. Apostolic excursions into the inner city or into the South were journeys into liminal places—and into possible futures in the process of renewal. They went as individuals, perhaps for the first time since entering vowed religious life.

Preconciliar norms of enclosure had meant not only that sisters' movements were largely confined to Catholic neighborhoods and institutions but also that non-Catholics, particularly those in the South, were not accustomed to encountering sisters. The first sisters who ventured outside traditional Catholic spheres into non-Catholic areas frequently met with surprise, bewilderment, and amusement. And because sisters often crossed these boundaries in order to work and live among African Americans, they also met with hostility from Southern whites who considered them outside agitators. In writing about their experiences in these locations, sisters stressed ways that their presence was novel. Stories describing the odd questions, comments, or behavior of non-Catholics were common in sisters' accounts of participation in projects of the racial apostolate. A report of a relatively benign exchange reads, "A wino who tried to read my open book as I waited for a bus was amazed to learn I was teaching at A&T. 'You a Catholic?' (Many asked this; a few 'Are you a *Roman* Catholic?')"[42] The man's curiosity and surprise was widely shared, as sisters reported in their narratives sent home. A sister from Eau Claire, Wisconsin, who taught summer courses at Albany State College through the NPB offered a more complicated interpretation of the relationship between sisters in the racial apostolate and the whites they encountered:

> A few of the white people we met in the city made it evident that they were not very happy with our contributions to the Negro. We did have the opportunity to acquaint many of the white people with the school system at Albany State, and informed them of the native ability of many of the students. Sister Fides, a Dominican who taught there too, felt that our contribution in changing the attitude of some of the Whites, perhaps was more valuable than our contribution at the college. I am not sure that I entirely agree with this.[43]

If not always unwelcome, sisters were at the very least an uncanny presence in much of the American South.

In Southern locations where Catholics were more numerous—for example, in Maryland, in Louisiana, and in some cities in Florida—the presence of sisters in the "new apostolate" proved problematic for a different reason. In such venues the arrival of sisters committed to the racial apostolate revealed the underlying racism of some white Southern

Catholics and the complicity of many Southern religious in segregation. A sister teaching black students in an Upward Bound program in Alabama commented on the difference between her work and that of neighboring sisters, "The OSB's (superior's name above) are living at the nearby (5 hilly blocks away) convent from which they go out to teach vacation school to an all white group in a nearby parish. Birmingham is still far behind."[44] Several sisters reported that Southern activists hoped that the presence of socially engaged religious would encourage local religious to become involved in racial issues. A sister who worked for Project Head Start in Abbeville, Louisiana, reported that the Head Start director had specifically arranged for her to stay with Carmelites in the area during her summer assignment, in the hope that she would interest them in the program. The sister returned to Durand, Wisconsin, in September unconvinced that she had influenced those religious who were "strongly favoring segregation."[45] Sisters involved in the new apostolate, performing work that was not directly tied to their congregations, also stood in marked contrast to local religious whose communities were less affected by conciliar *aggiornamento*. A sister teaching through CHOICE at Bethune-Cookman College in Daytona Beach, Florida, reported a conversation with a Presbyterian minister who was "shocked to learn that I would teach at B-C of my own choice—rather than being 'ordered to do so by my superiors.'" She explained the minister's dismay in terms of the contrast between herself and the local religious: "The Catholic Institutions here are staffed by Irish priests, Irish Sisters of Mercy, and New York Dominicans, and have been virtually unchanged by the Vatican Council."[46]

Sisters working through the NPB, who attempted to integrate the parishes and schools they found themselves in, proved most vexing to segregationist Catholics. In a lengthy, handwritten reflection on her experiences teaching in an Upward Bound program at Texas College in Tyler, Texas, a sister named M. Bernadette mentioned several "staring incidents" that occurred when she entered public spaces such as restaurants in the company of her black students. She reported her distress at encountering "another of those staring experiences" when a representative from Upward Bound and his young daughter volunteered to drive her to Mass at the Immaculate Conception Church one Sunday. Trying to explain the stares she attracted when she entered the church alongside her companions, Bernadette commented that:

> perhaps I did look a little different, with my white habit, a little six year old negro girl holding my hand and a tall handsome negro on the other side of me. It would be interesting to know what these people think. I'm sure they

> must have mixed emotions about such a strange trio. In fact, the little girl Yolanda remarked to me last Sunday, "Yo should see how all those people are lookin at yo, they must think what is that white sister doin with a negro girl!" To which I replied, "if they ask, I will tell them, we go to Mass with our friends."[47]

Sisters of the racial apostolate were outsiders to several worlds—to Southern society, to segregationist Catholics, and finally to African American students.

If activist sisters felt conspicuous among white non-Catholics and often unwelcomed by Southern white Catholics, they were even more foreign in African American communities and educational institutions, which were the focus of the racial apostolate. With few exceptions, the sisters who undertook racially oriented apostolic work were white. This compounded their otherness to African American students, most of whom were unfamiliar with nuns. One sister observed of her students that "what they know of Catholic is little and bad."[48] Sisters frequently comment that they were the first nuns that many of their students had ever encountered. Sister M. Bernadette, who taught in the CHOICE program in Tyler, Texas, reported, "I am the only sister here, and with one other member of the faculty, the only white face among the students. . . . They respond well, but insist on calling me m'am. I have some who say 'm'am sister.'"[49] Sisters alluded to ways in which their race seemed to complicate relationships with black students. Some, like M. Bernadette, recognized in students' responses to them patterns of deference often reserved for whites in Southern society; other sisters saw in such exchanges the opportunity to attach a friendly face to whiteness. Sister Rosarita, teaching in Texas, wrote of her students that "most of them are meeting Sisters for the first time," adding that "it may also be their first pleasant association with a white person, too."[50] Sisters' reports suggest that they were keenly aware of the many ways that, as vowed religious and as whites, they were outsiders within the African American institutions they served.

Sisters' search to find points of connection with their black students was aided by the fact that sisters' strangeness in these locations destabilized their own religious identities. The racial apostolate challenged familiar models of religious life and religious identity, which were otherwise constantly reinforced in Catholic settings. A sister arriving at a black college in South Carolina, for example, faced the task of maintaining her religious identity in a context in which no one immediately understood what her sisterhood meant, much less which words to use in addressing her. This internal process had an external counterpart: the stark differences between sisters and the African Americans they encountered—the absence of racial, regional, or religious frames of reference for understanding each other—necessitated that they find new bases for their relationships with students.

Ultimately, sisters claimed their experiences of marginalization in the South as something they shared with African Americans and employed it as a rhetorical basis for mutual understanding with black students. Because the racial apostolate was specifically directed toward remedying the consequences of white racism, sisters who participated in racial-justice programs were accustomed to thinking about African Americans largely in terms of discrimination and marginalization. Experiencing themselves as outsiders in Southern society, women religious identified with familiar tales of the racial stigmatization that blacks endured. Sisters' narratives directly linked their own experiences of social marginalization with those of African Americans by citing situations when both groups together suffered discriminationy, as when Sister M. Bernadette described the hostile stares directed at her and her African American companions entering church. Sisters also conveyed indirect identification with African American marginalization by including African Americans and themselves in the same "we"—"we go to Mass with our friends"—together facing common adversaries.

Sisters' embrace of outsider status deepened the significance they attached to experiences of belonging, particularly within the black community. A recurrent theme in sisters' writings is the extent to which they felt accepted and appreciated by African Americans. A typical account, written in this case by a sister who taught "a predominance of black" students at Hampton Institute in Virginia, reads, "I was accepted as a person. I was accorded much courtesy and friendliness. I never felt that I was looked upon as an 'outsider.'"[51] African American kindness to these sisters, who were so aware of their own otherness, exemplified a type of grace that sisters employed as a standard to judge the responses of Southern whites to them. Sisters often contrasted the hostility and gracelessness that Southern whites exhibited toward blacks and sisters to the courtesy they experienced from black students. One sister wove these elements together in a story that compared her relationship with African Americans to that of a Southern white woman:

> My reward for the entire summer was a statement made to me as I left a poverty-stricken home. While I was there a white woman came to the door and berated the negro mother for letting her son go to pick peppers. After completing my survey I thanked her and told her I was sorry to have inter-

rupted her wash day work. Her reply . . . 'Sister, come anytime, you are always welcome at our house . . . you understand us and we understand you.' Such a remark can make even a five footer feel tall![52]

Such accounts make clear that sisters felt both accepted and wanted in African American institutions. A sister whose regular assignment was at Mary Manse College in Toledo, Ohio, reported that she was "extremely well received as a nun and as a white" in her summer assignment at Virginia Union College. "I felt as if I really belonged to the community, was wanted," she explained, "and when the summer session came to an end, I felt sad to leave my classes and Virginia Union."[53] This sister's sense that she was leaving a place and a community rather than simply an educational institution reflects many sisters' descriptions of the racial apostolate as one of presence. Sisters' letters describe a daily apostolate of constant contact with students as the ideal, within and beyond classroom hours—living among, eating with, counseling, spending time at "picnics, cookouts, movies, art shows, social science forums,"[54] and even worshipping alongside their students. To the extent that sisters understood work among blacks as a ministry of presence—"we feel, hope and pray that our presence here may count for something"[55]—their reports of belonging, acceptance, and inclusion in black communities suggest that they felt successful in this endeavor. "Finally, but most important, this summer confirms what I learned last year in Mississippi. I really feel that I received special treatment here by the faculty and the Job Corps women, not as a person but as a 'Sister,'" wrote one sister from her assignment in Guthrie, Oklahoma. "So it seems, that our way of life means very much to the world and that the world stands very much in need of those who are witnesses to the 'invisible life,' the life of grace, and the Source of grace, Himself."[56] Sisters interpreted the acceptance and appreciation they encountered in the black community as both an affirmation of the institution of religious life and an endorsement of an expanded apostolate that combined service with presence.

It should be noted that a few sisters described a different, less-accepting reaction from African Americans. These infrequent accounts in the NPB papers stress ways in which African Americans, regardless of sisters' perceptions of them, may have had quite complicated reactions to the presence of white sisters within their educational institutions, particularly with the emergence of the Black Power movement and separatist ideologies. Sisters' accounts of the openness of African Americans to their presence should be understood purely as sisters' perspectives on the issue and not as a reflection of African American experience. A letter from 1969, typical of those few describing a certain distance between white sisters and black students, comments: "We were treated with cool acceptance. They—students and the few faculty members that we met—were by no means 'waiting to be saved' by any whites. They were nice to us but less than friendly."[57]

Sisters' obvious delight at African American reactions to them and their surprise at their own sense of belonging (as well as the enthusiasm with which they reported this to other sisters) contain an implicit comparison between black institutions of the racial apostolate and Catholic institutions of the traditional apostolate. The graciousness and gratefulness that sisters report in black students' responses to them unearthed sisters' feelings that they were not equally appreciated and valued in Catholic institutions, where women religious were a taken-for-granted presence. Aside from correspondence written from the field, most sisters wrote interpretive reports about the racial apostolate at the conclusion of their assignments, after they had returned to their usual teaching posts. As they settled back into appointments within Catholic educational institutions (and to a lesser degree within Catholic hospitals and congregational structures), many sisters wrote about the new apostolate, recording their experience of black communities as they reoriented themselves to white Catholic suburbia. Thus, sisters' reports contain comparative information about how the racial apostolate differed from a purely Catholic one and specifically how work in locations where their presence was a surprise rather than an assumed element affected them. "My students were surprised to learn that Sisters were only for the summer," one sister commented. "They seemed genuine in their appreciation of their courses. This made my spade work in English worthwhile."[58] Sisters regularly reported with astonishment that black students were grateful for their work and that administrators in black educational institutions valued their contributions to the academic environment. The exclamation point in Sister De Porres Conway's comment that African American students "were so very grateful that I took my time (!) to come and be interested in them" suggests that gratitude was an unexpected component of her interactions with students.[59] It also implies that Sister Conway expected her sister-reader to understand and share her surprise.

"Tall, Huge, in Every Way and Wearing Dark Glasses"

Sisters who worked through the NPB found many astonishing things in their interactions with African Americans. Their letters are punctuated with stories that portray black students as unpredictable and in some ways unknowable. For all the tales of connection and belonging woven into sisters' accounts of the racial apostolate, sisters occasionally reminded their readers that such work involved crossing boundaries, entering unfamiliar cultural worlds, and exposing themselves to uncomfortable or simply puzzling situations. Anecdotes about awkward encounters with African Americans illustrate the limits that sisters reached in attempting to experience solidarity across racial boundaries. The specificity of lived racial experience complicated sisters' efforts to understand African Americans; sisters could identify with African American experience but could never fully enter into it. "You can't fathom what deep meditating one does when a roomful of Afro-Americans discuss the cruelties of slavery and you are the only Anglo-American present," one sister wrote of her experience auditing a course in black history at the CHOICE college where she had been assigned. "I've found that to take a class with suffering people is not just an experience; it's a HAPPENING."[60]

Sisters surrounded black youth with an aura of mystery and seemed both amused and perplexed by the remarkable comments that they occasionally fielded from them. Sisters' anecdotes about these surprising exchanges always took the form of conversations, with the voices of black students counterpointing that of the sister involved. A baffled sister reported, for example, a conversation she had had with a student during her first week on campus as she entered the auditorium for orientation. "One of the boys said to me 'are you gonna teach?' I said, 'yes, I am,' so he asked what, I answered, 'Reading,' he just remarked, 'Oh baby.' I don't really know what he meant and never had the time to figure it out."[61] Sisters paraphrased students when reporting other types of conversations with them—"my students have been nice about saying they learned some things"[62]—but used direct quotes when relating conversations they found perplexing. Separating a student's words from the larger narrative, sisters acknowledged that baffling student comments were cultural elements that defied translation and interpretation. The comments stood with a mysteriousness and otherness that sisters could not fully assimilate into their own stories. Still, sisters approached these memories with amusement and wonder. Sister Carol Grochowska, who had taught at Jackson State College in Mississippi, wrote, "The greatest moment of joy came to me at the end of the first summer session when one of my students remarked: 'O Sister, it is so nice to have nuns on campus!' I asked why. She responded: 'They are SO VIRGINAL.' Need I say more!"[63] In these anecdotes sisters acknowledged that they had been transported to a cultural universe that was not completely within their mastery or even their understanding.

The most salient and transformative of these baffling interactions for sisters was the convergence of cultural worlds in the title "sister." Sisters reported with astonishment that their black students used the word "sister" in a way that was very different from its familiar use in Catholic enclaves. Where the title "sister" was a formal title among Catholics—one that often introduced a certain distance between those who were and were not vowed religious—among African American students the word retained many of its familial connotations. Used both casually as a term of friendly affection and racial respect by young people and formally as a term of connection toward co-religionists, the word "sister" emphasized connection and intimacy in the African American community. A sister wrote from her assignment at Bethune-Cookman College that her arrival had precipitated "ecstasy" among students. "My name is 'Sister Campbell,'" she explained. "Apparently 'Sister' has soul, and the students give me a big unearned grin when they say Sistah!"[64] The power of overlapping meanings for sisters and for African Americans should not be underestimated. Sisters referred to this coincidence frequently and with absolute wonder. The term "sistah" provided women religious with a much-desired entrée into black culture, allowing them to form unique connections with black students, particularly with young black women. The sister-sistah convergence placed women religious and African American women in the same vocative category, increasing the resonance of the concept of sisterhood in the process.

The term "sistah" generally altered the tenor of interactions between sisters and students. As Sister Benedicta observed in the passage that introduced this chapter, being able to call their new white teachers "sister" may have diffused or subverted the pressure black students felt to respond to women religious with patterns of racial deference otherwise enforced in the segregated South. In that regional context, the term "sistah" introduced humor and irony into conversations between black youth and white women religious, opening space for improvisation and play. Sisters suggest that students employed the word "sistah" as a way to claim them as their own, to rename them, and to integrate them into their world. Empowering African American students to exercise proprietary liberty with sisters, the sister-sistah convergence opened space for a richer reciprocity to emerge in sister-student relationships. One sister related that female students felt comfortable enough to ask "Sister" questions about—and offer critiques of—her lay attire. "The word 'Sister' seems to mean something special to the girls," she noted. "Most of them questioned me about why I was wearing regular dress. My explanation seemed to satisfy, though a good many expressed the opinion that they liked the 'Sister dress.' Interesting?"[65]

The term "sistah" also opened space for improvisations and revisions of ways of being a Catholic sister. Sisters evoked "sistah" status to legitimate the work of the racial apostolate: by placing women religious temporarily inside the specifics of black culture, the title "sistah" confirmed activist sisters' desire to be in a unique relationship with African Americans, that their religious status allowed them to enjoy a higher degree of trust and intimacy with blacks than other whites experienced.[66] The multiple uses of the term "sister" positioned women religious in the middle of an ever-widening gap between pre- and postconciliar visions of religious life, bridging familiar patterns of apostolate and religious life and emergent revisions to those preconciliar norms. Sisters' ways of understanding themselves were subverted and expanded when they claimed the title "sistah." And when young African American women addressed them as "sistah," women religious experienced simultaneously a traditional Catholic and a racial-activist religious identity.

At the same time that sisters identified with African Americans, claiming inclusion in the community via the title "sistah," they qualified this solidarity by drawing contrasts between themselves and black students. Sisters racialized the voices, bodies, and experiences of their students. Sisters presented student voices in dialect form. They gratuitously attached race to individuals who appeared in their reports, as did one sister in describing Dr. Edam, a colleague, as "delightful as he is black."[67] Many sisters indulged in common racial stereotypes to describe African American students, seemingly unaware that they were drawing upon racial tropes that often had been employed to discredit African Americans. Thus images of happy, majestic, soulful, spiritual people were woven into many sisters' accounts. "They are friendly & hard-working & earnest, but they write a form of English quite unknown to any speaker of the language, including themselves," observed another. She then added that "the people are charming and I love being here."[68] Even when they borrowed empowering language from the civil rights movement, sisters drew attention to differences between themselves and their students. "Physically and temperamentally, in personality, grooming, charm, I was surrounded with beauty," wrote one sister, "yet our part of town might almost have been Africa."[69] Though not all of these racializations were explicitly negative, most served to open an ontological distance between sisters and African Americans.

Underneath and alongside language about the "beautiful black students" in their classrooms, some sisters also displayed an acute awareness of the size of African Americans, particularly males. Writing to Traxler about her experience in a historically-black college, Sister M. Bernadette contrasted her own diminutive size with that of her students, writing:

> The other day something funny happened in class, (you must know that I am *barely* 5 ft. tall and weigh about 108 lbs). Well anyway, some of the boys were getting a little too friendly with one another so, when they came into class I told one of them, I thought it better if he would sit in the front seat—this is to a boy named Ivan, tall, huge, in every way and wearing dark glasses, he stood up—way up, and said to me—"you know, m'am, I has allergies to front seats," but, said I, "way down there, just try it Ivan you might even be cured!" To his companion, another fine big fellow, I said, "there's a nice place over there, 3rd desk, 3rd row," he arose (all of him) went to his place, and said with a big grin, "you know, I is scared all by myself like this." But nothing daunted I replied "how sad for you." But both of them took it well and we're still good friends.[70]

Sister M. Bernadette's anecdote about reseating unruly boys in the classroom—a common procedure for teachers—is punctuated by references to the size of her male students. One is a "fine big fellow"; another, "tall, huge, in every way." When they rose from their seats, their stature was remarkable to her; they didn't just stand, they stood "up—way up," bringing their full height, "(all of him)" to bear.[71] "The night I was going to Washington by bus," another sister reported in a typical review statement, "a 6'4" black man came up to me in the station at 10:45 to ask, 'Are you Sister Mary?' He wanted to get into one of my classes."[72]

Such currents of anxiety and ambivalence ran through sisters' encounters with African Americans, complicating their reports of joy at being accepted into the private world of the black institutions where they taught. Sisters' anecdotes about baffling students with strange ways of speaking and immense bodies suggest that sisters were not universally comfortable with immersion, much less inclusion, in African American communities. Rather, a complex dynamic of simultaneous identification with and distance from black students emerges in sisters' reports to the NPB about their work in the South.

Sisters expected that apostolic experiences in the South, among racial minorities, would be transformative. They went with this expressed intention: to be broadened culturally, deepened spirituality, challenged professionally, and made more human or more compassionate or more fulfilled. They wanted to be liberated in some way from facets of religious life with which they were uncomfortable. These expectations invested the South with particular resonance as a location where sisters could imagine the realization of the transformations they desired. Though sisters' experience of the racial apostolate was shaped by legacies of the Catholic past and contingencies of present-day Catholicism, it was also an expression of their vision of the future of the institution of religious life. Sisters engaged in the racial apostolate in response to changes in the social and theological orientation of the Catholic Church in America, but they entered these landscapes with expectations of and desire for personal transformation already in place. These desires functioned as lenses through which sisters interpreted the people they encountered. Sisters were unprepared, though, for the ways in which work in African American communities in the South challenged their experience of themselves as apostolic women religious. Removed from the familiar rhythms of enclosure within Catholic institutions, sisters of the NPB were forced to craft provisional identities that were shaped by their relationships with African American students. Thus sisters of the NPB became neither fully sister nor "sistah" but something of both.

Conclusion: Endings and New Beginnings

Sister June Fisher of the Sisters of the Blessed Sacrament, an African American congregation of women religious, wrote to Sister Margaret Traxler in 1969 looking for someone to direct a women's residence at Xavier University, a historically black university run by her order in New Orleans. "A Black person would be preferred," Fisher stated in her letter. "But if she is not available then a person who 'thinks black' as we say, and who has the proper attitudes towards the Black People, and her relationship with them [would be acceptable]." Sister Fisher's list of the qualities of a person who "thinks black" included:

> one who comes to learn and not to teach
> to become aware of, and not to impose
> one who comes to receive, and not to give in condescension
> a "with" attitude, not a "for" attitude.[1]

It is no surprise that in searching for a sister who either was black or who "thinks black" Fisher turned to Traxler. Through the auspices of the NCCIJ's Department of Educational Services, Traxler had initiated prominent projects in the racial apostolate, consulted in the development of similar programs in various orders of women religious, and kept a watchful eye and a cabinet of active files on racial-apostolate programs run by other people. Traxler spent the 1960s and early 1970s corresponding with, encouraging, and guiding women religious who wanted to contribute to the cause of racial justice. If there was a black-thinking white sister out there, Traxler likely either knew her or knew of her.

The emphasis on black self-determination in Fisher's request offered a foretaste of the trajectory toward which the racial apostolate was heading in the late 1960s. As we have seen, the apostolic revolution among American women religious occurred in tandem with significant shifts in the Catholic Church and in American society, and the path of sisters' engagement with racial justice in the civil rights era was inextricably intertwined with both the trajectory of the civil rights movement as well as that of conciliar reforms in the Catholic Church. As the 1970s dawned, a coalescence of factors similar to the ones that created the phenomenon of the "new nun" again emerged to significantly slow the momentum of the racial apostolate. A growing ethos of Black Power made the presence and assistance of white sisters increasingly unwelcome in the civil rights movement and in black communities. Congressional battles and the restructuring of the Office of Economic Opportunity during the Nixon administration curtailed federal appropriations to agencies engaged in the War on Poverty, starving the racial apostolate of reliable funding. And sisters were increasingly preoccupied with internal matters, devoting their energies to the general chapter meetings and self-studies that were the mechanism of postconciliar congregational reform. Sisters also were drawn into costly conflicts with American bishops and curial officials who objected to some of the reforms sisters had implemented in their communities. As a result, the number of racial-apostolate programs declined sharply after 1972 as sisters turned their attention to other issues and other apostolates.

The racial apostolate emerged at the same time that ideologies of black power were gaining prominence in the civil rights movement and, by extension, in African American culture. As the fragile coalition of young activists and seasoned ministers that had comprised the organizational foundation of the civil rights movement weakened in the mid-1960s, the movement's consensual emphasis on racial integration fragmented into competing ideologies of interracial cooperation and black separatism. Frustrated by the violence of white resistance to integration, angered by paternalistic attitudes of whites in the civil rights movement, and convinced that previous strategies of accommodation and compromise had yielded little real progress in securing racial equality, leaders like SNCC's Stokely Carmichael increasingly called for African Americans to claim more pronounced autonomy from whites in the movement. The slogan "Black Power!" encompassed more than a demand for racial self-determination; it also reflected growing confidence and racial pride in African American communities.[2] Sister Fisher's first preference for a black sister in the passage quoted above, and her stipulation that white sisters applying for the position not demonstrate attitudes of condescension toward African Americans, sounded strikingly similar to Stokely Carmichael's insistence on black autonomy in his oft-quoted 1966 essay, "What We Want." "We want to decide who is our friend, and we will not accept someone who comes to us and says: 'If you do X, Y, and Z then I'll help you,'" he insisted. "We cannot have the oppressors telling the oppressed how to rid themselves of the oppressor."[3]

This emergent separatist ethos complicated the presence of white sisters in civil rights organizations and in African American neighborhoods. Though the racial apostolate grew steadily through the 1960s, adding new programs and gaining new volunteers every year, the reception sisters received in African American communities progressively cooled after 1966. By the late 1960s, black communities—when they accepted the presence of sisters at all—expected nuns to approach African Americans with an attitude of openness and respect, ready to learn and to receive in equal measure with what they gave and taught. By the early 1970s, as separatist currents within black-power discourse gained strength, sisters were largely unwanted in the black neighborhoods and communities in which they endeavored to serve. Though some sisters seemed puzzled by these developments, many understood the anger that animated young black activists, having witnessed firsthand the brutal effects of white supremacy in their work. Some sisters welcomed the new assertiveness of African Americans as a positive development, a sign that, despite ongoing inequities in areas like income and education, the civil rights movement had successfully opened space for African Americans to claim ownership of their own culture, destiny, and place in American society. Writing Margaret Traxler to decline a second summer of placement in a historically black college in the South, a Benedictine sister from Wisconsin interpreted the growing preference in African American schools for African American teachers as a cause for optimism. "I am certain that the colored folks would prefer their own as teachers even when they do not have them readily available," she noted. "They show a growing sense of identity and I hope it will soon be fully realized."[4] In most cases sisters respected the limits that the black community placed on their ministries. They either stepped aside, moving from directive positions to supporting roles as black lay leadership emerged in racial-apostolate programs, or they discontinued racial-apostolate programs that were the most vulnerable to such criticisms. The Department of Educational Services scaled back the number and range of its racial-apostolate programs after 1970, shifting the structure of remaining programs to make them more responsive to the initiative and priorities of local African American leaders. In a few instances directors of racial-apostolate programs attempted to recruit African American sisters to replace white sisters on staff.

Some congregations responded creatively to the implicit (and at times explicit) charge that ministries like the racial apostolate were little more than intrusive meddling by know-it-all whites who were insensitive to the distinctive culture of black communities. In 1967 when the Sisters of Mercy in Detroit decided to develop a program to help the congregation relate "in a meaningful and positive way to urban problems," they acknowledged upfront that "imposed programming by paternalistic outsiders" was both "irrelevant and unwanted" in inner-city Detroit. Instead of forging ahead with a traditional program of direct service, the Sisters of Mercy instead moved cautiously, devoting a year to comprehensive research. Conceding that "limited personal and community experience in ghetto areas, lack of acquaintance with the people and their problems, and conflicting popular opinions as to the role of the white, professional, religious woman" all complicated their apostolic activities in inner-city Detroit, the congregation determined that "a program of research would be most beneficial to the individuals involved and to the religious community as it looks toward future apostolic planning."[5] Through the summer of 1968, a select group of sisters immersed themselves in a single neighborhood, gathering information about the community and its needs. They collected statistical data, interviewed community leaders, built relationships with residents of the neighborhood, and developed a list of thirty-three recommendations to guide the congregation in any future undertakings in the "inner-city apostolate." In their final report the sisters advised humility and restraint, arguing that sisters should assume a "supportive role in the present day Inner-City Community" and "assist in the development of self-determination within minority communities."[6]

While sisters were learning to scale back their racial-justice ministries to accommodate a growing desire for institutional autonomy and community control among African Americans, changes in the Office of Economic Opportunity reduced the amount of federal money available to fund racial-apostolate programs. From its inception the OEO had always been vulnerable to its political opponents on both sides of the aisle. As the war in Vietnam deepened, President Lyndon B. Johnson had less political capital to devote to defending the War on Poverty against its critics in Congress and in state governments. Though Congress continued to reauthorize the Economic Opportunity Act at two-year intervals in 1967 and 1969, it also weakened the effect of the law by adding cumbersome new requirements to the act while effectively decreasing the total appropriation to fund it. With the election of President Richard Nixon in 1969, the vulnerability of the OEO increased further. Nixon appointed Donald Rumsfeld, then a young congressman from Illinois, to head the OEO, and Rumsfeld immediately set about restructuring and transforming the agency. Rumsfeld divested the OEO of many of its operating programs, transferring programs like Head Start and the Job Corps to other federal departments (the Community Action Program, the most controversial of the OEO's operations, remained under the agency). He refocused the agency's resources on initiating new programs and evaluating existing ones. Nixon's opposition to the agency intensified during the course of his tenure in the oval office. In 1971 he vetoed the amendments to the Economic Opportunity Act, forcing Congress to create compromise legislation that further limited the scope of the OEO. By 1973 Nixon had moved the remaining functions of the OEO to state and local jurisdictions through the revenue-sharing programs of his New Federalism initiative, appointing Howard Phillips to oversee the final dismantling of the agency's federal offices. Though challenges in federal court and stopgap congressional appropriations kept the OEO nominally alive through successive years when the Nixon and then Ford administrations allocated zero dollars to the agency in the presidential budget, the Community Services Act of 1974 moved the remaining, anemic vestiges of the OEO to a successor agency, the Community Services Administration.[7]

To the extent that sisters in the racial-apostolate had been dependent on federal agencies of the War on Poverty to provide financial support for racial-justice programs, they found themselves and their ministries tied to an increasingly unstable federal bureaucracy. With each successive diminishment of the OEO and related agencies, fewer and fewer of sisters' grant proposals were successfully funded. Sisters who were reliant on the salaries they earned in federally funded projects were forced either to return to traditional apostolic assignments within Catholic institutions or to seek funding through private foundations. "We were turned down by the OEO for an Upward Bound program so we will have to start out with a tin cup," wrote one sister, attempting to explain the limited scope of her summer program for "disadvantaged ninth-graders."[8] Though organizations like the Ford Foundation sometimes came through with last-minute support for some racial-apostolate programs, the failing health of the War on Poverty in the early 1970s slowly starved the racial apostolate of the financial resources that had facilitated its euphoric expansion in the mid-1960s.

Following the conclusion of the Second Vatican Council in 1965, American women religious entered a period of rapid institutional transformation that siphoned the attention of sisters in the racial-apostolate away from these logistical and financial challenges toward internal matters of congregational mission and governance. Before the Council, American religious had pursued institutional modernization and reform through organizations like the Sister Formation Conference. *Perfectae Caritatis,* the conciliar document on religious life, transferred the locus of renewal from such large organizations to individual congregations, thereby increasing the responsibility of individual sisters for conciliar reform. Congregations were to formulate specific reforms through careful study of the Gospels and the charism of the founder, consulting with all members of the community as the process of reform unfolded. While most congregations made communitywide participation a priority in the renewal process, the forms this participation took varied greatly from community to community. Some congregations conducted anonymous surveys of their members. Others assigned sisters to committees or discussion groups that focused on a specific facet of religious life. While some congregations adopted strictly democratic models of majority-rule voting on renewal decisions, other congregations experimented with dialogic models that made consensus a prerequisite for the adoption of any change. Most congregational reform processes culminated with general or special chapter meetings that brought together all members of the congregation.[9] Congregational self-studies, general chapters, and other renewal mechanisms temporarily turned sisters' focus inward in the late 1960s and early 1970s, away from broad social problems like race as sisters considered more intimate, specific questions about religious dress, congregational finance and regulation, and community structure. "Only in part does one realize the blood, sweat and tears that went into the loving toil of the chapter. Or of the anguish of the time following," reflected one sister about the investment sisters made in religious reform in the closing years of the 1960s.[10]

The racial apostolate was especially hard hit by the demands of conciliar reform. Because of their experiences in new forms of mission, sisters who were involved in the racial-apostolate frequently volunteered, or were asked by their congregations, to participate in committees that studied the congregational charism or reform of its apostolic commitments. While this meant that a number of sisters were unable to participate in racial-apostolate programs during the central years of congregational reform efforts, it also meant that the perspective of sisters who pursued an expansive interpretation of the religious apostolate shaped congregational policies on this issue. "I am on a Committee on New Structures in Religious Life and New or Different Apostolic Works of the Communities," one sister wrote to Margaret Traxler. "I am taking along your June 26 report on the NCCIJ programs that need Sisters, and hope that I can make them realize more and more of us are thinking of this type of service."[11] After 1967, Sister Margaret Traxler was forced to juggle assignments within DES programs to accommodate the schedules of sisters who needed to attend committee or chapter meetings. "I hope I am not gumming up the works any further," one member of the Traveling Workshops faculty wrote to Margaret Traxler, "but our Self Study dates have been extended to June 20. I am the chairman of the Apostolate Committee and have to be on hand to meet with the Advisory committee."[12] "Sister, I would love to join the Traveling Workshop again next summer," wrote another, "but we are having our Extraordinary Chapter the first part of June and I am a delegate to the Chapter."[13] Another sister declined placement in a summer program because she needed to devote herself to her current assignment but then added, "if I needed more reasons I could add that we are to have a summer of renewal—with all of us concentrating on theology and the study of the religious life. That I need, too, and I'm not sure I could miss even two weeks of it. So, my dear Sister Peter, the answer must be a 'no'—reluctantly."[14]

The implementation of *Perfectae Caritatis*, and with it the reform of congregations of religious in the United States, was complicated by the unusually large number of papal directives that interpreted the conciliar document for religious, often sending them confusing and even contradictory messages about the nature and extent of appropriate reform. The initial papal documents that governed the implementation of *Perfectae Caritatis* (*Ecclesae Sanctae* in 1966 and *Renovationis Causam* in 1969) encouraged innovation, providing sisters with a period of relative freedom from external regulations and from precedent, in which they could experiment with new configurations of religious life. While some communities walked a cautious path toward renewal, many congregations initiated reforms that departed substantially from traditional patterns. Sisters abandoned the habit in favor of modest secular dress and eliminated many of the regulations that had limited sisters' movements, activities, and contact with laypeople and their families. They developed informal living arrangements and experimented with collegial models of authority in congregational governance. In 1969, papal directives reversed course, interpreting the *Perfectae Caritatis* through an increasingly narrow lens that restricted both sisters' freedom to depart from preconciliar norms and their ability to dissent from the hierarchical forms of authority exercised by bishops, curial officials, and the pope himself.

This reversal in Roman interpretations of the Council's intentions about reform in religious congregations exacerbated the already tense relationship between some American sisters and their bishops over experimental reforms that some congregations had implemented. In the late 1960s and early 1970s, sisters in the United States faced criticism and occasionally sharp reprimand from priests and bishops who objected to the abolition of the habit or the softening of rules of enclosure in their parishes or their dioceses. Communities who vigorously resisted pressure from indignant or angry bishops to renege on hard-won reforms faced difficult, even tragic choices. When conflicts could not be quickly or quietly resolved, officials from the Sacred Congregation for Religious and Secular Institutes (CRIS, the curial body that governs religious institutes) were called in to adjudicate, drawing sisters into exhausting investigations and interviews. With few exceptions, CRIS representatives supported the authority of the bishops, forcing sisters to choose between holding fast to the reforms or losing canonical status (and with it congregational assets like schools and buildings). Congregations that had formulated reforms through intricate processes of community consultation and conscientious study—believing such reforms to be consistent with the goals of the Council—resented what they saw as the intrusion of the male hierarchy into their internal affairs. "Women's congregations will be fearful in taking initiative," observed one sister of the chilling effect these conflicts had on the renewal of some congregations. "They look to 'the Church' for leadership. Someone must have courage; instead we seem to be paralyzed by multiple, mutual fears."[15] The infamous public dispute between the Immaculate Heart of Mary sisters and Los Angeles Cardinal Archbishop James Francis McIntyre in 1968 over reforms the congregation had implemented is but one example of a widespread pattern of increasingly acrimonious conflicts between women religious and male ecclesial authorities in the postconciliar period.[16] Sisters who had joined the racial-apostolate to protest the racist subjugation of African Americans in society increasingly were forced by circumstances to instead invest their energies in resisting male domination in the Church.

Even the DES, the main organization that had initiated and coordinated major programs in the racial-apostolate, gradually changed from an organization that focused on the civil rights of African Americans to one that primarily promoted the rights of women religious in the Church. Through its focus on the apostolate, the DES had become nominally engaged in reform issues through its 1967 workshop, "Adaptation and Renewal." One result of the 1967 workshop was the creation of a new newsletter, *Trans-Sister,* published under the auspices of the NCCIJ and co-edited by Sister Margaret Traxler, Sister Maryellen Muckenhirn, CSC, and Traveling Workshops veteran Lillanna Kopp, SNJM. *Trans-Sister* focused entirely on religious renewal, providing a literary venue for sisters to share new ideas about renewal and community structure as well as information about common struggles. In 1969, the editors of *Trans-Sister,* alarmed at the escalating seriousness of conflicts between sisters and the hierarchy, formed the National Coalition of American Nuns (NCAN), an advocacy group to speak publicly about unwanted interference of male clerics in renewing congregations of women religious. NCAN's founding statement boldly stated, "As religious women of the Church, we protest any domination of our institutes by priests, no matter what their hierarchical status. We have founded a National Coalition of American Sisters defending themselves against those who would interfere with the internal administration and/or renewal we alone must and can evolve in our communities."[17] On the twentieth anniversary of the NCAN founding, Margaret Traxler reflected, "This forthright call shocked many in the Church, including nuns themselves. But others welcomed such frankness. Sister Mary Luke Tobin wrote, 'You have thrown down the gauntlet, and it's about time.'"[18] NCAN quickly evolved into a major organization with a substantial membership roster, a monthly newsletter, annual meetings, and its own independent funding. As the racial-apostolate waned, and as the NCCIJ encountered some financial difficulties during a period of "low civil rights resources," the resources, staff, and loyal following of the DES became those of NCAN.

Embedded in these calls for the autonomy and the right to self-determination of American sisters was an emerging feminist consciousness among women religious. "I feel that our days of being male dominated have come to an end," one sister optimistically stated in a 1969 letter to

Margaret Traxler.[19] Commenting on the "dictatorial decrees" of the American bishops for women religious, another sister opined that "it seems very hard to get the idea into some of the episcopal minds that women are adults and able to manage their own affairs."[20] Reporting on the positive resolution of her grievance against a parish priest who had arbitrarily cancelled her employment contract with his parish, a sister from West Virginia commented hopefully, "This will greatly strengthen the position of the professional and will certainly do away with the idea that sisters can be shoved around by clergy pressure on superiors."[21]

Though the emergent feminism among sisters in the racial-apostolate who objected to the interference of male clerics was not entirely dissimilar to the link historian Sara Evans has described (in her book *Personal Politics*) between Caucasian women in the civil rights and student movements and the origins of the women's movement in the 1970s, the analogy between sisters in the racial-apostolate and the early leaders of second-wave feminism is partial at best. Racial activism was but one of several factors that contributed to and shaped the feminism that emerged among Catholic sisters in the 1970s and 1980s.[22] Catholic feminism thus developed in ways that paralleled second-wave feminism but remained largely separate from it. In fact, many of the sources that nourished nascent feminism among sisters were distinctively Catholic and specific to the experience of vowed religious. Sisters read foundational books of Catholic feminism by Mary Daly, Rosemary Ruether, and Sally Cunneen rather than works like Betty Friedan's *The Feminine Mystique*. Living and working in autonomous women-identified communities, sisters possessed a rich tradition of solidarity with other women that was unmitigated by intimate relationships with men. The feminism of Catholic women, and particularly of women religious, drew deeply on Catholic theological currents in the conciliar period that underscored the dignity of each human person. Since the 1950s, sister organizations like the Sister Formation Conference and the Conference of Major Superiors had trained women religious to view themselves and each other as competent professionals, and to work cooperatively for progressive change. In the 1970s the Conference of Major Superiors, in its new incarnation as the Leadership Conference of Women Religious, began to actively advocate on the behalf of congregations and individual religious in their battles with the male hierarchy. And though sisters discovered the transformative power of talking about common challenges and frustrations, they did so while participating in congregational self-studies and chapter meetings mandated by Vatican II rather than in traditional consciousness-raising groups.[23]

"Someone Must Have Courage"

Though the majority of sisters' projects promoting racial justice had disappeared by 1973, the demise of the racial apostolate did not signal the end of sisters' apostolic engagement with the world beyond convent walls. The racial apostolate declined but the larger apostolic revolution of which it was a part continued unabated in the 1970s. Sisters who left assignments in African American communities did not necessarily return to parish schools and convents. Rather, they threw themselves into new apostolic works that ministered to such groups as migrant workers, drug addicts, college students, battered women, and incarcerated persons. Many religious who had initially joined the racial apostolate in the mid-1960s as a way to push against the apostolic limitations of their congregations found that by the early 1970s their communities had caught up with them, allowing and even encouraging a wide range of apostolic activities outside of Catholic institutions.

Though the racial apostolate had largely played itself out by the 1970s, the lessons sisters learned and the transformations they had experienced within the racial apostolate had left a permanent mark on sisters' lives and on their institutions. The unanticipated symbiosis of racial activism and religious reform recast the spiritual and institutional world of Catholic women religious in the 1960s. On an institutional level the racial apostolate reinforced and in some cases accelerated the process of postconciliar reform that altered normative standards of enclosure, religious authority, devotional practice, and religious dress for apostolic women religious. Participation in the racial apostolate also transformed sisters on a more personal level, challenging conceptions of religious vocation and religious identity that sisters had brought with them from the novitiate into the new apostolate.

Because work among African Americans usually removed sisters from convents and Catholic institutions, the racial apostolate often required sisters to adjust certain logistical components of religious life. Sisters lived in small communities of five or fewer sisters, making decisions by community consensus rather than following the orders of a designated superior. They adopted informal devotional schedules and, for practical reasons, many sisters abandoned the religious habit altogether. By pushing against the institutional restrictions of convent life, sisters in the racial apostolate experimented with adaptions and reforms that later became normative for most communities of nuns. From her assignment in Newark, New Jersey, Sister Joan Bauer observed that sisters who chose assignments in African American neighborhoods "must realistically be prepared for little support from their religious community, her family and other white people who cannot understand. She must know herself well to wisely decide before God if she can stand the heat and dryness of the desert that will be her daily portion and still remain a woman of HOPE. This is not pessimistic; it is realistic."[24] Other sisters experienced the novelty of the new apostolic programs in more positive terms, as freedom from external bureaucracies and as an opportunity for adventure. A list of "ideas for possible experimentation" sent to Margaret Traxler by a group of "interested sisters" (as they signed their letter) who taught at Saint Bartholomew's School in Wayzata, Minnesota, reflects typical innovations that occurred in the racial apostolate. The sisters suggested the following ten ideas:

1. Break down large communities into small units, each with phone and discussion rooms
2. Individual budget for each unit
3. Family visit allowed
4. Individual choice of dress, possible ring for identification
5. Table reading discontinued
6. Chapter discontinued
7. Rule reading replaced by community discussion
8. Schedule revised to each sisters' needs and ministry
9. Convent tables not set during day, but set attractively at night
10. Community workshops on religious holidays[25]

The list also reads like a description of the organizational structure and rules that would characterize most communities of women religious from the 1970s onward.

On a basic level, the racial apostolate provided sisters with invaluable practice of the skills they would need in order to reconstruct religious life. As sisters learned from other participants in the civil rights movement how to endure seemingly endless planning meetings, navigate bureaucracies, negotiate with federal agencies, and respond fluidly to ongoing change, they also gained practical training in how to reform outdated institutions and bring new ones into being. Their experiences in the new apostolate gave sisters a certain confidence in their capacities that was noticeable in their later dealings with the male hierarchy in the 1970s.

Because sisters had become accustomed to meeting with community leaders, federal officials, city bureaucrats, and journalists in the course of their work, they were less easily intimidated when meeting with bishops and curial officials to discuss controversial facets of religious reform. They also were less likely to immediately cave in to pressure from people in positions of authority.

The racial apostolate also changed sisters by challenging familiar models of religious identity. Apostolic engagement in places like Selma and central Chicago removed sisters from the relative racial and economic privilege of Catholic schools and hospitals. Sisters entered Southern and urban landscapes liberated from the behavioral expectations they encountered in Catholic institutions and gripped by the anticipation of further transformations. Sisters characterized their encounters with African Americans as simultaneously unsettling and transformative. The salience of this dynamic is most evident in the ways in which sisters' self-understandings were simultaneously subverted and expanded when they claimed the title "sistah," incorporating new notions of self, religious consecration, and mission into their identities. The habit made sisters chameleons, allowing them to assume different racial and gender characteristics to suit particular situations. It also served as a form of camouflage. They could use it to be noticed—in a protest rally—or they could use it not to be noticed—to be able to drive into the heart of Cabrini Green—and to be able to move freely through the world. Through their letters and reports, sisters of the racial apostolate often served as translators, making the black community knowable (or viewable) to white Catholics in segregated areas.

The most striking examples of transformation through the racial apostolate were deeply personal in nature. The racial apostolate often stripped women religious of their familiar public identities of "the good sisters" and forced them to develop new ways of interacting with laypeople. As Sister Maigread reflected from Project Cabrini, women religious in the racial apostolate became virtuosos at "playing by ear," at adapting to new people and new situations, often on the spur of the moment. Sisters in the racial apostolate also became accomplished at manipulating racial and religious symbols. In African American communities, where whiteness often served as a symbol for white-supremacist oppression, the malleability of race attributed to sisters sometimes allowed them to move from the category of oppressor to a category of neutrality, if not solidarity, with blacks. It was not simply that sisters were not white in such moments; rather sisters who were transported across the binary system of racial signification confounded and complicated categories of black and white. Neither white nor black, according to the respective standards employed by both African American and white communities, sisters then constituted a third racial category, the category of "sistah."

Through proximity to African Americans, sisters in the racial apostolate also learned critical vocabularies to describe their experiences of oppression and gendered inequality within the Catholic Church. They developed strategies for confronting the male magisterium that they would later employ in conflicts with the Vatican throughout the 1970s and 1980s. When the racial apostolate immersed sisters in African American neighborhoods and social institutions, it gave sisters a close-up view of discrimination and its effects. To the extent that sisters identified with African Americans and recognized in the black experience the barriers, stigmas, and dynamics that evoked their own experience in the Catholic Church, sisters were able also to learn from the African American struggle for liberation. When Catholic sisters occasionally slipped through to the other side of segregation—when the black community or the white one occasionally cast sisters racially as black—their identification with African American experience took on additional resonance. Sisters who were discriminated against because of their affiliation with black people gained direct experience of segregation's sting. And when the black community claimed a sister as one of its own, sisters experienced the power of solidarity.

Through the confluence of their worlds with those of African Americans, particularly in the Jim Crow South, sisters were able to observe various strategies that African Americans used to manage white supremacy. They observed blacks using strategic silence to give the illusion of assent to discrimination not worth fighting and holding their tongues when there was nothing but violence to be gained from confrontation. Following the example of their African American neighbors and knowing that they needed every possible medical person's help, sisters held their tongues on Bloody Sunday in Selma as white doctors chastised wounded marchers for "stirring up trouble" even while they stitched up their wounds. Sisters learned that feigned complicity sometimes cost less than open defiance and that a well-placed "No, Sir" could deflect unwanted scrutiny. Sisters watched blacks manipulate racial symbols occasionally to pass as white when it was possible or strategically wise to do so. In the civil rights movement sisters learned the power of solidarity and the strategic value of carefully chosen symbolic protests. They learned how to resist rhetoric that reduced them to stereotypes. "That is something that I have over and over again reflected on," said a sister who was present through the events in Selma in 1965, "the courage of people and their own discovery of their self-worth, and that the messages that they had lived with were not true, and some of them always knew it, but not all."[26]

Finally, through the racial apostolate, sisters learned the power of imagination and hope. "God *is* in his heaven," wrote one sister in a note of encouragement to Margaret Traxler the autumn after Selma, "and God *is* just. And He and you and we and they *will* overcome!"[27]

Notes
Bibliography
Acknowledgments
Index

Notes

Introduction

1. To reduce redundancy of terms, in these pages I occasionally use the term "nun" in a colloquial rather than a canonical sense to denote vowed women in Catholic religious congregations, recognizing that the formal canonical definition of the term denotes women religious who are otherwise commonly referred to as cloistered or contemplative nuns.
2. Sister Barbara Lumm, SSJ, interview with author, December 14, 2000, Rochester, New York.
3. Sister Gertrude Joseph Donnelly, CSJO, *The Sister Apostle* (Notre Dame, Ind.: Fides, 1964), 125.
4. Dana L. Robert, *American Women in Mission: A Social History of Their Thought and Practice* (Macon, Ga.: Mercer University Press, 1997), 317–328.
5. Carol Coburn and Martha Smith, *Spirited Lives: How Nuns Shaped Catholic Culture and American Life, 1836–1920* (Chapel Hill: University of North Carolina Press, 1999), 4. For further reading on the history of Catholic women religious in the nineteenth century, see also Mary Ewens, *The Role of the Nun in Nineteenth-Century America* (New York: Arno Press, 1978); Maureen Fitzgerald, *Habits of Compassion: Irish Catholic Nuns and the Origins of New York's Welfare System, 1830–1920* (Urbana: University of Illinois Press, 2006); Mary J. Oates, *The Catholic Philanthropic Tradition in America* (Bloomington: Indiana University Press, 1995); and Barbara Misner, *Highly Respectable and Accomplished Ladies: Catholic Women Religious in America, 1790–1850* (New York: Garland Press, 1988).

6. For further reading on congregations of African American women religious see Cyprian Davis, *The History of Black Catholics in the U.S.* (New York: Crossroad, 1992); Tracy Fessenden, "The Sisters of the Holy Family and the Veil of Race," *Religion and American Culture* (2000): 187–224; and Diane Batts Morrow, *Persons of Color and Religious at the Same Time: The Oblate Sisters of Providence, 1828–1860* (Chapel Hill: University of North Carolina Press, 2002).
7. Robert, *American Women in Mission,* 332.
8. Mary Ewens provides an excellent exploration of the historical development of the apostolate and canon law in her essay, "Women in the Convent," in Karen Kennelly, SCJ, ed., *American Catholic Women: A Historical Explanation* (New York: Macmillan, 1989), 17–47.
9. Suellen Hoy, *Good Hearts: Catholic Sisters in Chicago's Past* (Urbana: University of Illinois Press, 2006), 73.
10. Suellen Hoy, "Lives on the Color Line: Chicago Sisters and African Americans in Chicago, 1890s–1960s," *U.S. Catholic Historian,* vol. 23, no 4., Fall 2005: 67–91.
11. For further reading on educational patterns among American women religious, including their history and effects on the institution of religious life, see Bridget Puzon, ed., *Women Religious and the Intellectual Life: The North American Achievement* (San Francisco: International Scholars Publications, 1996).
12. John T. McGreevy, *Catholicism and American Freedom: A History* (New York: Norton, 2003), 190–215.
13. Mary Ewens, OP, "Women in the Convent," in Kennelly, ed., *American Catholic Women,* 41.
14. Sister M. Charles Borromeo, CSC, "Can Sisters Be Relevant?" in *The New Nuns,* ed. Borromeo (London: Sheed and Ward, 1968), 38.
15. Rebecca Sullivan, *Visual Habits: Nuns, Feminism, and American Postwar Popular Culture* (Toronto: University of Toronto Press, 2005), 22–59.
16. Sister Mary Evangeline, RSM, to Sister Margaret Ellen (Mary Peter) Traxler, SSND, typewritten letter, 1968, series 4, box 2. National Catholic Conference for Interracial Justice papers, 1961–1969, Marquette University Archives (hereafter referred to as NCCIJ-MUA).
17. Sister Mary Antona Ebo, FSM, to Sister Margaret Ellen (Mary Peter) Traxler, SSND, typewritten letter, May 13, 1967, series 4, box 1. NCCIJ-MUA.
18. Louis Marie Bryan, *History of the National Black Sisters' Conference, Celibate Black Commitment* (Pittsburgh: National Black Sisters' Conference, 1971).
19. "Summer of HOPE," *Nuns Newsletter,* issue #6, November, 1965. NCCIJ-MUA.

20. The National Catholic Conference for Interracial Justice (NCCIJ) kept limited files on most of these projects, primarily in series 19, box 14, but also in correspondence files in series 4. Many projects also were mentioned in issues of *Nuns Newsletter,* also in the NCCIJ collection. NCCIJ-MUA.
21. Sister Peter to Sister Margaret Ellen (Mary Peter) Traxler, SSND, handwritten letter, September 19, 1967, series 4, box 4. NCCIJ-MUA.
22. For further reading on narrative, history, ethnography, and the politics of representation, see Joyce Appleby et al., *Telling the Truth about History* (New York: Norton, 1994); James Clifford and George E. Marcus, eds., *Writing Culture: The Poetics and Politics of Writing Ethnography* (Berkeley: University of California Press, 1986); Michael Jackson, *Minima Ethnographica: Intersubjectivity and the Anthropological Project* (Chicago: University of Chicago Press, 1998); Peter Novick, *That Noble Dream: The "Objectivity Question" and the American Historical Profession* (Cambridge: Cambridge University Press, 1988); Thomas Tweed, ed., *Retelling US Religious History* (Berkeley: University of California Press, 1997), especially Tweed's introduction, "Narrating U.S. Religious History," 1–26. I am grateful to John Demos for his guidance and encouragement on this subject.

1. Church and Society

1. Sister Evangeline Meyer, SSND, "Parish Servant to a Pilgrim People," in *New Works of New Nuns,* ed. Sr. Margaret Traxler, SSND (St. Louis: B. Herder, 1968), 1.
2. Meyer, "Parish Servant to a Pilgrim People," 2.
3. One well-known example of this genre of thought is Ann Carey, *Sisters in Crisis: The Tragic Unraveling of Women's Religious Communities* (Huntington, Ind.: Our Sunday Visitor, 1997).
4. On Catholic sisters in the nineteenth century, see Mary Ewens, *The Role of the Nun in Nineteenth Century America* (New York: Arno Press, 1987); Dana Robert, *American Women in Mission: Asocial History of Their Thought and Practice* (Macon, Ga.: Mercer University Press, 1997); Sisters, Servants of the Immaculate Heart of Mary, *Building Sisterhood: A Feminist History of the Sisters, Servants of the Immaculate Heart of Mary, Monroe, Michigan* (Syracuse, N.Y.: Syracuse University Press, 1997); Carol K. Coburn and Martha Smith, *Spirited Lives: How Nuns Shaped Catholic Culture and American Life, 1836–1920* (Chapel Hill: University of North Carolina Press, 1999); Margaret Susan Thompson, "Discovering Foremothers: Sisters, Society and the American Catholic Experience," in *The American Catholic Religious Life,* ed. Joseph P. White (New York: Garland Press, 1988); and "Sister-

hood and Power: Class, Culture, and Ethnicity in the American Convent" *Colby Library Quarterly,* 25, no. 3 (September 1989): 149–175.

5. Mary Ewens, OP, "Women in the Convent" in *American Catholic Women: A Historical Exploration,* ed. Karen Kennelly, CSJ (New York: Macmillan, 1989), 36–37.
6. Lora Ann Quinonez and Mary Daniel Turner, *The Transformation of American Catholic Sisters* (Philadelphia: Temple University Press, 1992), 34.
7. Mary Jo Weaver, *New Catholic Women: A Contemporary Challenge to Traditional Religious Authority* (San Francisco: Harper and Row, 1985), 71.
8. Ewens, "Women in the Convent," 36.
9. Patricia Byrne, "Saving Souls and Educating Americans, 1930–1945" in *Transforming Parish Ministry: The Changing Roles of Catholic Clergy, Laity, and Women Religious* (New York: Crossroad Publishing Company, 1990), 140. The essays by Byrne collected under the heading "In the Parish but Not of It: Sisters" in the above volume provide an unparalleled narrative of the history of American women religious in the twentieth century. Byrne's subtle and detailed essays are a good starting point for further reading on the patterns of change and continuity among American sisters in this period, which this chapter briefly summarizes.
10. Pius XII, "Sponsa Christi" in *The States of Perfection,* Abbe Gaston Curtois (Westminster, Md.: Newman Press, 1961), 153–154.
11. Patricia Byrne, "Success and the Seeds of Change, 1945–1960," 140.
12. Pius XII, "Counsel to Teaching Sisters" (sec. 14), 6.
13. Very Reverend Francis J. Connell, CSSR, "Opening Remarks," *Religious Community Life in the United States: Proceedings of the First National Congress of Religious in the United States* (New York: Paulist Press, 1952), 2.
14. Quinonez and Turner, *Transformation of American Catholic Sisters,* 17.
15. Joseph Haley, CSC, ed. *Proceedings of the 1953 Sisters' Institute of Spirituality* (Notre Dame, Ind.: University of Notre Dame Press, 1954).
16. Haley, *Proceedings of the 1959 Sisters' Institute of Spirituality.*
17. Byrne, "Saving Souls and Educating Americans, 1930–1945," 117.
18. Byrne, "Success and the Seeds of Change, 1945–1960," 135.
19. Madeleva Wolff, CSC, "The Education of Our Young Religious Teachers," in *The Education of Sister Lucy: A Symposium on Teacher Education and Teacher Training* (Notre Dame, Ind.: Saint Mary's College, 1949), 9.
20. Sister M. Madeleva Wolff, CSC, "Theology for Sisters," in *Religious Community Life in the United States: Proceedings of the First National*

Congress of Religious in the United States (New York: Paulist Press, 1952), 46.

21. Weaver, *New Catholic Women,* 82.
22. Joe Chinnici provides an extremely helpful extended analysis of the influence of Catholic Action on conciliar and postconciliar ideas and orientations among American Catholics in "*Dignitatis Humane Personae:* Surveying the Landscape for Its Reception in the United States," *U.S. Catholic Historian,* Spring 2006.
23. James Hennessey, SJ, characterized this change as a lessened "psychological defensiveness" among American Catholics in *American Catholics: A History of the Roman Catholic Community in the United States* (Oxford: Oxford University Press, 198), 309.
24. Sr. Marie Augusta Neal, SND de Namur, *From Nuns to Sisters: An Expanding Vocation* (Mystic, Conn.: Twenty-Third Publications, 1990), 32.
25. Karen M. Kennelly, CSJ, "Women Religious and the Intellectual Life" in *Women Religious and the Intellectual Life: The North American Achievement,* ed. Bridget Puzon (San Francisco: International Scholars Publications, 1996), 60.
26. Patricia Byrne, "A Tumultuous Decade, 1960–1970" in *Transforming Parish Ministry,* 156.
27. Kennelly, "Women Religious and the Intellectual Life," 59.
28. Sister Ritamary, CHM, ed. *Planning for the Formation of Sisters: Studies on Teaching Apostolate and Selections from Addresses of the Sister Formation Conferences 1956–1957* (New York: Fordham University Press, 1958), ix–xii.
29. Joseph E. Haley, C.S.C., ed., 1.
30. The results of the 1966 survey, as well as those of a comparative 1982 study also conducted by Neal for the CMSW, were published as Marie Augusta Neal, SND de Namur, *Catholic Sisters in Transition: From the 1960s to the 1980s* (Wilmington, Del.: Michael Glazier, 1984).
31. Sister M. Charles Borromeo, CSC, introduction to *The New Nuns,* ed. Borromeo (London: Sheed and Ward, 1968), 2.
32. Byrne, "A Tumultuous Decade, 1960–1970," 156.
33. Borromeo, "Can Sisters Be Relevant?" in Borromeo, *The New Nuns,* 38.
34. Erving Goffman, *Asylums: Essays on the Social Situation of Mental Patients and Other Inmates* (New York: Doubleday, 1961).
35. Leon Joseph Cardinal Suenens, *The Nun in the World: Religious and the Apostolate* (Westminster, Md.: Newman Press, 1963), 18.
36. Ibid., 127.
37. Ibid., 143.
38. Ibid., 120.
39. Ibid., 150.

40. Ibid., 45.
41. Ibid., 143.
42. Byrne, "A Tumultuous Decade, 1960–1970," 157.
43. John T. McGreevy, *Parish Boundaries: The Catholic Encounter with Race in the Twentieth-Century Urban North* (Chicago: University of Chicago Press, 1996), 80.
44. Hennessey, *American Catholics,* 289. For further reading on Catholic suburbanization see Jay P. Dolan, *American Catholic Experience: A History from Colonial Times to the Present* (Garden City, N.Y.: Doubleday, 1985), 352–370, and Andrew Greely, *The Church and the Suburbs* (New York: Sheed and Ward, 1959).
45. Sister Mary Lourdes, SSND, to Mr. Ritchie, typewritten letter, January 26, 1967, series 4, box 3. NCCIJ-MUA.
46. Sister M. Rosalie Noder to Sister Margaret Ellen (Mary Peter) Traxler, SSND, typewritten letter, September 28, 1969, series 4, box 4. NCCIJ-MUA.
47. Sister Joan M. Fallon, OSU, to Sister Audrey Kopp, SNJM, typewritten letter, October 4, 1969, series 4, box 2. NCCIJ-MUA.
48. See McGreevy, *Parish Boundaries,* and the substantial introduction to Robert A. Orsi, ed., *Gods of the City: Religion and the American Urban Landscape* (Bloomington, Ind.: Indiana University Press, 1999).
49. Sister Mary Ellen to Traxler, typewritten letter, September 26, 1967, series 4, box 2. NCCIJ-MUA.
50. Sister Margaret Hutton to Traxler, typewritten letter, December 11, 1970, series 4, box 2. NCCIJ-MUA.
51. Sister Margaret Mary, IHM, to Jack Sission, typewritten letter, July 8, 1965, series 4, box 3. NCCIJ-MUA.
52. Sister Mary Fides Gough, OP, to Traxler, handwritten letter, September 21, 1968, series 4, box 2. NCCIJ-MUA.
53. "History-Making Statement from Cardinal Spellman Relates to Committee Efforts," *Sister Formation Bulletin,* vol. X, no. 4, Summer 1964.
54. Sr. Ritamary Bradley, SFCC, interview with author, August 20, 1998, Davenport, Iowa. For the original study, see Rose Thering, *Jews, Judiasm and Catholic Education: Documentary Survey Reports of Catholic Institutions' Implementation of 1965 Conciliar Statement on the Jews, 1974 Roman Catholic Guidelines/Suggestions, 1975 U.S. Bishops' Statement on the Jews; Prepared for the Twentieth Anniversary of the 1965 Promulgation of Vatican II Document Nostra Aetate* (New York: Anti-Defamation League of B'nai B'rith, 1968).
55. Rabbi Marc H. Tanenbaum, "An Ecumenical Re-Examination of Christian-Jewish Relations," *Sister Formation Bulletin,* vol. X, no. 4, Summer 1964. For further reading on changes to Catholic perceptions of Jews in the concilar period, see Egal Feldman, *Catholics and Jews in*

Twentieth-Century America (Urbana: University of Illinois Press, 2001), in particular Feldman's chapter the "Revolt of the Bishops, 1960–1975," 103–125.

56. *Sister Formation Bulletin,* vol. X, no. 4, Summer 1964.
57. Sandra Schneiders, IHM, *Finding the Treasure: Locating Religious Life in a New Ecclesial and Cultural Context* (New York: Paulist Press, 2000), 169.
58. Prayer service, Urban Apostolate of the Sisters, Maria High, May 15, 1965, box 5, "Programs." Urban Apostolate of the Sisters, archives of the University of Notre Dame, South Bend, Indiana (hereafter referred to as UAS-ND).
59. Most Holy Second Ecumenical Council of the Vatican, *Gaudium et Spes* (Pastoral Constitution on the Church in the Modern World) in *The Documents of Vatican II,* ed. Walter Abbott, SJ (New York: Herder and Herder, 1966). On the Second Vatican Council and its effect on American Catholicism, see Guiseppe Albergio, Jean-Pierre Jossua, and Joseph A. Komonchak, eds., *The Reception of Vatican II* (Washington, D.C.: University Press of America, 1987), and John Tracy Ellis, *American Catholicism* (Chicago: University of Chicago Press, 1969), 163–254.
60. Sister Eugene Reynolds, OSU, to Traxler, typewritten letter, August 29, 1969, series 4, box 2. NCCIJ-MUA.
61. Sister Mary Louise, SSND, to Traxler, typewritten letter, December 21, 1966, series 4, box 3. NCCIJ-MUA.
62. *Perfectae Caritatis* (Decree on the Adaption and Renewal of Religious Life) in *The Documents of Vatican II,* ed. Abbott.
63. This did not always translate into congregational tolerance for such choices. Some sisters in the racial apostolate were labeled "rebellious" by their orders and either given grudging permission for assignments in black neighborhoods, or were expressly forbidden to pursue such apostolic work. But *Perfectae Caritatis* did provide such sisters with some measure of psychological autonomy from reticent congregational authorities.
64. *Perfectae Caritatis.*
65. For a detailed portrait of the complex ideological Catholic landscape on matters of race in the twentieth century, see McGreevy, *Parish Boundaries.*
66. William Osborne, *The Segregated Covenant: Race Relations and American Catholics* (New York: Herder and Herder, 1967), 234.
67. Ibid., 239.
68. Ibid., 242.
69. Helen Rose Ebaugh, *Women in the Vanishing Cloister: Organizational Decline in Catholic Religious Orders in the United States* (New Brunswick, N.J.: Rutgers University Press, 1993), 26.

70. David Southern, *John LaFarge and the Limits of Catholic Interracialism, 1911–1963* (Baton Rouge: Louisiana State University Press, 1996), and McGreevy, *Parish Boundaries,* 41–47.
71. Proposal, National Conference on Religion and Race, undated. Cardinal Albert Meyers papers, Archdiocesan archives, Chicago, Illinois (hereafter referred to as CAM-AAC).
72. Cardinal McIntyre later would become notorious for his resistance to the conciliar reforms enacted by the Immaculate Heart of Mary sisters in his diocese. Albert Cardinal Meyer to James Francis Cardinal McIntyre, typewritten letter, August 31, 1963. CAM-AAC.
73. Dr. Benjamin E. Mays, "Introduction," in *Race: Challenge to Religion,* ed. Mathew Ahmann (Chicago: Henry Regency Company, 1963), 3.
74. Rabbi Abraham J. Heschel, "The Religious Basis of Equality of Opportunity—The Segregation of God" in Ahmann, *Race: Challenge to Religion,* 55.
75. Monsignor John J. Egan, "The Responsibility of Church and Synagogue as Institutions of the Community," in Ahmann, *Race: Challenge to Religion,* 99.
76. R. Sargent Shriver, "America, Race and the World," in Ahmann, *Race: Challenge to Religion,* 152.
77. Dr. Martin Luther King Jr., "A Challenge to Churches and Synagogues" in Ahmann, *Race: Challenge to Religion,* 157.
78. Margaret Traxler, SSND, "The Great Tide of Returning," in *Midwives of the Future: American Nuns Tell Their Story,* ed. Ann Patrick Ware (Kansas City: Leaven Press, 1985), 132.
79. For further reading on LaFarge and the early history of the NCCIJ, see Southern, *John LaFarge and the Limits of Catholic Interracialism, 1911–1963.*
80. For further reading on Catholics in the 1965 Selma protest see Greg Hite, "The Hottest Places in Hell: The Catholic Church and Civil Rights in Selma, Alabama, 1937–1965" (PhD diss., University of Virginia, May 2002), or the forthcoming book with this title from the University of North Carolina Press.
81. Traxler, "Great Tide of Returning," 134.
82. David Farber, *Age of Great Dreams: America in the 1960s* (New York: Hill and Wang, 1994), 112.
83. Sr. M. Dennis to Traxler, handwritten letter, April 5, 1968, series 4, box 1. NCCIJ-MUA.
84. Sister Mary Patrick to Sister Margaret Ellen (Mary Peter) Traxler, SSND, typewritten letter, April 22, 1968, series 4, box 4. NCCIJ-MUA.
85. Sister Mary Evangeline, RSM, to Sister Margaret Ellen (Mary Peter) Traxler, SSND, typewritten letter, 1968, series 4, box 2. NCCIJ-MUA.

86. Sister Alice Rita, OSB, to Sister Margaret Ellen (Mary Peter) Traxler, SSND, handwritten letter, February 27, 1969, series 4, box 4. NCCIJ-MUA.
87. Robert F. Clark, *The War on Poverty: History, Selected Programs, and Ongoing Impact* (Lanham, Md.: University Press of America, 2002), 32.
88. Alice O'Connor, *Poverty Knowledge: Social Science, Social Policy, and the Poor in Twentieth-Century U.S. History* (Princeton, N.J.: Princeton University Press, 2001), 167.
89. O'Connor, *Poverty Knowledge,* 167.
90. Clark, *War on Poverty,* 48.
91. Osborne, *Segregated Covenant,* 199–200.
92. Clark, *War on Poverty,* 29.
93. *Nuns Newsletter,* 7, January 1966. NCCIJ-MUA.
94. Ibid., 9, September 1966, 4.
95. Sister Mary Elizabeth Dye, National Placement Bureau application, January 18, 1969, series 2, box 4. NCCIJ-MUA.
96. Sister M. Greyar to Traxler, typewritten letter, March 15, unspecified year, series 4, box 2. NCCIJ-MUA.
97. Sister Mary Audrey Kopp, "Valley of the Shadow," in Traxler, *New Works of New Nuns,* 14. Emphasis in original.
98. Sister Mary Peter Champagne, "Newman Communities," in Traxler, *New Works of New Nuns,* 105.
99. Sister Mary Peter Traxler, "The Ministry of Presence" in Traxler, *Split-Level Lives,* 1.
100. Sister Mary Peter Champagne, "Newman Communities," in Traxler, *New Works of New Nuns,* 99.
101. Sister Evangeline Meyer, "Parish Servant to a Pilgrim People," in Traxler, *New Works of New Nuns,* 5.
102. Sister Evangeline Meyer, "Parish Servant to a Pilgrim People," in Traxler, *New Works of New Nuns,* 8.
103. Sister Mary Audrey Kopp, "The Myth of Race," in Traxler, *Split-Level Lives,* 139.
104. I'm grateful to Father Joe Chinnici for his assistance in understanding the "religious sensibility of compassion" (his words) that pervades postconciliar devotional discourse.
105. Prayer service, Urban Apostolate of the Sisters, Maria High, May 15, 1965, box 5, "Programs." UAS-ND.
106. Muckenhirn, introduction to *New Works of New Nuns,* ed. Traxler, vii.
107. Prayer service, Urban Apostolate of the Sisters, Maria High, May 15, 1965, box 5, "Programs." UAS-ND.
108. Kopp, "Valley of the Shadow," in Traxler, *New Works of New Nuns,* 15.

2. Education and Training

1. The NCCIJ was the national coordinator of local Catholic Interracial Councils, founded by Father John LaFarge in New York in 1934. For histories of the Catholic interracial movement and the National Catholic Conference for Interracial Justice, see David Southern, *John LaFarge and the Limits of Catholic Interracialism, 1911–1963* (Baton Rouge: Louisiana State University Press, 1996); Gregory Nelson Hite, "The Hottest Places in Hell: The Catholic Church and Civil Rights in Selma, Alabama, 1937–1965" (PhD diss., University of Virginia, May 2002); and John McGreevy, *Parish Boundaries: The Catholic Encounter with Race in the Twentieth-Century Urban North* (Chicago: University of Chicago Press, 1996).
2. John Sisson, typewritten speech (with handwritten margin notes) labeled "Re: How nuns can effectively involve themselves in the struggle for interracial justice. A consideration of policy, training, programs, and so forth. To: Leadership Group (about 25) of the Sister Formation Conference: National Comm., Regional Directors, Exec. Sec. At: St Teresa's College Winona, Minn. Monday, August 26, 1963 at about 2 PM." series 20, box 23. NCCIJ-MUA.
3. Ibid.
4. Philip Gleason, *Contending with Modernity: Catholic Higher Education in the Twentieth Century* (New York: Oxford University Press, 1995), 320.
5. For a detailed analysis of this episode, see Sr. Judith Ann Eby, RSM, " 'A Little Squabble among Nuns'?: The Sister Formation Crisis and the Patterns of Authority and Obedience among American Women Religious, 1954–71." (PhD diss., Saint Louis University, 2000). Eby's description of the "stormy session" of September 26, 1963, is on pp. 139–145. See also Marjorie Noterman Beane, *From Framework to Freedom: A History of the Sister Formation Conference* (Lanham, Md.: University Press of America, 1993), 122–124.
6. Lora Ann Quinonez and Mary Daniel Turner provide a concise history of the Conference of Major Superiors in *The Transformation of American Catholic Sisters* (Philadelphia: Temple University Press, 1992), 14–16. Mary Jo Weaver places these developments in a larger context in *New Catholic Women: A Contemporary Challenge to Traditional Religious Authority* (San Francisco: Harper and Row, 1985), 81–85.
7. Beane, *From Framework to Freedom,* 1–30; Quinonez and Turner, *Transformation of American Catholic Sisters,* 6–13; Eby, "A Little Squabble among Nuns?" 45–52.
8. Description of the SFC-CMSW relationship as a "polite tug-of-war" is from Gleason, *Contending with Modernity,* 233.

9. Eby, "A Little Squabble among Nuns?" 118.
10. For example, the SFC had irritated the CMSW by advocating for certain changes within religious institutes that would have limited the authority of religious superiors. A part of a larger effort to help sister-run colleges attain outside accreditation, the SFC had advocated that sister-colleges establish governance structures that were separate from the internal structure of religious congregations. The SFC also had established an "educational resources committee" that served as a clearinghouse to match sisters with PhDs with faculty positions in sister-colleges, a role traditionally undertaken by superiors. Beane, *From Framework to Freedom,* 100–104.
11. Annette Walters, CSJ, "The Local Superior as Spiritual Leader," *Sister Formation Bulletin* (Spring 1963): 1–8. For accounts of the effect of Sister Annette Walter's article, see Eby, "A Little Squabble among Nuns?" 146, and Beane, *From Framework to Freedom,* 122.
12. For further reading see Patricia Byrne's excellent summary of this transformation in "In the Parish but Not of It: Sisters" in *Transforming Parish Ministry: The Changing Roles of Catholic Clergy, Laity, and Women Religious* (New York: Crossroad, 1990), 133–167.
13. In his lecture at the 1957 Sisters' Institute of Spirituality, Father Elio Gambari, SMM, a representative of the Congregation for Religious and a supporter of the SFC, used the phrase "directly apostolic" to distinguish the apostolic work of sisters "in immediate contact with the faithful" from the expression of the religious apostolate by contemplative sisters. Gambari, "The Mandate of the Religious Engaged in the Active Apostolate," *Proceedings of the 1957 Sisters' Institute of Spirituality,* edited by Joseph E. Haley, CSC (Notre Dame, Ind.: University of Notre Dame Press, 1958), 75. At the 1957 SIS, Gambari presented in embryonic form the ideas about the apostolic component of the religious vocation that he would later develop in his 1962 lecture tour of SFC workshops and conferences. Those lectures were collected and published by Fordham Press as P. Elio Gambari, SMM, *The Religious-Apostolic Formation of Sisters* (New York: Fordham University Press, 1964).
14. A. Ple, OP, "Apostolic Action—A School of Perfection" (Winter 1956); Ritamary Bradley, SHM, "Activity or Activism?" (Winter 1957); Elizabeth Ann, IHM, "Apostolic Formation through the Curriculum" (Spring 1958); P. Elio Gambari, SMM, "Religious Women and the Apostolate in the Modern World" (Summer, 1959).
15. I'm grateful to Father Joseph Chinnici, OFM, for his assistance in understanding the "religious sensibility of compassion" that pervades this new understanding of the religious apostolate. For further reading, see Joseph Chinnici, OFM, "Religious Life in the 20th Century: Discover-

ing the Languages," *U.S. Catholic Historian,* vol. 22, no. 1, 2004, 27–47, and "From Sectarian Suffering to Compassionate Solidarity: Joseph Cardinal Bernardin and the American Catholic Language of Suffering," manuscript in author's possession.

16. Quinonez and Turner, *Transformation of American Catholic Sisters,* 34. Angelyn Dries, OSF, offers incisive analysis of the internal shifts within the Sister Formation Movement in "Living in Ambiguity: A Paradigm Shift Experienced by the Sister Formation Movement," *Catholic Historical Review,* 79 (July 1993): 478–487.
17. For further examination of the intellectual context of American sisters in the 1940s, 1950s, and 1960s, see Bridget Puzon, ed., *Women Religious and the Intellectual Life: The North American Achievement* (San Francisco: International Scholars Publications, 1996).
18. Sister Mary Emil Penet, IHM, ed., "Report of Everett Curriculum Workshop" (Seattle: Heiden's Mailing Bureau, 1956), 21. Records of Providence Heights College of Sister Formation, Box 2, PHC-SP.
19. Quinonez and Turner, *Transformation of American Catholic Sisters,* 38. See also Beane, *From Framework to Freedom,* 112–113.
20. Beane, *From Framework to Freedom,* 111. Also Sr. Ritamary Bradley, SFCC, interview with author, August 20, 1998, Davenport, Iowa.
21. Beane, *From Framework to Freedom,* 111. Also Bradley interview with author, August 20, 1998, Davenport, Iowa.
22. At the same time, the SFC also began to open itself to the world financially, actively pursuing funding from sources outside the Church to support its programs. The SFC held workshops to train sisters in public affairs and fund-raising techniques, and established the Sister Formation Graduate Study and Research Foundation to solicit money for graduate education for sisters. The Overseas Project received grants from the State Department to visit and survey colleges in India. The SFC's newsletter to major superiors alerted sisters to scholarships from federal sources such as the U.S. Department of Education and the National Academy of Sciences.
23. Beane, *From Framework to Freedom,* 118.
24. Bradley, interview with author, August 20, 1998, Davenport, Iowa. See also Rabbi Marc H. Tanenbaum, "An Ecumenical Re-Examination of Christian-Jewish Relations," *Sister Formation Bulletin,* vol. X, no. 4 (Summer 1964).
25. Bradley, interview with author, August 20, 1998, Davenport, Iowa.
26. Letter quoted in Beane, *From Framework to Freedom,* 111.
27. Bradley, interview with author, August 20, 1998, Davenport, Iowa.
28. Eby, "A Little Squabble Among Nuns?" 134–176; Beane, *From Framework to Freedom,* 119–128.
29. Beane, *From Framework to Freedom,* 111.

30. Sister Mary Audrey (Lillanna) Kopp, SNJM, interview with author, March 16, 1996, Portland, Oregon. See also Lillanna Kopp, *The New Nuns: Collegial Christians* (Chicago: Argus, 1968), and *Sudden Spring: 6th Stage Sisters; Trends of Change in Catholic Sisterhoods* (Waldport, Ore.: Sunspot Publications, 1983).
31. Sister Mary Audrey Kopp, SNJM, "Evaluation of the Pilot TW of '56," typewritten memo, undated, series 19, box 8. NCCIJ-MUA.
32. Ibid.
33. For more information about the Chicago picket and its historical context see Suellen Hoy, "Lives on the Color Line: Catholic Sisters and African Americans in Chicago, 1890s–1960s," *U.S. Catholic Historian,* vol. 22, no. 1, 2004: 67–91. Hoy contextualizes this protest among other racial activities of Chicago sisters in her chapter "Marching for Racial Justice in Chicago in the 1960s" in *Good Hearts: Catholic Sisters in Chicago's Past* (Urbana: University of Illinois Press, 2006), 125–153. See also McGreevy, *Parish Boundaries,* 143–144.
34. Sisson speech, "Re: How nuns can effectively involve themselves in the struggle for interracial justice."
35. Ibid.
36. Ibid.
37. John P. Sisson to Sister M. Emmanuel, typewritten letter, September 25, 1963, series 20, box 23. NCCIJ-MUA.
38. Mathew Ahmann to Sister Annette Walters, CSJ, typewritten letter, November 5, 1963, series 20, box 23. NCCIJ-MUA.
39. Mathew Ahmann to Sister Annette Walters, CSJ, typewritten formal letter to be forwarded by Walters to Mother Superiors, February 4, 1964, series 20, box 23. NCCIJ-MUA. Ellipses are in original text.
40. Ibid.
41. Quinonez and Turner, *Transformation of American Catholic Sisters,* 78.
42. Eby, "A Little Squabble Among Nuns?" 181.
43. Sister Annette Walters, CSJ, to John O. Butler, typewritten letter, August 25, 1964, series 20, box 28. NCCIJ-MUA.
44. The DES's first report from August 1965 begins, "A little over a year ago when planning long-range goals for the then non-existent Department of Educational Services of the National Catholic Conference for Interracial Justice, one of the primary concerns was . . ." Margaret Ellen Traxler, SSND, typewritten memo, "Report of the Director of Department of Educational Services," August 20, 1965, series 19, box 2. NCCIJ-MUA.
45. Ibid.
46. The first director of the DES was Franciscan Sister Claire Marie Sawyer, OSF. She was followed by Sister Mary Peter (Margaret) Traxler, SSND. Traxler was initially assisted by Sister Maura Coughlan, CSJ, and later

by Sister Mary Audrey (Lillanna) Kopp, SNJM, and Sister Mary Kathleen Sparks, OSF, each of whom assumed primary responsibility for one or more of the department's projects.

47. Sr. Lilanna Kopp, SFCC, interview with author, March 16, 1996, Portland, Oregon.
48. Traxler, typewritten "Report of the Director of the Department of Educational Services," August 1969, series 19, box 2. NCCIJ-MUA.
49. I am grateful to Greg Hite for pointing out this particular dynamic in the DES.
50. Traxler, typewritten memo, "Report of the Director of Department of Educational Services," August 20, 1965, series 19, box 2. NCCIJ-MUA.
51. For the larger story of Catholics in the Selma marches, see Hite, "The Hottest Places in Hell."
52. Traxler, "Report of the Director of Department of Educational Services," August 20, 1965, series 19, box 2. NCCIJ-MUA.
53. Ibid., December 1965, series 19, box 2. NCCIJ-MUA.
54. Ibid., August 20, 1965, series 19, box 2. NCCIJ-MUA.
55. *Nuns Newsletter,* 1, October 1964, 1, series 8, box 1. NCCIJ-MUA.
56. Sister M. Josella, OSF, to Traxler, May 22, 1966, series 19, box 3. NCCIJ-MUA.
57. Traxler, typewritten "Staff Report," June 1967, series 19, box 2. NCCIJ-MUA.
58. Sr. Anne Michele to Traxler, June 7, 1968, typewritten letter, series 4, box 3. NCCIJ-MUA.
59. Sr. Janice Jackson, SNJM, interview with author, March 16 1996, Eugene, Oregon.
60. Traxler, typewritten press release, "Traveling Workshops, a Tale of Many Cities," undated, series 19, box 8. NCCIJ-MUA.
61. Sister Claire Marie Sawyer, OSF, to Mother M. Lorenza, CPPS, typewritten letter, November 10, 1964, series 19, box 7. NCCIJ-MUA.
62. Mathew Ahmann and Margaret Traxler, typewritten "Report of the Traveling Workshops on Inter-Group Relations, Summer 1965," undated, page 1, series 19, box 8. NCCIJ-MUA.
63. Traxler, typewritten memo, "Report of the Director of Department of Educational Services," March 1966, series 19, box 2. NCCIJ-MUA.
64. Traxler, typewritten "Staff Report of the Director of Department of Educational Services," May, 1967, series 19, box 2. NCCIJ-MUA.
65. Traveling Workshops brochure, 1966, series 19, box 8. NCCIJ-MUA.
66. Traxler, typewritten "Annual Report, Educational Services Project, 1966–1967," series 19, box 2. NCCIJ-MUA.
67. Traxler, typewritten "Annual Report of the Director of Department of Educational Services," August, 1969, series 19, box 2, NCCIJ-MUA.

68. Typewritten flier, "The Traveling Workshop on Intergroup Relations," 1969, series 19, box 8. NCCIJ-MUA.
69. Traxler, typewritten memo, "Report of the Director of Department of Educational Services," March, 1970, series 19, box 2, NCCIJ-MUA.
70. Ibid., August, 1970, series 19, box 2. NCCIJ-MUA.
71. Traxler, typewritten letter to "Dear Sister of the Traveling Workshop Faculty," March 20, 1967, series 19, box 2. NCCIJ-MUA.
72. Traxler, typewritten memo to "Sisters of the Traveling Workshops," April, 1968, series 19, box 8. NCCIJ-MUA.
73. Traxler, typewritten letter to "Sisters," May 7, 1969, series 19, box 2. NCCIJ-MUA.
74. Traxler, typewritten "Staff Report," March 12, 1966, series 19, box 2. NCCIJ-MUA. Later, in a more clearly frustrated mood, Traxler commented, "The appropriations committee of the House gave the EEO three million dollars for a summer title IV institutes. A million here and a million there adds up to a bit more than our three two-week workshops need." "Staff Report," May 15, 1966.
75. Traxler, typewritten letter to "Sisters," October 21, 1966, series 19, box 8. NCCIJ-MUA.
76. Traxler, typewritten memo, "Report of the Director of Department of Educational Services," March 1966, series 19, box 2, "Project Cabrini" file. NCCIJ-MUA.
77. Traxler, typewritten memo to "Sisters of the Traveling Workshop Faculty," March 20, 1967, series 19, box 8. NCCIJ-MUA.
78. Sister Mary Audrey Kopp, SNJM, "The Myth of Race," in *Split-Level Lives: American Nuns Speak on Race,* edited by Sister Mary Peter Traxler, SSND (Techney, Ill.: Divine Word Publications, 1967), 153.
79. Mother Bessie Chambers, RCSJ, "The Psychological Effects of Segregation," in Traxler, ed., *Split-Level Lives,* 52.
80. But even these forums of "native informants" could produce odd results, placing African Americans on display to describe details of their lives, as in a conversation reported in a DES press release about "sixteen white teachers" learning a "lesson of the streets" in one such encounter group with "a self-described former hustler and pimp" at a workshop session:

Harold Steigger, 22: "I grew up in the street. Everything I know I learned on the street—hustling and pimping."

Nun: "What do you mean—hustling?"

Steigger: "Well, like the handkerchief game. Say, a white man would come down to the street looking for something—."

Michael Lawson, a sociologist and civil rights leader involved in rehabilitation programs: "Looking for what, Harold?"

Steigger: "Looking for Black women."

Untitled Associated Press press release, series 19, box 8. NCCIJ-MUA.

81. Sister Mary Heffernan, OP, "Equality and 'The System'" in Traxler, ed., *Split-Level Lives,* 105.
82. Sister Mary Kenneth, OSB, handwritten note on NCCIJ pledge reminder, November 25, 1968, series 19, box 8. NCCIJ-MUA.
83. Anthony E. Kessel to Sister Mary Kenneth, typewritten letter, December 13, 1969, series 19, box 8. NCCIJ-MUA.
84. Kopp, "The Myth of Race," in Traxler, ed., *Split-Level Lives,* 139. As I've noted, there is a distinct tendency among some of these sister-authors to dwell closely on, and perhaps even relish, the details of the poverty they discuss, describing its minutiae with a curious enthusiasm. Joseph Chinnici, OFM, explores the possible devotional roots of this romance for the poverty of others in "Religious Life in the 20th Century: Discovering the Languages," and in "From Sectarian Suffering to Compassionate Solidarity."
85. Kopp, "The Myth of Race," in Traxler, ed., *Split-Level Lives,* 140.
86. Sister Mary L. Mangan, SL, "Unwritten History," in Traxler, ed., *Split-Level Lives,* 94.
87. Mangan, "Unwritten History," 89.
88. Mathew Ahmann, preface to Traxler, ed., *Split-Level Lives,* v.
89. Sister Mary Peter Traxler, SSND, "The Ministry of Presence," in Traxler, ed., *Split-Level Lives,* 1.
90. Traxler, "The Ministry of Presence," 6.
91. Sister Loretta Ann Madden, SL, "Challenge to the Churches," in Traxler, ed., *Split-Level Lives,* 10.
92. Madden, "Challenge to the Churches," 17.
93. Sister Mary Eric Zeis, SSND, "Forming a Christian Social Conscience," in Traxler, ed., *Split-Level Lives,* 38.
94. Zeis, "Forming a Christian Social Conscience," 38.
95. Sister M. Gabriel, OP, typewritten "Personal Evaluation of the Traveling Workshop," undated but from 1965, series 19, box 8. NCCIJ-MUA.
96. Ahmann and Traxler, typewritten "Report of the Traveling Workshops on Inter-Group Relations, Summer 1965," undated, page 4, series 19, box 8. NCCIJ-MUA.
97. Sister Maura Coughlan, CSJ, typewritten form letter to "Sister Superior," February 27, 1967, series 19, box 5. NCCIJ-MUA.
98. Traxler, typewritten form letter to "Mother Superior," May 16, 1967, series 19, box 2. NCCIJ-MUA.
99. Ibid.

100. Traxler, typewritten "Staff Report," Department of Educational Services, May, 1967, series 19, box 2. NCCIJ-MUA. Subsequent DES/NCCIJ records provide no evidence that the CMSW adopted the (Adaptation and Renewal) workshop.
101. Sister M. Peter Traxler, SSND, ed., *New Works of New Nuns* (Saint Louis: B Herder Book Co., 1968).
102. Traxler, typewritten memo to "Sisters of the Traveling Workshops," April, 1968, series 19, box 8. NCCIJ-MUA.
103. Sister Providencia, FCSP, to Traxler, typewritten letter, May 30, 1968, series 4, box 4. NCCIJ-MUA.
104. Sister Charitas to Traxler, handwritten letter, June 22, 1968, series 4, box 1. NCCIJ-MUA.
105. Sister Patricia Barrett, RSCJ, to Traxler, typewritten letter, May 21, 1968, series 4, box 1. NCCIJ-MUA.
106. Typewriten program, "New Works of New Nuns," July 8–11, 1968, series 32, box 3. NCCIJ-MUA.
107. "Slum-oriented" quote taken from "World Report on Trans-Sisters," *Trans-Sister,* vol. 1, no. 5, July 1968: 3. Explanation of the origins of "The Black Ghetto and the White Nun" conference is in confidential typewritten "Report to Staff," July 1968, series 19, box 2. NCCIJ-MUA.
108. Sister Catherine Barrickman, OSB, and Sister Theresa Demarks, FSM, "Sisters Study the Big City," *Sisters Today.*
109. Traxler, confidential typewritten "Report to Staff," July 1968, series 19, box 2. NCCIJ-MUA.
110. Typewriten program, "Sisters' Survival Strategy Seminar," May 28–June 1, 1969, series 19, box 2. NCCIJ-MUA.
111. Traxler, typewritten "Staff Report," September, 1966, series 19, box 2. NCCIJ-MUA.
112. Tentative schedule for SUE, as attachment to Margaret Ellen Traxler, SSND, typewritten "Staff Report," May 1967, series 19, box 2. NCCIJ-MUA.
113. Coughlan, typewritten form letter to "Sister Superior," February 27, 1967, series 19, box 5. NCCIJ-MUA.
114. Sister M. Louise to Maura Coughlan, typewritten letter, June 3, 1967, series 19, box 5. NCCIJ-MUA.
115. Sister Prudence Moylan to "SUE Participants," typewritten letter, May 8, 1968, series 19, box 5. NCCIJ-MUA.
116. Barrickman and Demarks, "Sisters Study the Big City."
117. Traxler, typewritten "Report of the Director of the Department of Educational Services," February, 1969, series 19, box 2. NCCIJ-MUA.
118. Ibid., August 1969, series 19, box 2. NCCIJ-MUA.

119. Traxler, Appendix C to typewritten "Report of the Director of the Department of Educational Services," August 20, 1965, series 19, box 2. NCCIJ-MUA.
120. Ibid.
121. Traxler, typewritten "Report of the Director of the Department of Educational Services," March 4, 1966, series 19, box 2. NCCIJ-MUA.
122. Traxler, typewritten "Staff Report," January, 1967, series 19, box 2. NCCIJ-MUA.
123. Ibid.
124. Traxler, typewritten "Report of the Director of the Department of Educational Services," February, 1969, series 19, box 2. NCCIJ-MUA.
125. Traxler, typewritten confidential "Report to Staff," July, 1968, series 19, box 2. NCCIJ-MUA.
126. Traxler, typewritten "Report of the Director of the Department of Educational Services," February, 1969, series 19, box 2. NCCIJ-MUA.
127. Ibid., December, 1969, series 19, box 2. NCCIJ-MUA.
128. Typewritten form, "Application for NCCIJ National Placement Bureau, 1969–1970," series 19, box 13. NCCIJ-MUA.
129. National Placement Bureau Announcement, undated, untitled folder in "Apostolate" records series, Archives of the Sisters of Saint Francis, Rochester, Minn.
130. Proposal for Project Bridge: Summer in Suburbia, Cleveland Ohio, April 18, 1968, series 19, box 5. NCCIJ-MUA.
131. Traxler, typewritten letter to "Sisters of Choice," undated, series 19, box 5. NCCIJ-MUA.
132. Traxler, typewritten "Report of the Director of the Department of Educational Services," February, 1969, series 19, box 2. NCCIJ-MUA.
133. Sister Marie Julie, SSND, to Traxler, SSND, handwritten letter, August 24, 1968, series 19, box 5. NCCIJ-MUA.
134. Traxler, typewritten "Report of the Director of the Department of Educational Services," February, 1969, series 19, box 2. NCCIJ-MUA.
135. Sister Adrian Marie Hofstetter to Traxler, typewritten letter, January 7, 1968, series 19, box 5. NCCIJ-MUA.
136. Ibid.
137. Margaret Ellen Traxler to Mother Provincial, typewritten letter, May 29, 1969, series 19, box 2. NCCIJ-MUA.
138. Sr. Adrian Marie Hofstetter, OP, typewritten letter to mailing list, May 19, 1969, series 19, box 5. NCCIJ-MUA.
139. A "Hurried-Up" Final Report prepared by Team Chairmen, typewritten report, undated, series 19, box 5. NCCIJ-MUA.
140. Sr. Adrian Marie Hofstetter, OP, and Rev. George Gibson to Sisters, typewritten letter, May 3, 1969, series 19, box 5. NCCIJ-MUA.

141. A "Hurried-Up" Final Report prepared by Team Chairmen, typewritten report, undated, series 19, box 5. NCCIJ-MUA.
142. Traxler, typewritten "Report of the Director of the Department of Educational Services," December, 1969, series 19, box 2. NCCIJ-MUA.
143. Syllabus, Ed. 313 "Man in Urban Society," Saint John College, Cleveland, Ohio, June 17–July 26, 1968, series 19, box 5. NCCIJ-MUA.
144. Exposures to the City, typewritten course assignment for "Man in Urban Society," series 19, box 5. NCCIJ-MUA.
145. Traxler, typewritten "Report of the Director of Department of Educational Services," March 4, 1966, series 19, box 2. NCCIJ-MUA.
146. Typewritten press release from the NCCIJ, April 14, 1966, series 26, box 3. NCCIJ-MUA.
147. Sister Maureen Mulcahy, OSB, to Nurses, typewritten letter, June 8, 1966, series 19, box 2. NCCIJ-MUA.
148. Typewritten press release from the NCCIJ, April 14, 1966, series 26, box 3. NCCIJ-MUA.
149. Charles P. Greco to Sister Claire Teeling, typewritten letter, July 6, 1968, series 26, box 1. NCCIJ-MUA. Teeling forwarded the letter to NCCIJ executive director Mathew Ahmann with the note, "Sounds very defensive, doesn't it?" attached.
150. Traxler, typewritten "Report of the Department of Educational Services," August 1969, series 19, box 2. NCCIJ-MUA.
151. Typewritten syllabus for "Sisters Urban Education Course," 1968–1969, series 19, box 5. NCCIJ-MUA.
152. Sister Alice Rita to Traxler, handwritten letter, February 27, 1969, series 4, box 4. NCCIJ-MUA.
153. Traxler, typewritten "Report of the Director of the Department of Educational Services," January, 1967, series 19, box 2. NCCIJ-MUA.
154. Traxler, typewritten "Report of the Director of the Department of Educational Services," August 20, 1965, series 19, box 2. NCCIJ-MUA.
155. Traxler, typewritten "Report of the Director of Department of Educational Services," March 4, 1966, series 19, box 2. NCCIJ-MUA.
156. Sister Barbara Louise, CPPS, to Traxler, typewritten letter, January 14, 1967, series 4, box 3. NCCIJ-MUA. Final quote from Sister Joann Carmen, OSF, *Lessons in Race Relations: A Fifteen-Unit Teaching Lesson Published for the National Catholic Conference for Interracial Justice* (Dayton, Ohio: George A. Pflaum, 1966), series 8, box 1. NCCIJ-MUA.
157. Traxler, typewritten "Report of the Director of Department of Educational Services," August 20, 1965, series 19, box 2. NCCIJ-MUA.
158. Sister Mary Callaha, RSC, to Harold, typewritten letter, February 19, 1968, series 4, box 4. NCCIJ-MUA.

159. Sister Gail Nolan to "Dear Friends," handwritten letter, September 17, 1970, series 4, box 4. NCCIJ-MUA.
160. Sister Mary Lynn, CSA, to Traxler, July 30, 1967, series 4, box 3. NCCIJ-MUA.
161. Sister Mary Lourdes, SSND, to Traxler, SSND, typewritten letter, April 7, 1968, series 4, box 3. NCCIJ-MUA.
162. Sister Mary Herman to "Dear Sister," handwritten letter, August 22, 1967, series 4, box 4. NCCIJ-MUA.
163. Sister Helen Suzanne Marx, OSB, to Traxler, typewritten letter, November 5, 1967, series 4, box 3. NCCIJ-MUA.
164. Sister Mary Jo Monfils to "Dear Sister," undated typewritten letter, series 4, box 3. NCCIJ-MUA.
165. Sister Vivian M. Coulon, MSC, to Traxler, typewritten letter, February 22, 1969, series 4, box 1. NCCIJ-MUA.
166. Traxler, typewritten "Staff Report, Department of Educational Services," June 1967, series 19, box 2. NCCIJ-MUA.
167. Traxler, typewritten "Report of the Director of the Department of Educational Services," March 4, 1966, series 19, box 2. NCCIJ-MUA.
168. Traxler, typewritten confidential "Report to Staff," July 1968, series 19, box 2. NCCIJ-MUA.
169. Sister M. Roland Sornsin, OSF, to Sister Maura Coughlan, handwritten letter, May 10, 1967, series 19, box 5. NCCIJ-MUA.

3. Vocation and Negotiation

1. Sister Jeanine Jacob to Sister Margaret Ellen (Mary Peter) Traxler, SSND, handwritten letter, April 9, 1972, series 4, box 3. NCCIJ-MUA.
2. Ibid.
3. Sister Joan M. Fallon, OSU, to Sister Audrey Kopp, SNJM, October 4, 1969, series 4, box 2. NCCIJ-MUA.
4. Sister Candace Nurse to Traxler, handwritten letter, April 15, series 4, box 4. NCCIJ-MUA.
5. Sr. Leah Marie Courillion to Traxler, undated handwritten letter, series 4, box 1. NCCIJ-MUA.
6. Sister Lisieux to Traxler, SSND, handwritten letter, January 7, 1967, series 4, box 3. NCCIJ-MUA.
7. Sister Sharon Ann Stanton to Traxler, handwritten letter, November 19, 1969, series 4, box 5. NCCIJ-MUA.
8. Sister M. Jeanette, SSND, to Traxler, handwritten letter, December 5, 1968, series 4, box 3. NCCIJ-MUA.
9. Sister Theresa Mary, SSND, to Traxler, undated typewritten letter, series 4, box 5. NCCIJ-MUA.
10. Sister Keuper to Sister Audrey Kopp, SNJM, handwritten letter, October 2, 1969, series 4, box 3. NCCIJ-MUA.

11. Weidig to Traxler, typewritten letter, October 6, 1969, series 4, box 5. NCCIJ-MUA.
12. Lisieux to Traxler, handwritten letter, January 7, 1967, series 4, box 3. NCCIJ-MUA.
13. Sister Jane Langer to Sister Claire, typewritten letter, August 13, 1968, series 4, box 3. NCCIJ-MUA.
14. Sister Mary Edward to Traxler, undated handwritten letter, series 4, box 2. NCCIJ-MUA.
15. Sister M. Teresa Frances, SSA, to Traxler, handwritten letter, May 5, 1969, series 4, box 2. NCCIJ-MUA.
16. "Marymount College Self-Help Program," *Nuns Newsletter,* September 1966. NCCIJ-MUA.
17. Sister M. Rosalie Noder to Traxler, typewritten letter, September 28, 1969, series 4, box 4. NCCIJ-MUA.
18. Sister Bernadette Marie Villeneuve, RSM, "Summary Report, Boulevard Research Project," Summer 1968, series 26, box 1. NCCIJ-MUA.
19. Sister Mary James to Traxler, typewritten letter, February 20, 1967, series 4, box 3. NCCIJ-MUA.
20. Sister Alice Marie Fox, BVM, to Traxler, handwritten letter, October 24, 1967, series 4, box 2. NCCIJ-MUA.
21. Sister Mary John, PVMI, interview with author, December 18, 2000, Marycrest, N.Y.
22. Sister Mary McDermott to Traxler, typewritten letter, February 23, 1970, series 4, box 3. NCCIJ-MUA.
23. Ann Sornsin to Traxler, handwritten letter, August 16, 1967, series 4, box 5. NCCIJ-MUA.
24. Sister Delores Mary Pint to Sister, handwritten letter found in Traxler's correspondence, September 27, 1971, series 4, box 4. NCCIJ-MUA.
25. "Dear Friend of Glenmary" and attached press release, typewritten letter, July 26, 1967, series 4, box 1. NCCIJ-MUA. See also Helen M. Lewis and Monica Appleby, *Mountain Sisters: From Convent to Community in Appalachia* (Lexington: University of Kentucky Press, 2003).
26. Sandra M. Schneiders, IHM, *Finding the Treasure: Locating Religious Life in a New Ecclesial and Cultural Context* (New York: Paulist Press, 2000), 123–152.
27. Courillion to Traxler, undated handwritten letter, series 4, box 1. NCCIJ-MUA.
28. Sister Margaret Ellen to Traxler, handwritten letter, September 19, unspecified year, series 4, box 2. NCCIJ-MUA.
29. Nurse to Traxler, handwritten letter, April 15, series 4, box 4. NCCIJ-MUA.
30. Sister Celestine Hoedel, SCC, to Traxler, typewritten letter, December 12, 1968, series 4, box 2. NCCIJ-MUA.

31. Sister Maureen Reidy, OP, to Traxler, handwritten letter, November 9, 1969, series 4, box 4. NCCIJ-MUA.
32. Sister Janet Levert to Traxler, typewritten letter, May 18, 1968, series 4, box 3. NCCIJ-MUA.
33. Sr. Annunciata and Sr. Philip to Traxler, handwritten letter, April 22, 1967, series 4, box 1. NCCIJ-MUA.
34. Sister Mary Lins to Traxler, undated handwritten letter, series 4, box 3. NCCIJ-MUA.
35. Jeanette, to Traxler, handwritten letter, December 5, 1968, series 4, box 3. NCCIJ-MUA.
36. Sister Christine Klop, National Placement Bureau application, January 25, 1969, series 3, box 4. NCCIJ-MUA.
37. Catherine Hartnett to Traxler, typewritten letter, May 8, 1972, series 4, box 2. NCCIJ-MUA.
38. Sister Mary Jane, SSND, to Traxler, typewritten letter, April 16, 1968, series 4, box 3. NCCIJ-MUA.
39. Sister Gabrielle, OP, to Traxler, typewritten letter, October 6, 1969, series 4, box 5. NCCIJ-MUA.
40. Sister Le Roy to Traxler, handwritten letter, October 8, 1967, NCCIJ correspondence, series 4, box 3, "I-Q" file. NCCIJ-MUA.
41. Noder to Traxler, typewritten letter, September 28, 1969, series 4, box 4. NCCIJ-MUA.
42. Sister Mary Anthony Scally, RSM, to Traxler, typewritten letter, May 3, 1969, series 4, box 4. NCCIJ-MUA.
43. Sister Sharon Ann Stanton, OSB, to Traxler, handwritten letter, November 14, 1969, series 4, box 5. NCCIJ-MUA.
44. Weidig to Traxler, typewritten letter, October 6, 1969, series 4, box 5. NCCIJ-MUA.
45. Sister Mary Lou Duffy to Traxler, typewritten letter, April 27, 1968, series 4, box 2. NCCIJ-MUA.
46. Sister Mary Angelica, OSF, to Traxler, typewritten letter, March 12, 1967, series 4, box 1. NCCIJ-MUA.
47. Sister Mary Anthony Scally, RSM, to Traxler, typewritten letter, May 3, 1969, series 4, box 4. NCCIJ-MUA.
48. Sister Margaret Mary, IHM, to Jack Sisson, typewritten letter, July 8, 1965, series 4, box 3. NCCIJ-MUA.
49. Sister M. Peter Raybell, OSB, to Traxler, handwritten letter, November 26, 1967, series 4, box 4. NCCIJ-MUA.
50. Sister Patricia Hyden to Traxler, undated handwritten letter, series 4, box 2. NCCIJ-MUA.
51. Sister Theresa Mary, SSND, to Traxler, undated typewritten letter, series 4, box 5. NCCIJ-MUA.

52. Sister Mary Liam to Mathew Ahmann, undated handwritten letter, series 4, box 3. NCCIJ-MUA.
53. Ibid.
54. Sister M. Kathleen to Harold, typewritten letter, February 21, 1967, series 4, box 3. NCCIJ-MUA.
55. Sister Noenie to Traxler, typewritten letter, November 4, 1967, series 4, box 4. NCCIJ-MUA.
56. Sister Christopher to Traxler, typewritten letter, September 29, 1967, series 4, box 1. NCCIJ-MUA.
57. Sister Lisieux to Traxler, handwritten letter, January 7, 1967, series 4, box 3. NCCIJ-MUA.
58. Mother M. Petronilla, CSJ, to Traxler, typewritten letter, May 31, 1967, series 4, box 4. NCCIJ-MUA.
59. Sister Mary Francis, OSF, to Traxler, typewritten letter, March 31, 1966, series 19, box 3. NCCIJ-MUA.
60. Mother M. Callista Hynes to Traxler, typewritten letter, March 11, 1969, series 4, box 1. NCCIJ-MUA.
61. Ibid.
62. Ibid.
63. Sister Patricia Hyden to Traxler, undated handwritten letter, series 4, box 4. NCCIJ-MUA.
64. Sister Eugene Reynolds, OSU, to Traxler, typewritten letter, August 29, 1969, series 4, box 2. NCCIJ-MUA.
65. Ann Ryan to Traxler, typewritten letter, January 8, 1970, series 4, box 4. NCCIJ-MUA.
66. Sister Joan Bauer, "Report for the General Chapter on Out Work in the Central Ward of Newark, NJ," series 4, box 1. NCCIJ-MUA.

4. Sisters in Selma

1. On the events in Selma 1965 and the march from Selma to Montgomery, see Michael B. Friedland, *Lift Up Your Voice Like a Trumpet: White Clergy and the Civil Rights and Antiwar Movements, 1954–1973* (Chapel Hill: University of North Carolina Press, 1998), 113–139; Charles E. Fager, *Selma, 1965* (New York: Charles Scribner's Sons, 1974); Howell Raines, *My Soul Is Rested: Movement Days in the Deep South Remembered* (New York: Penguin Books, 1977), 187–226; Henry Hampton and Steve Fayer, eds., *Voices of Freedom: An Oral History of the Civil Rights Movement from the 1950s through the 1980s* (New York: Bantam Books, 1990), 209–240; J. L. Chestnut Jr., *Black in Selma: The Uncommon Life of J. L. Chestnut, Jr.* (New York: Anchor Books, 1990).

2. For an outstanding study of the Catholics who came to Selma as "outside agitators" in 1965, see Gregory Nelson Hite, "The Hottest Places in Hell" (PhD diss., University of Virginia, 2002).
3. Sister Barbara Lumm, SSJ, interview with author, December 14, 2000, Rochester, New York.
4. Ibid.
5. Sister Mary Paul Geck, SSJ, interview with author, December 13, 2000, Rochester, New York.
6. Quoted in Patricia Cavanaugh Creighton, "What Were You Doing in Selma, Sister?" B.A. thesis, Department of History, SUNY Purchase, May 1988, unpublished, 10. Sisters of Saint Joseph, documentation of Saint Elizabeth's parish and Good Samaritan Hospital in Selma, Alabama, 1940–1970, archives of the Sisters of Saint Joseph, Rochester, New York (hereafter referred to as SSJ-NY).
7. Ibid., 8.
8. Ibid., 9.
9. "Outline of Selma History," 1940–1964, Selma series, box G-13–1–2, "Selma, 1940–68." SSJ-NY. Lewis would recover from his wounds and go on to represent Georgia's fifth district as a member of Congress.
10. Sister Jean Agnes, SSJ, interview with author, December 15, 2000, Rochester, New York.
11. Lumm, interview with author.
12. Convent chronicle, 10/14/40, Selma series, "Convent Chronicle 1940–1960." SSJ-NY.
13. Lumm, interview with author.
14. Geck, interview with author.
15. Lumm, interview with author.
16. "Outline of Selma History," 1940–1964.
17. Lumm, interview with author.
18. Sister Paul Marie Dougherty, typewritten memoir, December 14, 1989. Selma series, box G-13–1–5, "Year of the South." SSJ-NY.
19. Sister Ligouri, "In Retrospect, an Essay of Selma 1965," typewritten memoir, June 1965. Selma series, box G-13–1–5, "Year of the South." SSJ-NY.
20. Sister Jean Agnes, interview with author.
21. Convent chronicle, 10/18/40.
22. Ibid.
23. Unsigned letter, December 19, 1940, from Selma mission to motherhouse in Rochester, New York, quoted in Creighton, "What Were You Doing in Selma, Sister?" 23.
24. At the fifty-year anniversary celebration of the founding of the Selma mission in 1990, Bishop Moses B. Anderson, SSE, reflected on the

meaning of sisters' labor in Selma: "The home visiting by the Sisters in the early days of the 40's was most touching and fundamentally Gospel oriented. Having white women doing menial work in the homes of poor Black people in East Selma was unheard of. They founded units to care for the old people who were sick, they cleaned and took care of their homes by physically scrubbing the floors . . . You were a real sign of contradiction. Your lives as White women, working as servants to Black men and women was noted not only by your White brothers and sisters in a time when they would not have been caught dead doing such things but you were a witness to them in what they ought to be doing." Selma series, box G-13–1–5, "Year of the South." SSJ-NY.

25. Convent chronicle, 12/23/40.
26. Ibid., 9/28/40.
27. For example, in our interview conversations Sister Barbara Lumm interrupted my question about the Assumption parish with the exclamation, "Oh, you mean the white church?" and Sister Mary Paul Geck only used the term "white school" to refer to the parish school attached to the Church of the Assumption.
28. Lumm, interview with author.
29. On racial malleability, see Matthew Frye Jacobson, *Whiteness of a Different Color: European Immigrants and the Alchemy of Race* (Cambridge, Mass.: Harvard University Press, 1998).
30. It should be noted that a few sisters described a different, less-accepting reaction from African Americans. These infrequent accounts in Selma papers stress ways in which African Americans, regardless of sisters' perceptions of them, may have had quite complicated reactions to the presence of white sisters within their neighborhoods, particularly with the emergence of the Black Power movement and separatist ideologies. Sisters' accounts of the openness of African Americans to their presence should be understood purely as sisters' perspective on the issue, not as a reflection of African American experience.
31. Lumm, interview with author.
32. Convent chronicle, 6/16/41.
33. Typewritten letter to (Monsignor) Very Reverend John S. Randall, Rochester, N.Y., February 21, 1951. Selma series, box G-13–1–2, "Selma, 1940–68." SSJ-NY.
34. Sister Remigia McHenry, undated typewritten memoir. Selma series, box G-13–1–5, "Year of the South." SSJ-NY.
35. Sister Mary Paul [Geck] to "My dear Sisters and friends" in the Rochester, N.Y., motherhouse, typewritten letter, February 7, 1965. Selma series, box G-13–1–2, "Selma, 1940–68." SSJ-NY.
36. Dougherty, typewritten memoir.
37. Quoted in Creighton, "What Were You Doing in Selma, Sister?" with

corrections added by the SSJ archivist in the passage in question, 24. SSJ-NY.

38. Geck, interview with author. Also related in Creighton, "What Were You Doing in Selma, Sister?"
39. Typewritten letter to Randall, December 21, 1951.
40. On racial passing, see Gayle Freda Wald, *Crossing the Line: Racial Passing in Twentieth-Century U.S. Literature and Culture* (Durham, N.C.: University of North Carolina Press, 2000).
41. Geck, interview with author.
42. Lumm, interview with author.
43. Creighton, "What Were You Doing in Selma, Sister?" 37.
44. Geck, interview with author.
45. Lumm, interview with author.
46. Sister Mary Christopher to Sister Mary John (and by implication the other sisters of the convent), typewritten letter, March 1, 1965. Selma series, box G-13–1–5, "Year of the South." SSJ-NY.
47. Convent chronicle, 9/22/40.
48. Ibid., 8/31/41.
49. Ibid., 10/3/40.
50. Ibid., 10/19/40.
51. Ibid., 2/20/41.
52. Ibid., 10/21/43.
53. Ibid., 12/30/46.
54. Ibid., 3/14/47.
55. Handwritten document by Sister David entitled "St. Elizabeth Mission, Selma, Alabama," April 1962. Selma series, box G-13–1–1, "Selma, 1940–68." SSJ-NY.
56. Undated letter, quoted in Creighton, "What Were You Doing in Selma, Sister?" 23.
57. Sister Dorothy Quinn, "Memories of the Old South," typewritten memoir, December 1989. Selma series, box G-13–1–5, "Year of the South." SSJ-NY.
58. Typewritten letter to Randall, December 21, 1951.
59. Sister Mary Corgan, "Alabama reflections," undated typewritten memoir. Selma series, box G-13–1–5, "Year of the South." SSJ-NY.
60. Quinn, "Memories of the Old South."
61. Convent chronicle, 1/9/41.
62. Ibid., 1/19/43.
63. Ibid., 1945.
64. Typewritten letter to Randall, February 24, 1951. G-13–1–2, "Selma, 1940–68," SSJ-NY.
65. Ibid.

66. Convent chronicle, 6/24/41.
67. Sister Mary Christopher to Sister Mary John (and by implication the other sisters of the convent), typewritten letter, March 1, 1965.
68. Lumm, interview with author.
69. Ibid.
70. Ibid.
71. Dougherty, typewritten memoir.
72. Geck, interview with author.
73. Lumm, interview with author.
74. Quoted in Creighton, "What Were You Doing in Selma, Sister?" 29.
75. Lumm, interview with author.
76. Ibid.
77. Geck, interview with author.
78. Lumm, interview with author.
79. Andrew Young, *An Easy Burden: The Civil Rights Movement and the Transformation of America* (New York: Harper Collins, 1996), 333–371.
80. Lumm, interview with author.
81. Ibid.
82. Ibid.
83. Ibid.
84. Ibid.
85. Fager, *Selma, 1965*.
86. Geck, interview with author. Toolen also objected to the visiting religious. In an address to the Saint Patrick's Banquet in Mobile on March 11, Toolen declared: "We are living in a strange age. They asked me why do the priests and sisters come from other states and Canada to take part in the demonstrations. Certainly the sisters are out of place in these demonstrations. Their place is at home doing God's work. I would say the same thing is true of the priests. As to whether they have permission to come in, they haven't asked for it. It is customary to ask permission in such cases. What do they know about conditions in the South? I am afraid they are only eager beavers who feel there is a holy cause." "Toolen rips King, says priests, nuns should go home," article from unnamed newspaper, March 18, 1965, series 20, box 25, "Selma" file. NCCIJ-MUA.
87. Lumm, interview with author.
88. Sister Mary Paul Geck, typewritten memo, March 9, 1965, Selma series, box G-13–1–2, "Year of the South." SSJ-NY.
89. Sister Mary Christopher to Sister Mary John (and by implication the other sisters of the convent), typewritten letter, March 20, 1965. Selma series, box G-13–1–5, "Year of the South." SSJ-NY.

90. Geck, interview with author.
91. Sister Mary Peter (Margaret) Traxler, SSND, "After Selma, Sister, You Can't Stay Home Again!" article from unnamed publication, series 1, box 8. NCCIJ-MUA.

5. Project Cabrini

1. Sisters said, "About four, five or seven in the afternoon, parents return to the neighborhood. Many of them have been hauling, cooking, cleaning, operating elevators at the lake shore apartments only about ten blocks away." *Project Cabrini Newsletter* 6, July 17–24, 1965, series 19, box 2, "Project Cabrini" file. NCCIJ-MUA.
2. Descriptions of Cabrini Green and the surrounding neighborhood are based on interviews with sisters who participated in the project and from a long description of the neighborhood included in the *Project Cabrini Newsletter* 6, which included the following description: "Odors of malting plants, paint factories, tanneries mingle with exhaust fumes from buses and big trucks. . . . Old sacks, candy wrappers, newspapers and other debris blow through the streets and accumulate on the church steps and in doorways . . . a number of new holes have appeared in the yard. . . . The children who play together do so on the tarred area (which is also fenced in) and are forever tripping over one another, shoe strings, or stepping into puddles, falling and skinning themselves, or getting 'unclean.' . . . If they need to go to a washroom they head for home which may be on the 18th floor of the riser. . . . They begin the trek up the concrete stairs but give up halfway and take care of the emergency where they are. Back down they go. The swings squeak as only swings can do, and their rhythmic screech goes on all day and most of the night . . . most people are outside, or want to be. The children are in the streets. The noises, the smells, the lights, the life is carnival-like. Even the polluted river looks gay at sundown . . . the night air filled with the sound of screeching swings and racing motors, clattering tin cans, merry-melody ice cream vans, crying children, drinking men, breaking bottles, screaming fire sirens and gun shots." Ibid.
3. "Little Boxes," lyrics by Malvine Reynolds. The NCCIJ records contain recordings of Sister Lisieux Wirtz, OSF, singing "freedom songs," including "Little Boxes" at Project Cabrini. NCCIJ-MUA.
4. Project Cabrini proposal, series 19, box 2. NCCIJ-MUA.
5. Sister Joachim Von Arx, interview with author, July 31, 2000, Assisi Heights convent, Rochester, Minnesota.
6. "Report of the Committee on the Apostolate," 1964, untitled folder in "Apostolate" records series. SSF-MN.
7. Ibid.

8. "Report of the Committee for Planning Study of the Apostolate in Our Community," April 9, 1965, untitled folder in "Apostolate" records series. SSF-MN.
9. "Report of the Committee on the Apostolate."
10. Ibid.
11. Mother M. Callista Hynes, OSF, to Monsignor William McManus, typewritten letter, January 19, 1965; and Mother M. Callista Hynes, OSF, to Monsignor Francis Byrne, typewritten letter, January 19, 1965, untitled folder in "Apostolate" records series. SSF-MN.
12. Hynes to Rev. John J. Sullivan, typewritten letter, January 26, 1965, untitled folder in "Apostolate" records series. SSF-MN.
13. Hynes to Sister William, DC, typewritten letter, February 4, 1965, "Apostolate-Summer Projects, Cabrini, Chicago, IL, 1965." SSF-MN.
14. Sister Margaret Ellen (Mary Peter) Traxler, SSND, to Sister M. Emmanuel Collins, OSF, typewritten letter, February 23, 1965, series 19, box 2. NCCIJ-MUA.
15. Collins to Hynes, typewritten letter, March 1, 1965, "Apostolate-Summer Projects, Cabrini, Chicago, IL, 1965." SSF-MN.
16. Ibid.
17. Hynes to Sister Claire Marie, OSF, typewritten letter, April 15, 1965, series 19, box 2. NCCIJ-MUA.
18. Monsignor William McManus to Hynes, typewritten letter, May 12, 1965, "Apostolate-Summer Projects, Cabrini, Chicago, IL, 1965." SSF-MN.
19. Hynes to McManus, typewritten letter, May 28, 1965, "Apostolate-Summer Projects, Cabrini, Chicago, IL, 1965." SSF-MN.
20. Collins to Traxler, typewritten letter, May 17, 1965, series 19, box 2. NCCIJ-MUA.
21. Sam Dennis and Sister Margaret Ellen (Mary Peter) Traxler, SSND, typewritten memo to Sisters of the Urban Apostolate, undated, "Apostolate-Summer Projects, Cabrini, Chicago, IL, 1965." SSF-MN.
22. Traxler to Hynes, typewritten letter, June 3, 1965, "Apostolate-Summer Projects, Cabrini, Chicago, IL, 1965." SSF-MN.
23. Hynes to Traxler, typewritten letter, June 6, 1965, series 19, box 2. NCCIJ-MUA.
24. Collins to Traxler, typewritten letter, June 7, 1965, series 19, box 2. NCCIJ-MUA.
25. "Project Cabrini—faith—hope—love," *Extension,* March, 1966.
26. Handwritten, mimeographed flier advertising Project Cabrini, series 19, box 2. NCCIJ-MUA.
27. The figure is a rough estimate. Sisters noted that it was difficult to get an accurate attendance count because children often visited multiple classrooms in a session or would switch classrooms each day.

28. Sister Maigread Conway to Hynes, undated typewritten letter, "Apostolate-Summer Projects, Cabrini, Chicago, IL, 1965." SSF-MN.
29. Project Cabrini Guest Book, "Apostolate-Summer Projects, Cabrini, Chicago, IL, 1965." SSF-MN.
30. Conway to Hynes, undated typewritten letter, "Apostolate-Summer Projects, Cabrini, Chicago, IL, 1965." SSF-MN.
31. Dennis and Traxler, typewritten memo to Sisters of the Urban Apostolate, undated, "Apostolate-Summer Projects, Cabrini, Chicago, IL, 1965." SSF-MN.
32. Dolores McCahill, "Results of Cabrini Day-Camp Project Displayed," *Chicago Sun-Times*, Wednesday, August 11, 1965, 26.
33. Joachim, interview with author.
34. Typewritten press release, "Fifteen Franciscan nuns conduct pilot project 'day camp' in Chicago's Cabrini Housing Development," undated, series 19, box 2. NCCIJ-MUA.
35. *Project Cabrini Newsletter* 1, June 14–20, 1965, series 19, box 2. NCCIJ-MUA.
36. Ibid., 4, July 4–10, 1965.
37. Ibid., 2, June 21–26, 1965.
38. Ibid., 6, July 17–23, 1965.
39. Ibid., 5, July 11–16, 1965.
40. Ibid., 4, July 4–10, 1965.
41. Ibid., 3, June 27–July 3, 1965.
42. Ibid., 5.
43. Ibid., 1.
44. Conway to Hynes, undated typewritten letter, "Apostolate-Summer Projects, Cabrini, Chicago, IL, 1965." SSF-MN.
45. Joachim, interview with author.
46. Conway to Hynes, undated typewritten letter, "Apostolate-Summer Projects, Cabrini, Chicago, IL, 1965." SSF-MN.
47. Anthony J. Grant and William R. Copney to Hynes, undated typewritten letter, "Apostolate-Summer Projects, Cabrini, Chicago, IL, 1965," typographical errors in original text. SSF-MN.
48. Pius XII, *Mystici Corporis Christi, The Papal Encyclicals, 1939–1958*, edited by Claudia Carlen, IHM (Raleigh, N.C.: Pierian Press, 1990).
49. On American interpretations of the Mystical Body, see John McGreevy, *Parish Boundaries: The Catholic Encounter with Race in the Twentieth-Century Urban North* (Chicago: University of Chicago Press, 1996), 43–44 and 52.
50. Pius XII, *Mystici Corporis Christi.*
51. *Project Cabrini Newsletter* 1.
52. Ibid., 5.

53. Ibid., 4.
54. Ibid., 4.
55. Ibid., 2.
56. Ibid., 8, August 1–12, 1965.
57. Sister M. Sean to Hynes, typewritten letter, June 19, 1965, "Apostolate-Summer Projects, Cabrini, Chicago, IL, 1965." SSF-MN.
58. *Project Cabrini Newsletter* 7, July 25–31, 1965.
59. Ibid.
60. Ibid.
61. Ibid.
62. Ibid.
63. Ibid.
64. Ibid.
65. Ibid.
66. Typewritten memo, "Quotable quotes from the weekend that was," undated, "Apostolate-Summer Projects, Cabrini, Chicago, IL, 1965." SSF-MN.
67. *Project Cabrini Newsletter* 8.
68. Ibid., 4.
69. Sr. Viatrix Mach, SSF, interview with author, July 31, 2000, Assisi Heights convent, Rochester, Minnesota.
70. *Project Cabrini Newsletter* 5.

6. The Placement Bureau

1. Sister Benedicta Claus to Benedictine Sisters, typewritten letter with handwritten addendum to Sister Margaret Ellen (Mary Peter) Traxler, February 1971, series 19, box 13. NCCIJ-MUA. Emphasis in original text.
2. Ibid.
3. Sister Rose Thering, OP, "The CARA Survey of Inner City Activities of Religious Communities of Sisters: A Preliminary Study," typewritten manuscript, August 1, 1966, series 20, box 5. NCCIJ-MUA. According to the study, these "extra involvements" ranged from federal relief and education programs to social work and adult CCD, to part-time volunteer work in tutoring programs, and to summer assignments to recreational or educational projects (like the Yellow Ball Centers on Boston area playgrounds, run by the Association of Urban Sisters).
4. The racial stereotyping of students, present in this passage, will be addressed later in the chapter. Sister Mary Paul Krasowski, National Placement Bureau application, February 9, 1971, series 19, box 3. NCCIJ-MUA.

5. Sister Susan Elizabeth Fitzwilliam, National Placement Bureau application, February 6, 1970, series 19, box 13. NCCIJ-MUA.
6. Sister Ann Julia Kinnirey, National Placement Bureau application, February 25, 1971, series 19, box 13. NCCIJ-MUA.
7. Sister M. Consolata Grace, National Placement Bureau application, March 25, 1971, series 19, box 13. NCCIJ-MUA.
8. Sister Clara L. Grochowska to Traxler, typewritten letter, October 16, 1970, series 19, box 13. NCCIJ-MUA.
9. Sister Leona Stenzel, National Placement Bureau application, November 1969, series 19, box 13. NCCIJ-MUA.
10. Sister Anne Mary O'Donnell, National Placement Bureau application, January 6, 1972, series 19, box 14. NCCIJ-MUA.
11. Sister Mary Elizabeth Cameron, National Placement Bureau application, February 23, 1972, series 19, box 13. NCCIJ-MUA.
12. Sister Francis Clara Schares, National Placement Bureau application, February 18, 1970, series 19, box 13. NCCIJ-MUA.
13. Sister Naomi Cunningham, National Placement Bureau application, February 15, 1970, series 19, box 13. NCCIJ-MUA.
14. Sister Evelyn Marie Houlihan, National Placement Bureau application, November 2, 1969, series 19, box 13. NCCIJ-MUA.
15. Sister Mary Frances Lippert, National Placement Bureau application, November 23, 1969, series 19, box 13. NCCIJ-MUA.
16. Sister Virginia Berry, BVM, to Traxler, handwritten letter, July 4, 1969, series 19, box 13. NCCIJ-MUA.
17. Sister Julie Marie Donahue, SND, National Placement Bureau application, January 5, 1970, series 19, box 13. NCCIJ-MUA.
18. Sister Anne Cyril Delaney, SND de Namur, National Placement Bureau application, November 10, 1969, series 19, box 13. NCCIJ-MUA.
19. Sister Cathan M. Miles, National Placement Bureau application, February 20, 1970, series 19, box 13. NCCIJ-MUA.
20. Sister Ann Dolores Weisner, National Placement Bureau application, May 8, 1971, series 19, box 13. NCCIJ-MUA.
21. Sister M. Celestine Hoedel, National Placement Bureau application, December 12, 1968, series 19, box 13. NCCIJ-MUA.
22. Sister Mary Helen Hromcho, National Placement Bureau application, April 5, 1971, series 19, box 13. NCCIJ-MUA.
23. Sister Mary Marcella Shields, National Placement Bureau application, February 23, 1972, series 19, box 14. NCCIJ-MUA.
24. Sister Ann Patricia Donovan, National Placement Bureau application, February 6, 1970, series 19, box 13. NCCIJ-MUA.
25. Sister De Porres Conway, OP, National Placement Bureau application, October 30, 1968, series 19, box 13. NCCIJ-MUA.

26. Sister Yvonne L. Desrats, National Placement Bureau application, undated, series 19, box 14. NCCIJ-MUA.
27. Sister Mary Agnes Drees, National Placement Bureau application, January 14, 1970, series 19, box 13. NCCIJ-MUA.
28. Sister Dolores Ann Brinkel, National Placement Bureau application, January 15, 1971, series 19, box 13. NCCIJ-MUA.
29. Sister Ann Wittman, National Placement Bureau application, January 27, 1970, series 19, box 13. NCCIJ-MUA.
30. Sister Miriam Ann Cunningham, CSC, National Placement Bureau application, January 12, 1971, series 19, box 13. NCCIJ-MUA.
31. Sister Maria Petruska, National Placement Bureau application, January 13, 1971, series 19, box 13. NCCIJ-MUA.
32. Sister Barbara Marie Hergenrother, National Placement Bureau application, March 8, 1972, series 19, box 13. NCCIJ-MUA.
33. Sister Margaret Ann Korkmas, National Placement Bureau application, November 26, 1969, series 19, box 13. NCCIJ-MUA.
34. Sister Theresa A. McGreevy, National Placement Bureau application, May 25, 1970, series 19, box 13. NCCIJ-MUA.
35. Sister Mary Ann Coyle, National Placement Bureau application, March 13, 1969, series 19, box 13. NCCIJ-MUA.
36. Sister Mary Ethel Byers, National Placement Bureau application, October 21, 1969, series 19, box 13. NCCIJ-MUA.
37. Sister Mary Louise Ante, National Placement Bureau application, February 18, 1970, series 19, box 13. NCCIJ-MUA.
38. Sister Mary Frances Honnen, National Placement Bureau application, April 25, 1971, series 19, box 13. NCCIJ-MUA.
39. Sister Mary Lorraine Castelein, SSND, National Placement Bureau application, December 1969, series 19, box 13. NCCIJ-MUA.
40. Sister Jean Ingrassia, National Placement Bureau application, undated, series 19, box 13. NCCIJ-MUA.
41. Sister De Porres Conway, OP, to Traxler, typewritten letter, July 23, 1970, series 19, box 14. NCCIJ-MUA.
42. Sister Mary O'Carlaghan to unnamed recipient, undated typewritten letter, series 19, box 13. NCCIJ-MUA. Emphasis in original text.
43. Sister Mary Magdalen Dunn, OSB, to Traxler, typewritten letter, August 20, 1968, series 19, box 13. NCCIJ-MUA.
44. Sister Mary to Traxler, typewritten letter, June 25, 1968, series 19, box 13. NCCIJ-MUA.
45. Sister Frances Frieiwer, OSB, to Traxler, typewritten letter, October 18, 1968, series 19, box 13. NCCIJ-MUA.
46. Sister Joan Campbell, SL, to Traxler, handwritten letter, February 18, 1970, series 19, box 13. NCCIJ-MUA.

47. Sister Bernadette to Sister Joseph, also titled "An Experience in Texas," undated handwritten letter, series 19, box 14. NCCIJ-MUA.
48. Sister Mary O'Carlaghan to unnamed recipient, undated typewritten letter, series 19, box 13. NCCIJ-MUA.
49. Sister M. Bernadette, RU, to Traxler, handwritten letter, June 28, 1968, series 19, box 13. NCCIJ-MUA.
50. Sister M. Rosarita, RSM, to Traxler, typewritten letter, July 10, 1968, series 19, box 13. NCCIJ-MUA.
51. Conway to Traxler, typewritten letter, July 23, 1970.
52. Frieiwer to Traxler, typewritten letter, October 18, 1968. Ellipses in original text.
53. Sister M. Vincent Heydinger, OSU, to Traxler, handwritten letter, August 25, 1969, series 19, box 13. NCCIJ-MUA.
54. Sister M. Rosarita, RSM, to Sister Margaret Ellen Traxler, typewritten letter, July 10, 1968, series 19, box 13. NCCIJ-MUA.
55. Rosarita to Traxler, typewritten letter, July 10, 1968.
56. Sister Rosarita Johnston, RSM, to Traxler, typewritten letter, August 18, 1969, series 19, box 13. NCCIJ-MUA.
57. Sister M. Liguori to Traxler, handwritten letter, August 1969, series 19, box 13. NCCIJ-MUA.
58. Sister Kathleen M. Smith, SND, to Traxler, handwritten letter, August 30, 1968, series 19, box 13. NCCIJ-MUA.
59. Conway to Traxler, typewritten letter, July 23, 1970.
60. Bernadette to Traxler, handwritten letter, June 28, 1968.
61. Sister Benedicta Claus to Benedictine Sisters, cc: with handwritten addendum to Traxler, typewritten letter, February 1971, series 19, box 13. NCCIJ-MUA.
62. Bernadette to Traxler, handwritten letter, June 28, 1968.
63. Sister Helen to Traxler, handwritten letter, July 10, unspecified year, series 19, box 13. NCCIJ-MUA.
64. Grochowska to Traxler, typewritten letter, October 16, 1970.
65. Sister Joan Campbell, SL, to Traxler, handwritten letter, February 18, 1970, series 19, box 13. NCCIJ-MUA.
66. Ibid. In her letter, Sister Campbell continued her explanation, "'Campbell' is the name of the main street through the honky-tonk section of the black community, and this fact secured the value of my student stock immediately!"
67. Again, it should be noted that sisters' references to the unique nature of the bond they shared with African Americans reflect the desire and self-perceptions of sisters only; it cannot and does not reflect the perceptions and experience of African Americans, whose experiences cannot be determined from NPB sources. African American voices are only present in NPB sources in quotations in sisters' letters.

68. Smith to Traxler, handwritten letter, August 30, 1968.
69. Sister Helen Coughlan to Traxler, undated typewritten letter, series 19, box 14. NCCIJ-MUA.
70. Handwritten report letter to unnamed recipient, undated, series 19, box 13. NCCIJ-MUA. Emphasis in original text.
71. Bernadette to Traxler, handwritten letter, June 28, 1968.
72. Handwritten report letter to unnamed recipient, undated, series 19, box 13. NCCIJ-MUA.

Conclusion

1. Sister June Fisher to Sister Margaret Ellen (Mary Peter) Traxler, typewritten letter, July 26, 1969, series 4, box 3. NCCIJ-MUA.
2. On the development and ethos of black power see Clayborne Carson, *In Struggle: SNCC and the Black Awakening of the 1960s* (Cambridge: Harvard University Press, 1981); Kwame Ture and Charles V. Hamilton, *Black Power: The Politics of Liberation* (New York: Random House, 1967); and Elaine Brown, *A Taste of Power: A Black Woman's Story* (New York: Pantheon Books, 1992).
3. Stokely Carmichael, "What We Want," *New York Review of Books,* (September 22, 1966), 8.
4. Sister Alice Rita to Traxler, handwritten letter, February 27, 1969, series 4, box 3. NCCIJ-MUA.
5. Sister Bernadette Marie Villeneuve, RSM, "Summary Report, Boulevard Research Project, Summer, 1968," series 26, box 1. NCCIJ-MUA.
6. Ibid.
7. Robert F. Clark, *The War on Poverty: History, Selected Programs and Ongoing Impact* (Lanham, Md.: University Press of America, 2002), 55–70.
8. Sister Noel Marie to Sister Maura Coughlan, undated typewritten letter, series 4, box 3. NCCIJ-MUA.
9. Sandra Schneiders, "Religious Life *(Perfectae Caritatis)*" in *Modern Catholicism: Vatican II and After,* edited by Adrian Hastings (New York: Oxford University Press, 1991), 157–162; Sandra Schneiders, *Finding the Treasure: Locating Catholic Religious Life in a New Ecclesial and Cultural Context* (New York: Paülist Press, 2000); Sr. Lora Ann Quinonez, CDP, and Sr. Mary Daniel Turner, SDPdeN, *The Transformation of American Catholic Sisters* (Philadelphia: Temple University Press, 1992).
10. Sister Therese Mary Rebstork to Traxler, typewritten letter, August 29, 1969, series 4, box 5. NCCIJ-MUA.
11. Sister Ann Michelle to Traxler, typewritten letter, series 4, box 3. NCCIJ-MUA.

12. Sister Mary Catherine Patch, OP, to Traxler, typewritten letter, March 6, 1967, series 4, box 4. NCCIJ-MUA.
13. Sister Jean Vianney, CSJ, to Traxler, undated typewritten letter, series 4, box 5. NCCIJ-MUA.
14. Sister M. Yolande to Traxler, typewritten letter, February 18, 1967, series 4, box 5. NCCIJ-MUA.
15. Unnamed sister at Rosemont College, Rosemont, Pennsylvania, to Traxler, typewritten letter, June 18, 1970, series 19, box 1. NCCIJ-MUA.
16. Anita M. Caspary, *Witness to Integrity: The Crisis of the Immaculate Heart Community of California* (Collegeville, Minn.: Liturgical Press, 2003), offers a detailed account of the conflict written by the superior of the IHM community at the time. For a broader portrait of the general conflict, see Mary Ewens "Women in the Convent" in *American Catholic Women: An Historical Exploration,* edited by Karen Kennelly, CSJ (New York: Macmillan, 1989), 17–47; and Mary Jo Weaver, *New Catholic Women: A Contemporary Challenge to Authority* (San Francisco: Harper and Row, 1986).
17. *Trans-Sister,* vol. 2, no. 5, July 1969, 7.
18. Margaret Ellen Traxler, "A Twenty-Year Purview," preface to *If Anyone Can, NCAN: Twenty Years of Speaking Out,* NCAN Anniversary Issue, vol. 19, nos. 3–4, summer and fall, 1989.
19. Sister Geri Wagner to Traxler, typewritten letter, September 8, 1969, series 4, box 5. NCCIJ-MUA.
20. Sister Ann Ryan to Traxler, typewritten letter, January 8, 1970, series 4, box 4. NCCIJ-MUA.
21. Sister Elizabeth Twomey to Traxler, handwritten letter, March 10, 1970, series 19, box 1. NCCIJ-MUA.
22. Sara Evans, *Personal Politics: The Roots of Women's Liberation in the Civil Rights Movement and the New Left* (New York: Random House, 1979).
23. Mary Henold offers a cogent, detailed history of the emergence of Catholic feminism in her 2003 dissertation, "Faith, Feminism, and the Politics of Sustained Ambivalence: The Creation of the American Catholic Feminist Movement, 1963–1980," (PhD diss., University of Rochester, 2003). For an interesting study of the practice of "discursive protest" by American women religious, see Mary Fainsod Katzenstein, *Faithful and Fearless: Moving Feminist Protest inside the Church and Military* (Princeton, N.J.: Princeton University Press, 1998).
24. Sister Joan Bauer, typed "Report for the General Chapter on Out Work in the Central Ward of Newark, N.J.," NCCIJ correspondence files, series 4, box 1. NCCIJ-MUA.

25. "Interested sisters" to Traxler, undated typewritten letter, series 4, box 1. NCCIJ-MUA.
26. Sister Barbara Lumm, SSJ, interview with author, December 14, 2000, Rochester, New York.
27. Sister M. Alcantara, OSF, to Traxler, typewritten letter, October 7, 1965, "Apostolate-Summer Projects, Cabrini, Chicago, IL, 1965." SSF-MN.

Bibliography

INTERVIEWS

Abhold, Sr. Cecelia (Sr. Mary Loretta), SP. April 7, 1995, Seattle, Washington.

Agnes, S. Jean, SSJ. December 15–17, 2000, Rochester, New York.

Bradley, Sr. Ritamary, SFCC. August 20–23, 1998, Davenport, Iowa.

Byers, Sr. Mary John, CHM. August 21, 1998, Davenport, Iowa.

Dermondy, Sr. Germaine, CHM. August 22, 1998, Davenport, Iowa.

Dieker, Sr. Alberta, OSB. March 7, 1995, Mount Angel, Oregon.

Jackson, Sr. Janice, SNJM. February 22, 1995, Eugene, Oregon.

Gaasch, Sr. Marguerite, OSF. July 30, 2000, Rochester, Minnesota.

Geck, Sr. Mary Paul, SSJ. December 15, 2000, Rochester, New York.

John, Sister Mary, PVMI. December 18, 2000, Marycrest, New York.

Kasper, Sr. Rosemarie, SNJM. February 21, 1995, Marylhurst, Oregon.

Kopp, Lillanna, SFCC. (Sr. Mary Audrey, SNJM). March 16, 1996, Portland, Oregon.

Loyola, Sr. Mary, PVMI. December 18, 2000, Marycrest, New York.

Lumm, Sr. Barbara, SSJ. December 16, 2000, Rochester, New York.

Mach, Sr. Viatrix, SSF. July 31, 2000, Rochester, Minnesota.

Ryan, Sr. Janet, SNJM. February 7, 1995, Eugene, Oregon.

Traxler, Sr. Margaret (Mary Peter), SSND. August 17, 1996, Chicago, Illinois.

Von Arx, Sr. Joachim, OSF. July 31, 2000, Rochester, New York.

ARCHIVES AND PAPERS

AUS Association of Urban Sisters papers, Archdiocesan archives, Boston, Massachusetts.

BS Benedictine Sisters, self-study file, 1974–1976, archives of Benedictine Sisters, Mount Angel, Oregon.

CAM-AAC Cardinal Albert Meyer papers, Archdiocesan archives, Chicago, Illinois.

CIP Catholic Interracial Papers, Archdiocesan archives, Chicago, Illinois.

CIC-CHS Catholic Interracial Council papers, Chicago Historical Society, Chicago, Illinois.

DC-CHS Very Rev. Msgr. Daniel Cantwell papers, Chicago Historical Society, Chicago, Illinois.

FH-CHS Friendship House papers, Chicago Historical Society, Chicago, Illinois.

JE Very Rev. Msgr. John Egan papers, Archdiocesan archives, Chicago, Illinois.

JE-ND Very Reverend Msgr. John Egan papers, archives of the University of Notre Dame, South Bend, Indiana.

MA-CHS Mathew Ahmann papers, Chicago Historical Society, Chicago, Illinois.

MET-MUA Sister Margaret Traxler, SSND, papers, Marquette University Archives, Milwaukee, Wisconsin.

NCAN-MUA National Coalition of American Nuns papers, 1969–1984, Marquette University Archives, Milwaukee, Wisconsin.

NCCIJ-MUA National Catholic Conference for Interracial Justice papers, 1961–1969, Marquette University Archives, Milwaukee, Wisconsin.

SLK Sr. Lillanna Kopp, SFCC, private papers, Sister Lillanna Kopp, Portland, Oregon.

SMB-ND Sr. Mary Benet papers, archives of the University of Notre Dame, South Bend, Indiana.

PHC-SP Sisters of Providence, documentation of the Providence Heights College of Sister Formation, 1966–1969, archives of Sisters of Providence, Seattle, Washington.

SRB Sr. Ritamary Bradley, SFCC, private papers, Sr. Ritamary Bradley, Davenport, Iowa.

SSF-MN Sisters of Saint Francis, documentation of Project Cabrini, 1964–1966, archives of the Sisters of Saint Francis, Rochester, Minnesota.

SSJ-NY Sisters of Saint Joseph, documentation of Saint Elizabeth's parish and Good Samaritan Hospital in Selma, Alabama, 1940–1970, archives of the Sisters of Saint Joseph, Rochester, New York.

UAS-ND Urban Apostolate of the Sisters, archives of the University of Notre Dame, South Bend, Indiana.

BOOKS

Abbott, Walter, S. J., ed. *The Documents of Vatican II.* New York: Herder and Herder, 1966.

Ahmann, Mathew, ed. *Race: The Challenge to Religion, Original Essays and an Appeal to the Conscience from the National Conference on Religion and Race.* Chicago: Henry Regnery, 1963.

Albergio, Giuseppe, Jean-Pierre Jossua, and Joseph Komonchak, eds. *The Reception of Vatican II*. Washington, D.C.: Catholic University of America Press, 1987.

Beane, Marjorie Noterman. *From Framework to Freedom: A History of the Sister Formation Conference*. Lanham, Md.: University Press of America, 1993.

Berenstein, Marcelle. *The Nuns*. Philadelphia: Lippincott, 1976.

Borromeo, Sr. M. Charles, CSC., ed. *The Changing Sister.* Notre Dame: Fides Publishers, 1965.

———. *The New Nuns*. London: Sheed and Ward, 1968.

Branch, Taylor. *Parting the Waters: America in the King Years, 1954–1963*. New York: Simon and Schuster, 1988.

Brick, Howard. *Age of Contradictions: American Thought and Culture in the 1960s*. Ithaca, N.Y.: Cornell University Press, 1998.

Brown, Dorothy, and Elizabeth McKeown. *The Poor Belong to Us: Catholic Charities and American Welfare*. Cambridge: Harvard University Press, 1997.

Brown, Elaine. *A Taste of Power: A Black Woman's Story.* New York: Pantheon Books, 1992.

Bryan, Louis Marie. *History of the National Black Sisters' Conference, Celibate Black Commitment*. Pittsburgh: National Black Sisters' Conference, 1971.

Byrne, Patricia, Jay Dolan, Scott Appleby, and Debra Campbell. *Transforming Parish Ministry: The Changing Roles of Catholic Clergy, Laity and Women Religious*. New York: Crossroad, 1990.

Campbell-Jones, Suzanne. *In Habit: A Study of Working Nuns*. New York: Pantheon Books, 1978.

Carey, Ann. *Sisters in Crisis: The Tragic Unraveling of Women's Religious Communities*. Huntington, Ind.: Our Sunday Visitor, 1997.

Carson, Clayborne. *In Struggle: SNCC and the Black Awakening of the 1960s*. Cambridge: Harvard University Press, 1981.

Caspary, Anita M. *Witness to Integrity: The Crisis of the Immaculate Heart Community of Los Angeles*. Collegeville, Minn.: Liturgical Press, 2003.

Chestnut, J. L. Jr. *Black in Selma*. New York: Anchor Books, 1990.

Chittister, Joan, et al. *Climb along the Cutting Edge: An Analysis of Change in Religous Life*. New York: Paulist Press, 1977.

Clark, Robert F. *The War on Poverty: History, Selected Programs and Ongoing Impact*. Lanham, Md.: University Press of America, 2002.

Coburn, Carol, and Martha Smith. *Spirited Lives: How Nuns Shaped Catholic Culture and American Life, 1836–1920*. Chapel Hill: University of North Carolina Press, 1999.

Congar, Yves. *The Catholic Church and the Race Question*. Paris: United Nations Educational, Scientific, and Cultural Organization, 1953.

Davis, Cyprian. *A History of Black Catholics in the United States.* New York: Crossroad, 1988.

Delgado, Richard, and Jean Stefanic, eds. *Critical White Studies: Looking behind the Mirror.* Philadelphia: Temple University Press, 1997.

Dolan, Jay P. *American Catholic Experience: A History from Colonial Times to the Present.* Garden City, N.Y.: Doubleday, 1985.

Donnelly, Sister Gertrude Joseph, CSJO. *The Sister Apostle.* Notre Dame, Ind.: Fides, 1964.

Eagles, Charles W. *Outside Agitator: Jon Daniels and the Civil Rights Movement in Alabama.* Chapel Hill: University of North Carolina Press, 1993.

Ebaugh, Helen Rose Fuchs. *Out of the Cloister: A Study of Organizational Dilemmas.* Austin: University of Texas Press, 1977.

———. *Women in the Vanishing Cloister: Organizational Decline in Catholic Religious Orders in the United States.* New Brunswick, N.J.: Rutgers University Press, 1993.

Echols, Alice. *Daring to Be Bad: Radical Feminism in America, 1967–1975.* Minneapolis: University of Minnesota Press, 1989.

Evans, Sara. *Personal Politics: The Roots of Women's Liberation in the Civil Rights Movement and the New Left.* New York: Random House, 1979.

Ewens, Mary. *The Role of the Nun in Nineteenth-Century America.* New York: Arno Press, 1978.

Fager, Charles. *Selma, 1965.* New York: Charles Scribner's Sons, 1974.

Farber, David, ed. *The Age of Great Dreams: America in the Sixties.* New York: Hill and Wang, 1994.

Feldman, Egal. *Catholics and Jews in Twentieth-Century America.* Urbana: University of Illinois Press, 2003.

Fialka, John J. *Sisters: Catholic Nuns and the Making of America.* New York: St. Martin's Press, 2003.

Fisher, James Terrance. *The Catholic Counterculture in America, 1933–1962.* Chapel Hill: University of North Carolina Press, 1989.

Fredrickson, George M. *The Black Image in the White Mind: The Debate on Afro-American Character and Destiny, 1817–1914.* New York: Harper and Row, 1971.

Fuchs, Lawrence H. *John F. Kennedy and American Catholicism.* New York: Meredith Press, 1967.

Gilmore, Glenda. *Gender and Jim Crow: Women and the Politics of White Supremacy in North Carolina, 1896–1920.* Chapel Hill: University of North Carolina Press, 1996.

Gitlin, Todd. *The Sixties: Years of Hope, Days of Rage.* New York: Bantam, 1987.

Gleason, Philip. *Contending with Modernity: Catholic Higher Education in the Twentieth Century.* New York: Oxford University Press, 1995.

Goffman, Erving. *Asylums: Essays on the Social Situation of Mental Patients and Other Inmates.* Chicago: Aldine Publishing, 1962.

Goldfield, David R. *Black, White and Southern: Race Relations and Southern Culture, 1940 to the Present.* Baton Rouge: Louisiana State University Press, 1990.

Gossett, Thomas F. *Race: The History of an Idea in America.* Dallas: Southern Methodist University Press, 1966.

Gray, Francine du Plessix. *Divine Disobedience: Profiles in Catholic Radicalism.* New York: Knopf, 1970.

Greeley, Andrew. *The American Catholic: A Social Portrait.* New York: Basic Books, 1977.

———. *The Catholic Experience: The History of American Catholicism.* New York: Image Books, 1969.

———. *The Catholic Revolution: New Wine, Old Wineskins, and the Second Vatican Council.* Berkeley: University of California Press, 2004.

———. *The Church and the Suburbs.* New York: Sheed and Ward, 1959.

Green, Elna, ed. *The New Deal and Beyond: Social Welfare in the South since 1930.* Athens: University of Georgia Press, 2003.

Griffin, Mary. *The Courage to Choose: An American Nun's Story.* Boston: Little, Brown, 1975.

Grollmes, Eugene E., SJ, ed. *Vows but No Walls: An Analysis of Religious Life.* St. Louis: B. Herder Book Co., 1967.

Hale, Grace. *Making Whiteness: The Culture of Segregation in the South, 1890–1940.* New York: Pantheon Books, 1998.

Haley, Joseph E., CSC, ed. *Proceedings of the 1957 Sisters' Institute of Spirituality.* South Bend, Ind.: University of Notre Dame Press, 1958.

———. *Proceedings of the 1959 Sisters' Institute of Spirituality: The Superior and the Personality Development of the Subject-Religious.* South Bend, Ind.: University of Notre Dame Press, 1960.

Harris, Sara. *The Sisters: The Changing World of the American Nun.* Indianapolis, Ind.: Bobbs-Merrill, 1970.

Hastings, Adrian, ed. *Modern Catholicism: Vatican II and After.* New York: Oxford University Press, 1991.

Henderson, Nancy. *Out of the Curtained World: The Story of an American Nun Who Left the Convent.* Garden City, N.Y.: Doubleday, 1972.

Hennessey, James, SJ. *American Catholics: A History of the Roman Catholic Community in the United States.* Oxford: Oxford University Press, 1981.

Henold, Mary. "Faith, Feminism, and the Politics of Sustained Ambivalence: The Creation of the American Catholic Feminist Movement, 1963–1980." PhD diss.: University of Rochester, 2003.

Hite, Greg N. "The Hottest Places in Hell: The Catholic Church and Civil Rights in Selma, Alabama, 1937–1965." PhD diss., University of Virginia, 2002.

Hoy, Suellen. *Good Hearts: Catholic Sisters in Chicago's Past.* Urbana: University of Illinois Press, 2006.

Jacobson, Matthew Frye. *Whiteness of a Different Color: European Immigrants and the Alchemy of Race.* Cambridge: Harvard University Press, 1998.

Kenelley, Karen, ed. *American Catholic Women: A Historical Exploration.* New York: Macmillan, 1989.

Kennedy, Sally. *Faith and Feminism: Catholic Women's Struggles for Self-Expression.* Sydney: Studies in the Christian Movement, 1985.

King, Margot H., ed. *A Leaf from the Great Tree of God: Essays in Honor of Ritamary Bradley.* Toronto: Peregrina Press, 1993.

Kolbenschlag, Madonna, ed. *Authority, Community, and Conflict.* New York: Sheed and Ward, 1986.

———. *Between God and Caesar: Priests, Sisters and Political Office in the United States.* New York: Paulist Press, 1985.

Kolmer, Elizabeth, ASC. *Religious Women in the United States: A Survey of the Influential Literature, 1950 to 1983.* Wilmington, Del.: Michael Glazier Publishers, 1984.

Kopp, Lillanna (Sr. Audrey), SFCC. *The New Nuns: Collegial Christians, a Sociological Analysis.* Chicago: Argus Communications, 1968.

———. *Sudden Spring: 6th Stage Sisters, Trends of Change in Catholic Sisterhoods, a Sociological Analysis.* Waldport, Ore.: Sunspot Publications, 1983.

Kung, Hans. *The Council in Action: Theological Reflections on the Second Vatican Council.* New York: Sheed and Ward, 1963.

Leadership Conference of Women Religious. *Widening the Dialogue: Reflections on Evangelica Testificatio.* Ottawa: Canadian Conference of Religious, 1974.

Leaman, Nicholas. *The Promised Land: The Great Black Migration and How It Changed America.* New York: Knopf, 1991.

Lieblich, Julia. *Sisters: Lives of Devotion and Defiance.* New York: Ballantine Books, 1992.

Marsh, Charles. *God's Long Summer: Stories of Faith and Civil Rights.* Princeton, N.J.: Princeton University Press, 1997.

McAdam, Doug. *Freedom Summer.* New York: Oxford University Press, 1988.

McDonogh, Gary Wray. *Black and Catholic in Savannah Georgia.* Knoxville: University of Tennessee Press, 1993.

McGreevy, John T. *Catholicism and American Freedom: A History.* New York: W. W. Norton, 2003.

———. *Parish Boundaries: The Catholic Encounter with Race in the Twentieth-Century Urban North.* Chicago: University of Chicago Press, 1996.

McNamara, Jo Ann Kay. *Sisters in Arms: Catholic Nuns through Two Millennia*. Cambridge: Harvard University Press, 1996.

Meconis, Charles A. *With Clumsy Grace: The American Catholic Left, 1961–1975*. New York: Seabury Press, 1979.

Meyers, Sr. Bertrand, DC. *Sisters for the 21st Century*. New York: Sheed and Ward, 1965.

Misner, Barbara. *Highly Respectable and Accomplished Ladies: Catholic Women Religious in America, 1790–1850*. New York: Garland Press, 1988.

Moran, Gabriel. *The New Community: Religious Life in an Era of Change*. New York: Herder and Herder, 1970.

Morrow, Diane Batts. *Persons of Color and Religious at the Same Time: The Oblate Sisters of Providence, 1828–1860*. Chapel Hill: University of North Carolina Press, 2002.

Neal, Sr. Marie Augusta, SND de Namur. *From Nuns to Sisters: An Expanding Vocation*. Mystic, Conn.: Twenty-Third Publications, 1990.

Oates, Mary J. *The Catholic Philanthropic Tradition in America*. Bloomington: Indiana University Press, 1995.

Oates, Stephen B. *Let the Trumpet Sound: The Life of Martin Luther King, Jr*. New York: Harper and Row, 1982.

O'Brien, David. *The Renewal of American Catholicism*. New York: Oxford University Press, 1972.

Ochs, Stephen J. *Desegregating the Altar: The Josephites and the Struggle for Black Priests*. Baton Rouge: Louisiana State University Press, 1990.

O'Conner, Alice. *Poverty Knowledge: Social Science, Social Policy, and the Poor in Twentieth-Century U.S. History*. Princeton, N.J.: Princeton University Press, 2001.

O'Doherty, E. F. *Vocation, Formation, Consecration and Vows: Theological and Psychological Considerations*. New York: Alba House, 1971.

O'Meara, Thomas, OP. *Holiness and Radicalism in Religious Life*. New York: Herder and Herder, 1970.

O'Neill, William L. *Coming Apart: An Informal History of the 1960s*. New York: Random House, 1971.

Ong, Walter. *Frontiers in American Catholicism: Essays on Ideology and Culture*. New York: Macmillan, 1964.

Orsi, Robert A., ed. *Gods of the City: Religion and the American Urban Landscape*. Bloomington, Ind.: Indiana University Press, 1999.

Osborne, William. *The Segregated Covenant: Race Relations and American Catholics*. New York: Herder and Herder, 1967.

Penet, Sr. Mary Emil, IHM, ed. *Report of the Everett Curriculum Workshop*. Seattle: Heiden's Mailing Bureau, 1956.

Pius XII. "Counsel to Teaching Sisters." September 15, 1951. Washington, D.C.: National Catholic Welfare Conference Publications Office, 1992.

Puzon, Bridget, ed. *Women Religious and the Intellectual Life: The North American Achievement.* San Francisco: International Scholars Publications, 1996.

Quinonez, Sr. Lora Ann, CDP, ed. *Starting Points: Six Essays Based on the Experience of U.S. Women Religious.* Washington, D.C.: Leadership Conference of Women Religious, 1980.

Quinonez, Sr. Lora Ann, CDP, and Sr. Mary Daniel Turner, SDPdeN. *The Transformation of American Catholic Sisters.* Philadelphia: Temple University Press, 1992.

Raboteau, Albert J. *A Fire in the Bones: Reflections on African-American Religious History.* Boston: Beacon Press, 1995.

Raines, Howell. *My Soul Is Rested: Movement Days in the Deep South Remembered.* New York: Penguin Books, 1983.

Robert, Dana. *American Women in Mission: A Social History of Their Thought and Practice.* Macon, Ga.: Mercer University Press, 1997.

Schneider, Mary. *The Transformation of American Women Religious: The Sister Formation Conference as Catalyst for Change (1954–1964).* South Bend, Ind.: Charles and Margaret Hall Cushwa Center for the Study of American Catholicism, University of Notre Dame, 1986.

Schneider, Sandra. *Finding the Treasure: Locating Catholic Religious Life in a New Ecclesial and Cultural Context.* New York: Paulist Press, 2000.

Shriver, Sargent. *Point of the Lance: The Need for a New Kind of Politics, Education, and Public Service—at Home and in the World.* New York: Harper and Row, 1964.

Sisters of Charity, BVM. *Proceedings of the Institute on the Problems That Unite Us.* Mount Carmel, Dubuque, Iowa: Sisters of Charity, 1966.

Sisters, Servants of the Immaculate Heart of Mary. *Building Sisterhood: A Feminist History of the Sisters, Servants of the Immaculate Heart of Mary, Monroe, Michigan.* Syracuse, N.Y.: Syracuse University Press, 1997.

Southern, David W. *John LaFarge and the Limits of Catholic Interracialism, 1911–1963.* Baton Rouge: Louisiana State University Press, 1996.

Suenens, Leon Joseph. *The Nun in the World: Religious and the Apostolate.* Westminster, Md.: Newman Press, 1963.

Sullivan, Rebecca. *Visual Habits: Nuns, Feminism, and American Postwar Popular Culture.* Toronto: University of Toronto Press, 2005.

Thering, Rose. *Jews, Judaism and Catholic Education: Documentary Survey Reports of Catholic Institutions' Implementation of 1965 Conciliar Statement on the Jews, 1974 Roman Catholic Guidelines/Suggestions, 1975 U.S. Bishops' Statement on the Jews; Prepared for the Twentieth Anniversary of the 1965 Promulgation of Vatican II Document Nostra Aetate.* New York: Anti-Defamation League of B'nai B'rith, 1968.

Tobin, Sr. Mary Luke. *Hope Is an Open Door.* Nashville, Tenn.: Abingdon Press, 1981.

Traxler, Maragret, ed. *New Works of New Nuns.* St. Louis: B. Herder, 1968.

———. *Split-Level Lives: American Nuns Speak on Race.* Techney, Ill.: Divine Word Publications, 1967.

Ture, Kwame, and Charles V. Hamilton. *Black Power: The Politics of Liberation.* New York: Random House, 1967.

Tweed, Thomas A., ed. *Retelling U.S. Religious History.* Berkeley: University of California Press, 1997.

Valentine, Sister Mary Hester, SSND. *The Post-Conciliar Nun.* New York: Hawthorn Books, 1968.

Ware, Ann Patrick, ed. *If Anyone Can, NCAN.* Chicago: National Coalition of American Nuns, 1989.

———. *Midwives of the Future: American Sisters Tell Their Stories.* Kansas City: Leaven Press, 1985.

Weaver, Mary Jo. *New Catholic Women: A Contemporary Challenge to Authority.* San Francisco: Harper and Row, 1986.

Young, Andrew. *An Easy Burden: The Civil Rights Movement and the Transformation of America.* New York: Harper Collins, 1996.

Acknowledgments

During the course of completing this project I have often felt that the universe was conspiring in my favor, placing directly in my path a wealth of rich archival sources, steady financial support, gifted advisers, and solid friends and colleagues. One of the pleasures of finishing a manuscript, I am discovering, is the opportunity it presents to publicly thank some of the people who encouraged and sustained me through the process of research and writing.

I am indebted to the archivists who assisted my research at the Chicago Historical Society; the Archdiocese of Chicago; the Archdiocese of Boston; the archives of the Sisters of the Holy Names of Jesus and Mary (SNJM) in Marylhurst, Oregon; the archives of the Sisters of Providence (SP) in Seattle, Washington; the archives of the School Sisters of St. Francis (SSF) in Milwaukee, Wisconsin; and the archives of the Benedictine Sisters (OSB) of Mount Angel, Oregon. One of the unique delights of this project has been the time I spent in the archives of religious communities, enjoying the company and hospitality of sisters and sister-archivists. It is not often that an historian ends an intensely tiring day of archival research with a communal meal and a goodnight hug, and I regularly received both from the gracious sisters who facilitated my research in congregational archives or in their homes. On this score I am particularly grateful for the warmth and generosity of Sister Jean Agnes, SSJ, and Kathy Urbanic in the archives of the Sisters of Saint Joseph in Rochester, New York, and Sister Mary Lonan Reilly, SSF, in the archives of the Sisters of Saint Francis at Assisi

Heights, Rochester, Minnesota. I am equally grateful to each of the women who made time to talk with me, especially those who were willing to plumb memories of painful or confusing moments in order to help explain the experience of sisters in the 1960s and 1970s. I owe special gratitude to Philip Runkel at Special Collections at Marquette University. Phil has carefully cultivated an extensive collection of records from various organizations of progressive American Catholics in the twentieth century, as well as the private papers of several noteworthy sisters. Not only did Phil preserve much of the archival material that made this study possible, but his meticulous cataloging and attentive assistance made it possible for me to efficiently process large bodies of archival material in the precious weeks I spent at Marquette. Charles Lamb, Kevin Cawley, and Sharon Sumpter all provided professional assistance at the archives of the University of Notre Dame during various research trips. Sharon went above and beyond the call of duty, opening her home to me during one research trip to South Bend when my graduate-student budget was stretched thin.

I claim full responsibility for any errors or omissions in this work. The book's shortcomings surely would be more numerous and more serious had it not been for the efforts of the individuals who read and commented on the manuscript at various stages of its development. Bob Orsi and John McGreevy's thoughtful responses to the original dissertation helped shape its transformation into a book manuscript. I am indebted to two readers for Harvard University Press whose comments sharpened the manuscript. Gregory N. Hite and Patricia Byrne, CSJ, read the entire manuscript, offering corrections and challenges that greatly improved the book. I owe special gratitude to Pat for her incisive comments and spirited encouragement. Charles Robinson also generously lent his vigilant eye and keen mind to the manuscript. My editor, Kathleen McDermott, offered helpful practical guidance. David Trautman lent his keen eye to the manuscript proofs and index.

Several sisters who participated in the racial apostolate also intellectually sharpened this project by discussing ideas or reading drafts of various pieces of this manuscript. Sister Janice Jackson, SNJM, offered early encouragement and intimate stories about the experience of convent life during and after the Second Vatican Council. Sister Lillanna Kopp, SFCC (formerly Sister Audrey, SNJM) was an invaluable partner in the early stages of this project. In addition to lengthy interviews and free books, Lil also offered what proved to be influential challenges to my earliest, inchoate thoughts about sisters, race, and reform. In her inimitable way,

Sister Margaret Ellen Traxler, SSND (formerly Sister Mary Peter, SSND) encouraged me to try to capture the spirit and wit of the women about whom I was writing. Sister Ritamary Bradley, SFCC (formerly Sister Ritamary, CHM) opened her home and her private papers to me, patiently sitting beside me in her living room, playing with her faithful dog Dulcie and answering questions as I tried to piece together the role of the Sister Formation Conference in the racial consciousness of sisters in the 1960s. Maryellen Muckenhirn (formerly Sister M. Charles Borromeo) graciously read the final manuscript and helpfully suggested that the original title was too dull (she was right).

This book grew out of my doctoral work at Yale University. My first year of research was funded by a fellowship through the Catholicism in the Twentieth-Century initiative of the Cushwa Center for the Study of American Catholicism at Notre Dame. The periodic weekend-long meetings at Cushwa, which brought together scholars working under the initiative, proved to be an intellectual lifeline for me. This project took shape during those lively meetings at Notre Dame. I was challenged and influenced by conversations with members of my working group on Catholic women, as well as by the comments, criticisms, and words of encouragement and guidance offered by other historians who attended the Cushwa conferences. I am especially grateful for words of encouragement offered at a crucial moment by Sister Patricia Byrne, CSJ; Father Joseph Chinnici, OFM; and Richard Fox. The Cushwa fellowship introduced me to the community of scholars of American Catholicism, whose conviviality I've come to appreciate deeply. My thanks to Scott Appleby, Carol Coburn, Tim Matovina, Jeff Burns, and Kathy Cummings for contributions they have made to this work. Margaret Susan (Peggy) Thompson and Thomas A. Tweed have both been a steady source of encouragement and guidance.

I am grateful for the financial support that assisted me at every stage of this project. The early research and writing were supported by a fellowship from the Institute for the Advanced Study of Religion at Yale and by a Charlotte W. Newcombe Fellowship from the Woodrow Wilson Foundation. A visiting fellowship through the Center for the Study of Religion at Princeton University provided me with a year of quiet immersion in substantial intellectual resources of Princeton, as well as the solitude to rethink the scope and direction of the project. The Council on Research and Creative Activity, Committee on Faculty Research Support at Florida State University (FSU), provided a COFRS Summer Award that allowed me to conduct additional archival research. Finally, a generous leave from the religion department at FSU gave me time to write new chapters and put all of them in manuscript form.

My initial interest in the experience of American women religious in the conciliar era took shape while I was a master's student in U.S. history at the University of Oregon. I am grateful for the encouragement and guidance I received from faculty in the history department there, especially Jack P. Maddex, Daniel Pope, Howard Brick, and Barbara Welke. I am especially grateful for the unique intellectual camaraderie I enjoyed with Charles Robinson, Chuck Waugh, Heather Miller, Sharon Smith, and Daniel Gilfillan at the University of Oregon. As a Ph.D. student at Yale University I had the privilege of being trained, mentored, challenged, and encouraged by Jon Butler and Skip Stout. I am grateful for their kindness, professionalism, and intellectual rigor. I realize more fully in retrospect how fortunate I was to have not one but two advisers who always treated graduate students with the utmost care and respect. Kathryn Dudley provided intellectual guidance and practical training in ethnographic methods. I benefited tremendously from the model of intellectual solidarity that Kate and her partner, Maria Trumpler, generously offered to female graduate students in American Studies. Glenda Gilmore offered incisive historical commentary. John Demos inspired me to think about my research in terms of story. My colleagues in the study of American religious history—Rachel Wheeler, Jacqueline Robinson, Jim Bennett, Jon Baer, Michael Alexander, Andrew Lewis, Mark Oppenheimer, and Joseph "Kip" Kosek—were stimulating conversation partners and good company.

I am grateful for the support of my colleagues and their families in the religion department at Florida State University: John and Rita Kelsay, Kathleen Erndl and Yakini Kemp; Barney and Pat Twiss, and especially for the camaraderie of Shannon (Burkes) Pinette, Aline Kalbian and Bob Cross and their daughter Eva, Nicole Kelley and Matt Day and their son Henry, Martin Kavka and Dan Casey and their mother Kamila Kavka, David Kangas and Inese Radzins and their sons Olaf and Sevrin, Bryan Cuevas, David and Cathy Levenson and their daughter Tovah, and Matthew Goff and Diane Rixson. I am grateful, also, for the intellectual vigor and thoughtfulness of my colleagues in American religious history, John Corrigan, Amanda Porterfield, and Curtis Evans, as well as the geniality of their partners, Sheila Curran, Keith Hull, and Janet Evans. The graduate students in American religion at FSU have challenged and invigorated my thinking, and I am especially grateful to Howell Williams, Kelly Baker, and Michael Pasquier. Finally, I'd like to offer special thanks to the students in my spring 2005 undergraduate seminar on American Catholicism in the conciliar era whose questions deepened my understanding of the Council and whose enthusiasm reminded me why it matters.

I'd like to extend very special thanks also to Katie Wasson, Steve (Auntie C.) Johnson and Mike Walker, Jude McKay, Axel Jansen, Sharon and Eric Smith, Bob Orsi, Simone Flynn and Andrew Campbell and their children Sasha and Soren, Nancy Hiller, Adam Malson, Shelly Scott and Jeremy Harmon and their son Aidan, Marie-Claire Lehman and Will Hanley and their daughter Emma, Melanie Simmons and Jason Hight and their daughters Samantha and Josephine, Cadence Kidwell and Mike Bozeman, Sylvester Johnson and Heather Nicholson, Rachelle and Chris Ashmore, and Will Hensick. I am especially grateful to Carol Simmons and Lee Williams for the grace of their friendship during a difficult time.

I am grateful to my family for their love and support, especially their unique way of reminding me that there is life beyond text. To Ralph Feldkamp, Lisa and Brian Griffin and Aubrey, and Jeff, Pam, Andrew, and Ryan Koehlinger—many thanks, I love you. Warm thanks also to Shirley and Ralph Robinson, Denis and Judy Koehlinger, and to my beloved grandmother, Marjorie Koehlinger.

Charles Evard Robinson has been a true partner in every sense of the word, making innumerable sacrifices, big and small, to bring this book to completion. I'm grateful to him and to our daughter Hannah Margaret Koehlinger Robinson for the sheer delight of life in their company.

Two friends who made this book possible did not live to see its completion. Shafali Lal's honest and unique style of friendship made the pressures of graduate school endurable and, often surprisingly enjoyable. Her untimely death in 2003 left the field of American studies, and all who knew knew and loved her, impoverished.

Those who knew my beloved golden retriever, Mona, will understand why she deserves special mention. Most every word between these covers was written as she lay beside my feet under my desk. I'm grateful for the years of companionship she shared with me.

I owe a great debt to my late grandfather, Erwin Wilhelm Koehlinger. Grandpa Erv delighted over every achievement of my graduate education and offered unbridled enthusiasm for my career. A lover of theology and books who spent his last years bent over his electric typewriter painstakingly translating the sermons of a mostly forgotten German-immigrant theologian, Grandpa modeled for me a love of knowledge for its own sake and a love of family that knows no bounds. It is to him and to his memory that this book is lovingly dedicated, with deep gratitude.

My mother, Judith Marie Feldkamp, has always been the mainstay of my life, forging a rare and genuine balance by encouraging my wanderings, adventures, and projects while providing for me a true home to return to when I'm ready to rest. She made this book—and so much more—possible. This book is dedicated to her, with all love and gratitude.

Index